Don't Count Me Out

The Irrepressible Dale Brown and His LSU Fighting Tigers

Bruce Hunter

Bonus Books, Inc., Chicago

©1989 by Bonus Books, Inc.
All rights reserved

93 92 91 90 89   5 4 3 2

Library of Congress Catalog Card Number: 89-62306

International Standard Book Number: 0-929387-03-1

Bonus Books, Inc.
160 East Illinois Street
Chicago, Illinois 60611

First Edition

Printed in the United States of America

To Janet and Daniel, for their love, support, encouragement and understanding

Contents

Foreword

I first met Dale Brown when he was an assistant coach at Washington State. He was a very outgoing, interested, inquisitive young man who was wrapped up in his profession. He was very ambitious and eager to progress in the coaching profession. I remember he was a good recruiter at Washington State; he was so open and outgoing and worked so hard that you couldn't help but like him. At the time, I didn't really know his qualifications. But he seemed to be a very bright, eager coach, and you couldn't help but feel that he would make it in the profession.

Like most young coaches, Dale wanted to learn from the coaches he respected. Usually, I don't give advice. I just answer questions and give my opinion. Dale always asked a lot of questions. He wanted to know everything. You might say he picked my brain. He wanted to know everything about practice organization, drills, conditioning, quickness, working with others, teaching methods. I always told him that a coach is only a teacher. Teaching is more than knowledge of what you're trying to teach. You must be able to get it across to your players. I never complicated the game. After all, basketball is a reasonably simple game.

I've always been impressed with people eager to learn. Denny Crum had that quality when he played for me at UCLA. I would tell people that he was born to coach. What I meant was he seemed to be interested in everything we did. He wanted to understand the reason for each action and decision. I felt in my early association with Dale that was his quest also. He was so eager to learn.

I gave him a recommendation when he applied for the LSU job. When he was hired, he came to see me and brought his assistant coach, Jack Schalow. He often called me to ask questions about various situations. He invited me to visit Baton Rouge and go on trips with him. I wasn't able to go, so we talked often on the phone. I think coaching under different coaches and always asking questions helped Dale develop into the coach he is today.

We've had a good relationship. I think our friendship is strong because we're both from meager backgrounds. Times were tough when we were coming up. There weren't any athletic scholarships. You had to work for everything you got. I think that realization made us closer.

When he went to his first Final Four in 1981, he called me a lot. I told him about my first Final Four in 1962. I felt I had overworked my players. I tried to add new things and wound up doing too much. We were eliminated by Cincinnati, and I think I might have done too much. I should just have kept them sharp. I suggested that Dale be careful about that.

I think what I like best about Dale is that he is such a caring person. I know his players can tell he is interested in them. Some people say he comes on too strong. They question his sincerity. I don't. That's just Dale. He's a motivator. He motivates in ways most people would find uncomfortable. A lot of coaches criticize him. They say he's a fake. I tell them, "I don't think you know him." I think I do.

Dale is like most coaches who are in a position to have a chance for a national championship. I think coaches who are close to winning a title can get obsessed with it. Had he stayed at Washington State, I don't think he would have been obsessed. It's difficult to recruit there, and the chances of winning a national championship are poor. When a coach is located at a school that has a chance, he wants it a little more. And, there is greater disappointment when he doesn't win.

Early in my career, when we had poor facilities at UCLA, I didn't think about winning a national championship. Then in 1962, we made it to the Final Four under those circumstances, and it changed everything.

I really don't know if Dale will win a championship. There are so many who come close. It doesn't mean they haven't done an outstanding job. The timing may just not be right. I remember Bob Boyd had a great team one year at Southern Cal. It just happened that we had an even better team. The only two games they lost were to us. So it's more than just having a great team. You have to have it at the right time.

If Dale wins one, he should not let it change him. He shouldn't do anything differently. Winning can affect people, it can become a problem. I've often said if I could wish something good for someone I respect in the coaching profession, like Dale, I would wish that he would win one national championship. If I could wish something for someone in the profession for whom I have little respect, I would wish that he would win several.

John Wooden
July 1989

A Prophecy

from Norman Vincent Peale

I want to reiterate a prophecy I made on Nov. 6, 1979, regarding Coach Dale Brown. I do not set myself up as being a prophet very much, but I am making a prophecy now that under Coach Brown's leadership, LSU will be the basketball champion of the United States. And I want to tell you why I believe that. I believe it because of Dale's coaching ability. I believe it because of the fine players he recruits. I am sure of it because of the spirit of his great educational institution, and I believe it because Coach Brown, his staff and players are positive thinkers. And it's very hard to defeat positive thinkers who keep being positive whatever the circumstances.

Dale Brown and his players and associates and friends among the team's vast following have been imaging the championship. And positive imaging, long held, strongly tends to become fact. A picture held persistently in the conscious mind by a process of intellectual osmosis proceeds finally into the subconscious. And when it dominates the subconscious, you have it because it has you totally. Thoughts and images certainly dominate the conscious and subconscious mind of Coach Brown.

And he has another powerful quality in full measure. He is a man of faith. He is a believer. Faith is widely recognized as the greatest power in the world. And the believer is an achiever. For these reasons, plus the mastering of the science of the game, I repeat the prophecy that LSU will be the champions for they are a team of champions.

Acknowledgments

This book would never have been written without Dale Brown's co-operation. There would have been no reason to write it if he wasn't the type of person and coach that he is. Dale opened up his program and his life to my scrutiny, with nothing to gain, financially or otherwise. For that, I will always be grateful.

If I respect any individuals more than Dale, it would have to be the young men who play for him. Chris Jackson and Ricky Blanton shared their most personal thoughts with me, again with nothing to gain. Russell Grant and Lyle Mouton were also instrumental to the book, but so were all the other players, assistant coaches, trainers, managers, and Athletic Department staff members. I thank you all.

Jamie Roth and his family were both helpful and inspirational to me. I can never thank them enough. Doc Broussard couldn't have been more helpful. I sometimes wonder if there would be an LSU without Doc.

Special thanks goes to Gus Weill, who convinced Dale to grant me access to the program and advised me throughout the process. Special thanks also goes to John Wooden and Norman Vincent Peale, who were so gracious in assisting me.

I thank my supervisors at the *Morning Advocate* for granting me time off to write this book.

Also, I thank John Feinstein for his advice and for setting the standard by which all sports books are measured with his master-piece, *A Season on the Brink*. I think I had better material to work with, however.

The Bonus Books' staff was tremendous to work with, and their editing greatly enhanced the book. I also thank my colleague Joe Planas for his advice, encouragement and editing assistance. Last but not least, I thank my favorite editor—my wife, Janet.

For all those I didn't mention by name, I wish I could pay tribute to each one of you. I can only say I am grateful for your assistance.

Counted Out

December 10, 1988—Deep inside, he wanted to dash off the court, arms raised, fists clenched, coattail flapping behind in the breeze. He felt as if he were back in Atlanta, Chicago or Cincinnati and had just upset some powerhouse in an NCAA Basketball Tournament game. Why shouldn't he run out of the University of Florida's O'Connell Center leading the victory celebration? This seemed a moment worthy of such jubilation.

Dale Brown did something he seldom has been able to do. He restrained himself and kept his emotions under control. It was not easy. On this Saturday night, in front of the ESPN cameras, lowly Louisiana State had turned David and knocked off mighty Florida. The Florida team picked by many to win the 1988-89 Southeastern Conference title, the team highly ranked in most preseason national polls. LSU, on the other hand, was picked to finish eighth in the SEC and wasn't even in the top 100 nationally. A sixth straight NCAA Tournament berth for the Fighting Tigers? An 11th consecutive national tournament bid? Another miraculous March? No chance. Not with this bunch of misfits. They would be lucky to avoid a losing season.

Even Brown, with all his positive thinking and creative coaching, couldn't pull this one off. One publication wrote that for LSU to have a winning season it would take a greater miracle than the raising of Lazarus. This team was counted out.

But after shaking hands with Florida coach Norm Sloan, Brown knew better than anyone else this was a special night. It was his secret, one that was painfully hard to keep. Had Brown been the only witness when Lazarus arose, it would not have been much more difficult to keep to himself. This was the kind of game he lived for. But he held it in, trying to mask his ecstasy, wanting to show some humility.

Granted, it was only December and the season was in its infancy. But beating Florida in front of a large, hostile crowd carried great significance. Some of Brown's most successful teams had not won in Gainesville. These young LSU players, going on the road for the first time, had shown amazing poise and executed his Freak Defense and offensive game plan to the letter. They had also absorbed Brown's proliferation of positive thoughts. As inexperienced as they were, they could go a long way performing like this.

More important, Brown believed this win would have residual effects. When it came time to go against national powers like Georgetown, Nevada-Las Vegas and Illinois, he could try to convince his players they were going to win. But there was nothing like the real thing to make his case. "Remember Florida. Just remember what we did there," he would stress. And they would recall that wonderful evening in the O'Connell Center when they played hard enough and well enough to beat anybody, to get back to the NCAA Tournament, to create another March miracle, to disprove those who had counted them out.

Inside the visitors' locker room, a celebration was going on that made it seem like March. These kids from LSU were going wild. It was bedlam—players shouting, clapping for each other and themselves, jumping, waving towels. Players were knocking over chairs, throwing cups of water and knocking over players. The noise was painfully loud. Most of all, everyone wanted to hug somebody. They didn't just slap each other on the back. They squeezed tight and held on. All 13 players, four assistant coaches, two managers and two trainers got into the act. Brown had not joined them yet.

In the middle of it all stood Chris Jackson, the child prodigy, a Mozart of the hardwood, and Ricky Blanton, the decorated veteran, a classic overachiever. Athletically, they were at opposite ends of the spectrum. Jackson measured 6-1 with a slight build and spindly legs. But he was a deceptively explosive player who mastered the game as a boy growing up in Gulfport, Mississippi. Blanton, a 6-7, 215-pound senior, was one of the strong men of college basketball who had delighted in outworking and pushing around opponents from the day he reported to LSU from Miami. But Jackson and Blanton had almost identical personalities. They were gentle, polite and thoughtful, kind to children, almost too good to be true. Most of the time, they were reserved. But not on this occasion.

This was a moment worth cutting loose and getting a little crazy. It reminded Blanton of the many wonderful victories he had experienced with Brown in the last four years. Now there would be more with Jackson. These were familiar times for Blanton, who had become the team captain and alter ego of Brown.

Blanton was just a freshman when the Tigers staged a dramatic late-season rally, hitting a high point by winning the 1985 Southeastern Conference championship. As a sophomore, Blanton was asked by Brown to move to center from guard. He responded by leading the Tigers to the pinnacle of college basketball, the 1986 Final Four. They became the lowest-seeded team in NCAA history to reach the Final Four, upsetting Kentucky, Georgia Tech, Memphis State and Purdue during a magical stretch drive to Dallas. LSU almost made tournament history again in 1987 but Blanton could only watch as he rehabilitated an injured knee, which gave him a fifth year of eligibility. He was a helpless, hurting spectator as the Tigers marched over Georgia Tech, Temple and DePaul before narrowly missing a return trip to the Final Four with a one-point loss to Indiana. Blanton returned in the 1987-88 season, this time as a forward and the team's leading scorer and rebounder. The deaths of former LSU players Don Redden and Pete Maravich weighed heavily on the team, but the Tigers still made it to the NCAA Tournament, beating national runner-up Oklahoma along the way.

A victory at Florida was the best gift his teammates could have given Blanton. He had gone out a winner in the last college game he would play in his home state. Many of his friends from Miami were in attendance. Others watched on television. Understandably, he got a little more emotional than his teammates.

"They didn't think we could beat them!" he shouted, latching on to his best friend, Wayne Sims, the only other returning starter on a pitifully inexperienced team. "They said we couldn't do it!" Then he went around the room hugging and thanking each teammate—starters and reserves alike.

When he made his way to Jackson, Blanton's eyes were beginning to get red and his words choked. They embraced, a little longer than the others. They clenched each other a little harder. Their combined performances had proved too much for Florida. Blanton had been brilliant in the first half, and Jackson had taken over after that, breaking the O'Connell Center scoring record with 53 points. Not even "Pistol Pete" Maravich, the leading scorer in the history of college basketball, had scored that many points in a game at Florida.

"C.J., they said we couldn't do it!" Blanton yelled into his teammate's ear. "They said we couldn't do it!"

Beaming with joy, like a boy who had just done something to draw his father's praise, Jackson gave a high-five to Blanton and twirled around, shouting, "Who said we couldn't do it!"

Just then, Brown strolled through the doorway. He had heard a faint rumble from outside. Once in the room, he saw how his team was reacting and instantly got caught up in the excitement. He raised his right hand in a fist and let out a yell that could be heard above the commotion. Then he lowered his head, shuffled his feet and danced around one side of the room. He never noticed his friend, Harvey Schiller, commissioner of the Southeastern Conference, enter behind him. He just kept dancing and rejoicing in the privacy of the locker room. Brown, 53, was beginning his 17th season at LSU. This night marked his 300th victory. But he felt like a rookie coach winning his first big game.

Even Brown, an eternal optimist, had wondered if there would be any nights like this. In their first four games, the Tigers appeared suspect. Already, they had been through trying times. In one game, they were tied at the end of regulation and managed to lose by four points without even playing overtime because Brown was called for a technical when he protested a foul that was called as time expired. The next outing, they lost by two points in overtime. In both defeats, a controversial call probably cost them the game on their own court in the Pete Maravich Assembly Center in Baton Rouge. Meanwhile, Brown was still getting a feel for the team. He had praised his players in defeat and raged at them in victory.

Before the Florida trip, there were the makings of a long, frustrating season. Everything pointed to a rebuilding year. Blanton was the only upperclassman. There was a lack of height, lack of experience, lack of depth and particularly, a lack of defense. They had not been able to stop anyone, especially big men. Their two centers, Richard Krajewski and Geert Hammink, had demonstrated an open door policy. Other teams' big men were waltzing through the lane for layups. Television commentator Dick Vitale was already calling it the Doughnut Defense, because there was a big hole in the middle.

Brown tried to implement his Freak Defense, which had been pivotal to the Tigers' success in the previous three seasons. It worked against Florida. But to play this complex combination of zones and man-to-man defenses, a team must have good defensive players who are experienced with using his system. Blanton was the closest thing to that. The rest of the team had to improve on defense. Only then could they take full advantage of the Freak, a defense Brown designed as a high school coach to neutralize an opponent's offensive superiority.

The battle cry heard round Baton Rouge was "Just wait till next year." If all went as planned, the Tigers would be adding a bonanza of talent: 7-footers Stanley Roberts and Shaquille O'Neal, the nation's top-rated high school centers in 1988 and 1989; 6-9 Parade Magazine All-American Harold Boudreaux; 6-8 forward Lenear Burns; 6-7 forward Shawn Griggs; and point guard Maurice Williamson, who averaged 39 points a game in high school. Roberts, Boudreaux and Williamson were ineligible for one season, having failed to meet the academic standards of NCAA Bylaw 5-1-(j), Proposition 48. O'Neal, Griggs and Burns still had a year of high school left. Once these six joined the returning players, many believed LSU would be one of the most talented college teams ever assembled. Ole Miss coach Ed Murphy said LSU would have the best talent since the glory years of John Wooden and UCLA. Nothing would please Brown more as a coach than to have his team compared to those of Wooden, his coaching idol and close friend. Wooden, who won 10 national titles at UCLA, was considered the greatest college coach of all time.

All the talk about what a great team LSU would have in 1989-90 didn't bother the younger players. They knew they would be part of it. But Blanton would not. This was his final year. It had to happen now. Brown wanted to make sure Blanton went out the way he came in, on a high note.

If anyone could provide Blanton with a memorable senior season, it was Brown. Being counted out only stimulates him to work harder, to get more out of his players and himself. The ability to motivate is by far his greatest strength. His players are bombarded with his positive attitude; they have no choice but to become Brown clones. He has an uncanny knack of taking just the right approach, depending on the situation. Usually, he speaks in a comforting tone and provides uplifting messages. But if he catches them loafing, he turns into a fierce, raging dictator. Through the course of a season, he nurtures his players with daily motivational messages. He hands out inspirational literature like candy on Halloween. Brown expects his players to improve and get mentally tough like him. So when the pressure of tournament time presents itself, they're ready.

"Coach Brown knows every part of the game, but his main asset is motivation," LSU sophomore Lyle Mouton said. "He is the preacher. He can motivate anything. That's what really gets us going. We believe in him. And if you believe in him, you can believe in yourself. You go as far as your leader takes you."

For Blanton's sake, they would have to get going right away.

No shouts of "Next year" could be heard in the locker room at Florida. Just more chants of "They said we couldn't do it!" As it grew to a peak, Brown slipped into the middle of the players. Just as spontaneously as he had started dancing, he bent to one knee and lowered his head to pray. He waited until the racket died down, which didn't take long. Almost everyone noticed him kneeling. Some seemed a little surprised. Most were not. They began to kneel around him, forming a circle. Once everyone was situated, they bowed their heads and waited.

In past seasons, Brown had not put much stock in praying with his team. Sometimes, they would say the Lord's Prayer together. Most often, he would give them time for silent prayer. This season, many things had changed. Everyone was praying. Brown had appointed a spiritual coach, Father Jeff Bayhi, a young, jolly, unconventional Catholic priest, ideally suited to Brown.

Father Bayhi spent almost as much time with the team as some of the assistant coaches. He counseled the players. He gave a short sermon before every game and led prayer before and afterward. He was just what his title implied, a coach in charge of spiritual matters. A prior commitment forced him to miss the Florida trip. So Brown took it upon himself to pray with the team.

Before then, he probably would have criticized any coach who prayed with his team. Brown would have called him a fake. In an ESPN interview before the Florida game, he was asked about his nickname "Preacher Man" and responded by making it clear he didn't want to be categorized with some preachers of the day.

"Well, I guess that can be a compliment and it can also be a negative, because there have been a lot of phony preacher men," he said, smiling but driving home his point. "Jimmy Jones in Guyana, Jimmy Bakker." He paused, considering adding another Jimmy to the list, but his Baton Rouge neighbor, Jimmy Swaggart, was not mentioned this time. "So I hope if that is a philosophy," he continued, "I am trying to speak from my heart. But when you open your mouth, obviously you get into trouble. And secondly, there are so many charlatans that you wonder, 'Is this guy counterfeit, fake or what?' That is why you have to look at yourself in the mirror each day."

Until that fall, Brown had looked into the mirror and seen a self-made man with great presence, power and integrity. Someone with few flaws. No one else, with the possible exception of his wife, Vonnie, and daughter, Robyn, saw quite the same image. Actually, Vonnie was often his sharpest critic when he needed to be told he was out of line. Even his closest friends, assistant coaches and players were keenly aware of his shortcomings.

Because of his troubled childhood, Brown believed he had to control everyone and everything in his life. He sometimes manipulated people as if he were playing a real-life game of chess. He altered facts to suit his needs, he ridiculed, and he condemned. Always, he justified it in his own mind. His chess match was no game. He played for keeps. Above all, he wanted to win a national championship. He had to prove to the world that a poor, neglected North Dakota boy could grow up and make it on his own. Make it to the top.

Brown, who bears a striking resemblance to the comedian Bob Hope, is both brilliant and bizarre. He has many of the characteristics of an eccentric genius. Almost everything he does is unusual. He has often gone days without sleeping, routinely worked 18 to 20 hours, regularly skipped two or three meals in a row, often splurged on eating binges (putting away a gallon of praline-caramel ice cream at a sitting), chewed gum until his jaws ached, and had enough energy to power a small nuclear plant. He is a fanatic about straightening up and cleaning things to the extent that he lines up his paper clips and polishes the plastic floor covering under his office chair. Anyone around him too long risks being driven crazy with his zany antics and non-stop gab.

For all of his faults, Brown is still a "people person." He has charm and charisma. He has an open wallet for anyone in need. Almost any other coach in his position, possessing his talent for public speaking, would have been a rich man at his age. Brown is so benevolent he still has financial concerns. By his own admission, he is a poor businessman and has lost money on many ventures. But he has the ability to talk convincingly, positively and creatively. Being recruited by Brown is like taking a one-year Dale Carnegie course. If a player signs with LSU, he gets the full five-year course.

Brown's ability to charge his players with positive thoughts is the key to LSU's basketball success. He inherited a program at rock bottom in 1972 and transformed it into a national power. His first Final Four appearance came in 1981. The glory years of the mid-80s elevated him to the ranks of elite coaches.

Brown's players are expected to think the way he does, or they don't play for him. In crises, he responds by turning a negative into a positive. It could be at halftime of a game. It could be in the midst of an academic or family problem involving one of his players. Regardless, he immediately changes the mood of the situation.

"When everyone else is down on us, Coach Brown changes it all around," Blanton once said. "We can be losing. People can be saying we aren't any good. But we believe in ourselves, because Coach Brown believes in us. He never gets down. He is always lifting us up."

Yet for all his positive thinking, Brown for years did not really have peace of mind. He had even come to understand that a national championship would not be enough to satisfy him. He would just have to win another. There would always be something else. He had to prove himself. He had to do it on his own.

But Brown found out there was something he could not control. When his wife had become seriously ill that summer, he finally realized where he had to find his peace. He and his wife turned toward God and committed their lives to Christ. Quietly, they began leading a crusade to lead others to a similar change. "We're on a mission now," Vonnie kept telling her husband. It was both a basketball and evangelistic mission. If LSU could win a national championship or just be a dominant team, Brown would have the chance to share his faith. He no longer wanted to win just to satisfy his ego. He wasn't using people any more. At Florida, he made no mention of his 300th victory. In other years, he would have talked about it at the postgame press conference. He would have made sure the school issued a press release about it. He didn't need to boast any more.

Praying became an important part of his daily life. It was almost an automatic response. So in the locker room at Florida, his prayer with the team was as natural to him as if he had been alone at home in his study.

"Father, we thank you for being with us tonight," he prayed, slowly and softly in the still room. "We thank you for showing us again that if we really love each other and care for each other, miracles can happen. This is one of the greatest wins in LSU basketball history. We thank you for showing us what hard work and believing in each other can do. Father, help us to just continue to play hard like this. In your name, God, we are going to conduct this season the way it should be and we can win the Southeastern Conference. Thank you, Lord."

As soon as Brown finished, there was one more rousing cheer, the players' way of responding to the prayer and the victory. It was just the fifth game of a season that would go at least 31 games, possibly well beyond, depending on how far they went in postseason play. There would be more victories, more celebrations, more prayers of thanksgiving. But there would be setbacks and blowups by Brown along the way. They would be handled differently, too.

His new beliefs affected everything he did. They had an impact on all aspects of the basketball program. At practice, he remained energetic, almost hyperactive. But his explosive outbursts, once a common occurrence, were few and far between. Occasionally he would scream at someone, but it didn't last long and didn't break his train of thought. During games, he seldom argued with the officials. He realized that was a losing battle and didn't play it. He concentrated on making adjustments to win the game. That made him a better coach; he was once rated among the worst bench coaches in the SEC.

Even in recruiting, Brown took a different approach. He spent more time with his recruits. His wife visited with them. The Browns even invited them to church. They invited a lot of people to church. They were continually reaching out, trying to share their new-found faith.

Often he went to great lengths to do this. Whenever he heard of a friend, acquaintance or even a former enemy in trouble, he acted. He called Eddie Sutton, Dana Kirk, Larry Brown and others experiencing problems to wish them well and to tell them he was praying for them. He got some reactions of surprise. Some wondered if it really was him on the phone. But his booming, nasal voice gave him away. It was Dale Brown, and he was sincere. He wanted to help. He hoped they would rise above their troubles. He was praying for them. He was even praying for Bobby Knight.

Since they met on the court for the first time in the 1981 Final Four, Brown and Knight had been enemies. They exchanged verbal blows in the media. It was obvious to anyone familiar with college basketball that they hated each other. Brown had once said of Knight, "I want to wrestle him naked in a dark room and may the best man come out alive."

Now his attitude had reversed itself. He was waiting for the right time to meet with Knight and share his deepest feelings and beliefs. He had found peace within himself. He wanted to make peace with everyone, including Knight.

Brown's players weren't sure what had happened to him. All they could tell was something had changed dramatically. This was not the Dale Brown they had known. Already, it was clear to everyone associated with the team that this would be a different type of season. It might, in some ways, be like the magnificent years of 1986 and 1987. But in no way had Brown ever dealt with his players and himself like this. There was a bond forming among them. Now they had to find a way to transfer this growing strength and unity into the way they played basketball.

2

Downright Dale

It's called March Madness, that scintillating time of the year when the NCAA Basketball Tournament comes to life. Dale Brown is enthralled by tournament time like no other part of the year. His teams gear up all season long for it. In the 1980s, only six schools reached the NCAA regional finals, called the Final Eight, at least four times. North Carolina and Georgetown led with six appearances. LSU, Louisville, Duke and Virginia tied with four. Each time LSU made it that far, it took the eventual national champion to eliminate Brown's team.

Millions have watched Brown in action. They've seen a strong-willed, high-strung coach who unfailingly grabs the spotlight with his theatrical style of flashing signals on every possession, pumping up his players and the crowd with emotional outbursts and taunting the officials. They've heard the remarks of a man who is candid and color-ful and wears his emotions on his sleeve. They've seen his teams pull off pulsating, miraculous upsets. As a result, they've formed an opin-ion of him. Typically, it is one of appreciation of his boldness or dislike of his brashness. You either love him or hate him. You can't be indif-ferent.

Portland Trail Blazers assistant coach Jack Schalow will tell you he loves the man. And because of it, he gets inquiries from fellow coaches. "Everyone knows we're friends," Schalow said, "and they all ask the same thing, 'Is Dale Brown for real?'"

The real Dale Brown has done his job and lived his life like no one before him. His coaching is most influenced by John Wooden, his philosophy by Norman Vincent Peale. But the greatest impact on his life has been his past. He is uniquely his own man.

Perhaps it is no coincidence that Brown was born on Halloween, coaches in an arena that looks like an alien spaceship and is most noted for creating a defense called The Freak. Even among the odd lot of college basketball coaches, he is a freak. The world probably is not big enough for two Dale Browns. College basketball certainly is not.

Those who know Brown best see that the good in him far outweighs the bad. Usually, the bad gets most of the attention. But Dale Brown is changing. He has a better understanding of his own flaws. He knows his prideful, abrupt manner has spoiled many of the good things he has done. He wants to be more humble. He would like to be real. But to many people and perhaps even to himself, he has not been.

To Schalow, Brown has always been real. Schalow has known him since they were teenagers. They both grew up in Minot, North Dakota. Schalow was the top assistant on Brown's first LSU teams. He stayed only three years, but they've remained best friends. Everywhere Schalow goes, it seems someone wants to know about Brown.

"A lot of coaches think he is a jerk and a phony," Schalow said. "A lot of people don't like him. But they've never met him. They've never spent any time with him. Dale Brown is real. I don't know of a better person. He cares about people. He *really* cares."

What Schalow sees in Brown is a man of character, compassion and devotion to those around him. He also sees a charismatic personality. In Brown, there is a powerful force at work that changes people. Justifiably, he has been called the "Preacher Man" and "Billy Graham in sneakers." Basketball may have never known a greater motivator. Brown has elevated motivation almost to an art form. For three days and two nights, he went without sleep to help get his team through the Southeastern Conference Tournament and into the NCAA Tournament. He has threatened numerous times to resign, sometimes to protest some issue, but more often to inspire his team. A few times, he has threatened his players with physical violence when they didn't perform up to his standards.

At team meetings, he has burned newspaper articles or shown video tape of a television report that slighted the team. Once when his players were in a shooting slump, he invited local reporters to shoot a game of HORSE against them. Another day, the team had to run backward for a mile, because Brown had read about a former boxing champ who used that training technique. Then there is his list of speakers. They come from virtually every walk of life—politicians, clergy, Olympians, coaches, administrators, actors, authors, musicians. Whoever can inspire his players is welcomed and pursued.

But Brown doesn't really need help. His players are motivated because he is with them every day. Without fail, he has a daily motivational message. It might take five minutes. He could go on for a half hour or longer. What he does is fill their minds with visions of success and what it takes to attain it. He gets them to dream, to believe in their teammates, to believe in him and ultimately, to believe in themselves.

Many ask Schalow if Brown could coach in the NBA. "That's just what we need in pro basketball," he answers. "When you play up to 100 games a year, you've got to have somebody or something to keep you going. Dale would be perfect for that. His kids will do anything he asks them. If he tells them to run through a brick wall, they'll be lined up and ready to go. They think just like he does. If another coach asked his players to do the things Dale does, they would say, 'The hell with it, I'm going home.'"

Few have a better perspective of Brown, but Schalow admits that he doesn't know all there is to this puzzling individual.

The making and shaping of Dale Brown involved a complicated, drawn-out process much like a carefully prepared Louisiana gumbo. The roux, or base stock, comes from a bitterly painful, tough childhood. Among the many ingredients is a rare blend of North Dakota pride, endless enthusiasm, child-like compassion, natural charm and piles of positive thinking. Added to that is a mixture of abrasiveness, vengeance and a touch of hypocrisy. The garnish consists of one giant-size mouth, one keen mind and enough energy to make it bubble over.

Brown is like gumbo in another way. Some people can't get enough. Others can't stomach the hot, spicy stuff.

What makes Brown unique are three facets of his personality that seem to affect his every action. Best known to fans and enemies alike is his "Don't dare try to stop me" attitude. He will attack anything he perceives to be injustice. But just as integral to his character are the traits of "You can always depend on me" and "I can only trust myself."

Recognizing the first trait is easy. No one knows that better than Schalow and Rueben Hammond, another close friend from Minot. They've seen Brown in his native environment. They identify with the fighter in him. Their first and favorite recollections of young Dale are fights.

Brown attended Minot State Teachers College and was involved in sports the year round. Schalow remembers a football game when Brown was having a particularly good day. Then someone on the other team angered him, and Brown exploded. "Dale was the fullback," Schalow recalled. "I mean he was a huge fullback. He stood about 6-3 and weighed 225 or 230. Heck, he was bigger than any of the linemen back then. And he loved to run hard, just try to run right over people. He was one of the best athletes, but most of all he was just tough, mean and strong. One time he ran up the middle and there were three or four guys on him. He just kept driving and driving his knees. Finally, a defensive back came up to tackle him, and Dale just raised up, cocked his fist and smashed the guy right in the face."

Helmets weren't equipped with facemasks in the early '50s. There was nothing to stop his punch. It landed squarely on the opponent's nose, bloodying both his and Brown's uniforms. Naturally, Brown was ejected from the game, but it was not his last fight. "He was a hell of a fighter," Schalow said.

Even before his playing days, Brown made a similar impression on Hammond, then the director of recreation in Minot. One afternoon, Hammond was on his way to the gym when he saw Brown, then a young boy, talking to a priest. As he got closer, he could tell the priest was angry. To his surprise, the boy got just as angry and gave a smart-aleck reply. The priest responded by rapping him powerfully across the face. "All I saw was white coming out of Dale's mouth!" Hammond recounted with a roar of laughter. "I thought the father had knocked his teeth out. He couldn't have hit him any harder with his fist."

Brown did not lose any teeth. He had been eating a vanilla ice cream cone, which was knocked from his mouth. He deserved the punishment, even if it appeared extreme. As Hammond would soon find out, Brown got into some kind of trouble almost daily. He also learned that Brown's father had deserted the family when Dale was born, leaving behind a sickly wife, two teenage daughters and a heart-broken son who grieved about not knowing his own father. Hammond tried to look after the boy. But Hammond couldn't ease the disgrace and bitter disappointment that haunted and drove Dale most of his life. Growing up, he rebelled at authority. No priest, no teacher would rule him.

Russ Smith, a Minot sportscaster who later would be the best man at Brown's wedding, saw him change from a teenage ruffian into a thoughtful, but still driven adult. "I'm very proud of Dale, where he's gotten from whence he came," Smith said. "He could have wound up with a life sentence for something. Instead, he overcame that difficult start in life."

Brown's "Don't dare try to stop me" outlook carried over into his professional life. He would have nothing to do with the coaching establishment. No way would he kiss up to anybody. He worked his way up the coaching ladder. His first jobs were high school positions in North Dakota. At both schools, there was a minor question over salaries for him or his wife, Vonnie. Each dispute led him to revolt against what he perceived as a slight. He abruptly quit those positions. Without jobs and with an infant daughter, the Browns packed up and left their home state. Dale managed to get a junior high coaching job in Berkley, California. Next was a high school post in Palm Springs. Then Utah State coach Ladell Andersen hired him as an assistant. After Andersen left, Brown was recommended to become Utah State's head coach. He didn't get the job and left to become an assistant at Washington State. A year later, LSU athletic director Carl Maddox took a chance and made Brown head coach.

"I chaired a five-person committee that interviewed Dale," Maddox recalled. "We were all very impressed with his industry and spontaneous enthusiasm. He was also very articulate. I didn't know much about his basketball background, so I called around. I just remember being sold on him as a very positive person and coach."

Only a few weeks on the job, Brown went nose-to-nose with the football empire at LSU. In this instance, it was the emperor himself, Charlie McClendon. In many people's eyes, McClendon was second in command in Louisiana behind only the governor. He had been an assistant under Paul Dietzel when LSU won its only national championship in 1958. He was promoted to head coach after Dietzel left in 1962. When Brown arrived on the scene, McClendon was at the height of his career, sending the Tigers to bowl games almost every year. Basketball was a poor stepchild. Basketball players lived in the athletic dorm and ate in the same cafeteria with football players, but it was an accepted rule that they stepped aside and let football players go to the front of the meal line.

Basketball coaches were expected to follow similar protocol, not only when it came to food, but in every athletic activity. After all, the football team filled Tiger Stadium on Saturday nights and brought in all the money. The basketball program, under former coach Press Maravich, couldn't fill a high school gym and was in the red. Maravich's son, "Pistol Pete," had been an interesting attraction for four years. But when he left in 1970, so did the fans. And LSU was trying to pay for the new, 14,000-seat Assembly Center.

Brown stated publicly that there was room for two successful programs. Secretly, though, he wanted to blow football out of the water. A collision between McClendon and Brown was inevitable.

LSU had a tradition that athletes in all varsity sports got together once a year to hear from each of the head coaches. It was understood that the coaches of minor sports, which included everything but football, would stand up, introduce themselves and sit back down. Then McClendon would give a speech. Naturally, that didn't sit well with Brown. His "Don't dare try to stop me" side overcame his better judgment.

When it was his turn to introduce himself, Brown did that and more. He talked on and on—about basketball, athletics in general, college life, discipline, conditioning. He stopped short only of politics and religion. McClendon grew more furious by the minute. As if that weren't enough, Brown closed by saying, "I want all of you athletes to know you're important to this university and important to us. And everyone will be treated as equals. There will be no favorites here."

The basketball players were almost in shock. Brown had taken a courageous stand for them. They wouldn't forget it. But they also expected McClendon to explode, which would have made things even more difficult for them. They didn't realize that Brown wouldn't back down from anyone, even if it were a fight he probably couldn't win.

McClendon began with some words of praise for the football team. Then he shifted his talk to "the big mouth" coaches on the athletic staff. He didn't name Brown, but the message was clear—back off or I'll crush you. Brown turned red with anger. One of his players, Collis Temple, remembered how Brown kept his head down and waited for McClendon to finish. As the athletes and coaches made their way out of the room, Brown stormed after his powerful adversary. He grabbed McClendon by the arm and jerked him to a halt.

"Coach Brown looked like he was going to hit Coach Mac," Temple recalled. "He told him, 'You better not ever try to embarrass me again. I'm going to build a program here, and you or nobody else is going to stop me. And another thing, I'll still be here when you're gone.' We couldn't believe he was saying that. But he was right."

McClendon's contract was not renewed in 1979, the same year Brown brought LSU its first Southeastern Conference basketball championship in a quarter of a century. LSU basketball was headed toward an unprecedented decade of success. The football program would have five different head coaches in seven years.

It didn't come easy for Brown. Louisiana was a staunch football state. Only by promoting the game of basketball did he stand a chance of making his program work. He and his assistant coaches, Schalow and Homer Drew, barnstormed the state handing out purple-and-gold nets, basketballs, bumper stickers and key chains. They talked up the sport everywhere they went. Austin Wilson, veteran New Orleans sports editor for The Associated Press, witnessed it all. "Dale Brown had the most profound impact of anyone on basketball in Louisiana," Wilson said.

Even during his winningest seasons, Brown never retreated from a confrontation, real or imagined. He had skirmishes with LSU's administration and the media. After a game at Kentucky in 1978, he had a memorable clash with the press corps. LSU had been beaten badly by a physically dominating UK team that featured Rick Robey, Mike Phillips and James Lee. Brown criticized the Wildcats and coach Joe B. Hall for "butchering" the game of basketball. This went on for about 20 minutes before Billy Reed, then a columnist for the Louisville Courier-Journal, broke into Brown's diatribe and asked, "Is your team simon-pure?"

Without taking time to think, Brown countered, "Do you masturbate?" His response was reported all over the country. The next day Brown called Schalow, who was coaching at Morehead State in Kentucky, and told him, "Jack, they really made me look like an ass this time. I should have kept my mouth shut."

Brown's bloodiest battles were with the National Collegiate Athletic Association and Indiana's Bobby Knight. Brown thought the NCAA ripped off athletes and tried to destroy his basketball program.

Knight ruined Brown's two best shots at winning the national championship.

Because Brown criticized the "Gestapo bastards" of the NCAA and their "inhumane" rules so feverishly, everyone thought he was breaking those rules. The NCAA enforcement staff obviously thought so. Its investigation of Brown and his program lasted three-and-a-half years, one of the lengthiest probes in the organization's history. Although Director of Enforcement David Berst would never admit it, he wanted Brown's head on a silver platter. But all he got was a clump of Brown's hair, which had taken on a silver tint during the long ordeal. The final NCAA report came out in 1986 and listed eight minor infractions, none involving Brown. LSU got a slap on the wrist—the loss of two scholarships that probably wouldn't have been used anyway.

Reports of large cash payoffs to players John Williams and Tito Horford were unsubstantiated. The NCAA had uncovered no payments, no cars, nothing of significance.

"The best bill of health that you can get is an NCAA investigation that shows nothing," Brown said repeatedly. "They could find that many nitpicky things at any school if they looked for four years. I always said we didn't cheat. Now everyone knows we don't."

But Brown wasn't satisfied. What about the recruits he had lost because of the cloud of such a long investigation? How about the indignation he, his family and his friends suffered? These questions continued to trouble him.

Even more so, Knight was a constant source of grief. Brown berated Knight whenever anyone would listen. There were many who also disliked Knight and wanted someone like Brown to go after him.

"I think a lot of coaches respect Dale Brown," said Ken Trickey, head coach at Oral Roberts University. "He's not afraid to speak out about what he believes in. Not many coaches would take a stand against Bobby Knight. I'm not going to say Knight gets every call. But I think there are five or six coaches in the country who run college basketball. Dale Brown is not going to sit back and let them get away with anything. The blue bloods of college coaching don't like him. They wish he would keep quiet."

Brown took great pleasure in showing video tapes that were sent to him by a television reporter in Indiana. One tape showed Knight and former Indiana star Isiah Thomas at a banquet in Indianapolis. Asked about what he had learned from Knight, Thomas gave a detailed explanation of several four-letter words. The audience laughed at first, but then grew silent, realizing this was no joke. In the background, Knight could be seen red-faced and muttering under his breath. The other tape was an interview conducted with Knight the day before a game. The reporter asked some basic questions, and Knight, caught in a bad mood, was belligerent in his responses. He cussed out the reporter and finally ordered him to leave. Both tapes made Knight look like a villain. Brown thrilled in showing off his treasures to fellow coaches, friends and especially reporters. "See what he's like," Brown would say. "He gets away with that stuff. He needs to be stopped."

Twice, Brown had a chance to stop Knight's teams. Both times he failed. And both times Indiana won the national championship, elevating Knight's status to that of the greatest active coach in the game. Meanwhile, Brown was still without the national championship he told everyone he didn't need, but inwardly had to have. Ever since he landed in Baton Rouge with $800, three suits and a Volkswagon bug, his sights were set squarely on an NCAA title. He was convinced that LSU should have won it in 1981 and 1987.

When the Tigers appeared in the 1981 Final Four at Philadelphia, Brown had coached them to a 26-game victory streak and had already been named national Coach of the Year by several publications. If he had won the title then, many of his friends speculate he would have retired. But it didn't get that far, because Indiana came from behind in the second half of the semifinal to rout LSU, 67-49. After the game, an LSU fan was taunting Knight, and the temperamental Indiana coach grabbed the man and stuffed him into a trash can. Brown took it as a personal affront, just as he did the defeat.

The next time they met was in the Midwest Regional of the 1987 NCAA Tournament. At stake was a trip to the Final Four, which would be played at the Louisiana Superdome in New Orleans. Brown was convinced if his team, despite being seeded 10th in the region, could get in front of a home crowd at the Superdome, the title would be theirs. But Indiana rallied to win by a point. A week later, Knight and the Hoosiers were crowned national champs in New Orleans.

Just months later, Brown took a shot at Knight in a SPORT magazine article, calling him "a despicable human being who has everyone—the NCAA, the referees, the media, other coaches—intimidated out of their pants by calling people cheaters and deciding who can and can't coach. Well, I defy intimidation." He accused Knight of being a cheater, because he bullied referees, used his influence to get certain players on the Olympic and Pan Am teams and robbed his players of enjoying their college careers. "Some smart man once said, 'Be proud of your enemies.' Well, I'm extremely proud to know that Bobby Knight can't stand me," Brown said.

In response, Knight delivered some blows of his own, saying, "As long as the Dale Browns of the world are in disagreement with me, then I think I'm in pretty good shape." Later, he talked about being behind and starting to worry about losing the 1987 regional final to LSU, "then I looked down the floor and saw Dale Brown, and I knew, well, we had a chance." At the 1988 regional, reporters tried to get Knight to talk about Brown. Knight said only, "When you ask questions about him, you should direct them to a psychiatrist, not me."

Brown also attacked the local and national media whenever he was the subject of a critical article or harsh comment. He always took it personally. Jordy Hultberg has seen both sides of Brown's dealings with the media. He played for Brown from 1976-80, coached for him from 1981-84 and then, as a sportscaster, began covering him. He remembers occasions when Brown would fume for days about an article in some small-town newspaper. He has also seen him work the media. "He knows how to get his message across. If he has a cause to promote, he will talk to you for a lifetime," Hultberg said. "But on other days, he rushes you in and out."

Now Hultberg, a Baton Rouge sports anchor and color analyst for SEC basketball games, tries to be careful in his dealings with Brown. In order to remain objective, he keeps his distance from the program. He thinks his connection with Brown has hurt him, because some consider him "Dale's boy."

"When I was a player, Dale was so fiery and cause-oriented," Hultberg said. "He was always fighting for something. He was also fighting for his basketball life. When I coached for him, he had already achieved some success and had security. By then, he was fighting the Kentuckys of the world to get on top. Now as a commentator, I see that Dale has gone through a complete evolution. He is really focused on what he is doing. He keeps things basic. He doesn't play mind games. He is a much better coach."

————●————

The second driving force behind Brown—"You can always depend on me"—occupies even more of his attention and time. Because of his impoverished childhood, he wants to provide for anyone in need.

He also wants others to trust him, which was another thing missing in his younger years.

Dale Duward Brown was born in 1935 in the midst of the Depression. Times were particularly tough in Minot, a small railroad town in the northwest corner of North Dakota. On that Halloween day, Agnes Brown tried to call her husband, Charles, to tell him the good news about their first son. Charles had already skipped town, leaving behind not so much as a note of explanation, much less any money.

By age 10, Dale Brown had two part-time jobs to help support his mother and himself. He washed windows in a jewelry store and sold papers on a street corner. The rest of their income came from a monthly welfare check of $42.50. It took more than half of that to pay the rent on their one-room apartment above a seedy bar and a hardware store. They had to pass through the bar to get to the stairway to their room.

Agnes Brown died in 1970. Dale remembers her as a sweet, gentle woman. But heart and liver ailments had aged her beyond her years. Her religion and her son were her life. She brought little Dale to mass almost daily. At five, he became the youngest altar boy Minot had ever known. But he soon grew bitter toward the Catholic church. "Why didn't any of those pious people ever invite this poor little boy home for dinner or take him to play ball?" he wondered. Before long, he was hostile about his circumstances. He thought he couldn't talk to his mother about anything because her religion had made her so guilt-ridden. "She would just tell me if you do anything wrong, you're going to hell," he said.

Brown did see his father twice before he died. Each visit lasted only minutes. Meanwhile, he heard stories of how his father had other wives and children in Minot and nearby towns. "The bigamist sonofabitch," Dale called him. Dale's two older sisters left home when he was a young boy.

Already developing in Brown was his "You can always depend on me" instinct. He always was hustling money. He went by stores, restaurants and hotels to check the pay phones for coins. He did whatever odd jobs he could find. He worked in a creamery, drove a taxi and then a school bus and hammered railroad ties. If he couldn't raise money, he tried to help his mother save it. He skipped meals. They rarely had meat to eat. When the landlady yelled at his mother for being late with the rent, he scuffed the linoleum to get back at her. He did everything he could to be the "man of the house." But he was still a boy. It bothered him that he couldn't take proper care of his mother.

When he got older, he did receive attention from two men—Hammond and Father John Hogan. Brown went to Father Hogan for man-to-man talks, not religious counseling. Hammond provided the fun and excitement that had been missing. Brown was on his way to becoming a juvenile delinquent before Hammond, who had two daughters but no son, took him under his wing.

"Dale wasn't really a bad kid," Hammond said. Yet Brown was often in trouble at school, usually for fighting. Once, he burned down an old vacant building. Another time, he broke a boy's leg in a fight. Other children were always teasing him. He didn't have a winter coat in a climate that is colder than parts of Alaska. His clothes were old and patched. His only pair of shoes had holes in the bottom. He would sneak into the movie theater to pick up popcorn boxes and put them in the bottom of his shoes to keep the snow out. Most of all, they teased him because of his father.

What Hammond gave Brown went beyond companionship. Hammond made Dale feel good about himself. He introduced him to sports. Finally, Brown found himself. He was the best athlete in Minot. At last, he was somebody, other than Agnes Brown's little ragamuffin.

"Basketball gave me my life, my identity," Brown once said, describing his youth. "Until I found basketball, I thought I was a piece of shit. I mean, I disliked myself immensely. I had no father, no friends, no nothing. But when I was in that gym, oh, I had peace. For the first time in my life, I could think of myself as someone."

Throughout his athletic career, Brown was one of the biggest, strongest and fastest athletes in North Dakota. He played everything, but basketball was his favorite. He led the state in scoring his senior year at St. Leo's High School. He decided to attend Minot State, primarily because he wanted to stay home and take care of his mother. Doctors had told him that she could die at any time. He lived at home until he was 21. Surprisingly, he also lacked the confidence to leave home. He had visited the University of North Dakota in Grand Forks, but felt intimidated. "When I went there for a visit, I stayed in a fraternity house," he recalled. "All the other guys had money, clothes and cars. I didn't have anything. I wasn't real confident in myself. So I didn't visit anywhere else."

At Minot State, he became the first athlete to win 12 varsity letters, four each in football, basketball and track. He got everything done the hard way in basketball. He was a punishing rebounder and defensive player. He didn't have a great outside shot, but Russ Smith who announced many of Brown's games, said he had never seen a more fierce competitor.

Back then, college players were permitted to play on select teams in the offseason. That was another way for Brown to make a little money. Hammond coached the Minot team. Once, Minot was playing the American Indian national champions. The crowd was hostile toward the Indians during warmups. That bothered Brown. When it came time for Hammond to give his pregame talk, he counted his players and found only six instead of seven. "I realized Dale was missing," he recalled. "I thought to myself, 'Oh, no, he must have left.' So I started to send somebody out to find him when I happened to glance over at the other end of the court. There was Dale shooting layups with the Indians."

Brown's "You can always depend on me" facet grew stronger through the years. After he got into a position of influence and financial means at LSU, it shifted into high gear. He gave away his time, his money and practically his home. If there was a sick child in Plaquemine, Gross Tete or Abbeville, Brown often was contacted. Then he called, visited or sent an inspirational message and autographed LSU basketball. Usually, he would either have the child brought to the Assembly Center to meet the team, or he would have a player or two make a visit. If someone came to him with an idea for a charitable organization, he volunteered to serve on the board and usually made a contribution. He was an active member of the NAACP, sometimes marching with the group.

Officials at the Louisiana State Penitentiary at Angola sought out individuals to speak to the inmates. Brown went regularly and took his team there for exhibition games. He corresponded with dozens of inmates, helping some get paroled.

Brown even spent time with convicted murderer Leslie Lowenfield as he awaited the electric chair on April 13, 1988. The native of Guyana had no relatives in the United States, so Brown tried to comfort him before his execution. They had exchanged letters for several years. "Regardless if he's guilty or not guilty, I imagined the fear he must be experiencing," Brown said after the execution, which he did not witness. "I saw no fear. I saw no bitterness. I never saw it in any letters, either." After that, Brown became an outspoken opponent of the death penalty.

An administrator at a hospital for lepers requested some LSU basketball souvenirs for the patients. Brown took souvenirs and the team. Drew remembered heading home after a recruiting trip with Brown to Mississippi and stopping off at a country store in some obscure town. They each got an ice cream cone, and Brown started a conversation with the clerk. He found out the girl was thinking about going to college. When he went to pay for the ice cream, he discovered he had only a 10-dollar bill, and Drew was out of cash. He told the clerk to keep the 10 dollars if she would promise to go to college.

On game nights, LSU's bench often looked like the front row at a faith healer's service. Sitting with the team would be Jerry Gandy, a special education student who had been Brown's assistant manager since 1981; and little Jamie Roth, a local boy who had been part of the program for several years, despite an ongoing battle with brain cancer. Behind the bench there usually would be two or three wheelchairs seating physically handicapped persons, including LSU administrative assistant Jim Childers' daughter, Amy.

Once a year, Brown would pay for Alphonse Ellis, another man with health problems, to travel by bus to LSU from his central Louisiana home. First thing, Brown would have a manager or assistant take Ellis to a barber shop for a haircut and then to a department store for some new clothes. During the 1985-86 season, Bill Bailey, a Baton Rouge public relations executive, became part of the program. He had brain cancer and pledged to live long enough to see the Tigers make it to the Final Four. He did. They made it that season; Bailey died the following summer.

Often, the media criticized Brown for "exploiting" the handicapped or terminally ill. "Sure it helps our kids think about how fortunate they are," he answered his critics. "But I'm doing it for another reason. All I want to do is bring a moment of happiness and joy into their lives."

Ironically, some of the same reporters who questioned his intentions were quick to come to Brown when they needed help. He was even called to bail a reporter out of jail.

But most of his good deeds were never reported. Just before Christmas in 1987, he found out about some poor children in the tiny town of Melville, Louisiana. He and his family decided to buy clothes and toys for the children rather than exchange gifts themselves.

Sometimes, his home became a shelter for misplaced coaches, old friends and new acquaintances. "Dale is like a little boy who brings home stray pets," Vonnie Brown once said. "But he brings home stray people."

Until the spring of 1988, one of his occasional house guests was Moacyr Cezar, a Brazilian coach who wanted to learn about American basketball. He spent two years at LSU as a volunteer coach. The players became fond of him and nicknamed him "Gato," which means cat in Spanish. Brown continually gave Gato clothes, food and cash. On holidays, he stayed with the Browns. The rest of the time he was a dorm proctor, living with the basketball team. But Cezar's visa prohibited him from collecting wages. Finally, Gato, who spoke little English, became desperate.

On a warm, sunny afternoon, Gato stole the keys to the cage holding Mike the Tiger, the school's live mascot. He locked himself in the outer compartment of the cage and put up a sign that read, "I protest Coach Brown." He threatened to let the tiger out. He also produced a gun and a bag, which he said contained a bomb. Panic broke out on the LSU campus. A SWAT team trained its sights on the cage, which is located between the Assembly Center and Tiger Stadium. To make matters worse, Brown was 700 miles away, speaking at a dinner in Orlando, Florida. It took several, tension-filled hours before basketball player Jose Vargas and Chancellor James Wharton persuaded Gato to surrender to police. It turned out he had no bomb and the gun was a toy.

"I could have gotten him out in a minute," Brown said privately. "All I had to say was, 'Gato, get the hell out of there or we're going to let the tiger in with you.' He is scared to death of that tiger. He is just a gentle, little man. Everyone knows that. He wouldn't hurt anyone."

Initially, Brown was angry with his friend. He felt betrayed. He considered leaving Gato in jail, but the next day Brown was overcome by his "You can always depend on me" emotions. Brown arranged for his release. Then Gato had to undergo evaluation at a mental hospital. He was found to be mentally competent, but was ordered to return to Brazil, where he faced imprisonment for failing to make child support payments. Once again, Brown took care of him. He bought the airline ticket and paid the child support of more than $2,000.

Despite being among the top earners in the coaching profession, Brown still has financial worries. He has never publicly disclosed his earnings, but estimates from close friends and associates place his annual income from $300,000 to $500,000. He is in great demand as a motivational speaker, usually giving more than 50 speeches a year. He gets a fee of $5,000 per speech. Many businesses pursue him for commercials. He was paid $50,000 for an advertising campaign with a utility company. Often he makes more money speaking and doing commercials than he does coaching. His salary at LSU is $88,000, plus a $60,000 guarantee for radio and television shows. The rest of his money comes from Dale Brown Enterprises, run by his daughter, Robyn. She arranges his speaking engagements and commercials and helps organize his summer basketball camp, which attracts more than 1,000 youngsters every year.

Robyn has often tried to persuade her father to stop giving away so much money. It got to the point that his checking account dwindled to just a few hundred dollars. "Daddy, you've got to keep more money for yourself and Mom," Robyn finally told him. "You can't keep giving it away. What would Mom do if something happened to you?" He heeded his daughter's advice—for a few weeks.

The Browns don't live an extravagant lifestyle. For 15 years, they lived in the same, modest home that they purchased for $38,000. They moved into a more expensive neighborhood in 1987, but still not the most exclusive in Baton Rouge. They own one car. They have few investments.

"Dale Brown is the most generous man I know," said Jim Talbot, a local businessman, politician and one of Brown's closest friends. Talbot recalls a trip they took together to Europe. They passed through a small French village looking for a place to eat. They came upon two teenage boys who couldn't speak much English, but managed to give them some directions to a restaurant. Naturally, Brown had done all the talking. He noticed one of the boys wasn't wearing shoes, even though it was a chilly night. He wanted to know why, and the boy explained he didn't own any shoes. "Right away Dale takes off his shoes and socks and hands them to the boy," Talbot said. "I mean it was freezing. I was already shivering, and Dale went barefoot."

In every impoverished child, troubled teenager, desperate prisoner and distraught parent, Brown sees a glimpse of his past. He is compelled to be a helper, because there really had been no one there for him. He wants people to trust in him, to take comfort in his strength. They can always count on him.

Yet, trusting others has been almost impossible for Brown. How could he depend on someone else? His father abandoned him. Growing up, he was told his mother could die at any time. He was a heart-beat away from being orphaned. It caused him to develop an emotional shield. At a young age, he prepared himself to be alone in the world. He built a barrier around his heart. Nobody was ever going to hurt him. As a result, there was little exchange of feelings in his relation-ships. He could give, but wouldn't take. He couldn't completely trust anyone or anything. It would make him too vulnerable. And he wanted to make sure nothing or no one ever hurt him again.

Thus, Brown developed the "I can only trust myself" facet of his personality. It extended into his coaching methods, outside interests, friendships, family life, relationships with his players and even his faith. "It's not that I don't want to trust people," he explained. "But when I give myself, I can get hurt."

On his wedding day, Brown prayed for a blizzard so the roads would be blocked and he couldn't get to the church. He knew he loved Vonnie. Theirs was a storybook romance. They had met at Minot State. He was a star athlete. She was a cheerleader. But he wasn't sure he could totally trust anyone, even her. Their marriage worked, even though it took some unusual turns. Of course, Dale Brown has rarely done anything the traditional way.

The time Dale and Vonnie spend together is special to them. They hold hands on walks, snuggle on the couch, even when guests are present. Most of all, they have supported each other's career pur-suits. Vonnie understood her husband had to work long hours and travel extensively to build a prominent basketball program. Dale was understanding of his wife's desire to become one of the best folk dance instructors in the country. Both achieved their goals through years of dedication and sacrifice.

During those years, Dale and Vonnie went weeks, sometimes months, without seeing each other. Dale would be in South America recruiting a player or the Middle East conducting a clinic, while Vonnie was in Yugoslavia studying dance. Even when they were both home, they led separate lives. Their main means of communication was leav-ing notes. Once when they were both in town, they went seven days without seeing each other. Dale actually spent more time with his daughter than his wife. He started taking Robyn on recruiting trips when she was two. Some of her fondest childhood memories are go-ing to road games with her father. "I love him because he's my dad, but he's also my friend," she said.

Brown's friendships are also non-traditional. He has developed an inner circle of friends who are supremely loyal to him. He would do anything for them, except completely trust them. His friends understand.

"I don't need to hear from Dale every day," said Tom Moran, one of the inner circle. "And he doesn't need to get a call from me. He knows he can count on me. When he needs me, I'm there. And I know he is there for me."

Moran is a successful restauranteur, called by some the "Restaurant King of Baton Rouge." Before he met Brown, he had made up his mind he didn't like him. From watching him coach and reading about him, Moran thought Brown was a fake and a flake. One night, LSU assistant football coach Lynn Amedee took Brown to eat at one of Moran's restaurants. Amedee introduced Brown to Moran. Within hours, Brown had convinced Moran to become coordinator of the summer jobs program for basketball players. Moran was hooked.

Others in Brown's friendship circle include Dr. Redfield Bryan, a renowned surgeon; Al Guglielmo, a businessman with international holdings; and Gus Weill, an author, playwright, political expert and public relations executive.

Undoubtedly, Brown's friendship with Weill is his most unusual. It has nothing to do with basketball. In fact, Weill had never been to an LSU game until he met Brown at a grocery store. At the time, Weill was in a sporting mood, going up and down the aisles whistling the theme song from the movie "Chariots of Fire," which he had just seen. He introduced himself to Brown, and they struck up a conversation.

Their relationship is mainly about conversations. They sit together or talk on the phone for hours, discussing books, philosophy, politics and anything else that comes to mind.

"I think Dale is intellectually frustrated," Weill said. "He is constantly searching for challenges and ways to utilize his intellect. The man is brilliant. He is so knowledgeable and conversant on so many subjects. He has a thirst for knowledge. The X's and O's of basketball just aren't enough for him. He has to have more than basketball."

Brown is fascinated by Weill's creativity. He calls on Weill whenever he needs to make an important public statement. Brown can make it sound good, but Weill can give it a special flare.

Brown particularly enjoys Weill's plays, perhaps because Dale once had aspirations to pursue an acting career. He played the lead role in a college play, "Gas Light," and received favorable reviews. He gave up acting because he took so much ribbing from his teammates.

Often, Brown's friends won't see or hear from him for months. Then out of the blue, he calls them and wants to know why he hasn't heard from them.

Brown likes to be surrounded with his friends and associates during the basketball season. Then he wants to be by himself. He usually travels and vacations alone. Talbot has joined him on some trips. Guglielmo on others. But even then, he often wanders off by himself.

On one summer excursion, Brown and Talbot drove to Utah State University, where Brown had a speaking engagement. They took a side trip to the Grand Canyon, arriving late at night. Since they had no idea where to find a hotel, they slept in the car. Shortly after sunrise, Brown was awake and stretching. "Get up, Jim," he called to his drowsy companion. "We've got some hiking to do. Who knows when we'll be here again. We're going down to the bottom."

Brown was sure Talbot would not follow him down the trail. So he set out on his own, enjoying the view and solitude. After a couple hours, Talbot was wide awake and wondering how much longer he had to wait. He walked about a quarter mile down the steep path and sat down on a large rock. He saw people with backpacks, others riding on mules. Then he began to worry. Brown was stubborn enough to try to hike all the way to the bottom with no food and water.

About five miles down the trail, Brown was nearing the bottom. He considered turning back, then remembered Talbot was there. "He's probably sitting up there watching me with binoculars," Brown said to himself. So he continued his descent. Even before he got to the bottom, he knew he was in trouble. All the other hikers were stopping to eat or drinking out of canteens. He passed them on the way down, but not on the way up. His legs ached and he was near exhaustion as he trudged up the rocky trail. The sun was sinking when he finally reached the top. He tried not to show the pain. But Talbot, who already had eaten twice, knew Brown had to be hurting, hungry and thirsty. "I'll go get you something," Talbot said. "What do you want to eat? How about something to drink?"

Brown just shook his head and motioned toward the car. "Let's get out of here," he moaned. "My legs are killing me." Little did he know the agony was only beginning. As they drove away, his legs began to cramp violently. Rubbing the muscles didn't help. Nothing did. "Get me to a hospital," he screamed. But after a half hour, the cramps subsided and he refused even to see a doctor. Brown had paid dearly for his independence.

On other vacation adventures, Brown has climbed more than three-fourths up the 14,700-foot Matterhorn in the Swiss Alps; raced the length of the Mississippi River in a speedboat; worn only a loin-cloth while he canoed down a section of the Amazon River and hunted crocodiles; and ended a trip to Baghdad the day before the airport was shut down by the start of the Iraq-Iran war. He often goes to West Germany to speak to U.S. military troops. Early in his career, he spent 30 days in South Korea giving motivational talks to soldiers. His travel plans include an expedition up Mount Ararat to find Noah's Ark and a dogsled trip to the North Pole to plant an LSU flag there.

When relaxing at home, nothing pleases Brown more than read-ing. He loves almost any kind of book, except those involving sports. His bookshelves are filled with biographies, great literature, history and psychology books, and, of course, books on positive thinking, self-help and more recently, religion. Once he opens the cover, he usually finishes a book in a single sitting, often reading until 4 o'clock in the morning. To facilitate his quest for knowledge, he developed his own style of speed reading. He analyzes the work and writes down his thoughts. He shares sections with his team or friends. Many times, he copies some inspirational message directly from the book and uses it on one of his many handouts. He reads 100 to 150 books every year.

Jogging is another way Brown makes time to be alone and reflect on the events of the day or season. Almost every year, he makes a bet with somebody that he will jog a mile every day for a year. It is a wa-ger he rarely loses.

Pastimes like golf, tennis and fishing frustrate him. They require too much patience and quiet for long periods of time. Once, when a friend took him fishing, Brown sat in the boat and talked the whole time. They never caught a fish. Another friend took him to the golf course. He whiffed a few times, knocked a couple balls into the woods and drove the rest of his shots into the ground. After four holes, he stormed off the course.

Besides, Brown can't be far from a telephone at any time. He spends most of his day with a receiver lodged between his neck and shoulder. Many times he will have people on two lines and his secre-tary will be placing more calls for him. He usually gets several dozen messages a day, occasionally as many as a hundred. Every call is re-turned.

Although he is genuinely concerned about his players and helps them long after their careers end, he is not really close to them. Not even to an alter-ego like Ricky Blanton. They have a business-like relationship. Brown thinks it is necessary to keep a certain distance while athletes are playing for him. He seems to be closer to his former players. Neboisha Bukumirovich, a Yugoslav who rarely contributed in four years at LSU, said, "I didn't realize how much I learned from Coach Brown until I got away from the program. He taught me so much about life. He is a psychologist, more than anything. In those years of being around him, he was always positive, never once down. You always left his office feeling better."

Nowhere does Brown's self-reliance show up more than in his coaching. If Schalow had stayed with him, it wouldn't have been so bad. He was so much like Brown that they claimed to actually think alike. Ever since Schalow left the team, Brown has missed their close relationship, the kind he has never really had with any other assistant.

In fact, Brown has had clashes with assistant coaches. He demands that one man—Dale Brown—run the show. Ron Abernathy, Brown's associate coach, was on the staff longer than anyone but Brown. When he was hired in 1976, Abernathy was the first black assistant coach in any sport at LSU. His basketball knowledge isn't as great as some older, more experienced coaches, but he is intensely loyal and supportive. "He motivates the motivator," Brown said. "He contributes so much. He charges me up. He deserves more credit."

For several years, Brown delegated some decision-making to assistants Rick Huckabay and Tex Winter. Brown liked both men, but eventually decided he needed to be completely in charge of everything.

3

Packages and Promises

Dale Brown dislikes many aspects of recruiting high school athletes. He has seldom attended the major summer camps that he says parade young players like cattle at a meat market. Overall, he thinks the recruiting process puts too much pressure on the players, on the parents and on the coaches. He contends the only other profession in which adults recruit teenagers is prostitution.

Nonetheless, Brown was born to be a recruiter. He can outtalk anyone in the business. He landed his first college coaching job by recruiting a player for Utah State before Brown had ever seen the campus. He built a program at LSU by first winning on the recruiting trail and then on the court. Through the years, he has refined his technique.

Some wise person, probably not a coach, first coined the phrase, "Great players make great coaches." Nowhere is that more true than in college basketball. Game strategy and motivation obviously come into play, but recruiting ranks right up there. It is the life blood of the sport. One elite player can turn around a program. The teams with the best talent have the best shot at winning championships. It is just that simple. Getting the talent isn't so easy.

Even before he gained fame as a coach, Brown could recruit. He knew what he was looking for, worked hard enough and long enough, and convinced young athletes they needed him. He has always gone after players from backgrounds similar to his own. His players must think and act like him or he can't coach them.

Before recruiting players on the West Coast, Brown sometimes asks Jack Schalow to watch them and make an evaluation. On one visit, Schalow was convinced almost immediately that the player was not cut out for major college. He recommended that Brown drop the boy from consideration.

"Dale, the kid can't play for you. I'm telling you he just can't play," Schalow reported over the phone. "And besides, he is a bad kid. I don't like his attitude."

There was a prolonged pause. Schalow waited patiently. Finally, Brown responded, "But Jack, the boy doesn't have a father. I think I should give him a chance. That's the kind of kid I can coach. He will listen to me." Brown gave the player a scholarship.

Brown's players tend to be tough-minded kids. They've grown up the hard way. They respond to his us-against-the-world mentality.

Early in his career, Brown learned he could pull remarkable upsets with young men who think like he does. But to complete his mission, he needed talented players who could also be motivated. That meant he had to adjust his recruiting. Originally, he went after the best in Louisiana and tried to pick off some second-level national recruits and foreigners. Then he realized if he wanted to win big, he had to recruit head-to-head with the elite of college basketball. His success in the late '70s and early '80s enabled him to do that. Those teams had good, but not great talent. None of those players made it more than a couple years in the NBA. There were no Magic Johnsons, Michael Jordans or Akeem Olajuwons at LSU. The Tigers played against the great ones, but for many years, they couldn't recruit them.

That changed in Brown's 12th season at LSU. The quest for his first premier player began when Ron Abernathy was contacted by a friend, who advised him to look at a player in Los Angeles. It turned out to be the man-child, John Williams. Only 16, he already had an NBA body. He stood 6-8 and easily carried 240 pounds on his broad-shouldered frame. He resembled another player in Los Angeles—the Lakers' Magic Johnson. Better yet, he could play like Johnson. During his senior season at Crenshaw High School, every major college power pursued him. By the spring of 1984, he still had not signed, and the recruiting was getting nasty. Accusations were being tossed back and forth. Some coaches considered pulling out. Others knew they didn't have a chance. Louisville, Houston, Nevada-Las Vegas, Kentucky, UCLA and yes, LSU, were the front-runners. As the days passed, conflicting reports came out. First, Williams had apparently committed to Louisville. Then it was UNLV.

Keeping a low profile, LSU was busy behind the scenes. Brown doesn't like to be in the recruiting spotlight. For many years, he has had a rule of silence. He does his best work in private. Sometimes his recruits are told not to let anyone know of their interest in LSU. That was the situation with Williams. While everyone thought Williams was headed to one of the more established programs, Brown had already locked up his first super recruiting deal.

Brown possesses qualities that suit him perfectly to the craft of recruiting, which is generally a business for eager, young coaches trying to make a name for themselves. There is never really such a thing as a day off. No time for vacations. Recruiting season begins in May and continues through April. Then another cycle starts. A recruiter must keep constant tabs on his prospects, calling in the morning and evening, sending letters in the afternoon and visiting whenever NCAA rules permit. In recent years, recruiting rules have become more restrictive in an effort to lessen the pressure on high school players. But it is still a mad rush to persuade a recruit to sign a national letter of intent, binding him to a school.

Recruits say Brown's outgoing, energetic personality puts a family at ease. But that is only the beginning. Depending on the situation, he can be entertaining, witty, charming, scholarly or any combination of those. What separates him from most coaches is the ability to blend into an environment. Whether it is a tenement in Watts, where Williams lived, or a plush home in suburban Houston, where Tito Horford resided, Brown makes all those around him feel he belongs.

Once he establishes a rapport with the family, he goes right to work with a polished pitch of positive thoughts. His recruits and their parents see a man who is thoroughly convincing and believes in himself and his program completely. If he sold vacuum cleaners, they would probably buy one. If it was life insurance, they would likely sign up.

Other coaches get to the point that they hate to recruit against him. His charisma is too much to overcome. Rival recruiters feel like they are trying to get a date with a woman who has just met Robert Redford.

"Dale Brown is the best head coach in recruiting that I know," Mississippi State recruiter John Brady said. Brady has an unusual perspective of Brown. When Brady was a high school coach in Crowley, Louisiana, Brown recruited two of his players. Both went to Mississippi State, along with their coach. Since then, Brady has tried unsuccessfully to break into Brown's recruiting territory. "I think he is a master of convincing people about what he stands for," Brady explained. "I just think he is the best. I think it is his personality. His personality is so strong, and he believes totally in what he does and the way he is doing it. That is what makes him great at it."

Beyond that, Brown has a knack for being able to find out who will make the decision. Usually, it is not the player. Either a parent, relative or coach generally has the greatest influence on a college choice. Brown concentrates most of his effort on that person. Often high school coaches are so close to their players they become like family. In those cases, Brown has gone after the player and his coach. For years, his staff has been made up primarily of coaches who had great high school players. To get the players, he hired the coaches. Many schools follow the same practice, which is permissible under NCAA rules. It is commonly called a package deal. It might as well be known as a "Package Dale."

At least a half dozen top players have come to LSU with their coaches or someone close to them who was hired by Brown. Most notable are Stanley Roberts, Howard Carter and Rudy Macklin. LSU might have signed these players anyway, but hiring their coaches was like purchasing an insurance policy. Roberts' high school coach, Jim Childers, announced in the summer of 1987 that he had accepted a position with LSU. Two months later, Roberts signed with the Tigers. LSU wasn't even among his top three schools until Childers went there.

The first "Package Dale" was worked out in 1976. Ron Abernathy was a promising young coach at Trinity High School in Louisville, Kentucky. He had an even more promising player in Rudy Macklin. Both signed up with Brown. Three years later, Howard Carter was the top recruit in Louisiana. To ensure getting him, Brown hired his coach from Baton Rouge's Redemptorist High School, Rick Huckabay. Macklin, Carter, Abernathy and Huckabay were part of the LSU team that went to the 1981 Final Four.

In another instance, LSU was about to lose a top prospect from Louisiana. Brown went to work and reversed the situation in a matter of minutes. Gary Duhe, then an LSU graduate assistant coach, remembers watching Brown make calls until he found out the player's mother was in charge of all important decisions. So he went directly to her and asked for a commitment. She said it was up to her son. To which Brown responded abruptly, "Look, ma'am. This is your child. You fed him. You clothed him. You took care of him. You raised this boy. Now don't tell me you're not going to help him make the right choice. He is YOUR boy." The mother was startled at first, but then took it as a compliment. She agreed she was going to make the decision. She said her son was going to LSU, and he did.

Most of the college coaches pursuing Williams thought his high school coach, Willie West, had the most influence. West was not family. Brown and Abernathy did some checking and discovered that John's mother, Marie Matthews, had come into the picture. Williams had been raised by his grandmother, but now his mother wanted to get involved. That was all Brown needed to know. He sent Abernathy to Los Angeles throughout the spring months. Abernathy lost count of how many trips he made, but he logged enough frequent flyer miles to fly around the world. He developed a close bond with Matthews.

When it came time to sign a letter of intent, LSU got Williams' signature and its first superstar. It also got Matthews. She moved to Louisiana with her son. She bounced from job to job, at least one of which was arranged through LSU contacts. Williams, meanwhile, bounced the ball with the brilliance that was expected of him. He led LSU to the Southeastern Conference championship and then to the Final Four. Having lived up to his prize billing, he departed after his sophomore season for the NBA. Only 19, the gifted youngster bid a tearful farewell to his basketball family. It was reported he had to leave because of his grades. Actually, he could have survived academically, but not financially. LSU coaches and others associated with the program learned that his mother had received $90,000 from an agent. The agent, whom Williams refused to name, gave him the choice of paying back the money or turning pro. If Williams did neither, the agent said he would report him to the NCAA and the player would be stripped of his eligibility. Williams' only real choice was the NBA. He was drafted in the first round by the Washington Bullets and immediately became a key player.

Recruiting Williams was the start of something big for Brown. He no longer went after just players who were close or had some contact with LSU. It was open season. Brown set out to land the best players in the world. He recruited Tito Horford, the nation's top-rated high school center in 1985. Then he became the first American coach to recruit in the Soviet Union, fervently pursuing 7-4 center Arvidas Sabonis, considered the world's greatest amateur player. Sabonis led the Soviets to the gold medal in the 1988 Olympic Games. When Brown couldn't get Sabonis, he settled for Hernan Motenegro, the center on the Yugoslavian national team that beat the United States in an early game at the 1986 World Basketball Championships. Back in the states, he successfully signed Fess Irvin, one of the nation's top-rated point guards in 1986. Irvin was LSU's last major player recruited by Abernathy. After Craig Carse became recruiting coordinator, LSU signed Stanley Roberts, the No. 1 center in 1988; Chris Jackson, the best point guard of the 1988 class; and Shaquille O'Neal, the top-ranked center in 1989.

It takes months of phone calls and letters just to capture the interest of top players. Then the personal visits have to go well. The pressure on these players and on the coaches trying to get them is intense. No price—a coach's time or sometimes money and other gifts—is too high to pay. These players can literally make millions of dollars for a school. Many coaches, alumni and representatives of the schools are willing to pay thousands, sometimes hundreds of thousands to get players of this caliber.

About the time Brown was diving head-first into the recruiting of high-profile athletes, the NCAA was breathing down his back with its long investigation. His coaching rivals were convinced he was cheating. They fully expected the NCAA to crush his program like a smoldering camp fire, and that would be the end of the nuisance in Baton Rouge. Yet, when the investigation concluded in 1986, amidst rumors of major violations, LSU was found to be almost spotless, to the amazement of some and disbelief of others.

What is cheating? According to the NCAA, it can be almost anything. There are thousands of rules. Many make little sense. Others are unenforceable. Only a handful are truly necessary to prevent any school from gaining an unfair advantage in recruiting.

A coach who drives one of his players to the dorm on a rainy day has committed an NCAA violation. If a recruit attending an athletic event gets a free soft drink or hot dog, it is a violation.

The violations that need to be more closely policed by the NCAA involve cash payments, cars, houses, monthly allowances and other major incentives that cause a young man to be swayed toward a particular program. These actions are not against the law. They are merely violations of NCAA rules, punishable by sanctions against the school and occasionally a player or coach. The strongest sanctions are typically two to three years of probation with no television and postseason appearances.

Major rules violations happen, usually without detection, because the NCAA doesn't have the manpower to investigate even the 300 Division I programs. Almost without exception, the only way the NCAA finds out about violations is through a disgruntled player, a coach or booster from another program, or an investigation by a newspaper or television station. Coaches are reluctant to expose their peers. In their fraternity, it isn't proper behavior to squeal. As for the players, the ones who take money aren't going to talk, and the ones who don't cash in are hesitant to blow the whistle on somebody else. Often, they don't trust the NCAA anyway.

Consequently, big-time cheating exists. It runs rampant in some programs. Anyone familiar with college basketball suspected that Kentucky cheated long before the program was exposed by the Lexington Herald-Leader in its Pulitzer award-winning investigation in 1985. Yet, it wasn't until the NCAA was handed evidence three years later that the UK program was investigated and put on three years probation.

Many of the outstanding college basketball programs in the country don't cheat. They don't need to. North Carolina, Indiana and Notre Dame are going to get their share of great high school players based on their basketball and academic reputations. Yet, a survey of basketball coaches indicated that the large majority think cheating is a serious problem.

Logically, one would think LSU could not have successfully recruited Williams, Horford, Irvin, Jackson, Roberts and O'Neal without offering something extra. LSU does not have tradition or a huge arena like Kentucky and North Carolina. It certainly does not have the academic reputation of Duke and Michigan. And it is not located in a major city like Temple and St. John's or a glamour spot like Nevada-Las Vegas. So how does LSU win recruiting wars?

A saint, Brown is not. He breaks some rules. But he is careful about which ones. Most of his infractions are humanitarian acts, his way of showing his players they can depend on him. When former LSU player Mark Alcorn died of cancer in 1981, several of his teammates wanted to go to the funeral in St. Louis, but did not have the plane fare. Brown contacted the NCAA and asked for special permission to pay for their transportation. When he didn't get it, he went ahead with his plans anyway. Friends of the program paid for the players' travel expenses. Other incidents involved arranging dental care for a player with an abscessed tooth, getting a freshman from a poor home some dress clothes to wear on a team trip, helping a player get bus fare home for Christmas and giving food to the families of several of his players. In the early years of his program, there was some minor cheating going on, though Brown was never a party to it.

"As a player, I saw things [money] passed around," Jordy Hultberg said. "They gave it to me to give to other players. Those kind of people aren't in the program any more. Dale never knew about it."

Like a crafty attorney, Brown uses the rules to his advantage. The NCAA permits colleges to hire a recruit's coach, so he takes it to an extreme. The NCAA allows schools to arrange summer employment for their athletes, so he gets them top-paying jobs. His players work for construction firms and industrial plants that pay $15 an hour or more for common workers. In a long summer, an LSU player can make close to $10,000. "We don't need to cheat," said Al Guglielmo, a friend of Brown and the program. "We get them good jobs. Dale teaches them they have to earn everything they get. They can buy a car if they want it. They don't need to be given anything."

Tom Moran, another LSU booster, maintains there have been no payoffs. "No player has ever gotten a cash payment or anything like that here," Moran said. "If we cheat, we cheat less than any other program in the country."

If Brown cheated, he certainly would not have publicly chastised the NCAA so vigorously. The NCAA and investigative reporters from national publications placed Brown and his program under a magnifying glass for most of the '80s.

They never found out about LSU backers offering money to Benoit Benjamin. In 1982, Benjamin, from Monroe, Louisiana, was one of the nation's top-rated high school centers. Brown had to get him. To make sure he would, a boosters group from north Louisiana secretly set out to raise $50,000 to give the player. Brown caught wind of it about the time they had collected $35,000. Without giving it a second thought, he shut off the transaction. Benjamin didn't get the cash. LSU didn't get Benjamin. He went to Creighton University with Willis Reed.

After that, Abernathy got caught in a precarious position. He was on a short recruiting trip to south Mississippi when his briefcase was stolen out of his car. It contained approximately $800 in cash and $1,200 in checks, all payments he had collected earlier that day from rented homes in Baton Rouge. He reported the theft to police. When the story hit the news, it was reported as $2,000 in cash and seemed to implicate him. Once the rumors started to spread, the amount of money involved grew to as high as $50,000 in cash. The LSU administration conducted an independent investigation and found Abernathy's account to be accurate. The NCAA checked into it, and discovered no wrongdoing.

Austin Wilson, who has covered LSU basketball about as long as anyone, said he is confident Brown does not cheat. "Dale Brown's integrity is flawless," Wilson said. "I don't think he has ever cheated. I do not believe Dale Brown would condone cheating. I just do not believe it. I would be shocked if it were true."

Brown's assistants know they would be fired if it were true of them. "Coach Brown would not tolerate buying somebody," Abernathy said. "He tells all of his coaches when they're hired that if they're caught cheating, they're going to be fired on the spot."

Even some of his adversaries are beginning to believe Brown doesn't cheat. When the NCAA spends as much time and money as it did to investigate LSU, it usually comes up with substantial infractions. That means almost automatic probation for at least two years. LSU lost only two scholarships for one season. In the end, by clearing its name, LSU gained more than it lost.

Furthermore, the actions of Williams and Horford are testimonials of LSU's innocence. Williams stayed only two years and left. Horford stuck around two months and departed. If they had been paid to play, they wouldn't have left. In fact, many of LSU's players have said they turned down major inducements, as much as $200,000, from other schools. Why? It isn't the weather, arena or basketball tradition. It apparently isn't the cash, either. So it must be Brown and what he teaches.

While other coaches talk about what their programs offer in terms of basketball opportunities, Brown sells himself and his philosophy. His recruiting visits have little to do with basketball. He discusses lifetime goals and pursuits. He stresses the value of developing a work ethic. He explains his own beliefs, based on his upbringing. He tells families what an education means to the recruit. He promises them that he will take a personal interest in the young man's development in every aspect of life. He assures them that this teenager will become a man of integrity and character. He goes on and on, sometimes for hours. He is convinced about what he tells them. As a result, he is absolutely convincing.

Initially, Roberts was overwhelmed by the vivacious coach from LSU. On his only visit to the family's home, located just outside Columbia, South Carolina, Brown walked up to Roberts and hugged him. "I thought the man was crazy at first," Roberts said with a laugh. "Then I found out he meant it. He cared about me as a person. I knew I wanted to play for him. That's the kind of family I wanted to be part of."

Vernel Singleton, recruited along with Roberts, knew immediately that Brown was the coach for him. "I just liked him right away," Singleton said. "It just seems like he knows you before you meet him. He was so friendly. He didn't really seem like a coach. He was just a friend."

During Brown's trip to the Singleton home in Natchez, Mississippi, he did not so much as mention basketball. No promises of playing time. No talk of national championships with Roberts and Jackson. It was a time for the Singleton family to get to know Brown and for him to form a relationship with them. "I knew I could talk to him," Singleton said. "Coach Brown was different. I guess that's why he's one of the best."

Most recruits are captivated by Brown. Not every parent feels that way, though. Jacqueline Jackson didn't hit it off with Brown at all. She tore up the letter of intent her son, Chris, signed with LSU. Basically, she told her son to go anywhere except LSU. But his attraction to Brown and the program was so strong that he temporarily broke off relations with his mother and left home.

The first time Jackson met Brown, Chris made up his mind he was going to LSU. They shared stories about their childhoods, growing up without a father and falling in love with basketball to the point it made up for everything else. But they didn't discuss the game itself or what Jackson could do as a player at LSU. Brown didn't give him a sales pitch and didn't try to force him to make a commitment. He just wanted Jackson to understand he had a friend, regardless of where he went to school.

Brown had no way of knowing the pursuit of Jackson would be his most draining recruiting effort. What made it so frustrating was that Brown knew beyond a shadow of a doubt that Jackson wanted to play for LSU. The problem was many of the residents of Gulfport, Mississippi, were trying to influence Chris and his mother. Another factor was Jackson had not met the requirements of Proposition 48. The rule stipulates that athletes must have at least a 2.0 grade point average in a minimum of 11 academic courses and must score at least 15 on the American College Test or 700 on the Scholastic Aptitude Test. If the athlete doesn't meet both requirements, he can still attend college on an athletic scholarship, but has to sit out the first year and lose a year of eligibility. Jackson squeaked through on the grade point average. But he failed to score 15 on the ACT on each of the first four times he took it. In June, he was down to his last chance.

Meanwhile, LSU was out of point guards after Darryl Joe completed his eligibility, Fess Irvin transferred to James Madison University and seldom-used backup Parker Griffith departed for Vanderbilt.

LSU had to get Jackson, and he had to be eligible. Other programs were just as anxious to attract him. Most had given up until the news broke in July that Jackson had passed the test requirement, scoring 16 on his last chance. While Brown and Craig Carse were expecting Jackson to show up in Baton Rouge at any time, he mysteriously vanished. That same week, a letter was sent to the Sun-Herald newspaper in Gulfport stating Jackson wanted to visit other schools. The letter had Jackson's signature at the bottom, but it was a fake.

Reports came out that Jackson was on his way to visit Georgetown, which had recruited him. Georgetown coach John Thompson, relaying his message through a school spokesman, denied it. Then there were reports that Chris was visiting North Carolina, Nevada-Las Vegas, Alcorn State and Mississippi State before making his choice. North Carolina had lost interest in Jackson long before that, because of his test problems.

But the other schools actively recruited him to the end. UCLA was the last to get involved. Jackson publicly denied that large cash offers had been made to him through Les Matthews, a family friend who is a wealthy, mysterious businessman in Gulfport. But privately, he told his teammates and coaches about them. He later told an NCAA investigator, who spent days in Gulfport tracking down Matthews and others who involved themselves in the recruiting of Jackson.

When Jackson had sat down with Matthews to talk about college opportunities, he thought they were going to discuss the basketball and academic programs. He was shocked when Matthews started talking about how much money he could get to sign with Mississippi State, UNLV or UCLA. Matthews told him that Mississippi State was offering $100,000, while UNLV and UCLA were both willing to pay $200,000 through anonymous representatives of their programs. No coaches' names were mentioned. But it was clear the payoff was his for the taking. Jackson reported it all to the NCAA.

The money did not tempt Jackson. Just the opposite, he was offended that Matthews had tried to cut a deal for him. That was the last time he talked to Matthews about college.

But his mother still wanted him to visit other schools. She didn't think he knew enough about college to pick one without comparing it to others. She also didn't like Brown. She had been told that he used players and was somehow connected with the Mafia. She believed it; her son didn't. They often argued about it. Eventually, he made up his mind he was going to LSU with or without his mother's permission. After all, he was 19 years old.

Jackson's disappearance took place late in the summer of 1988. It was a week before Brown or Carse heard from him. When he finally did call, he explained that he had to get away from the pressure. So he had spent several days at a friend's house. They had also gone to Mobile, Alabama, for two days. Until then, he had been a nervous wreck. He didn't want to disappoint his mother. He didn't want the family's friends to be angry with him. But he knew that he wanted to go to LSU. Many times he stayed up almost all night, finally crying himself to sleep.

On the last day of July, Jackson finally got to Baton Rouge. A cousin, Len Jackson, found out about the confusion and was concerned enough to travel from his Detroit home to Gulfport. Actually, Matthews had asked Len Jackson to talk with Chris, thinking he would persuade him to visit other schools. On the contrary, Len told Chris to make up his own mind.

Convinced of Chris' desire to attend LSU, Len Jackson drove his cousin to Baton Rouge. Upon his arrival, Chris contacted local newspapers and issued the following statement:

"I have signed the Southeastern Conference scholarship form and will be attending Louisiana State University this fall. I want to get my degree from LSU, and I want to play basketball there. I made that decision a couple of years ago. My reasons were simple. I liked the coaches. I liked the school. I liked the area, and I liked the people. As hard as it may be for some people to accept, those were my reasons.

"The last year has been a difficult one for me. Others have chosen to speak for me. Never with my permission. Others have written letters for me. Never with my permission. Others have reported conversations with me. Those conversations never took place. This is not the time or the place to air these matters, perhaps some day. Perhaps they will help some young man to make his way more easily. Now I would like to get on with my life and my future. I earnestly ask that I be allowed to do that."

Jackson was not the only LSU recruit to have turned down inducements. Williams and Roberts were promised large sums of money and cars from other colleges. Even Ricky Blanton, not considered a major recruit, could have cashed in. But they invested their basketball talents in Brown.

Stanley Roberts, at 7-foot, 270 pounds, could have played for any school in the country. He could have named his price at some. Even NBA teams pursued him.

"You got offered cars," Roberts recalled. "You got offered money. You think it's great at first. But then after a while you realize it's not worth it. Look what happens to guys who get caught. They can't play. It was tempting. But I knew it wasn't worth it. Besides, my mom is a Christian lady, and she doesn't believe in that."

Roberts said about half the schools that were recruiting him played it straight. The others were willing to make concessions. The offers he received weren't quite as attractive as Jackson's, but they would have made him very comfortable for four years in college. Schools were willing to pay him $50,000 to $75,000 for a signed letter of intent. Once enrolled, he would have received a car, clothes, money to send home and spending money for himself. He would not name the schools, saying he had friends at some of them.

The University of South Carolina wanted desperately to keep Roberts at home to play for the Gamecocks. It got to the point where strangers were involved in his recruitment. A local magistrate, Harold Hill, admitted calling Roberts' mother, Isabella Davis, to encourage sending her son to South Carolina. Hill just happened to be handling the case of Roberts' brother, Wayne, who was being tried on murder and assault charges.

When Brown learned of the magistrate's call, he contacted a friend in the Federal Bureau of Investigation. There ensued a major investigation by the FBI, South Carolina Law Enforcement Division, NAACP and NCAA. All charges against Wayne Roberts were eventually dropped. It was ruled he acted in self-defense after being attacked in the Starlight projects in Columbia. He was beaten with a baseball bat. Then he pulled a gun and shot three of his attackers. Although his brother was not convicted, Stanley Roberts was made to feel like a villain himself. Many people in his hometown were hostile about his decision to go to LSU.

On the pro level, the NBA team most interested in Roberts was Atlanta. A scout for the Hawks first contacted him after his sophomore year in high school. Another Atlanta scout pursued him after his senior year. That was when the Detroit Pistons also made a contact. Both clubs assured Roberts it would be worth his while to skip college and turn pro. Neither team made an exact offer, but he was told it would be a large sum, probably in the $1 million range.

Pro basketball was not what Isabella Davis had in mind for her son. She wanted him to attend college, earn a degree and then consider the NBA. She trusted Jim Childers, his coach at Lower Richland High School. Stanley trusted Childers, sometimes calling him his second father.

At one point, Roberts had narrowed his list of college choices to South Carolina, Georgia Tech and North Carolina State. That was before Brown learned how close Roberts was to Childers. It was clear the way to Roberts was through his coach. It just so happened that Brown had an opening on his staff for a graduate assistant or part-time coach. So Brown offered Childers a job. Childers already had an offer from South Carolina coach George Felton. But he considered joining Brown a better opportunity, so he jumped at it. Felton later denied offering a job to Childers.

Rather than keep it a secret, Childers announced his intention to go to LSU during the summer of 1987. He thought it would be more up front to reveal his plans, even though he was going to coach another season at Lower Richland. That way, he reasoned, there would be no allegations of impropriety on his part. Just the opposite, everyone else screamed foul. The NCAA stepped in to investigate. But it was absolutely permissible to hire the high school coach of a recruit. Many schools had done it at one time or another, although few had taken advantage of the rule as often as Brown.

As a direct result of Childers' decision, Roberts made a verbal commitment to enroll at LSU, even before he had laid eyes on the place. There was little doubt Roberts would have ignored LSU if not for Childers going there first. What did his coach mean to him? "If it weren't for him, I'd probably still be running the streets, having fun, getting drunk and hanging out," Roberts said.

Blanton was pursued by a school close to his home, but not to his heart—the University of Florida. Blanton was the Player of the Year in Miami in 1984, and Florida wanted to keep him in state. A representative of the school went so far as to offer to pay off the family's note on a condominium. Blanton declined the offer. He narrowed his choices to LSU and Michigan. Both had talented players and well-known coaches. He selected LSU because of its proximity to his home.

That same year, Williams' recruitment overshadowed everyone else signing with LSU. Although LSU had the inside track to him through his mother, Marie Matthews, major obstacles were in the way, mostly in the form of cash. At one point, Brown got fed up and made a statement that Williams was being offered $150,000 to play for another school. He said he was considering taking a briefcase packed with $150,000 and giving it to Williams' mother, along with a dollar bill on top of it. But he didn't have to.

Who was willing to put up the money? Brown never would say. But Abernathy said he was in Matthews' home when a representative of UNLV brought by a brief case with $150,000. Abernathy said he saw the cash. Matthews saw it, too, but turned it down. She was relying on her friendship with Abernathy.

Later, about the time Williams was ready to turn pro, the LSU coaches found out he had an agent. They never knew his identity, but were sure he had been paying the player and his mother all along. There had also been a car given to Williams in his freshman season. When Brown found out about it, he told Williams to return it immediately. There was nothing Brown could do about the agent. Williams had to go pro.

The Tito Horford affair, if not as well publicized as the Williams case, was just as messy. Horford was a poor kid from the Dominican Republic, who left his home to play basketball at a private high school in Houston. He had been more or less recruited at the age of 15.

Horford, a 7-footer, closely resembled a great foreign player who had played at the University of Houston and was the star of the Houston Rockets—Akeem Olajuwon. By all rights, UH had Horford in its hip pocket. There was no way anybody was going to get him out of town. Except maybe Brown. Dale went after Horford with a passion. Some help came from Ed Gomez, a Dominican living in Baton Rouge. Gomez had known Brown for years. He had already helped bring Jose

Vargas, a childhood friend of Horford's, to LSU. Horford was several inches taller and vastly more talented than Vargas. He was regarded the finest high school center in the country. Brown had never been able to get a great center. In his mind, Horford would be the one. Dale would somehow persuade him to leave Houston. Another ace in the hole was the vice president of the Dominican Republic, Carlos Morales. He was an LSU graduate and had steered many Dominicans to his alma mater. Throughout the 1984-85 school year and into the summer, Brown committed most of his spare time to recruiting Horford. Even after Horford signed with Houston, Brown continued to go after him. He believed Horford had been forced to sign. Brown claimed the letter of intent was invalid because Horford's mother had never signed it. Instead, Robert Gallagher, who had housed Horford in Houston, signed as his guardian. Officially, he was not a legal guardian. But the NCAA upheld the letter of intent. Later, allegations surfaced that a UH recruiter visited Horford in the Dominican Republic in the summer when direct contact is not permitted by NCAA rules. Horford was ruled ineligible to play for the Cougars. Brown expected him to head straight to LSU. He didn't.

Brown grew angry at Horford for not leaving Houston. When he learned Horford had gone home to the Dominican Republic that summer, he went there to check on him. It was a dead period in recruiting when coaches are not permitted to visit recruits. Brown, though, was willing to take a chance, just like UH had done. "I wasn't really doing anything wrong, because Tito told me on the phone he wanted to come to LSU," he said. "They [Horford's Houston connection] just wouldn't let him."

Gomez arranged a meeting at a country home. But Horford was late. That was one thing Brown would not tolerate. His conscience was also bothering him. Finally, he left the house and got out of the country. Then he said LSU had no more interest in Horford. "I would not take Tito Horford if he crawled up the steps of the Assembly Center," he announced.

Late one Sunday night that fall, Brown got a phone call at his home. It was Horford on the line. He said he was in Baton Rouge, ready to enroll at LSU. Caught off guard, Brown did not want to commit himself. He told Horford to call back in the morning. After sleeping on it, Brown made up his mind that he should give Tito another chance. Brown didn't even ask him to crawl up the steps. Any 7-foot center, even an unpredictable character like Horford, was worth a shot, he reasoned. But before he committed himself to Horford, Brown made him swear out an affidavit that LSU broke no NCAA rules in recruiting him. Brown claimed the affidavit was legally binding. "If Tito lied, he is going to Angola," he said. In fact, it was not a court document and there was no possibility of Horford being sent to the state penitentiary.

The only chance Horford had of going to Angola was to play an intrasquad game there. Ironically, the prison was the only place he ever wore an LSU game uniform. The inmates loved him. They chanted "Tito, Tito, Tito." They asked for his autograph and wished him luck in leading LSU to a national championship. A week later, Horford said adios to Brown and LSU. Actually, he did not even stick around to say that. He was gone as mysteriously as he had arrived. Supposedly, he had no money. But he had been seen at Baton Rouge's Metro Airport leaving on weekend plane trips to Houston, Washington, D.C. and New York. Each time, he paid for his ticket in cash, usually with hundred-dollar bills.

What actually caused his departure was an argument over money. Horford fully expected LSU to provide some cash as well as an apartment for his fiancee, Arelis Reynoso. Brown said no chance. When Horford's car payment became overdue, he told assistant coach Johnny Jones he would not practice until he got money to pay the note. When Jones reported it to Brown, he exploded, "That's it! Tell him to pack his bags. He's through." The next day LSU had another intrasquad game out of town. Horford heeded Brown's command. He packed his bags and left. Brown announced that Horford was indefinitely suspended from the team. It did not matter. Tito was gone for good.

Horford eventually turned up at the University of Miami. It was one of the schools recommended to him by NCAA investigator Doug Johnson. The recommendation was made by Johnson during an interview with Horford concerning his recruitment by LSU. The year after Horford went to Miami, the university hired Johnson as an assistant athletic director.

Even though Horford was no longer connected with LSU, Brown continued to keep tabs on him. "They gave him a $25,000 car, a place for Arelis Reynoso, immediate eligibility, protection by Doug Johnson, got his two brothers to Miami," Brown said. "They let him drive that car for almost a year before they made him take it back. I've got that Tito Horford documentation down so thick and deep. I could have put

Miami out of business. But I told myself there's going to be a time and a place. That's going to be in Dick Schultz's office at the NCAA. And Doug Johnson is going to be there.'' Horford stayed at Miami two years before turning pro and going to the Milwaukee Bucks in the NBA draft.

Still determined to land the elusive center of his dreams, Brown ventured into even deeper water. This time his target was Soviet star Arvidas Sabonis, a 7-4 center who was playing in the World Basketball Championships in the summer of 1986. Brown would be there, ready to sign him. In the early stages of recruiting, Brown ran into Rima Janulevicius, an American with relatives in Lithuania, the Soviet republic in which Sabonis was born. Her contacts were instrumental in getting Sabonis interested in LSU.

Assured that Sabonis wanted to come, Brown began to tackle the red tape that stood in the way of Sabonis becoming the first Soviet to compete on an American team. It was the same year of the inaugural Goodwill Games between the U.S. and USSR. Both countries appeared eager for cultural exchange.

Getting the backing of the State Department was essential. That posed little problem for Brown. He contacted his good friend Norman Vincent Peale, who wrote to his good friend President Ronald Reagan. The doors to Moscow were open. The problem was Brown did not have any contacts in the Kremlin. So he worked through industrialist Armand Hammer to open channels of communication. Then he went to Moscow to talk in person with Soviet officials. He spent a week there, meeting daily with the Soviet hierarchy. The last step would be getting in to see Soviet leader Mikhail Gorbachev. A meeting was going to be set up by Hammer, but he became seriously ill that same week. Communications fell through, and Brown didn't get to see the Soviet leader.

Nonetheless, he was given a commitment that the matter would be considered. In the back of his mind, he feared the proposal would be vetoed. The Olympics were only two years away, and the Soviets wanted Sabonis to spend most of his time with the national team preparing to make a run for the gold medal.

During his Moscow visit, Brown spread some LSU good will. Everywhere he went, he handed out LSU key chains, T-shirts and other souvenirs. The Soviets were eager to get anything American. They clung to Brown. He was enchanted by a little girl he met one afternoon in a park just outside the gates of the Kremlin. The child reminded him of his daughter. He cleared his pockets of trinkets. People were warm and receptive to him. They wanted to meet Americans. Brown soon realized why.

"It was such a depressing place to visit," he remembered. "Nothing worked. The elevators got stuck. The hot water wouldn't come on. People were really sad. Drab buildings. Terrible conditions. I don't know how they could ever win a war. But I really liked the people. They were very pro-American. I enjoyed being around them."

Once back in the states, Brown got off the plane and wanted to kiss the ground. "Right then, I knew what the immigrants felt like coming to Ellis Island," he said. Then he went back to work trying to get his center. He was assisted by U.S. Senator Russell Long and Louisiana state Representative Donald Ray Kennard, an LSU athletic official. Brown and Kennard spent a week in Washington, D.C., meeting with officials at the Soviet Embassy. Each day they moved up the ladder of command visiting with higher ranking officials. Getting in to see Ambassador Anatoly Dobrynin was their goal. Toward the end of the week, a meeting was set up with him. But at the last minute, Dobrynin had to travel to New York. Brown and Kennard went home empty-handed.

Throughout the recruitment, Brown had been in contact with the Portland Trail Blazers. They had selected Sabonis in the NBA draft and had a vested interest in him. Team officials thought a year or two of college basketball would help prepare him for the pros. They were willing to let LSU have him first. But Brown was disappointed they didn't do more to help.

"I think I could have swung the deal if the Portland Trail Blazers would have gone with me and did what I said. We could have got him. We were that close," Brown said. "We were going to have a press conference at the base of the Statue of Liberty and then have one in Moscow. We would say, 'We will let him play at LSU, we will let him go to the Olympics and give the Soviet Union a chance to win the gold medal, and as soon as the Olympics are over, here is the largest contract in the history of basketball.' He was better than Ralph Sampson and Patrick Ewing and all those guys put together. I believe the Soviets would have bought that."

The press conferences never came off. Brown continued to correspond with Sabonis through their Lithuanian friend. But even that broke down. Sabonis suddenly disappeared. Brown found out he had been placed in a hospital just outside Moscow for undisclosed medical problems. Dale had no way of contacting him again. The recruitment of Sabonis was finished.

Frustrated by the near miss, Brown pledged never to recruit another foreign player. He finally got his center, or centers, when Stanley Roberts and Shaquille O'Neal signed with LSU. Those two, combined with Chris Jackson, represented by far the greatest force Brown had ever assembled.

Adding to his satisfaction, they were his kind of players. Jackson and Roberts were raised by their mothers in harsh conditions. O'Neal had some comforts as well as both parents. But his father was an army sergeant. He was hard-nosed and regimented.

These young men would have no difficulty relating to Brown's philosophy. They could follow his commands.

4

The Miracle Years

Walking down a back hall in the University of Dayton Arena, Dale Brown felt angry and discouraged. His team had worked so long and hard to win the Southeastern Conference championship. Then it all came apart in their faces. The U.S. Naval Academy, of all teams, had just destroyed LSU in the first round of the 1985 NCAA Tournament. Navy's sophomore center, David Robinson, simply overpowered the Tigers. The game was decided by halftime. LSU had just lost its 10th consecutive postseason game.

Brown was in a stupor as he prepared to exit the arena. He never heard the footsteps coming from behind. But he felt a heavy arm being placed around his shoulders. Glancing to his left, he saw that it was John Williams. Though soft-spoken and shy around everyone but his closest friends, Williams was a tender, compassionate young man. He squeezed Brown's shoulder. For a moment, they just smiled at each other. It wasn't a joyful smile. More like a thanks-for-caring look.

Williams broke the silence. "Coach, don't worry about this one," he said, almost whispering. "We're going to come back. I'm going to help us get to the Final Four next year."

Until that moment, the 1986 Final Four was the furthest thing from Brown's thoughts. It was scheduled for Reunion Arena in Dallas. It might as well have been in Beijing for all he cared. But Williams recharged him. "You're right, John," Brown said. "You're absolutely right." They walked a few more steps arm-in-arm. Then he added, "And thank you, John."

Those words of encouragement stayed in Brown's thoughts for the next year. Part of the puzzle would be solved with a lineup change. All five starters were due back from a team that won its final six regular-season games to capture the SEC championship. But he knew it wasn't the right combination. Skinny Nikita Wilson was playing out of position at center. They had to have a legitimate big man, who could dominate inside. If LSU could get Tito Horford, that would be the answer.

Then there was the question of Jerry Reynolds. Here was a defensive standout who could be potent offensively on some nights and horrendous on others. Reynolds just did not fit into the program. Even though he came from a rough background growing up in New York, he never responded to Brown's coaching techniques. Finally, Brown asked him to turn pro. Publicly, Reynolds and Brown said the early departure was for financial reasons. That was part of it, too. His mother was deaf and lived in a dangerous neighborhood. Soon after Reynolds was signed by the Milwaukee Bucks, he built his mother a home in Atlanta. He also found himself in the NBA, where he could utilize his freelance style.

The versatility of Williams allowed Brown some freedom to make a move like that. Williams could play any position. He was as effective at point guard as he was at power forward, his natural spot. He could even play center if necessary.

During the brief weeks Horford was on the team, Brown could easily picture LSU in the Final Four. That image became fuzzy the day Horford flew into the sunset, leaving the erratic 6-9 Jose Vargas and slowly improving 7-footer Zoran Jovanovich as the centers for the 1985-86 season.

Before the season tipped off, Sports Illustrated decided to make Dale Brown a cover boy. But with all that was going on with the recruitment of Horford and ongoing NCAA investigation of the LSU program, the magazine's story was anything but flattering. Brown was pictured on the cover looking like he had just pulled off the deal of the century. Just above his picture was the title, "Crazy Days at LSU." There was a three-story special report on the recent recruiting escapades and LSU athletic director Bob Brodhead's arrest for plotting to bug an NCAA investigator. Brodhead obtained the recording devices through a contact of Brown's.

Eventually, there was some basketball played at LSU that year. Brown started Vargas and brought Jovanovich off the bench. Vargas was inconsistent, but the Tigers were winning. In practice, Jovanovich showed signs of developing into a dominating big man. He was blocking shots and pushing people around under the basket. It caught Brown's attention. Just before Christmas break, Brown decided he would start Jovanovich. But he never got a chance. Jovanovich was spending the holidays with Ricky Blanton in Miami and tore up his knee in a pickup game. He was going up for a routine layup and came down wrong. The ligaments were shredded. His season was over. Maybe his career as well.

Two months into the season, both of the team's 7-footers were gone. Vargas had to handle the middle. If not him, it would have to be Nikita Wilson again. Or would it? Wilson, a team captain with a bright basketball future, was not as committed to his academic progress. In the fall semester, he flunked two courses, making him academically ineligible. He had until the start of classes in early January to appeal the grades, make up the work or take correspondence courses to boost his grade point average. He tried all three avenues. None worked. One of the courses he flunked was taught by Billy Seay, a psychology professor and chairman of the Athletic Council, which oversees the operations of the Athletic Department. Even though Wilson was flunking, Seay never contacted Brown to inform him of the situation. Seay believed it was the student-athlete's responsibility to maintain his grades without assistance. When Brown found out Seay had failed Wilson and not forewarned the coaching staff, he hit the roof. He called a press conference and gave the "system" a 21-gun blast. He said the university "used" Wilson. He had even harsher words for Seay.

"I hope it is not a personal vendetta and because he can't get me, he's going to try to get Nikita," Brown thundered before the media. "I think a tremendous unfairness has been done. That's exactly how I feel. If the facts are wrong, fine. But I would sure feel terrible if I had that on my conscience today. I believe you go into class an F and I think if you learn anything, you should come out a D-minus. But maybe I've got it all screwed up. Some teachers at this university should have their records published. Instead of giving 45 F's and 5

B's and thinking you're a great teacher, to me your record is 5-45 and you deserve to get fired.''

Brown said there was a Judas on the university staff. As his half-hour harangue drew to a close, he became even more critical, saying, ''One reason LSU will never rise to its height, in my opinion, is because of that kind of gutless people who go behind the scenes and try to hurt other people.''

The speech didn't save Wilson. He continued to play basketball until his eligibility ran out at the start of the next semester. In the process, LSU got off to a school record-tying start, winning its first 14 games. The streak came to an end at Alabama, where the Tigers played without Wilson for the first time.

Losing Wilson was more of a blow than the loss of either Horford or Jovanovich had been. Wilson, though built like a rail, was quick, aggressive and experienced. At 6-8, he could play forward or center. Without him, it seemed Jose Vargas had to play. But Vargas never responded to the call and as a result, LSU struggled. The Tigers won only seven of their last 17 regular-season games. They tied Florida for fourth place in the Southeastern Conference, both with 9-9 records. They fell fast and hard.

That LSU managed to win even nine league games was remarkable considering what happened midway through the SEC season. If the loss of three centers weren't enough, the Tigers almost lost John Williams and backup forward Bernard Woodside for the season with, of all things, chicken pox. Williams and Woodside contracted the chicken pox on a road trip to Florida. Upon the team's return, they were both hospitalized. Jovanovich had a mild case and was treated as an outpatient.

Team physician Dr. Jim Osterberger recommended that the team be placed under quarantine until everyone could be tested. He notified the Southeastern Conference of the situation. LSU was scheduled to play at Auburn that Saturday. Based on league policy, only the home team can postpone a game, and Auburn did not want a delay. Brown was outraged. He called Auburn coach Sonny Smith and pleaded with him to postpone. Smith sympathized with Brown, but could not help him. He said the decision would be made by the athletic administration. His hands were tied. LSU was told to play the game or forfeit.

Never one to back down from a challenge, even against all reason, Brown made up his mind he would put a team on the court Saturday no matter what. He rounded up as many athletes as he could. Football coach Bill Arnsparger gave him permission to borrow several of his players. It would be an odd array of tight ends, linebackers, running backs and defensive backs. But it would be a team. No way would Brown forfeit.

As game day approached, Auburn finally gave in to pressure from the LSU administration and SEC officials and agreed to delay the game a week and a half. LSU had to play then or forfeit. At least Brown would have most of his players available by then. The only problem was LSU had to play at Georgia on Saturday, meet Georgetown in a nationally televised game in Landover, Maryland, on Sunday, come back to play at Auburn on Tuesday and then travel to Mississippi State on Wednesday. Even NBA teams don't play that kind of schedule. Auburn turned down Brown's request to postpone the game until the end of the season. Brown was sure they were doing it because they expected Williams to be healthy by then. Initially, doctors feared Williams would be too weak to play any more games. His illness was severe, thought to be potentially life-threatening. The prognosis was a hospital stay of two to three weeks, followed by two months of rest.

The doctors based their projections on how the average adult responds to a severe case of chicken pox. But Williams was not a typical patient. His powerful body withstood the illness remarkably well. By the end of the week, he wanted to leave the hospital. Doctors finally released him the following Wednesday. He attended the LSU-Kentucky game that night in the Assembly Center, his presence bringing prolonged cheers from the crowd. LSU lost the game on a last-second shot by Roger Harden. It was LSU's first heartbreaking loss of the season to the Wildcats. They would meet again in the regular-season finale and twice in the postseason.

After the Kentucky game, the whirlwind road swing was next for the Tigers. They left for Georgia on Friday afternoon. Williams accompanied the team, but was not expected to play at least until the last two games of the trip. If at all possible, Brown wanted him to play at Auburn. No other game really mattered. But in the early going at Georgia, the score was close, and Williams wanted to play. Brown agreed to put him in for a few minutes. Once on the court, he would not come out. He played most of the game. LSU led at halftime, but could not hold on in the second half, even with Williams' help.

Their team leader was back, but the Tigers had a long road ahead of them. Losing all four games was a real possibility. Shortly after the Georgia game, the team's charter flight left for Dulles International

Airport. LSU would go on the court in less than 24 hours against Georgetown, which was battling for the Big East championship. Reggie Williams led a cast of quality players left over from the Patrick Ewing era. John Thompson's team was a big favorite playing before a home crowd and against a tired, depleted LSU team. Georgetown had not played in four days and was fresh.

Somehow Williams regained his strength in time for his first appearance in the Capital Centre, where he would later play regularly for the Washington Bullets. He showed no signs of the illness and put on a brilliant performance. He almost single-handedly broke the Hoyas' vaunted full-court press and scored a career-high 28 points. Late in the game, LSU had a chance for the winning shot and called time out. Brown wanted Williams to take the last shot. He didn't want Vargas to so much as touch the ball. But on the inbounds play, Williams was covered. Anthony Wilson passed to Vargas, who put up a lame shot, missing everything. Don Redden fouled Georgetown's Michael Jackson going for the rebound. Jackson got two free throws. LSU lost, 74-72.

Two nights later came the showdown at Auburn, Alabama. Another healthy, rested, talented team awaited LSU. "We are going to beat their ass tonight," an emotionally charged Brown told his players. "They tried to screw us out of this game. We'll show them not to mess with us." LSU went out and won a moral victory and an important basketball game, 63-61. The next night, the Tigers beat Mississippi State to take a split on their grueling road adventure. "Beating Auburn the way we had to, playing four games in five days, is one of our biggest accomplishments at LSU," Brown said.

Through the remainder of the season, the Tigers were up and down. Brown made a major lineup change in the final two weeks, inserting 6-6 sophomore Ricky Blanton at center in place of the unpredictable Vargas and bringing Anthony Wilson into the lineup at off guard for Oliver Brown. They joined Williams, and seniors Don Redden and Derrick Taylor. At first, Brown was not pleased with the change and threatened to bench Blanton and Wilson. "You haven't done a damn thing in two weeks," he shouted at them one afternoon. "We have got to turn things around. But you are not doing the job. You will do it or you won't play."

How could Blanton be expected to play center? He was not tall enough. He could not jump very high. He had never dunked the ball in a game. But he possessed brawn and heart. What he did not have physically he more than made up for mentally. "I totally understood my role," Blanton said. "I had to rebound on both ends and play defense. I did not have to worry about anything else. I had to come up with something more than points. Coach Brown made me understand exactly what I had to do." The extra scoring would come from Anthony Wilson. When he was hot, he could hit four or five in a row and change the complexion of a game. He and Blanton eventually responded to Brown's directive and made an impact.

Despite losing at Kentucky in the last game of the regular season, LSU was in decent shape to get an NCAA invitation. To lock it up, the Tigers needed to beat Florida in the quarterfinals of the SEC Tournament at Rupp Arena. Before tipoff, Brown gathered his players together in the locker room and told them, "You have got to beat these guys to have any chance. We will not play in the NCAA Tournament unless we win this game. It is do or die. This is your season."

Williams scored 20 points and took down a tournament-record 20 rebounds. LSU won easily to advance to the semifinals and a third game with Kentucky. It would be their second meeting with the Wildcats on their home court in six days. The game was much like their first clash in Baton Rouge. The lead seesawed back and forth, but Kentucky always seemed to be in command. In the closing seconds, Roger Harden drilled a long jumper to put the Wildcats ahead by three. With the three-point shot not yet in effect, LSU was out of it. A third loss to Kentucky in one season. The visitors' locker room was deathly silent when Brown finally made his way there. His first words caught everyone by surprise. "We will meet them again," he said in a most confident tone. At first, the players weren't sure what was on his mind. Then they realized Brown was already looking ahead to the NCAA Tournament. "I'm telling you right now that we will play them again," he continued. "We have a big opportunity. We have a regional in our gym. We can win two games there and then just watch us go from there. Somewhere we will play Kentucky for the fourth time. And we will win that one."

When the NCAA pairings were announced that Sunday, LSU was seeded 11th in the Southeast Regional and had a difficult draw. A team seeded that low has little hope of winning more than a game or two. But just as Brown had predicted, the Tigers would have a chance to play two games on their home court in the Assembly Center. Their first-round opponent was sixth-seeded Purdue, the Big Ten runner-up. A victory probably would send LSU up against third-seeded Memphis State, the Metro Conference champion. From there, it would be on to The Omni in Atlanta, where the Tigers just might get their chance for a rematch. Kentucky was the top seed in the Southeast Regional. To get to the Wildcats, LSU would likely have to face second-seeded Georgia Tech on its home court. There were a lot of "ifs" on the board. But Brown had a way of making it sound like a certainty that his team would have its day with UK.

The 1986 version of March Madness began as usual on a Thursday at four first-round regional sites around the country. LSU played Purdue in the final game on opening day at Baton Rouge. There was a sellout crowd in the Assembly Center.

But even playing at home, the Tigers had trouble with the physical Boilermakers. The game was nip-and-tuck for 40 minutes. Then for 45 minutes. Finally, in the second overtime, LSU managed to pull away at the free-throw line. It was after midnight when the Tigers left the floor with a 94-87 verdict. "We had the momentum and that game put us into high gear," Ricky Blanton recalled. "We were gone. We believed what Coach Brown told us. We thought we would play Kentucky again."

As expected, Memphis State was the next opponent. Dana Kirk's Tigers had it all—7-footer William Bedford, cat-quick point guard Andre Turner and a stable of outstanding jumpers and shooters. Even so, Kirk wasn't happy about having to play in LSU's arena. On the first play of the game, Derrick Taylor collected the tipoff and spotted Blanton on a breakaway. But Bedford caught him from behind and swatted the shot away. LSU was in trouble. Memphis State took control in the first half and began to pull away in the second. Down by 11 points, LSU called a timeout. Brown used every second of it to rip into his outmanned players. "You guys aren't playing with any intensity," he screamed. "You're going to get embarrassed in your own gym. You look like you don't even want to win. Well, I want to win. You start playing like you mean it or you won't play. Now get your ass out there and do it."

They reacted like Brown had hoped. They caught fire and made a run at Memphis State. Helped by Bedford's foul trouble, LSU got back in it and ignited the home crowd. It went down to the wire. There were several close calls that went LSU's way, infuriating Kirk. LSU went ahead by two points, but Bedford hit a shot to tie the game. LSU got the last shot. Redden worked free for a jumper in the lane. His shot rolled around the rim and came off for a miss. Several players scrambled for the ball and it ended up in Anthony Wilson's hands. Never hesitating, he went straight up with the shot. It went off the glass, on to the front of the rim and down through the net as the buzzer sounded. Delirium broke out in the arena and around the state. Teammates piled on top of Wilson. Bodies were sprawled all over that end of the court. Brown quickly went to shake Kirk's hand. All he got was a slap on the wrist and a few choice words. He did not care. The moment belonged to LSU. He dashed around the court hugging players, coaches, managers, trainers. It went on like that for several minutes. The celebration revived Deaf Dome, the name given to the Assembly Center in the late '70s.

Having clinched a spot in the Final Sixteen, LSU moved on to The Omni in Atlanta. Still alive was its hope of playing Kentucky. The Wildcats had advanced through the first two rounds. In the regional semifinals, LSU was matched with home-standing Georgia Tech and Kentucky had to play SEC rival Alabama for the fourth time.

Once again LSU had to go up against the big boys. Georgia Tech had won two games in Baton Rouge and was a huge favorite to end LSU's joy ride. But already these upstart Tigers were gaining national attention. They were the lowest-seeded team among the 16 still alive. And they were the kind of team that attracted fan support. Most of the players were baby-faced underclassmen, especially Blanton. They looked like mere boys going up against Memphis State, and they seemed to really like each other. When they huddled to call offensive or defensive plays, they always put their arms around each other. They were bright-eyed and smiling. They were enjoying their favorite sport. Then there was the flamboyant Brown, standing beside the bench flashing defensive and offensive signals like he was giving a speech in sign language. It was a made-for-TV cast of characters.

Georgia Tech, though, was not sympathetic. John Salley and Mark Price were primed to send the Tigers home and then take on the SEC's real force, Kentucky. LSU had other plans. Blanton never remembered Brown being more positive than in his pregame talk on that day. ''I have got so much confidence in you guys,'' he told his players. ''You are going to win this game, and we are going to play Kentucky on Saturday for the regional championship. I believe in you guys. No one gave us a chance. Here we are. Who says we can't go any farther?''

Not Georgia Tech, as it turned out. Redden and Taylor could not seem to miss from 20 feet and beyond. Their blazing shooting more than made up for Williams' off night. Blanton held his own with Salley, and Price never became a factor. Surprisingly, LSU controlled the game and took its easiest victory of the tournament, 70-64. In the second semifinal, Kentucky beat Alabama for the fourth time in a row.

Back at the hotel that night, the LSU players were mobbed by Kentucky fans thanking them for beating Georgia Tech. They anticipated a quick trip to the Final Four in Dallas. After all, the Wildcats had beaten LSU three times already. Everyone assumed they would win again.

On the day of the regional championship game, Atlanta was ablaze with SEC basketball fans wearing Kentucky or LSU colors. Rarely had teams from the same conference met in a regional final. Atlanta was right in the middle of SEC country, readily accessible to anyone in the league who wanted to see the game.

That afternoon no player or coach uttered a sound on the LSU bus as it made its way from the hotel to The Omni. In the locker room, even Brown was quiet in a self-assured, unintimidated way. "What did I tell you?" he asked rhetorically. "We made it this far. We are going to beat Kentucky today, just like I said we would. This is our game. You just have to do what we tell you."

Early in the game, the Wildcats, especially Kenny "Sky" Walker, were more dominating than they had been in any of their previous victories over LSU. Obviously, they expected to earn the Final Four berth. But so did the Tigers. They settled down and began to chip away at the UK lead, finally pulling within a point at halftime. It was close the rest of the way. If the Wildcats scored, the Tigers answered back. When LSU slipped ahead, UK responded. It would not be decided until the final seconds.

An unlikely hero, Blanton sat on the bench for much of the second half. He came back in with seven minutes left and got a couple key rebounds and free throws. Then he found himself in the right place at the right time. With LSU ahead by a point in the final minute, the Tigers were trying to work the shot clock and then get a basket or pick up a foul. Don Redden finally penetrated and got past Ed Davender. That forced Walker to come out and cut off Redden, leaving Blanton open. Redden threw a bounce pass around Walker's outstretched arms. Blanton grabbed the ball and layed it in for the clinching points in a 59-57 victory. In utter jubilation, Blanton flew down court, alternately pumping his powerful arms in the air, each movement punctuating the conquest. His victory dance came to be known in Louisiana as

"The Blanton." The replay was shown hundreds of times state-wide and nationally. On the fourth try, Kentucky had finally been beaten. Brown's words had come true. His team was indeed the Cinderella story of the tournament. The Tigers put on "Destination Dallas" hats, cut down the nets in The Omni and celebrated the rest of the day. Much of the nation shared their joy. They were in the Final Four.

When it came time to report to Dallas, the Tigers knew all they needed to know about their opponent, Louisville. Denny Crum's Cardinals were bigger and more talented than Kentucky. They had wanted to play state rival Kentucky in the Final Four, but would have to settle for the other team from the SEC. Louisville had been the top seed in the West Regional and was favored to beat LSU and play the winner of top-ranked Duke and second-ranked Kansas for the national championship.

But for Brown, just making the Final Four was not enough. LSU had achieved that in 1981, when it lost to Indiana in the national semifinals. "We can win it all now," Brown repeatedly told his players. "We got Kentucky out of the way. The national championship is ours."

For a while, it appeared he was right. The Tigers came out looking like they were at least on their way to the championship game. They answered Louisville basket for basket in the early going and began to ease in front toward the end of the half. Their lead was eight points at halftime. They were 20 minutes away from the championship game and 60 minutes away from winning the national title. But they were also 20 minutes away from being eliminated. The second half belonged to Louisville. LSU couldn't keep up with the speed of Milt Wagner, Billy Thompson and Pervis Ellison. The Cardinals won 88-77.

But who would have thought it possible? LSU—chicken pox, injuries, ineligibility and all—in the Final Four? Only Brown could have dreamed up such a plot. In the locker room, he was already talking about New Orleans, the site of the 1987 Final Four. And why not? If this team could make it to Dallas, anything was possible.

A month after Louisville beat Duke for the national title, LSU suffered a major blow to its 1986-87 hopes. Williams announced his decision to turn pro. The man-child was headed to a league where his superb basketball skills could be utilized to the fullest. LSU had lost its star. Along with Williams' early departure, Taylor and Redden had completed their eligibility. Only Blanton and Anthony Wilson remained from the starting lineup. Brown spent most of the summer trying to get the Soviet Union to allow Arvidas Sabonis to play at LSU. But his efforts were fruitless. The Tigers were strengthened by the addition of All-America point guard Fess Irvin from nearby Gonzales. Also recruited that year was 6-7 forward Ben McDonald from another small town near Baton Rouge. His favorite sport was basketball, but his best was baseball. He would develop into an Olympic hero and the finest pitcher in college baseball. He played only one season of basketball, spending most of his time on the bench.

So when the season opened on October 15, Brown had Blanton, Wilson, Irvin and leading reserves Jose Vargas and Oliver Brown. Nikita Wilson was well on his way toward regaining his eligibility. If he picked up 12 hours in the fall semester, he could rejoin the team in mid-December. Then came a fateful night in November. LSU had to play an exhibition game, but Brown's mind was on the NCAA hearing he had to attend the next day in Kansas City. It was the culmination of three and a half years of investigating Brown and his program. It would be Dale Brown Day at the NCAA. He wished he wasn't coaching that night. Later, he wished the game had never been played.

Brown could hardly believe his eyes as he watched Blanton writhing on the floor. Blanton's left knee was twisted after he slipped on a wet spot. He had fallen in his own best asset—the sweat of his brow.

Only moments earlier, Blanton had dived for a loose ball. Such plays were his trademark. Nobody noticed the glistening streak in front of the LSU bench until it was too late. The next time Blanton hit that spot, he severely damaged his knee. Brown quickly went to his side, but could offer little help. Brown felt numb all over his body, except his stomach. It was in knots. How could this happen? What possible reason was there? Searching his mind, he found no answers.

The only thing he hated worse than watching Blanton get hurt was the mere thought of the NCAA trying to penalize his program. He was proud to have overstepped many of the NCAA's minor rules, which he considered ridiculous and unfair. He made his disdain for the NCAA known to everyone in the country, constantly attacking the organization.

Once, he threatened to blow the whistle on the top 10 programs in the country if the NCAA messed with him. He sent out thousands of letters to every university president, athletic director and basketball coach in the country, condemning many of the current rules and calling for revisions. Needless to say, Brown was not a popular fellow around the NCAA offices just outside Kansas City.

Many coaches expected the NCAA to lower the boom on Brown. Most thought his program would be placed on probation with no television appearances or postseason play for two to three years. Even his friend, TV analyst Al McGuire, publicly warned, "Dale Brown is so vulnerable, they'll reopen Devil's Island if he's done anything wrong."

On judgment day for his basketball program, he was anxious to get in front of the Committee on Infractions, which is made up of professors and athletic officials from universities around the country. The infractions committee hears evidence from the NCAA enforcement department, headed by David Berst. Then the school has a chance to respond.

Brown had much to tell the committee. LSU's attorneys feared he might get out of hand and hurt his own cause. They cautioned him to keep quiet. He paid no attention. Only minutes after the hearing commenced, committee chairman Thomas Niland announced that the three charges, all minor issues involving Brown, had been expunged. Brown raised his hand and asked to be acknowledged.

"Mr. Niland, I would like to respond to the allegations against me," Brown said. Everyone else in the room stared at him. There was silence for many tension-filled seconds. Finally, Niland tried to explain there was no evidence to support the charges, so they had been wiped off the slate. "I understand that, sir," Brown responded politely. "But those allegations were made public. I think I should have a chance to respond to them."

Unsure how to handle such a request, the four-member committee huddled. After several minutes, Niland said he appreciated Brown's desire to state his case, but there was really no reason to do so.

"Well, I've got just one thing to say," Brown fumed. "Those allegations are all a bunch of lies. They were all made up, and they were made up by one person." By then, he was standing and looking directly at Doug Johnson, the NCAA investigator who had handled the probe of LSU. "You are a liar," he shouted at Johnson. "You lied about these. You were out to get me, and you lied!" They glared at each other for a moment. Then Brown sat down and said to Niland, "Thank you, that's all I had to say."

Seven hours later, the LSU delegation emerged from the meeting room in a triumphant mood. Brown was ecstatic. The NCAA found nothing but a handful of minor rules violations. There would be no major sanctions. Having won perhaps his greatest battle, Brown pledged to work with the NCAA. He reasoned he could be part of the system and make it better. But he wasn't completely satisfied.

"Dale, we did all right," LSU Chancellor James Wharton told Brown on the flight home. "I was just telling everyone, 'I know Dale isn't going to fight this.' I know you're not going to appeal, right?"

A nod from Brown brought a smile to Wharton's face. It didn't disclose Dale's true feelings, though. He wanted to clear LSU of everything, even if there were only a few meaningless charges. But he also had Blanton and the upcoming season on his mind. That had to take precedence. As feared, Blanton needed surgery and eventually elected to sit out the season and get an extra year of eligibility.

Just before the season opener, Jovanovich crashed his car into a telephone pole on a rainy day, sustaining near-fatal head and neck injuries. He would miss his second consecutive season. That same week, Vargas sprained an ankle.

The Tigers looked so bad in the early going that they were nicknamed the "Uglies" by a local sportswriter. They stumbled through November and December, splitting their first eight games. "They'll be lucky to win four more games," Al Guglielmo said.

Even after Nikita Wilson regained his eligibility, LSU was not much of a basketball team. Wilson was rusty after a year on the sidelines. The offensive load fell on the shoulders of guards Anthony Wilson and Irvin. Wilson carried them with his three-point bombs against some teams. Against others, he could not score. Irvin was a major disappointment. As a high school player, he was deadly from outside. In college, he faced taller, quicker players and couldn't get open shots. Eventually, Brown had to pull Irvin from the starting lineup and replace him with junior college transfer Darryl Joe, a superior athlete. How bad could it get for a team just coming off a Final Four appearance? Almost as bad as Guglielmo predicted. For the first third of the Southeastern Conference season, the Tigers were on track to win only three league games. A loss to Alabama dropped them into 10th place, dead last in the league, with a 1-5 mark. Overall, they were 6-8 against Division I competition. The season appeared to be a lost cause.

Undaunted, Brown kept telling his players they could turn it around, that they could even make it back to the Final Four. "Talent is in your mind," he told them the day after the loss to Alabama. "I look at talent differently. Some people say we don't have much talent." Actually, almost everyone familiar with the team said it was hopeless. Most thought LSU would not finish as high as seventh in the SEC, where it had been picked at the start of the season. Brown looked at it another way. "Talent is an attitude," he said. "Talent is not just ability. Talent is believing in yourself and your teammates. It is the love you have for each other. I think we've got the most talented team in the country. I'm not happy about the way we're playing right now. But we will get better."

In the midst of gloom and doom, Brown guaranteed his players that they would play in a national tournament if they played hard, intelligent and together and followed his instructions. A few observers saw a glimmer of hope as well. Sportscaster Bucky Waters came over to Brown after announcing LSU's close loss to Oklahoma at The Myriad in Oklahoma City. He shook Brown's hand and told him, "Your kids won't quit. They just won't quit. The next time I have you on TV is one month from now. You're going to be tough by then. You just don't know how to quit."

The first indication that the season was not a lost cause came at Rupp Arena, of all places. Until Brown became head coach, LSU had never defeated Kentucky in Lexington. In 14 years, Brown had won there only twice. But this trip would be different. Only three days after losing to Alabama, LSU was a different team. Nikita Wilson was too quick for Rob Locke. Rex Chapman and Ed Davender weren't picking up Anthony Wilson on the perimeter. The Wilsons were taking target practice, and the Wildcats were being embarrassed in their own arena and on national television. Coach Eddie Sutton sat helplessly on the UK bench. Nothing he tried could stop LSU. The lead grew up into the teens, then the twenties and finally the thirties.

On the LSU bench, Ron Abernathy suggested pulling the starters with about nine minutes left. "It's not over yet," Brown shot back. "Remember what they did to us a few years ago. They beat us by 30, and I said some day we were going to do that to them. Well, we are going to beat them by more than that. Nobody is coming out." Finally assured of a 30-plus margin, Brown cleared the bench. The Tigers won, 76-41. It was the worst defeat ever handed a UK team at Rupp Arena. Coincidentally, it matched the 35-point margin by which Kentucky beat LSU in 1975. Brown was supremely satisfied to have crushed the Big Blue.

If LSU could win like that in Lexington, Brown was convinced the Tigers could win anywhere against anybody. He put together a lineup that was a blend of offensive stalwarts Nikita and Anthony Wilson and defensive experts Bernard Woodside, Darryl Joe and Oliver Brown. Irvin and Vargas came off the bench. Things started to click.

Still, there was a serious setback. In the regular-season finale at Auburn, LSU had a chance to finish in the top five in the SEC and greatly enhance its chances for an NCAA bid. What happened was similar to the Lexington massacre. Only on this day LSU took the blow. A sizzling Auburn team, led by Chris Morris, raced to a 20-point lead in the first half. Brown could see the writing on the wall and yanked his starters. Auburn rolled to a 100-62 victory, equaling Brown's worst loss.

On the sideline, Brown walked to the end of the bench to speak to his starters while the game was still in progress. ''I want you to look up at the scoreboard,'' he said. They looked, but didn't see anything they didn't already know. It may have reinforced the embarrassment. ''I did not pull you out because I didn't think there was a chance we could win this game,'' he continued. ''There's always a chance. But it's so slim that I need to let the other guys play and get the experience for the tournament. I am now convinced that if you don't give up, we will play Alabama in the championship game of the SEC Tournament. And we will win it.'' Another dire moment. Another bold prediction by Brown. Another group of players who listened and believed.

Actually, LSU had to reach the SEC tournament final to have any chance to get back into the NCAA field. Some thought the Tigers had to win it outright. They were 16-10 against Division I competition. They had finished 8-10 in the league, tying Ole Miss for sixth place. Thanks to a tie-breaking procedure, LSU drew the seventh seed, which meant a first-round game in the SEC Tournament. The top six teams receive first-round byes. Brown had never brought his team into a first-round SEC game. Just getting to the final would take three victories in three days. But LSU had an emotional edge because the tournament was at The Omni, where it had clinched the Southeast Regional title the previous March.

The first victory proved little trouble. LSU dispatched Mississippi State with relative ease, beating the Bulldogs for the third time that season. Next in line stood an opponent of a different caliber. Florida was poised for its third victory of the season over LSU. The first two were decided quickly by sharpshooting guards Vernon Maxwell and Andrew Moten. LSU had not come within 20 points of the Gators. But this time, Brown put the Freak Defense on Moten and Maxwell, and it deflated Florida, causing the upset of the tournament.

Even though the victory probably clinched LSU's invitation to the NCAA Tournament, Brown wanted to take the whole shooting match. He would not be satisfied until the Tigers were SEC Tournament champions.

Brown stayed awake for 60 hours, refusing to sleep until his team won the tournament. He wanted to show his players he shared their mission and was willing to fight the fatigue of four games in four days. To stay awake, he called sportswriters in town covering the tournament, watched TV with his daughter and went jogging through downtown Atlanta in the middle of the night.

Georgia was LSU's semifinal opponent. The Tigers threatened to make it a rout, building a 20-point lead in the second half. But Georgia fought back. It developed into a thriller that lasted two-and-a-half hours and two overtimes. LSU survived 89-88.

In the championship game, the Tigers were matched with regular-season champion Alabama, just like Brown had predicted. Once again, LSU battled nose-to-nose with a favored team and never flinched. Brown looked pale and had dark circles under his eyes from lack of sleep. He waved his fist in the air and stomped back and forth in the coaches' box. His fiery spirit helped for a while, but Alabama began to pull away. LSU lost the title, 69-62, but won the war. Later that afternoon, LSU was made the 10th seed in the Midwest Regional. That was a notch higher than the previous year. And there was a familiar foe—Georgia Tech. They would meet at the Rosemont Horizon just outside Chicago.

The day before the game, Brown spent most of the allotted practice time working with Darryl Joe on his three-point shot. He turned the rest of the team over to Ron Abernathy. Against Alabama, Joe had made one of his 10 three-point attempts. Brown gave him some advice on positioning his right elbow properly before shooting. Joe listened and watched. He put it into practice the next afternoon.

Georgia Tech coach Bobby Cremins had instructed his guards to give Joe that shot. Their defense focused on Nikita Wilson. But for the next 40 minutes, Darryl was no average Joe. He shelled the Yellow Jackets with seven three-point shots and a career-high 28 points. That sent LSU into the second round against Temple.

Even though Temple was 32-3 and seeded second in the region, Brown believed it posed less of a threat than Georgia Tech. Indeed, the Owls were overrated. LSU bothered them with the Freak Defense and was in control all the way, winning by 10.

Suddenly, the last-place Tigers were back in the Final Sixteen. CBS called it Cinderella II. Could Brown's down-and-outers get back to the Final Four? They moved on to Riverfront Coliseum in Cincinnati to face third-seed DePaul, which had won 28 of its 30 games. In the other regional semifinal, it was Duke against Indiana, the top-seeded team in the region. Brown couldn't help but ponder a rematch with Bobby Knight.

DePaul, though, may have been a better team than Indiana. The Blue Demons had Dallas Comegys, Rod Strickland and Kevin Edwards. They could be devastating. But against LSU's tough, switching defenses, the Demons weren't so difficult to contain. Still, the game swung back and forth. Then the Tigers held DePaul without a field goal in the final four minutes and won 63-58. Indiana held up its end, too. Knight beat his protege, Mike Krzyzewski. The stage was set. All the attention focused on the two generals. Everyone knew Brown and Knight intensely disliked each other. Reporters hoped to make it a war of words. But neither side obliged. "I think Dale has been extremely successful," Knight offered. "I don't necessarily go about things in the same way. How he has gone about things is good and works for him. That is what I like about college basketball." Brown bit his tongue.

On game day, they had a private confrontation before tipoff. Brown was strolling down the hallway to the LSU locker room, his head lowered in deep thought, when he heard a strange but somehow familiar voice calling out, "Hi, Dale." It was Knight. Caught off guard, Brown hesitated. "Good to see you," Knight said, extending his hand. Again, Brown paused. What crossed his mind was a similar meeting they had in Philadelphia before LSU played Indiana in the 1981 Final Four. Knight had ignored him. Finally, Brown decided not to turn away. "Hello, Bobby," he said. Then he shook Knight's hand.

"Dale, I really like the way your team is playing," Knight told him. "I told my team if North Carolina, with all the talent they've got, could play as hard as you guys play, we just would send them the trophy. None of us would have to play. Your team is the hardest-working team and you have the best defense. You play harder than anyone in the country."

The North Dakotan in Brown told him he was getting a snow job. He nodded to acknowledge Knight's praise. Then he returned the favor, doling out compliments of his own. His administrative assistant, Bo Bahnsen, saw them in the hall together and worried there may be trouble brewing. When he got close enough to overhear the conversation, he was shocked. It sounded like two buddies getting together at a reunion. They couldn't say enough nice things about each other. Finally, they shook hands and went to work.

In the LSU locker room, Brown reported the meeting to his players. "They are scared of us!" he shouted, like a battle cry. "I just met Knight, and he is scared. I know we've got them whipped. We will win today."

For 39 minutes, 52 seconds, Brown's prediction looked like it would come true. Neither team could shake loose in the first half. The biggest moment came when Knight walked onto the court in protest of a traveling call. He drew a technical foul and then stormed over to the scorers table. He screamed at tournament officials and slammed his fist down on a telephone. A second technical was not called, even though Knight was later reprimanded and fined $10,000 by the NCAA.

Early in the second half, LSU made a bold run and threatened to blow out the Hoosiers. The lead jumped to 12 points with just over 12 minutes left. But LSU couldn't sustain it. Brown called for a spread offense to use up time; the move backfired.

Trapping the LSU guards, Indiana forced several turnovers and began to inch closer. The Tigers led by nine points with five minutes left, but scored only one more point. Indiana scored seven unanswered points to close within 75-73 with less than a minute to play. Joe finally hit a free throw for the Tigers, but Keith Smart sank two for Indiana to make it 76-75. Irvin had a chance to build the lead back to three, but missed a one-and-one free-throw chance, barely grazing the front of the rim. On the other end, Ricky Calloway followed up a miss by Darryl Thomas and the Hoosiers led 77-76 with seven seconds left. Nikita Wilson attempted a turnaround jumper, but couldn't get the shot off before the buzzer. It missed anyway. Indiana celebrated. LSU was crushed. Its Final Four dreams were ended.

After Indiana had left the court, the Tigers were still out there. In those painful moments, they remembered what they had accomplished and how they got there. They wrapped their arms around each other—Brown, the players and assistant coaches. Once more, they shared the camaraderie that had carried them from last place in the SEC to the Midwest Regional championship game and within a basket of the Final Four.

"You didn't make the game bigger than the lesson," Brown said, consoling his players. "That makes me feel really good. We are not whipped by this. Sometimes you can make the game so big and winning so important that you lose the real meaning of what you did: the love, the hard work, the sacrifice, the unselfishness, the discipline. We may be judged by others on whether we won or lost. What did we lose? Another Final Four ring? That doesn't compare to what we did this year."

The disappointment passed quickly for the players. After they had showered and dressed, they were in an upbeat mood—even with the media. Nikita Wilson was one of the last to leave the locker room. As he walked down the hall, he ran into Indiana's Smart, who grew up in Baton Rouge. Wilson put his arm around his shorter opponent and like a father hugging his son, he squeezed him around the neck. "Way to go, Smart," he said. "Now you're going to win it all." They walked off together toward their respective buses, Wilson's college career over and Smart's about to soar. Smart would hit the shot to give Indiana its third national championship under Knight. It was a title that LSU, just like in 1981, could have won.

On the flight home, Brown sat next to his daughter. Shortly before takeoff, he leaned over to talk to her. "I have a funny feeling," he said. Then he smiled.

"What do you mean, Daddy?" Robyn asked.

"In the midst of despair," he said, smiling even more, "I feel we're going back to Baton Rouge with more than they're going back to Bloomington with. We accomplished our mission. We never lost our vision. We never stopped believing."

That faith in themselves was about all the Tigers had left for the 1987-88 season. Gone were their scorers—Nikita Wilson and Anthony Wilson—and their best defensive player and rebounder—Oliver Brown. For the first time in Dale Brown's years at LSU, he did not have a returning player who had averaged in double figures. The well was dry, or so it seemed from afar. The Tigers were picked to finish anywhere from fifth to eighth in the league, sixth being the consensus. That kind of season would mean no NCAA trip and quite possibly not even an NIT bid. But no one who pulled on purple-and-gold uniforms that fall believed the school's string of nine consecutive national tournaments would end. Brown refused to let anyone think that way.

"We are good common laborers," he told them on October 15. "We work hard. Maybe you can't get to the moon with hard work, but

I'll tell you what, you can get to the top of a lot of mountains. And that is better than being in a rut all your life. We will get to the top of some mountain. We're going to be playing in a national tournament in March.''

It was clear to everyone that Blanton and Vargas had to carry the load. Even though they had never been consistent scorers, they would be called on to fill the void left by the Wilsons. There was also Irvin, back for his sophomore season, and Wayne Sims, a burly freshman forward, who sat out the previous season because of academic problems. Before long, Brown realized he had to work Sims into the lineup. Irvin was benched again, and Bernard Woodside was moved to guard from forward.

The missing link was a shooter or inside threat, someone who got the ball at crunch time. Who would it be? Blanton could not beat many people one-on-one. On his good days, Vargas filled the role. But on his bad days, everything was an adventure for Vargas. He dribbled the ball off his foot. He threw it over his teammate's head. He missed wide-open dunks.

Without a doubt, Vargas frustrated Brown more than any player he had coached. Vargas just missed setting what would probably be an NCAA record: starting at center four years and being benched before the season ended each time. He probably would have been benched the fourth time if Argentine center Hernan Montenegro had not broken his ankle and quit the team to turn pro. Strangely enough, Brown adored Vargas, a thoughtful, gentle giant with a brown belt in karate. But he wasn't easy on him. One time, Vargas was having such a bad practice that Brown ran up to him screaming. Dale slammed his fist in his hand, right in front of Vargas' face. The impact caused Brown's watch, a present from his wife, to burst apart. Pieces went everywhere. As Brown raged on, Vargas bent over and picked up the pieces of the watch.

That fall, many things happened to the team. First, Parade All-Americans Stanley Roberts and Harold Boudreaux signed with the Tigers and Chris Jackson made a verbal commitment. Then the legendary ''Pistol Pete'' Maravich came home to LSU. Before his recent Christian conversion, Maravich had vowed never to set foot again on the LSU campus. But his bitterness over the firing of his father, Press, as head basketball coach had subsided. Brown convinced him to be a part of the program. The players were thrilled by his presence.

Before practice one afternoon, Maravich talked to the whole

squad. Standing near midcourt of the arena that would soon bear his name, he told the players, "I think you are going to do a lot better than you were picked in the Southeastern Conference. You have really come together as a team and a family. Coach Brown has seen to that. I hope you win the Southeastern Conference championship and the national championship. I hope you accomplish all the goals you have set for yourselves. But just remember, there is more to life than basketball. I played a lot of years, made a lot of money and did a lot of things. But I found out basketball is not the most important thing. We all need to prepare for our spiritual lives. We need to turn our lives over to the Lord Jesus Christ and serve him."

Here was Pete Maravich, the all-time leading scorer in college basketball history, telling 11 young basketball players that their priority should not be the game. Coming from Maravich, those words had a powerful impact. Several players had private meetings with him to discuss their spiritual needs. But as a team, they had heard from him the final time.

On the morning of Tuesday, January 5, the news spread through Louisiana and the rest of the nation like wild fire. Many thought a terrible mistake had been made. No one wanted to believe it. At age 40, Maravich had died of a heart attack, suffered playing a pickup basketball game at a California church, where he had gone to share his Christian testimony. His last words to the team rang louder than ever. Later that day, the Tigers had to fly to Nashville to begin the most grueling stretch of their season. They were already struggling at 4-4 and many thought they were on the way to a losing season.

In the next eight days, they had to play Vanderbilt, Ole Miss, Oklahoma and Tennessee, all on the road. They had to miss the funeral, but carried the memory of their friend with them, each wearing a black band on his shoulder strap. Whether it was for Maravich or themselves, they played inspired basketball.

Against a Vanderbilt team that had already beaten top-ranked North Carolina, the Tigers played a slow-down game, working the shot clock inside 10 seconds before shooting. The tactic kept Vanderbilt off balance, and LSU won easily. At Ole Miss, they stayed with a slow-paced attack and rallied for an overtime victory, their first there in three years. Then in New Orleans, they changed gears and stunned third-ranked Oklahoma with an up-tempo game. Finally, they rallied from 13 down to defeat Tennessee. Those four victories figured prominently into their getting an NCAA Tournament bid. After finishing 15-

12 in the regular season, it would come down to the Southeastern Conference Tournament.

LSU and Vanderbilt tied for fourth in the league and would meet again in the tournament quarterfinals. LSU had won both regular-season games, but had to win this one to get into the NCAA field. LSU had the advantage of the SEC Tournament being held at the Assembly Center. Vanderbilt, already assured of an NCAA berth, had no pressure.

On the morning of March 8, another Tuesday, tragedy rocked the LSU campus again. Heart failure claimed another member of their basketball family. This one was even more unbelievable. Don Redden, 24, a hero of the 1986 Final Four team, died in his sleep. The team was crushed, especially Blanton, who was a close friend of Redden's and even dated his sister, Roxanna, a freshman on the LSU women's basketball team.

The day before playing Vanderbilt, the Tigers buried one of their own. Blanton and several other players were pallbearers. They dedicated the game to their former teammate. On their shoulder straps, they attached a piece of the gray LSU T-Shirt that Redden was wearing when he died.

Two deaths, just two months apart, were too much. Somehow the Tigers pulled themselves together in time to play Vanderbilt. Led by an emotional Blanton, who scored 30 points, they beat Vanderbilt for the third time and virtually locked up an NCAA bid. The most meaningful moment of the season came at the end of that game. Blanton led a procession of players and coaches into the stands to present the game ball to Redden's parents. It sent chills through the huge, silent crowd.

"As God is my judge, that was the most important victory I have ever been part of," Brown said. "I don't care if we ever win another game."

The Tigers did not. They played SEC champion Kentucky to the wire the next day. The game was tied with less than a minute left, but the Tigers ran out of emotional fuel and lost. In the NCAA Tournament, they played Georgetown in the first round of the East Regional at Hartford, Connecticut. Again, they were tied in the final minute. But Hoyas point guard Charles Smith fired a 25-foot desperation shot at the buzzer with Bernard Woodside right in his face. It slammed into the backboard and banked into the net. The miracles of March belonged to Georgetown, Rhode Island, Kansas State and ultimately, national champion Kansas. The Tigers went home early. The memories of the 1986 and 1987 tournaments had been enough to take them through another season. The memories of Redden and Maravich would be with them forever.

5

Heartbreak

During those final days of the 1987-88 season, Dale Brown had never been more frustrated. At the same time, he had never been more encouraged.

This had been the most unpredictable, emotionally draining group of players he had ever coached. The only thing that tempered his frustration was the recruiting class lined up for next season. The Tigers had landed arguably the finest crop of high school talent in the country, unquestionably the best class to ever play basketball at LSU. But it couldn't help this team, which could go from wonderful to abysmal at the bat of an eye.

The string of road victories over Vanderbilt, Ole Miss, Oklahoma and Tennessee had been incredible. If LSU had played like that all season, it would have been in Kansas City for the Final Four. On other nights, it could be the most inept team in the SEC. The Tigers lost both regular-season games to Mississippi State, which won only four other league contests and finished last.

After an especially disappointing loss to Auburn on the next-to-last day of the regular season, Brown seemed to hit rock bottom. It appeared the Tigers might not make the NCAA Tournament.

"I believe it will turn around, but only under certain circumstances," he told his players. "I have done all that I can do as a motivator and as a positive thinker. As far as making you believe in yourselves, I think I believe in you more than you believe in yourselves. I can't do any more. I can be an encourager, I can be an instructor, and I can be a coach. But it's like my daughter. Robyn left home and is on her own. If she can't carry on without her daddy, then she's not going to succeed. You guys are the same way. You have to do it. You have to play the game. You have to go beyond your normal effort, like you did early in the year. If we're going to win, we have to play like we did against Oklahoma.''

Ricky Blanton, finishing his fourth season under Brown, had never seen him more upset. He ranted and raved at the least provocation. No one attracted his wrath more than Jose Vargas, easily the most inconsistent player to ever suit up for him. Sometimes Vargas deserved the tongue-lashings. Other times, he did not. After the loss to Auburn, Brown chastised him in front of his teammates. ''Jose, I love you, man,'' he thundered. ''But I'll be so damn glad when you leave. I never know what to expect from you.''

Vargas responded to Brown's criticism with a superb performance against Vanderbilt in the quarterfinals of the SEC Tournament. He dominated Will Perdue, the league's Player of the Year, and LSU played extremely well in beating the Commodores for the third time in two months. Vargas was sharp against Kentucky in the semifinals, and the Tigers took the league champion to the wire before losing. But in the NCAA Tournament, he reverted to his old ways, and LSU went home early.

Brown had trouble keeping his spirits up, much less motivating his team. He became dejected as the defeats piled up, and there was little progress to show. This team didn't improve through the course of the season like most of his teams. Dale would not take the blame for the lack of progress. So he laid it on his players and his assistant coaches.

''I'm not going to take responsibility for everything,'' he said privately. ''I've carried this program on my back for too long. I've got to get players who can play. I need administrators. I need professional people. I've carried the thing on my shoulders long enough. They're using my strength, but my strength can't go out there on the court. My strength can't put the effort out. I can prepare them. I can set the physiological and psychological terminology. But sometimes you need more than that. I believe without a doubt in my mind that talent is inferior to total dedication, belief in the system and total commitment. I believe talent loses to that. Now if talent has the same commitment, talent beats you.''

The talent was signed, sealed and waiting to be delivered. His greatest recruiting class was only six months away from suiting up in purple and gold. There was Stanley Roberts, the center of his dreams. Complementing Roberts inside would be forward Harold Boudreaux, who had remarkable touch from outside. To get them the ball, there would be Chris Jackson, the slick, quick, high-scoring point guard.

LSU added some role players to further strengthen the class: Maurice Williamson, Connecticut's Player of the Year; Steve Cooke, Oregon's Athlete of the Year; Scott Guldseth, Mr. Basketball in North Dakota; and Kevin Moses and Vernel Singleton, two highly rated players from Mississippi.

If these recruits had come a year earlier, LSU probably would have had an all-freshman starting lineup. Blanton, only because of his desire, would have been the only veteran to have stood a chance against such talented players. Vargas and the others would have taken a back seat.

Brown couldn't wait until next year. ''I wonder what it will be like to have equal or greater talent?'' he said one day. ''For once, we won't have to scratch and dig our way out of trouble. It won't be that great burden on my shoulders. We don't have to always be the underdog, do we?''

Brown wanted a break from the stress of pulling rabbits out of his hat every season. He imagined how easy it would be to get Roberts, Jackson, Boudreaux, Williamson and the other recruits ready to play. Just throw in Blanton with those fabulous freshmen and write your ticket to the Final Four, he thought.

But there was a snag. Brown considered it a minor hurdle to clear. It turned out to be a Mount Everest. He couldn't even get three-fourths up this mountain.

Roberts, Jackson and Boudreaux shared a problem, along with three of the late signees. They were only partial qualifiers under Proposition 48. They had graduated from high school with the required 2.0 grade point average in academic courses. But they had not scored high enough on the ACT or SAT. If they didn't make the score, they couldn't play as freshmen.

Most coaches would have played it safe and signed only two or three partial qualifiers. They would have taken Roberts, Jackson and

Boudreaux, who were Parade All-Americans, sought after by just about every school in the country. With the possible exception of Williamson, the others who had yet to qualify weren't worth the risk. If they failed to score high enough on the tests, it could be crippling to the team to have six ineligible players. It also would be a black mark on the program and university.

Being optimistic—and a little naive—Brown hoped they would all make it and believed at least half would. He never seriously considered the consequences if they all missed. They were so close, needing only to improve a point or two on the ACT or a comparable percentage on the SAT. Brown reasoned that all they had to do was prepare a little harder for the tests and they would all pass with flying colors. Then he would have his dream class of All-Americans and assorted other stars. They would make the ride to the top so much smoother, almost effortless.

The final test dates were in June. Roberts had been tutored by Larry Mills, a high school teacher in Columbia, South Carolina. Mills had trained many athletes to take the SAT. None had failed to score at least the required 700. Jackson was studying in a special ACT preparatory program in Gulfport. Lil Jenkins, wife of his high school coach, drove him to it every day. Boudreaux was reviewing the ACT test guide on his own. The others were making some kind of special preparation, too. Brown and Craig Carse kept tabs on all the recruits to make certain they were doing everything possible to improve their scores. Well, almost everything.

Because of the pressure to make sure their freshmen became eligible, coaches across the country were putting their recruits through similar test training. Some were doing more than that. There were numerous incidents of athletes caught cheating on the ACT or SAT. Either they were looking at someone else's test sheet or they had someone take the test for them. That was one of the major allegations against Kentucky's basketball program. Prize recruit Eric Manuel had taken the ACT in Lexington along with the coach's son, Sean Sutton, who had already met the ACT requirement. The Auburn football program was also being investigated that summer on a similar charge. In 1986, three LSU football recruits had submitted almost identical answers after taking the ACT in a small Louisiana town far from their homes.

Brown didn't want more trouble with the NCAA, and he didn't want to risk losing any of his prize recruits. So he emphasized to his coaches and recruits that under no circumstances should they even consider cheating on the tests.

Before leaving for a two-week trip to West Germany, where he would give motivational talks to U.S. soldiers, Brown told Carse, "Make sure nobody fools with the kids on these tests and gets them thrown out."

Carse was indignant at Brown's insistence on checking up on the recruits. But a few days later, Carse found out why Brown had been so concerned. An LSU alumnus wanted to make sure Boudreaux didn't have to sit out his first year. He knew the player and wanted to help him out. So he was in the process of getting someone else to take the test for Boudreaux. Another LSU supporter tried to call Brown to inform him of the situation. Carse took the call. He immediately got in touch with Brown. That same day, the deal was cut off.

Boudreaux never even heard of the plan. "I wouldn't have let it happen anyway," he said. An athlete caught cheating on the test may lose a year of eligibility or even be ruled ineligible to play for the school that recruited him.

After returning from West Germany, Brown could only wait. It was agonizing for him to be confined to Baton Rouge at a time of year when he was usually on a trip to another continent. He longed for adventure. His expedition to Mount Ararat in search of Noah's Ark had been postponed. Later that summer, he had scheduled a second trip to Medjugorie, Yugoslavia. He was also going to Guatemala as a host on a medical relief mission. After that, he would head to China for a series of basketball clinics. Still, sitting around his office and not being able to control his own destiny proved a trying time for him.

The test results came in piecemeal during the first two weeks of July. For Brown, each score felt like a blow from a sledge hammer. Boudreaux, ineligible. Williamson, ineligible. Roberts, ineligible. Moses, ineligible. And finally, Cooke, ineligible. There was no report on Jackson because of an unexplained delay in the testing system. Five were in, and five were down. It didn't look promising for Jackson, who had already come up short on four tests. The glimmering recruiting class was tarnished. The bottom had fallen out. Brown and his new players were crushed.

On the afternoon Roberts received his SAT score, he had been day-dreaming about playing for LSU in the fall. There was no indication that he would not score at least 700 on the SAT. He had been scoring in the 900's on sample tests given to him by his instructor. He knew he had not done that well under the pressure of an actual test. But he fully expected to be close to 800. When he opened the envelope, the numbers shocked him. He had scored 670 and wouldn't be playing for anyone in the fall.

Boudreaux didn't get a chance to open his test report. His twin, Carroll, was so anxious to find out the score that he opened it for Harold. Carroll broke the news as gently as he could. But Harold Boudreaux was overwhelmed. For two months, he had studied the ACT material. He was convinced he was ready. "When I went to the test center, I felt really good," he said. "I thought for sure I made it. I said to myself, 'Give me my uniform, I'm ready to play.'" He couldn't believe the score was accurate. There must have been some mistake. He went to his room and stared at the number. It was an 11 on the ACT, well short of the minimum, 15. Finally, he fell back on the bed and closed his eyes. "I thought, 'Oh, my gosh, maybe I don't belong in college.' I felt like crying," he recalled.

Maurice Williamson called it the worst day of his life. The others had similar reactions. It was one of the low points of Brown's coaching career as well. But it also caused him to re-evaluate his priorities.

"The first thing that I thought was, 'Boy, I was sure selfish then,' " he said later. "I was wondering why I ever thought I had it made." Instead of having the most talented team in the SEC, he was left with the least talented.

Blanton was the only upperclassman. At 6-7, Blanton and Wayne Sims would be the tallest veterans. Sophomore Richard Krajewski was 6-10, but he had missed the previous season because of Prop 48 and was not expected to contribute significantly any time soon. He was a North Dakotan, but didn't have the same spark Brown had. Sims, a cousin of Johnny Jones, from DeRidder, Louisiana, was an avid weightlifter like Blanton. He also had a delicate touch on his shot. He was quiet and shy and needed to be more aggressive.

Sophomore guards Lyle Mouton, Russell Grant and Kyle McKenzie were coming off unspectacular seasons. Mouton, from nearby Lafayette, Louisiana, was built like a small John Williams and had a wealth of potential, but little drive. McKenzie had been recruited out of Cincinnati for his shooting ability, and Grant was a walk-on from Louisville who survived on sheer determination, a true Brown player.

The only other scholarship players available were freshmen forwards Vernel Singleton, from Natchez, Mississippi, and Scott Guldseth, from Edinburg, North Dakota. They had been signed only because they already had met the Prop 48 guidelines. They were projected as role players, although Singleton had exceptional athletic ability.

Brown was in a bind, especially at point guard. He didn't have one. He couldn't even dream a scenario to get this kind of team into a national tournament.

"I thought that I was going to lay back, cross my legs and just coach," he recalled. "I imagined how nice it would be not to have to fight for everything. It was almost a lesson to me that life is a continual battle. This isn't the way it should be. You're not going to lay back and relax. So it hit me how selfish I was being. I wondered if I was getting old and lazy, or I just lost my drive, that I was just going to sit on the bench and be the genius. All I had to do was give them a few basic things to do and we would win easily."

He thought of himself as the "spoiled American." He came to grips with the dilemma and realized he would have to keep struggling, continue his fight and climb another mountain. The national championship would not be shipped to his doorstep. He had to go out and win the thing.

Soon, his mind was abuzz with thoughts of how to make it work. He could teach Blanton how to play point guard. True, Blanton wasn't quick enough. But he had played every other position on the court. Brown convinced himself that Blanton could handle the point. He could mold the rest of the team around him. Perhaps, it would work out. Yes, he knew it would.

Once recovered from his self-pity, Brown realized how his recruits must be feeling. Sitting out a year presented an imposing obstacle for an 18-year-old accustomed to being treated as a star athlete. So Dale turned his attention to them.

The five who failed to qualify had similar personalities. They were soft-spoken, somewhat shy. Even Roberts and Boudreaux, who were physically imposing, kept their feelings to themselves. They were sensitive and in some ways, lacked confidence. Dealing with this setback was difficult, even devastating. Brown knew he had to rebuild their self-esteem. He accepted it as another challenge.

Despite the risk of being called a hypocrite, he publicly denounced Prop 48. He argued that all freshmen should be ineligible to play varsity sports, which had been the policy before 1972. "They've got the mark of Cain now," he said shortly after the scores came in. "They're Prop 48 kids. It's not right. It's just not right. It's like there is ignorance in them. It's a stigma, and people will keep on bringing it up. Instead of saying, 'Stanley Roberts, who redshirted last year at LSU, is averaging 20 points and 12 rebounds.' They'll say, 'Prop 48 Stanley Roberts, who didn't make it last year, is averaging . . .' And the same person who is saying that probably couldn't make the test score himself.''

For much of the summer and on into the next season, Brown divided his time between coaching basketball and campaigning for revisions of Prop 48. His main point of disagreement was taking away a year of eligibility. In fact, he promised his recruits that they would have four years of eligibility. It was a promise he expected to keep, but he had no way of knowing how. Selfishly, he wanted these players to be eligible for four years because they would present a dominating force. For their sakes, he sought the change so they could have the same number of years as all other college players to develop socially, academically and athletically.

Brown counseled and reassured each one that he could overcome this setback. He advised Cooke and Moses to attend junior college and then return to LSU in two years. Roberts, Boudreaux and Williamson enrolled at LSU and spent the summer in Baton Rouge, working to make some money and working out with their future teammates to develop some comaraderie and a sense of belonging. As the weeks passed, the pain eased. They accepted their fate and Brown helped them develop a positive approach to it.

''Coach Brown has a way of making you feel better,'' Roberts said. ''He has a lot of philosophies. He threw those philosophies on me, and what he said was true. This year can help me out. I can make it be positive or I can let it be negative. It's up to me. I think it's really going to help me be a better student, a better person and a better basketball player.''

Boudreaux went to see Brown and was quickly cheered. He remembered being told by his coach, ''Don't worry about it. You're not the first guy to have to sit out. Just keep your head up. We're going to have everybody in next year. You just have to work on your game and school work and you'll be ready to play. This is going to be a blessing in disguise academically and athletically. For the first time in your life, you can sit back and watch other people play. You all need a year just to learn how to play anyway. So here's your chance to improve your basketball skills. Academically, you won't have any pressure on you, so you can get in and get your feet on the ground. You won't have to be struggling the whole time. It really is going to be a blessing. You will be better off for it. I don't think any freshmen should have to play anyway."

Boudreaux came around quickly. "I don't feel bad at all," he said. "I've got this year to work out with the weights and work on my dribbling and shooting. I'm going to be a totally different player inside and outside. And I'll be a better student, too."

So much for convincing his players. Now Brown had to explain the situation to the university and LSU fans. The fans had expectations of a third trip to the Final Four in the '80s. The university wasn't expecting to get a black eye. But it did.

Ironically, the SEC had spearheaded the drive to upgrade academic standards for athletes. Initially, the league supported Prop 48. But the chancellors and presidents in the conference decided that wasn't enough, so they adopted more stringent rules. Eventually, student-athletes who failed to meet all the Prop 48 requirements would not be allowed to receive an athletic scholarship at an SEC school. That legislation was passed by the conference at its annual meeting that June. Brown missed the meeting because he was in West Germany. The SEC's ruling led to the adoption of a similar rule by the NCAA, called Proposition 42.

No other SEC basketball program had stockpiled partial qualifiers like LSU had just done. No other school in the country had five Prop 48 basketball recruits. Naturally, the university's administration wasn't thrilled with the idea of being the leader in such a dubious statistic. But Brown has never been overly concerned with what LSU's hierarchy has thought about his program. Often, he has been too busy criticizing the academicians to worry about what they think about him.

Throughout the summer, local and national media beseiged the LSU basketball office with inquiries about the status of the recruits. If most or all were eligible, it would be a major story because LSU would automatically become a national contender. If they didn't make it, it would still be news because of the magnitude and number of recruits involved.

LSU was sitting on top of a gold mine or powder keg, depending on which way the test scores came out. There was national interest because the large majority of the nation's premier high school basketball players were in the same situation, hoping to qualify on their last tests. According to one recruiting service, 16 of the country's top 20 recruits had not qualified under Prop 48 to play as freshmen. Roberts and Jackson were in the top five. Boudreaux was in the top 20. No other school in the country had three recruits rated so highly. No other coach was in the dilemma in which Brown found himself.

There was nobody to blame but himself. Surely, no one was going to volunteer to explain the situation to the media. Brown had to do it. He carefully considered how to offer something positive, for the sake of the program and the recruits. Like always, he approached a disastrous situation with the hope of turning it into a promising one.

The television cameras were set up and the reporters seated, reading a news release, when Brown made his way to the L Club Room in the basement of the Assembly Center on that July afternoon. He was dressed in a dark suit and was wearing his reading glasses and a half smile. He greeted several friends before stepping up to the podium.

By then, everyone in the room was aware of what had happened. So he skipped the formalities and went right to work on his mission. Before he had finished the half-hour talk, he had claimed a spot for LSU in the 1993 Final Four to be played in New Orleans. "Obviously, we're disappointed," he began, peering into the packed room. "There is no sense in approaching it any differently than to say you're heartbroken about it, for them and for us. But that's the way the cookie crumbles. We're not done yet."

For the next few minutes, he explained that the coaching staff had anticipated the possibility of losing some of the recruits. There was a contingency plan. They had been busy making contacts with players who could join the program in a hurry. Without naming anyone, it was clear he meant foreign players or Americans who weren't recruited by other major schools. There was little chance he could come up with quality players at such a late date. But he insisted there was just that possibility.

In fact, he had been working on bringing Geert Hammink to LSU, although Brown didn't name him at the press conference. Hammink was a 6-11 center and star of the Dutch junior national team. Brown had contacts in Holland who told him Hammink was comparable to Rik Smits, the "Dunking Dutchman" and second player picked in the NBA draft that year. And there was still the hope of Jackson being eligible to play as a freshman.

Changing subjects, Brown started to discuss revising Prop 48 so that partial qualifiers would sit out their first year but not lose a year of eligibility. "We need to upgrade academics on a national level, not just for athletes,'' he said. ''And so I think the upgrading of academics is a good idea. But for anyone to lose a year is totally wrong, and I don't think it will happen.''

If Roberts, Boudreaux and Williamson were granted four years of eligibility, they would be able to play through the 1992-93 season and have a chance to send LSU to New Orleans for the Final Four. ''But still, good manages to come out of it,'' Brown said. ''And I am convinced, particularly in 1993, I am convinced, because there are going to be some fifth-year players on this team, and the Superdome has the Final Four. So it will work out.''

Brown complimented Carse for doing an honorable job as recruiting coordinator. He also promised that all of the recruits would eventually earn degrees from LSU. About 75 percent of the players who stayed in his program the full four years earned college degrees. In a brief conversation after the press conference, he assured reporters that the 1988-89 season was not being written off.

''I think this program has established itself that we're either going to be good or great,'' he said confidently. ''We've been to 10 straight national tournaments. We'll go to our 11th.''

Right then and there, if the chairman of the NIT selection committee had offered Brown a bid for its 1989 tournament, he would have jumped at it. Not that he was fond of the NIT. It is a poor sister to the NCAA Tournament. His teams had been to it twice and lost in the first round both times. Nonetheless, it was a national tournament. There was a championship at stake. He would have gladly accepted the opportunity to win it.

But postseason bids are not awarded in July. In the next eight months, Brown had to assemble a team that could be somewhat competitive and then manufacture a winning season. Even the NIT does not take teams with losing records. Many thought LSU to be incapable of winning more games than it lost. Others contemplated a disastrous season.

Brown's critics rejoiced at the chance to lash out. One columnist wrote, ''You think last October 19th was Black Monday? The Dow's plummet was a minor setback compared to what happened to LSU's hopes for next season. What might have been the nation's best recruiting class looks like Chicago after the fire, Johnstown after the flood and Jimmy Swaggart after Debra Murphree.'' Another story read, ''LSU has lost the best recruiting class it never had.''

Despite the inglorious reviews of the recruiting class, LSU's fans were excited about the prospects of watching these athletes perform, whether it was this season or next. They had waited 25 years for an SEC championship, which Brown delivered in 1979, 1981 and 1986 along with an SEC Tournament title in 1980. They had waited 28 years for a Final Four team, which he produced in 1981 and 1986. So they were certainly willing to wait another year to see the greatest collection of talent ever put together at LSU.

At first, Brown liked the talk about how tremendous next season would be. He used it to soothe the anxiety of his sidelined players.

"It is going to hurt at times to sit out this season," he told them. "But we are going to get everyone together next year. With the players we'll have, we're going to win it all."

Having the ineligible players on campus that summer helped. He was able to talk to them regularly and keep them involved in the basketball family.

Roberts enjoys working with kids, so he helped out in the summer basketball camp. One day, Brown caught him by surprise, asking him to speak to the whole camp, about 400 high school boys. Some were almost his own age. He reluctantly agreed.

"What do you want me to talk about, Coach?" he asked.

"I want you to talk about the importance of education and academics," Brown replied.

Roberts roared with laughter. He patted Brown on the back. Still laughing, he asked, "What do you really want me to talk about?"

As they walked toward the field house, Brown convinced him that he was serious. He reasoned that no one knew more about how important it is to study and avoid suffering the consequences than someone like Roberts. So he introduced his freshman center, who looked like a skyscraper compared to some of the younger boys sitting on the floor of the gym.

Roberts paused to collect his thoughts. Then he began talking about academics. He even surprised Brown. "Coach Brown asked me to speak on education," he said loudly and clearly. "I thought he was just kidding. But let me just say something to you all. If you want to stay away from the hurt that I'm feeling right now, you had better get serious about it. I was the class clown. Don't be the class clown. I was kind of a fat kid when I was younger. I got attention by clowning around, not listening to the teacher, throwing erasers, stuff like that. Some of you aren't going to listen, either. You think it's funny. But you're wrong.

"Coach Childers got a hold of me in the 10th grade. I never dreamed I could be anything. He told me I could be a basketball player, that I could get a basketball scholarship and go to college. I tried to study, but I didn't even know how. I didn't know some of the stuff in math I was supposed to know, because I used to daydream in class. I finally learned how to study, and I learned a lot. But I could have just been the class clown. Where would I be now? Listen. Don't be the class clown. Do your work, and you can make it.''

Most of the boys' parents were waiting to pick them up and heard the speech. Many came over to thank Roberts for giving such wise advice to their sons. Afterward, Brown took him aside and told him, "You did more good there, what you said to those kids and how you acted, than if you had been eligible. Isn't that amazing? You can't let this thing get in your way. This can be a great year for you, Stanley.''

Just when the commotion over the ineligible players was dying down, a new controversy came to life. Jackson's test score had finally come in, and he was eligible. Brown rejoiced, at least temporarily. He had his point guard, the missing link. Then his point guard disappeared.

Even Brown was beginning to lose hope as the days passed and there was no word from Jackson. It was an agonizing week in the midst of a stifling month. When Jackson finally made his way to Baton Rouge, Brown was elated. The odds were still long, but not impossible. Once Jackson got cranking, nothing would be impossible.

Eventually, Brown completely accepted the dilemma of being short-handed again. Just ahead lay perhaps the most difficult challenge of his career, behind only his first season at LSU. At least, he had established a winning tradition. The handful of veterans expected to win. Better yet, they knew how to win. He had Blanton as the captain, and Jackson would be a tremendous addition.

Certainly, this wasn't going to be a picnic, trying to mold something out of almost nothing. But it was just the kind of challenge that invigorated Brown and kept him up all night working on new defenses, better inbounds plays and creative ways of motivating his players. This team might not make a national tournament. It might even have a losing season. But in situations like these, Brown is at his best. And his teams are the most dangerous.

6

Like Knight and Day

Throughout the summer, something else troubled Dale Brown. Still to be settled was the score with Bobby Knight. The 1987 loss to Indiana was ever so vivid in Brown's mind. He could not forget the pot-bellied gray-haired Hoosier coach slamming his fist on a telephone and getting away with it. He wanted a chance to put Knight in his place. How he would love to grab him by the fold of his chubby belly and toss him in a trash can.

It almost happened earlier that year in Kansas City. Both men were there for the Final Four and coaches meetings. Brown was sitting in a hotel coffee shop talking to Bob Boyd, a former coach at Southern Cal and Mississippi State. To Brown's delight, Knight walked in and headed toward the table. Brown actually wanted to start a fight and get this thing over with, having no doubt he would flatten his rival. So he stuck his foot into the aisle. "If that bastard touches my foot, I'm going to knock him out," he said to himself.

But Knight detoured from his path, went over to Boyd and patted him on the back. He passed by Brown without so much as a glance. Brown seethed. He had missed his chance to have it out with his chief adversary.

"I never had a problem, a major problem, with him until what happened in the game," Brown said. "I didn't enjoy being critical like that. But I think something good came out of it. He was fined, and the referees who worked the game didn't advance. If he was fined and the referees didn't advance, then obviously something should have been done at the time.

"It was a losing cause for me, because somebody could immediately say it was sour grapes. It was not sour grapes. It was standing up for what I thought was right. I reached my saturation point with him. There were a lot of people who did not have courage. It looked like they were trying to get his blessing to coach international teams and to get him to say they were great coaches. I had to do what I thought was right. I would have to say I was looking for a fight. I was looking for anything. I would have liked to lock myself in a room with him."

Mutual friends had tried unsuccessfully to smooth the waters between Brown and Knight. Brown was not willing to listen, especially to C.M. Newton, who was coaching at Vanderbilt.

Newton told Brown that he disagreed with his actions. "Even if Dale's perception of the events that went on was accurate, it seems to me it was totally the wrong forum and timing," Newton said. "I think if you have that kind of problem, you don't address it like that. I think he really put Bobby in a position where he had no other recourse but to strike back at him."

Brown brushed it off as a typically conservative response from Newton. Besides, Newton and Knight were close friends. Newton even served as an assistant under Knight on the 1984 U.S. Olympic team that won the gold medal.

Brown was envious of Knight's Olympic conquest, not to mention his three national championships. But there was something about the Olympics that meant even more to Brown.

After Joe Dean became LSU's athletic director that spring, Brown sought his help in becoming the Olympic coach. Dean, formerly vice president of the Converse shoe company, knew all the coaches and was friends with many of them, including Knight. He understood the crony system. To coach any international team, you have to know the right people, attend the right meetings and say the right things. Dean was close enough to Brown to be able to tell him the truth. If Dale didn't play the game, he had no chance to coach the Olympic team, no matter how successful he was.

Brown also wanted Dean to arrange a game between LSU and Indiana. Brown had tried to set one up through his friends at the television networks, but it couldn't be worked out. Maybe Dean could pull it off.

Dean did everything he could. He suggested a Dome-and-Dome series. LSU would play Indiana in the Hoosierdome at Indianapolis. Then Indiana would come to New Orleans to play LSU in the Superdome. Brown didn't care where or when they played. It didn't even bother him that he wouldn't have his top recruits. He just wanted another shot at Indiana. But Knight refused to play regardless of the terms. Brown was resigned to the fact his only shot would be in the NCAA Tournament.

With his player emergency over and battle with Knight on hold, Brown ran head-on into the most devastating crisis of his life. It would shake him up more than he thought possible and transform much about his life.

All summer, Vonnie had complained of back pains. She was able to accompany Dale and Robyn on the trip to Yugoslavia in August. But upon their return, she decided it was time to see a doctor.

A series of tests produced alarming results. She had a large tumor in the uterine area. It could be removed, but the prognosis was not favorable. It was life-threatening.

Brown canceled his mission trip to Guatemala and the basketball clinics in China. He would not leave town until he knew his wife was going to be all right. Suddenly, basketball and everything related to it seemed unimportant.

One night, shortly after the diagnosis, Brown was alone in his study at home. It was late, which was when he did his most constructive work. He was confused and unsure of himself. Before long, he found himself praying harder than he had ever prayed. If he had been the one with the serious ailment, he still would have prayed. But it would have been a much different prayer. He would have asked for strength to fight it himself. After all, he had overcome every other obstacle in his life. He could take care of something like this, too.

But he was not the one who had to beat this illness. Vonnie, his sweet, darling wife of almost 30 years, could be dying. She just had to make it. Never had he realized just how much he needed her. Even more so, he recognized he had to depend on something greater than himself. He prayed that God would heal her and make them both more spiritual. He sensed he must turn his life over to a higher power. And he did. So did his wife.

Dale and Vonnie had similar responses as they waited to hear more from the doctors in the final days of August. With their busy careers, they had rarely taken time to stop and think about where they were going. The illness stopped them in their tracks. It brought them to their knees. They had no place else to look but up.

Together, they sought answers. Who was really in control of their lives? In whom had they been trusting? Dale had disassociated himself from the Catholic church for more than 20 years. Vonnie was brought up in the Lutheran church, but had not attended regularly since their marriage.

For weeks, they went to Christian book stores and bought every book and pamphlet that seemed to apply to their situation. Friends, learning of their quest, gave them more books. They read, discussed, debated and prayed. Their housekeeper, Clara Gerard, was a tremendous help. She told Vonnie how much she was praying for her, that her whole church was praying for her and they believed she would be healed. Everything seemed to be pointing them in one direction.

It built up up inside until one afternoon when Vonnie was feeling particularly anxious about her condition. She asked Dale if he had time to sit down and talk. They went upstairs in their house, sat on the floor together and talked for what seemed like hours. They prayed. They talked. Then they prayed some more. Ultimately, they put their complete trust in God.

Almost immediately they had a peace about themselves and even about her health. Robyn saw the difference. Their friends noticed it. At the office, Brown was a different person. He no longer looked tense, pale and drained. The color was back in his face, and so was his smile. Even more telling, he didn't work long hours at a break-neck pace. For once, he was learning to relax and enjoy himself. He was in the office for only seven or eight hours a day, instead of 12 or 13. His players, coaches and staff noticed it right away. It was obvious that something had changed drastically.

During that same traumatic week, Brown was sorting through some correspondence when he thought he heard a light knock on his office door. A moment later, he was sure there had been a soft tap. "Come in," he said, still looking down at a letter from a fan. Just as he was glancing up, a tiny girl with wavy bangs and sweet brown eyes leaped into his lap.

"Crystal!" he said, opening his arms to catch her. They hugged for several moments, then he propped the girl on his left knee. By then, her father, Marvin Willett, had followed her into the room.

"Here, I've got something for you," Brown said with a chuckle, pulling out a dollar bill. "I'll give you this for an ice cream cone if your daddy promises to let you have it."

Beaming with delight, Crystal thanked him and then turned toward her father, who nodded his approval. Willett had come to check on Vonnie's condition and to see how his longtime friend was handling it. They had first met when Brown tried to recruit Willett at Utah State. Marvin turned down the scholarship offer, but they had remained friends. When Willett's wife was killed in an auto accident, leaving him with a toddler, Brown had arranged for him to become the manager of LSU's athletic dormitory.

"Coach, we just wanted to stop by and tell you that we've been thinking about you and wishing you well," Willett said. "Are you doing all right?"

"You know about Vonnie, so you understand it's tough," Brown said. "She has that tumor, and they say it's as big as an orange." He motioned with his hands to show the approximate size. Then he shook his head and looked up at the ceiling for a moment.

"Marvin, I'll tell you it has been some kind of experience for both of us," he said. "You know what I'm talking about. When you have to face death for the first time, when you have to face cancer, it hurts deeply."

Once again, he paused to reflect on what he was saying. He stroked the back of Crystal's head. She remained oblivious to the conversation.

Changing his tone, he looked back at Willett and said, "But I feel a real peace about it. I told Vonnie, 'This is the last hurdle.' I've always had a speech about the four hurdles of life. The last one is getting to know yourself. You can't really know yourself without knowing God.

"I've always believed in God. All of my life. But now I'm reading the Bible and getting closer to him. Everything makes sense to me. It's like everything was written for me. I know now that I can't depend on myself for everything. I have always done that, and Vonnie has always depended on me. Now we're depending totally on God. You know that gives you such a feeling of peace."

It was obvious that he wanted to keep talking. Willett remained quiet and still, other than occasionally nodding or responding, "That's right."

"Marvin," Brown went on, "it's really interesting how you

change during something like this. Basketball has never been the most important thing to me. You know that. It has been a way for me to reach out to others. But now basketball means noth...''

He cut himself off and leaned forward in his chair, still holding the girl. ''It really means nothing to me. I don't care about championships any more. I just want to work with young people and try to give them some direction. I want to try to help them grow up and mature. Isn't that what is really important? Winning championships is so insignificant when you think about watching Ricky Blanton develop into the kind of young man he is.''

For much of the afternoon, he talked about Blanton and the new players on the team. Willett said how much he had enjoyed Blanton and now was getting close to the others. They all took an interest in Crystal, treating her like a little sister. Stanley Roberts carried her around under his arm as if he were carrying a football.

Brown thanked Willett for complimenting the players and maintaining discipline in the athletic dorm. Mainly, he thanked him for paying a much-needed visit.

''You two really helped me. I was feeling good. Now I feel even better,'' he said, kissing Crystal on the cheek. ''Thanks so much for coming by. It means a lot to have friends like you. In times like these, you're really grateful for your friends.''

''Coach, everything is going to be all right,'' said Willett as they walked toward the door. ''Vonnie is such a wonderful person. Please give her our best.''

''Thanks again,'' Brown told them. ''Say a prayer for her. That would mean so much.'' Willett nodded as he walked out holding his daughter's hand.

During those days, Brown asked many of his friends to pray for his wife. He once was private about such things, but no longer. There were many things he did differently. He got up at 5 o'clock every morning to pray and read the Bible. He had never done that before. Much of his free time, which he normally saved for pleasure reading, was spent on studies of Christian biographies, testimonials, commentaries and related works. Often, Vonnie would read the same books.

His office hours, though greatly shortened, provided him with a chance to discuss his beliefs with others. He either called friends on the telephone or invited them to his office.

Father Jeff Bayhi, the team's spiritual coach, paid numerous visits to Dale and Vonnie while she was sick. He also came by the basketball office occasionally.

On one of those visits, Brown told Father Bayhi, "Sit down, I've got something very important to tell you. There are so very few of us who have ever heard the truth. I have flirted with the truth for so many years, always trying to do the right things. I have flirted with being a totally committed person. And now, all of these things that have happened the last week have showed me something. I am totally, completely committed to the Lord. No matter what happens, I am going to live the rest of my life to serve the Lord. I know now that is the most important thing in my life."

Brown explained that nothing was quite the same in his life any more. Particularly his marriage. He and Vonnie had never felt closer. "I love my wife so much right now," he said. "I have never had anything close. And it's not because she might die. I just see things differently now. Everything is different."

He described how Robyn had come to the house the previous night and quickly sensed something had changed. She watched her parents carefully as they talked to each other, sharing thoughts and passages from scripture and books. She told them how happy she was for them.

What bothered Brown was that he had waited so long to find this kind of happiness. What if he had waited too long? Vonnie's condition was not good. Toward the end of the month, her doctors decided she needed surgery. The sooner it was done, the better her chances. It was scheduled for the last day of August.

She was wheeled out of her hospital room at 11 o'clock in the morning to go to surgery and didn't return until 7 that night. In the meantime, Brown's mind flashed through all the years, the joys and the disappointments they had faced together. Robyn was by his side, and Father Bayhi spent part of the day with them. Dale kept thinking about how much time he had wasted, that could have been spent with his wife. Father Bayhi advised him not to dwell on the past, but to pray for wisdom in the future. They prayed together that Vonnie would survive.

Brown expected the doctors to find a malignancy, but prayed that the tumor would be benign. The pap smear had been positive. Every indication was cancer.

But late that evening, they were given some wonderful news. The tumor was benign. Vonnie faced some painful months recovering from the surgery. But she would recover. She and Dale believed she had been healed by God. "I know it was a miracle," she told everyone who inquired.

Brown was exuberant for days. "I feel so much gratefulness," he told a friend one day. "I feel like there is something I must do to repay God."

Vonnie's recovery only served to strengthen the Browns' faith. They were convinced it was God's way of allowing them to be servants. Getting started posed a problem, especially for Dale. If he paraded his beliefs in public—particularly in the media—he knew that he would be labeled a charlatan. Some people thought he was the Elmer Gantry of coaching, anyway. He had to be careful about his approach.

"I don't want to say a lot about it," he explained one day. "It's like if you give money to something, you shouldn't tell anybody. You should do it in private. But where do you deliver your Christian philosophy? You should do it in your actions. That's very important. That's the key way."

On the other hand, he recognized that he could influence more people by going public.

Finally, he settled on the private approach. "I hope my actions will display what I believe," he said. "And I hope people who know me, if I do lose my temper or something, will say, 'He's still a human being.' I am still going to make mistakes. I am still going to have temptations. I am still going to have flaws. But I still think I can make a difference. I want to help people. I really do."

But Brown would face an ongoing struggle of reconciling his new faith with his old self.

One thing kept popping into his mind—he needed to help others. The first idea that he and Vonnie came up with was starting a home for abused and abandoned children. They knew they could do that without calling too much attention to themselves. But they weren't sure how to go about it. Brown decided to get the ball rolling by contacting some of his friends in real estate and public service. He knew it would take time to set up everything, which was fine because Vonnie needed about a year of rest to be fully recuperated and he had a season just ahead.

Even before his wife's surgery, Brown had started a quiet crusade. Whenever he felt somebody would listen without judging him, he talked about his commitment to God and the peace and joy he had found. Instead of handing out strictly motivational material, he was giving away Christian books and tapes. He was also taking to heart the command to love your enemy and pray for those who persecute you. He began praying daily for his family, players, coaches, friends, neighbors and especially his enemies.

To avoid forgetting someone, he started a prayer list. Every morning, he prayed for everyone on the list. Many of the names surprised him. Sometimes he wondered how he could possibly be praying for these people. Then he simply remembered the purpose of his prayers.

The list included Bobby Knight, former NCAA investigator Doug Johnson and former LSU athletic director Bob Brodhead. He felt each one had slighted him. Each had been considered the enemy. But now they were his concern.

The first time Brown prayed for Knight, he could hardly get the words out. But after several days, it became routine. Knight was just another person who needed to be helped.

"I really want to sit down with Bobby Knight someday," Brown explained. "I want to tell him why I said the things I did about him. I don't take any of it back. I think what he does is wrong. But I want to tell him why it's wrong. I think I can help him. I really do. He doesn't need to treat people the way he does. Sometimes I think he is going crazy. But he can change. Somebody needs to help him."

Trying to help Brodhead was easier. Dale had always liked Brodhead, even though he didn't think he could completely trust him. He heard the rumors that Brodhead wanted to fire him after LSU's loss to Navy in the 1985 NCAA Tournament. But Brodhead, after being forced to resign his LSU position in 1986, needed a friend. Brown was willing to let bygones be bygones.

Johnson was a similar case. Brown thought Johnson must have been an unhappy person to treat others the way he did. In Dale's mind, Johnson had tried to hurt him and his basketball program by attempting to slap LSU with major NCAA sanctions.

Despite harboring some hard feelings, Brown resolved to keep praying for his former enemies. There were many on his list.

"I know you're going to be a dog if you don't totally try to involve God in your life," he told Father Bayhi. "Now more than ever I feel armed in what I am doing because I feel closer to God than ever before. Victory isn't necessary. The final result doesn't always have to be victory. Like in the Indiana game, I felt I wanted to win desperately. I didn't humble myself enough to God. I recognize things like that now. And I feel so good about it. I never knew I could feel this good."

Understanding his need for humility was not easy in itself. Putting it into action would be a major struggle.

First, there were symbolic things that needed to be removed. He considered taking the trophies out of his office. The room is filled with large, ornate trophies and plaques awarded for Final Four appearances, Southeastern Conference championships and Coach of the Year in the conference and nation. "As God is my witness, these don't mean anything to me," he often said. "I laugh at them every day." But he decided they had to stay for recruiting purposes.

What mattered most to him were the team and individual player pictures and mementos from his years at LSU. They lined virtually every inch of his walls. There were also inspirational messages on a small bulletin board next to his desk, where he could look at them while he talked on the phone. The trophies were kept in the back of the office near the window.

He decided his own awards could be given away. There were watches, plaques and many rings. He had two Final Four rings and four SEC championship rings. He made up his mind to give them to someone who would enjoy having them, a friend or just a fan. The rings were on the kitchen cabinet one night when Robyn stopped by for a visit.

Puzzled, she asked, "Daddy, why do you have all your rings out?"

"I am going to give them to people who would like them. I don't want to wear them any more. They don't really mean anything to me. I am not wearing them."

Robyn was alarmed. All she knew was how hard her father had worked and how much the family had sacrificed to build a program at LSU.

"You shouldn't give those away," she told him. "Those are important."

"I don't need them anymore, Robyn. Why should I keep them? They're worldly. They don't mean anything to me."

"But that's not it at all," she said, picking up one of the rings and holding it up for him to see. "It was the philosophy that got these. That is what should mean something to you. It was the philosophy. The ring is just something that shows what you stand for."

Finally, he agreed to keep the rings. They did symbolize the basis of his program, what he was all about. But actually, that had changed dramatically. He was almost glad to have another great challenge ahead of him. It would have been almost too easy having Ricky Blanton back for his fifth year and bringing in all those great freshmen.

Rather than flounder in self-pity, he was eager to get to work. He felt well-equipped for the task at hand.

Over the next six weeks, he found a different way to prepare for the season. Instead of getting his practice plans together for October 15, the traditional opening day of college basketball practice, he spent most of his time taking care of his wife, reading Christian books, going to church or Bible studies, visiting friends, speaking at churches, schools and clubs, and just sharing his faith.

He and Vonnie visited many churches. Everywhere, they enjoyed the worship. But they felt a special revival every time they visited Church Point Ministry, which was their housekeeper's church. Often, they were the only whites in the congregation. "I always feel so close to God there," Vonnie said. "Sometimes, I'll be driving to another church and I'll just end up there."

Brown was comfortable at Church Point, but he would not join the church. He didn't believe only one church was the right one. Part of that was his distrust of organized religion. He was sure of what he believed and sure he wanted to tell others about it. But he still wasn't sure about churches.

Father Bayhi offered to take him on a retreat to Manresa Home, a former college owned by the local Catholic diocese. Brown thought it would be a perfect opportunity to completely unwind before the season started, as well as strengthen his faith. He knew it would take plenty of praying to get through the season.

Brown invited his friend, Tom Moran, to come along. He hoped that Moran and Father Bayhi might discuss their problems and beliefs. Brown could sense Moran was struggling, just as Dale had been only weeks before.

So they scheduled the retreat for Wednesday night, October 12. It would last about 24 hours. Moran was initially intrigued by the idea. Just being around the entertaining Brown would be fun. Then, too, he might just get something out of it.

At about 8 o'clock Wednesday night, Moran arrived at Brown's house in his long, white limousine, accompanied by Jeb Andrews, his executive assistant, and Stan Harris, one of Brown's former basketball managers and now the manager of one of Moran's restaurants in

Nashville. Andrews was driving, and Harris was just coming along for the ride, having spent the day with Moran discussing business matters. They soon headed south to the Sunshine Bridge, about 25 miles away. Father Bayhi was to meet them at Lafitte's Landing, a restaurant near the bridge.

The drive was just long enough for Brown to tell Harris a couple of highlights of his two trips to Medjugorie. He had witnessed what is known as the miracle of the sun on his first visit in the summer of 1987. He recalled looking up at the sun without even squinting and seeing several disks spinning around and a golden crucifix extending below the sun. The second time Brown went there, he had an even more startling experience.

"I felt evil all around that place," he said, leaning over toward Harris. Moran had already heard these accounts, but listened attentively anyway, because Brown is a wonderful story teller. "It was a terrible, eery feeling. But I was the only one who felt that way. Vonnie and Robyn really enjoyed the trip."

Brown went on to recount what is called the miracle of the birds. He was walking in a cornfield by himself when suddenly thousands of sparrows swarmed around him. "I thought I was in a Hitchcock movie," he said, shuddering. "Those birds were everywhere, for as far as you could see in any direction. Then as quickly as they appeared, they vanished."

He described running through the field until he met another American tourist. To Brown's relief, the man said he, too, had seen the birds and watched them disappear into thin air.

"I believe God is telling us to get our act together," Brown said as the limo approached the bridge spanning the Mississippi River. "I think he is tired of us messing things up, and he wants to let us know we need to straighten up right away."

At Lafitte's Landing, Moran led the way inside and went right over to greet John Folse, the celebrated Cajun chef who had prepared meals at the Moscow Summit that summer. Brown was right behind Moran and once again did most of the talking.

"Good to see you again, John," Brown said, smiling and extending his hand. "I thought the KGB might have kept you over there to cook for them."

Folse laughed and they all took a seat at the bar. Brown and Folse began to discuss the conditions in Moscow. Brown asked how Folse had obtained all the ingredients he needed for cooking. Then they talked about the Russian people. Folse seemed to agree with everything Brown said. Before long, Father Bayhi joined them and suggested getting over to Manresa, located about 10 miles south.

Brown rode with Father Bayhi. Moran, Andrews and Harris followed in the limo. Brown told the priest how excited he was about the retreat. He hoped and prayed it would be a meaningful time for Moran. But he also wanted to get away and rejuvenate himself before the five-month grind of the season started. He couldn't wait to put his feet up and start reading, or just get alone by himself to pray. He also enjoyed being in the company of Father Bayhi. This was no ordinary priest, certainly like none Brown had ever known. He valued his wisdom and candor. If there had been more priests like Father Bayhi, Dale would not have been alienated from the church.

As the cars pulled through the gates at Manresa, Brown grew quiet and gazed at the grounds. The meticulously groomed lawns, lush gardens and shrubbery were illuminated by floodlights. Majestic live oaks were everywhere, enhancing the beauty of the 1,300-acre estate. The well-maintained buildings looked like they were still part of Jefferson College in the 1800s.

On this night, the grounds were deserted. The priests who managed the campus had already gone to bed. After saying farewell to Andrews and Harris, Brown and Moran began their retreat with Father Bayhi. For several minutes, they stood silently absorbing the serenity. Then Father Bayhi left to get the keys to the dormitory.

"This is an unbelievable place," Brown said to Moran, breaking the silence. "It's so gorgeous here. It just makes you feel closer to God, doesn't it?"

Moran was skeptical of the religious kick his friend was on. Past experience told him that Brown could easily get carried away with a new idea or approach to something. But despite some doubts, Moran noticed a marked difference in Brown. Perhaps it was only an emotional response from Vonnie's illness. But just maybe there was something to it.

Several minutes passed before Father Bayhi returned. Brown was eager to get started. He inquired, "Father, is this going to be like one of those silent retreats? I mean are we supposed to keep quiet now that we're here?"

Father Bayhi explained that the weekend retreats were always silent to add to the peacefulness of the campus and give individuals more time to do what they went there to do. Since this was a private retreat, silence was optional. He left it up to Brown, although both Father Bayhi and Moran knew all too well that Dale could not possibly keep quiet for 24 hours. Even 24 minutes would be a test. Moran had earlier joked with his business associate that he would pay $1,000 to personally witness Brown remain speechless for a whole day.

"Why don't we go ahead and talk," Brown said in all sincerity. "I've got some questions I need to ask you, Father. We can still have some quiet time to read. But maybe we should talk, too."

After putting their overnight bags in the tiny cubicles used for sleeping quarters, they met in the library. Brown was the first to arrive and went directly to the shelves that lined three walls of the room with hundreds of Christian books, all in paperback.

Putting on his glasses, he browsed through book after book, reading the jacket of one and then skimming a chapter of another. He couldn't decide which one to read first. Soon he had a half dozen in one hand and was reaching for more with the other. Moran joined him but wasn't quite so enthused.

"Tom, this is a great book," Brown said, grabbing a copy of Imitation of Christ. "I really got a lot out of it. I am going to buy you a copy."

When Father Bayhi joined them, Brown interrupted his book search and pulled out a legal pad covered with numbered questions. It was only a little after 9 o'clock, and Father Bayhi knew that Brown would want to stay up most of the night. He suggested going to the priests' lounge, where there were more comfortable chairs. He realized he had his work cut out.

The lounge was in the main building that housed the dining hall, on the other side of the grounds. On the way over, Father Bayhi gave them a brief tour. Everything was immaculate, in perfect order and repair. Brown and Moran told him how impressed they were with the beauty of the campus. They especially liked the little chapel, where Father Bayhi said he would conduct a mass the next day just for them.

Having made their way to the lounge, they got comfortable and prepared for a long discussion. Father Bayhi got them soft drinks and coffee. Moran, meanwhile, didn't let Brown get rolling with his thousand-and-one questions about Biblical history.

Brown was a history buff and could never get enough background information on any subject. To sidetrack him, Moran began talking about himself. Before long, Brown and Moran were sharing family and personal histories. Father Bayhi sat back, smoking a pipe and taking it all in.

They talked about growing up in the Midwest during the Depression. Both knew poverty all too well. Neither had much association with his father. Brown's father abandoned him at birth in North Dakota; Moran's father left when Tom was a small boy in Chicago. For both men, sports had been about the only happiness they had known.

"Tom, I didn't know that about your father," Brown said. "We had it pretty hard, didn't we? I wonder who had it the hardest."

Moran didn't take long to respond. "We had days when we only had a nickel and we had to decide to buy bread or bologna," he said. "But we wouldn't take anything. Nobody ever gave us a thing. Not one thing."

Brown and Moran had come a long way financially. Brown made close to $500,000 a year. Moran earned several times that in a good year. Even so, they would not, or could not, forget their painful pasts.

Talking about it was an important step, especially for Moran. Brown was delighted that Tom was opening up to them. He sensed his mission was moving in the right direction. He started to talk about Father John Hogan, a Catholic priest in his hometown, who had been so influential in his childhood. He explained that if it had not been for the kindly, old priest, he didn't think he could have survived.

"I never had a Father Hogan in my life," Moran said sullenly. "I grew up scared as hell of the church. That was the only way I knew. I was guilty or scared of everything."

Even though Brown and Moran had been friends for almost 10 years, they had never felt as close as they did then. They shared their heartaches and deepest secrets. Moran had been on Brown's prayer list for weeks. Brown could see his prayers being answered that night. He believed it wasn't so important that Moran return to the Catholic church, but that he just put his trust in God and not himself.

Father Bayhi offered some advice during their long conversation. His relaxed, non-traditional manner caught Moran by surprise.

"Priests weren't like this when I was going to church 30 years ago," he exclaimed. "Dale, I've missed something. I know I like this a lot better."

It was well after two in the morning, and Brown was still going strong. But his companions were tired and hungry. They suggested getting something to eat. He told them he had eaten his one meal of

the day—corn chowder and a ham sandwich—and didn't need anything else. But he followed them to the kitchen, where they found a
smorgasbord of leftovers. Brown ended up eating more than anyone
else, feasting on four pieces of baked chicken and two pints of frozen
strawberry yogurt.

After raiding the ice box, they walked back to the dormitory, so
Moran and Father Bayhi could sleep and Brown could read some of
the books he had picked out. They agreed to meet for breakfast at 8.
Brown said he wouldn't stay up too late. But by the time he had reviewed several books, it was well past 4.

As usual, he had overexerted himself. He was so exhausted and
the campus was so quiet that he slept through breakfast. Likewise,
Moran and Father Bayhi overslept. Brown was already in the library
again when Moran found him just before 9. Since their host could still
be heard snoring, they decided to go for a walk on the grounds.

Strolling alongside a row of moss-shrouded oaks, they chatted
about anything that came to mind. Brown inquired about Moran's net
worth. He had never bothered to ask before, knowing only that his
friend had plenty of money. Without hesitating, Moran told him he had
accumulated more than $30 million, but his assets had dropped in
value during Louisiana's economic decline. They discussed the economy. Then Brown changed the subject.

"Do you think politics will ever change in this state?" he asked.
"Will it always be so corrupt?"

"Dale, the only way it will change is if we get somebody in office
who doesn't owe anything to anybody," Moran answered. "That is
why I wanted you to run for governor last time. If you had been in it,
you would have won easily. I told you that. It would not have been
close."

Brown didn't respond. He reflected on the two times he had considered running for political office. Moran and other influential friends
had offered to fund his campaign for U.S. senator in 1986 and governor
in 1987. Both times he had seriously considered the opportunity. Public office interested him, but not as much as basketball.

"How large is this place?" Brown inquired, shifting the conversation again. "It is so beautiful here. I am so glad we came. It just
makes you feel so close to God to come to a place like this. We need
to come here for a whole week. I want to bring the team here."

By then, Moran had warmed to the purpose of the retreat. "This is an amazing place," he said. "And Father Bayhi is an amazing priest."

As they made their way back toward the dormitory, Father Bayhi had spotted them and was walking in their direction. They had time for a quick cup of coffee before mass.

In the quaint, little chapel, Brown and Moran tried to follow the order of service in the Catholic liturgy. They listened intently to the scripture reading, songs and sermon given by Father Bayhi. They both took communion. It was the first communion for Brown in 20 years. It had been even longer for Moran.

"I just got a tingling feeling all over," Brown whispered to his friend. "That was such a spiritual thing."

"Dale, that was just beautiful. The church has changed. How did I miss it?"

"I missed it, too, Tom. This isn't what it was like when I was an altar boy. I feel good about church now. I feel like I'm really worshiping God. I'm not just afraid of God any more."

That afternoon, Brown went on another long walk, this time along the levee of the Mississippi River and without Moran. He wanted to give him time alone with Father Bayhi. He climbed up the steep bank of the levee and went almost two miles before turning around to come back.

After he thought enough time had passed, he returned to the library and pulled out his list of questions. For the next several hours, he quizzed the priest on details of the Bible.

"Father, how long was Noah in the Ark? It was longer than 90 days, wasn't it?" he asked.

Father Bayhi said he would have to look that up in a commentary to get an exact number of days. Many of the other questions were of a similar nature. Brown wanted to know every detail of hundreds of Biblical stories. They had covered about 30 questions when Moran's limo arrived to take them back to Baton Rouge.

The retreat was over. Brown's quest was accomplished. Moran announced the next day that he was going back to church.

Now Brown could start thinking about basketball. He was eager for the start of the season. He had never felt so full of strength and so good about himself.

No longer did he feel compelled to beat Knight. He told friends that the matter was over and done with. All was forgiven on his part. He even admitted that he should have handled it differently.

"It's over, and I have totally forgiven him," he said. "It's off my mind. If I had it to do again, I would do it a different way. I wanted to get back at him. That's not what I believe in now. That's not a Christian attitude."

To forget that part of his life would be difficult. But he would try his best. For now, his full attention was focused on the season. He felt sure of success, despite seemingly insurmountable odds.

7

Belle Rose

Ricky Blanton's Diary, October 15—This is my fifth year, and I've still got butterflies. It isn't really nerves. I'm more excited than anything else. This is what I've been looking forward to for months. I'm in good shape, but I know I'm going to get winded today. It always happens. You get the adrenalin pumping so much. There's nothing like it. You feel exhausted, but you're so pumped up it doesn't matter.

Thousands of fans were milling around outside the Assembly Center waiting for the game to start. It was a cool, cloudy fall afternoon, ideal for outdoor activities. Later, the LSU football team would enter Tiger Stadium, just across the street, to play Kentucky.

But October 15 also meant something special to basketball players, coaches and fans alike, and always has. It is the first day of practice. A time to begin another season. A chance to realize hopes of success.

A new season was in the making on this Saturday for LSU and hundreds of other basketball teams across the country. Many schools had already held special practices, opening the season at one minute past midnight.

At Kentucky, Memorial Coliseum had been packed with more than 11,000 fans. Dale Brown had never held a midnight practice and vowed he never would. This was a time for his team to begin taking shape. This was not a time for fans and hoopla. This practice, like most of LSU's, was closed to the public and media. Brown wanted no distractions. As usual, he opened with some comments. He was already beginning the motivational process that would make his team a little bit different from any other in the nation.

The players were called back to the locker room to hear his first address of the season. They were eager to get started, but no more so than their coach. This was his special talent, and he knew it. If these players had any doubts about themselves or the team, he would erase them.

''You all have been hand-picked,'' he started. Then he paused to glance around the room at each player. There were only eleven on scholarship, including late additions Geert Hammink, the Dutch center, and Lester Scott, a Baton Rouge freshman guard who was not recruited by any other major program, and four walk-ons who made the team in a tryout that morning. ''I believe you represent what has made us successful. Our secret is very simple: we care for each other, we love each other, and we play hard and together.

''See, this guy sitting right here.'' He walked over to Ricky Blanton and put his arm around his shoulder. ''If I can't put my hand on his neck and say, 'I love you, Ricky,' or if I can't coach you for some reason, then you can't play for us. But I know you all. You will all learn to love each other and be a family and a team. So that's why we've hand-picked you all. We've rejected a lot of people, but we picked you.''

Then he displayed several newspaper and magazine articles that predicted a losing season for LSU. He read excerpts from each one, putting emphasis on parts that he thought were most demeaning. All the while, he knew his players would respond. If athletes are anything, they're competitors. And they don't like to be told they can't do something.

Brown, on the other hand, would tell them they could do anything. ''Don't be mad about what they say. Feel sorry for them. They don't understand what we're about. They don't have the kind of love and concern for each other that we have. They can't understand our system. If you believe what they write, you will finish exactly where they said you'll finish. But if you can use this as a stimulant to understand that God doesn't make any junk, that you're as good as anyone else, we're going to get something special out of this season. We will go back to our eleventh straight national tournament, even if it looks impossible. We've got one guy who is a junior or senior. It is the youngest team we've ever had. It is the toughest schedule we've ever had. But if you take to heart what I am telling you, you can beat any team in the country. You can do anything that you want to do. You can get to the NCAA Tournament. I believe you can get to the Final Four. But it's got to start today."

Reaching the Final Four is the dream of every college basketball player and coach. During the last decade, the Final Four has blossomed into a major sports happening. Some rank it with the Super Bowl and World Series. The nation was captivated by the Larry Bird-Magic Johnson showdown in the 1979 Final Four. Then North Carolina State's dramatic victory over Houston in 1983, coupled with Villanova's 1985 upset of Georgetown, further elevated the event. Brown and LSU were a part of it twice. He wasn't about to give up on trying for a third trip in the '80s.

There was nothing fancy about his practice plan for opening day. Like always, every minute of the two-hour session was mapped out. They started by working on the basics: dribbling, passing and shooting. The shooting drills were the only fun moments for the players.

Chris Jackson, his first time in an LSU uniform, put on an exhibition in the opening drill. Each player had two minutes to shoot, with a teammate getting the rebound and returning the ball. Jackson, who had not warmed up, backed to the three-point line and began working on his jump shot.

His shots whizzed through the net with spectacular efficiency. He moved from side to side and into the corners, hitting everything he put up. His streak soon hit double figures. He made his first 17 attempts. When his next shot skipped off the rim, he shook his head vigorously and got ready to shoot again.

As quickly as Lyle Mouton could get the ball back to him, Jackson flicked another jumper through the hoop. The handful of guests sitting in the stands watched in amazement. Brown couldn't help but notice. He shook his head in disbelief. Without question, he had never seen anyone shoot like that.

The C. J. File (First person from Chris Jackson)—I don't really know what to expect from college ball. I'm anxious and excited to see what it's going to be like. A lot of players do well in high school but have trouble in college. I don't want that to happen to me. I'm prepared to score. Offense is my game. I work all the time on my shot. In high school, I didn't worry much about defense. I know I need to play better defense here. That's something I'll work on. I'll do whatever they want me to do. But scoring is the best part of my game.

Once shooting practice ended, the drills got tedious for the players. They worked on bounce passes, overhead passes, chest passes, baseball passes, hook passes. They practiced crossover dribbling, pivoting and stop-and-go. At times, they looked bored. At other times, they seemed confused. Often, they looked sloppy.

Brown saw there was much work to be done. "You know we really look bad in drills," he said to Ron Abernathy during a break. "You have to have talent to look good in drills. You need some athletic ability to do these things. We just don't look very good. But we know what we have to do."

"You're right, Coach," said Abernathy. "We've got to get the fundamentals down. We've got to push them to get better."

"We're not that good right now," Brown said. Then he winked at his associate. "But we're going to get better. We're going to get a lot better."

It would take time, which they had. The season opener was a month and a half away. It would also take patience, which Brown was beginning to have. Blanton and Wayne Sims were his only returning starters. Mouton was the only other true veteran, who had played when it really counted. There was no question Jackson would be the starting point guard. But after that, nothing was certain. The centers, Hammink and Richard Krajewski, had a long way to go. Several of the scholarship players were not major college material. Perhaps some of the walk-ons would have to play. Included in that group were guards Dennis Tracey and Jason Cormier and small forwards Tony Doyley and Stephen Ussery. Doyley was a former high school teammate of Blanton's in Miami. The other three were from Louisiana. Basically, they were on the team to help in practice.

But even if all of the freshmen had been eligible, Brown could not have been more enthusiastic at the first practice. He was almost bubbling over with excitement. It had been seven months since their last practice. He missed the interaction with these young men. He was eager to teach the game he loved. During individual drills, he bounced around the court, carefully studying each player's technique. When they worked together as a team, he moved from one end of the court to the other. He was constantly on the go, ready to point out some small correction whenever he could.

Just short of his fifty-third birthday, Dale Brown looked as vivacious as ever. He was the picture of health. Standing 6-3, he was a trim 205 pounds and probably could have worked out with the players. Only the streaks of gray in his hair gave away his age.

This was his 17th opening day. And yet there was no staleness. He wasn't there to finish his career and retire. He vowed to keep pushing and driving himself every time he stepped on the court. He required the same thing of himself that he demanded from his players.

Through the years, he has mellowed in his approach. He learned that he got more done by teaching and preaching than by screaming and hollering. He lost his temper only once on the first day. That happened when he thought some players were loafing. That was the worst thing anyone could do.

"Look, we've only been practicing an hour and 25 minutes," he said, stopping the drill and pointing to the clock. "I can tell who busted their butts to get in shape and who didn't. OK? Some of you are already dragging your damn heads, because you haven't pushed yourselves on your own. Don't make it our responsibility to get you in shape. This is a team. There's no coach's name or player's name on that jersey. It says LSU. We play for the team. You know who's in the best condition of everybody here? Two guys."

He pointed to Blanton and Sims, who showed no signs of fatigue from a full-court, full-speed offensive drill. Then he turned back to face the other players. By then, he was shouting, his voice echoing through the arena.

"We've got a couple of you who are sucking air! You're going to be the same guys who are going to complain when you don't play. If some of you don't start moving, I'm going to keep you after practice and run your ass. As gently as I can say this, you guys cannot play for us unless you're aggressive. Fatigue makes cowards of us all. OK, we're going to work on the same drill. This time, I want to see you hustling and working hard."

Immediately, the pace picked up. There was another half hour of drills, and then the players shot free throws before showering. They had to shoot 50 times unless they made 10 in a row, in which case they could leave. After running hard for two hours, it was difficult to concentrate on free throws. Even though most were well-conditioned, their legs were weary and their arms felt heavy. No one made 10 in a row. Not even Jackson.

Despite his brief outburst, Brown was pleased with the practice. There wasn't great talent out there, but it was similar to what he had worked with the last several years. It was already clear that Jackson was special, maybe even better than anyone had anticipated. He had the shooting ability to score more than 20 points a game. Blanton and Sims were capable of getting 20 a game, as well. LSU had not possessed that kind of offensive potential since the 1984-85 season with John Williams, Jerry Reynolds and Nikita Wilson, who all went on to the NBA.

Mouton could develop into a major threat. Brown worried that Lyle was too soft. He came from a prominent family in the state. His father, Lyle Sr., was highly successful in the oil business. His mother, Phyllis, was appointed head of the state Department of Labor. That wasn't the kind of background that created the gritty, hard-nosed athlete Brown liked to coach.

But it was evident Mouton had to contribute for LSU to succeed. Brown called him aside after the opening practice and told him that he would have to win the starting job at off guard. His competition would be Kyle McKenzie, a gifted shooter, but too slow to be a factor at this level of play.

"I want you to fight for this," he told Mouton. "If you don't do it, I want you to quit the team. We don't need you as a backup any more. You've got to play for us or we don't want you."

If Mouton produced, Brown was certain they could turn out another memorable season. He didn't think finding a fifth man would be a problem. Somebody would step up in practice or early in the season and show he wanted to play. It could be one of the centers. It might be Vernel Singleton, a 6-6 freshman who had the jumping ability and quickness to play almost anywhere. It might even be a walk-on. Regardless, Brown liked the prospects for this team.

The only thing he didn't like was not having Marty "Doc" Broussard around. The feisty head trainer was at home recovering from coronary bypass surgery. Doc was important to the program. Not only did he take special care of the players' medical needs, but he pushed them just as hard as Brown. He was demanding, but well liked. Furthermore, he had influenced the hiring of coaches, athletic directors and even chancellors. He had been at LSU for nearly a half century and knew all the right people. Broussard was especially fond of Brown. The feeling was mutual.

Brown's first objective was to mold the players into a team. That was as important, if not more so, to Brown than honing their skills. So he sent them on a trip to Belle Rose, a tiny south Louisiana town about 40 miles from campus, in an economically depressed area. It is also the parish of Father Jeff Bayhi. Brown wanted his players to get a first-hand look at life in rural Louisiana. He also wanted them to spend time with Father Bayhi.

When the team bus pulled away from Broussard Hall (it is not named after Doc, although many think it is), the athletic dormitory, at 8 o'clock Sunday morning, most of the players thought they should have had the day to study for midterm exams that began the next day. "I didn't really agree with going," Sims said. But he and the other players would find out why Brown deemed it worthy of their time. Even Stanley Roberts, Harold Boudreaux and Maurice Williamson came along. They had to pay six dollars for their bus fare, as required by the NCAA. Otherwise, it would be considered a benefit not afforded to other students.

It was a beautiful morning. The bus passed through countryside with flat, open fields beginning to fade to brown. Then it traveled through a stretch of sugar cane, most of which had already been harvested, leaving nothing but crumbled stalks. Finally, it crossed the Sunshine Bridge and pulled into Belle Rose a little before 9. And after passing a few small stores, the team arrived in front of St. Jules Catholic Church.

St. Jules is a small, red-brick church with a tall steeple. The grounds are landscaped with large spruce trees and azalea bushes. The lot is bordered on two sides by cane fields, which were still lush and green with stalks growing to 14 feet. Even Roberts couldn't touch the tops.

Already, the parking lot was filling. Tom Moran's white limo had just arrived with Brown and Vonnie, and Moran and his girlfriend, Judy Byers. They joined the players in the rectory, where the first meal of the day was waiting for them. Belle Delaune and Nellie Savoie, two grandmotherly ladies, and some other members of the church had worked all weekend to prepare food for some of the largest guests their parish had ever known. They served doughnuts, pastries, orange juice and coffee for a quick breakfast before the service began.

In the church, three rows near the front had been reserved for the team. The rest of the pews were packed for the biggest event to ever hit the Beautiful Rose. Only five of the players were Catholic. Most had never attended a mass.

But Father Bayhi's message was a meaningful lesson for the young athletes. "All the great ones are dead. Have you ever heard people say that?" he began. "Let me say you don't have to be dead to be one of the great ones. But what is a great one? There's a difference between being famous and being great."

His example of greatness was an elderly woman in the Belle Rose community who was always doing thoughtful acts for neighbors. He also used as an example his own grandmother—or Maw Maw in Cajun lingo. She made her dozens of grandchildren feel like they were each someone unique and important. He said that is the kind of greatness everyone should seek, not fame and fortune.

"Before closing, I want to say something to the LSU players," he said, turning to face them. "I believe in you. Your coaches believe in you. Some people are counting you out. It was written in some magazine, 'For the LSU Tigers to have a winning season, it would take a miracle greater than raising Lazarus from the dead.'"

Laughter rang through the chapel. When it died down, he digressed from his message momentarily. "I'm asking you people to pray for these young men. Not that they win championships, which I think they will. But I want you to pray for them to become a family, to learn to love each other like brothers and to share their love with others.

"And fellas," he said, looking again at the players. "Coach Brown is a miracle worker. If you do what he tells you, you can do anything you set out to do. But remember being famous isn't as important as being great."

After the service, the team was directed to the auditorium behind the church. There, they met church members, signed autographs and posed for pictures. The parishioners were given team posters and schedule cards. Little boys brought their basketballs to be signed, and then they dribbled around the crowded floor. After about an hour, the crowd began to disperse.

The players went back to the rectory for lunch. Nellie and Belle had lined up pots, pans and casserole dishes filled with delicious food of all kinds, mainly specialties of the area. There was a large roast and gravy, sweet potatoes with praline topping, Cajun dirty rice, asparagus casserole, a fruit tray, homemade rolls and homemade candies and pastries galore for dessert.

While the players feasted, Father Bayhi took Brown and his guests for an unforgettable trip down Belle Rose Lane. They rode in the limo for about a mile before coming to a narrow paved lane. About halfway down the street, they stopped in front of the home of Gertie Landry.

Gertie is one of Father Bayhi's great ones. She is a gentle, kind-hearted lady who has done many things for the church, despite being deaf and blind. She lives with a sister, who is also deaf and blind, and a brother, who is deaf but has some peripheral vision. The brother grows parsley and green onions in a garden behind their small, modest frame house. When Father Bayhi was organizing the church's annual food fair, Gertie contributed a freezer full of parsley and green onions.

Gertie had found out Brown and the team were coming to town. Through sign language, she instructed her sister-in-law to write a note on a brown paper bag, telling Father Bayhi to invite Brown to her house. After hearing about her, Brown was eager to come.

Her sister-in-law, who lives across the street, greeted the guests and led them into the house where Gertie was waiting, dressed in a freshly cleaned and ironed outfit, her hair neatly done up. Her sister-in-law signed into Gertie's hand the message that Father Bayhi, Coach Brown, his wife and friends had arrived. Brown reached out and gave her a hug. Her face lit up with a joyful glow. She was so delighted that she trembled. She kept holding Brown's hand as the others greeted her with hugs.

Communication was slow, but Gertie's warmth filled the room. She indicated that she wanted to show everyone around the house. In each room, everything was immaculate. The linoleum floors and wood paneling shined. Pictures and other wall hangings were neatly arranged. She took them into her bedroom, where the bed was tidily made and every item on the dresser was carefully arranged. Her closet held about a dozen dresses, each spaced evenly. She coordinated her clothing every day by feeling the texture of the fabric. Even in the kitchen, there was not a thing out of place. It was hospital-clean. She and her sister took care of it all, even though they couldn't see it.

After the house tour, they went out to the porch and took pictures to commemorate the visit. Soon neighbors, having seen the limo, were coming by to meet Brown. He shook hands and spoke to them all. He talked about the Midwest to a neighbor who said he was from Nebraska. He spoke to another about the LSU basketball team.

When their visit to Belle Rose Lane ended, Brown got into the limo and told his wife, "Vonnie, I'm so glad we went to see Gertie. You know a lot of people would have taken us to see the wealthiest family in town first or maybe the mayor. But not Father Bayhi. You can tell he really loves people. I'm so glad we came here. I really love people like her. She hardly has anything, but she keeps her place spotless. I admire that. That is a lesson for us all."

Back at the rectory, the players were finishing their second and third helpings when the limo returned. Brown and the rest of his group got something to eat. The food was splendidly prepared and seasoned with a hint of cayenne pepper and other Cajun spices. "If you think this is good, you need to come for our food fair in the spring," Belle told them. Brown said he definitely would come to the next one.

After lunch, Brown assembled the players in the library of the rectory. He wanted to tell them about a retreat they would be going on with Father Bayhi. "I don't want you guys to think I'm trying to convert you to Catholicism or something," he said, explaining the reason for the trip. "You can be an atheist and still play on the team. So don't think you have to get baptized in the Mormon church or something to play for us. That has nothing to do with it."

Some of the younger players had wondered what going to a Catholic church in some out-of-the-way place had to do with getting ready to play Georgetown, Nevada-Las Vegas, Illinois and Kentucky. Jackson did not make the trip. He had received permission from Brown to go home to see his family and take a girlfriend to her high school homecoming dance. The others were beginning to understand the value of traveling, eating and spending time together. Even worshipping together.

"I did this today," Brown continued, "because this is a community that has had some hard times. You lifted their spirits immensely today. And the biggest reason we did this is you'll spend a lifetime meeting a lot of people and a lot of people will tell you stuff that is often bullshit. People don't live like they speak. If most of us preached just what we practiced, there wouldn't be as many phonies out there in the world. This guy you're about to spend time with is one hell of a man. You'll have a friend for life. It don't make any difference if you're

Communist, Lutheran, Catholic or Baptist. Religion doesn't have anything to do with it. He's just a good man. He's so wise for his years. He's only 35 years old. I've spent a lot of time with him. He's totally trustworthy. He's a guy I think you're really going to profit from.

"Most of us are out getting ready for basketball, or chasing girls, or making money, or trying to win the national championship, and sometimes we kind of let our spiritual life go. Without a spiritual life, there's zero. So I think you'll get a lot out of being with him and have a lot of fun. That's why we're here."

Only the players accompanied Father Bayhi to the home of J.P. and Katherine LeBlanc on the outskirts of town. They were left to talk about anything that was on their minds. Father Bayhi's casual manner relaxed the players. They related well to him and opened up.

Singleton and Krajewski talked about the pain of their parents splitting up. Doyley described the grief he felt when his younger sister died, and Mouton shared feelings about his grandmother's death earlier that year. They discussed their goals in life and basketball, too.

"OK guys, Lyle and Wayne and Ricky played last year," Father Bayhi said during a brief talk near the end of their time together. "These are the three you've got to beat. If you want Coach Brown's attention, make them look bad. You just have to outplay them. But if you go through the next four years just beating up on each other, all you're going to beat is each other. If you learn to love each other and help each other become the best, ain't no stopping you. Ain't no stopping you."

After their discussion time, several of the players went up to the priest and thanked him for his advice. "Father, that was just what I needed to hear," Boudreaux said. "This has been a great day for us."

"God is the one who is in control of this team," Sims said. "If we have a losing season, that's up to God. And if Coach Brown is going to work out another miracle, that's up to God, too. We just need to believe in God and keep him first in everything we do."

After that, the LeBlancs treated the players to more food. There was a long table covered with smoked turkey, ham, roast beef, white beans with ham, Cajun rice and desserts. The players spent the rest of the afternoon eating, playing pool and watching football on TV.

While the players were with Father Bayhi, Brown and his group were taken on a tour of the cane fields and a local sugar mill. Sugar production was the main provider of jobs and income for the residents of Belle Rose and surrounding communities.

After the tour, Brown, the assistant coaches and the team managers went to the LeBlanc home. The guests returned to Baton Rouge in Moran's limo. There was plenty of food left when the coaches joined the players. Brown said he wasn't hungry again, but ended up picking the turkey clean. They visited for about an hour before returning to St. Jules on the bus.

For the next two hours, the players met in the auditorium with about 40 to 50 high school students. No parents, coaches or other older adults were allowed to stay. The players and students had a rap session about the importance of academics, staying drug-free and committing one's life to something.

Later, many of the students followed the team bus to nearby Donaldsonville to watch a practice. Brown had planned a routine workout. But word got around town that the Tigers were going to Ascension Catholic High School and several hundred fans showed up. So Brown decided to hold a short scrimmage.

They had had only one practice. There had been no time to work on offense or defense. Brown wasn't sure what to expect. Abernathy had driven down late in his own car and Jackson got a ride to the gym with his Gulfport friends Evans and Joe Walters. So there definitely would be some excitement, even if everything was somewhat new. The players had played pickup games together, so they had a semblance of each other's abilities. The likely starting lineup of Jackson, Blanton, Sims, Mouton and Hammink formed the Purple team. Krajewski, Singleton, McKenzie, Doyley and Scott made up the Gold.

Surprisingly, it was a close game. Not so surprisingly, it was high-scoring, especially since the court was about 15 feet shorter than regulation length. Jackson led the Purple team's running game, hitting long jumpers and feeding off to Blanton and Mouton. But Singleton was more than holding his own inside against his more experienced teammates. He and McKenzie kept the game close. Then Russell Grant came off the bench to hit a three-point shot that won the scrimmage for the Gold. Both teams had scored more than 70 points in the 20-minute exhibition.

The intensity delighted Brown. He and Abernathy talked enthusiastically about the team's prospects as they drove home in Abernathy's car.

"Look at the way we played tonight," Brown said. "I was really pleased with the way things went. Look at Chris Jackson and Richard

Krajewski. Did they do a nice enough job? Both teams scored 70 points in one half. That says something about these guys.''

Abernathy was enthusiastic and supportive. "Coach, that's what I like about these kids. These are good kids. It's what's inside that counts, now so much more than at any other time. When I was going to school and you were going to school, it was hard-nosed. It was knock-down, drag-out type of stuff. Everybody was that way. But now you've got so many kids whose minds are on themselves. They get the ball and all they want to do is show off to somebody.''

Brown nodded in agreement. "They're just spoiled. That's all there is to it. But not our kids. They really work hard. Here was a little meaningless scrimmage in a little tiny town, where we spent the whole day. They ate all day. They could have been tired and bogged down. Hey, they played well out there.''

"And it's only the second day!'' Abernathy exclaimed. "We've got some great possibilities.''

"But we're not going to say one thing to the media,'' Brown said, continuing his assessment. "I thought Richard had a nice practice. Chris did a nice job. Scott Guldseth probably had his best day. Those three caught my eye. But you know we're not going to say one thing. We're going to accept our cellar spot that everyone is putting us in. And then when we win, we're not going to say, 'We told you so.' I think we've been overly humble. I'm not mad at anybody, but they don't understand our system. Al Guglielmo doesn't think we can win seven games. What everybody doesn't understand is our family. You can join a foster family and the father is an alcoholic and you'll have a screwed up life. But you join a foster family where there's love and in time you can be happy and have a productive life.''

Just how productive this team could be was still in doubt. Brown sensed on this second day of the season that the signs were good. But there was much that needed to be accomplished.

8

The C.J. Phenomenon

Ricky Blanton's Diary, October 17—We're going to do a lot of running. That's fun from a player's standpoint. C.J. gives us that added dimension. Everything comes easy for him on the court. He is so fluid. He is a natural. And this is a good situation for him because he can play his game with no restrictions. We know the only way we can win is to get up and down the floor.

Nobody associated with this team had to wait until the season started to find out what kind of player Chris Jackson would be. They had watched in awe as he ruled pickup games during the summer and early fall. It took only a few minutes of observing his masterful skills to appreciate and admire just how talented he already was and how remarkable he could become.

Years of intense drills have given Jackson the feeling that the ball is but an extension of his hand. He handles a basketball like an artist with a delicate brush or a musician at the keyboard. He darts left, then right, dribbles between his legs, flicks a pass through a crowd or suddenly explodes, soaring higher than three feet, like a ballet dancer, and releasing his shot.

And oh, what a beautiful sight his shots are. Picture perfect. Elbow pointed straight at the goal. Wrist cocked like a loaded gun. Release at the peak of the leap. Just the right arch. Enough backspin to make it stick to the rim. More often than not, it rips through the net without so much as caressing the iron.

To watch Jackson is to understand what athletic grace and greatness are all about. Like Carl Lewis on the long jump runway or Greg Louganis on the diving platform, Jackson performs at his own level. At times, he seems out of place, like a maestro leading a kiddies' choir. Yet, he enhances everyone around him, making them excel within their own capacities.

Many casual observers were already trying to compare him to the legendary "Pistol Pete" Maravich. But there really is no comparison. They are magnificent, unique players from two vastly different eras. Maravich was the greatest showman to ever play the game. Jackson's game is geared to one thing: scoring. His every move is made to free himself for a shot or to position himself to hit an open teammate. No frills. No wasted motion. Just C.J. looking to score.

His scoring ability was evident to every LSU player the first few sweltering days of summer. Even before he came to stay at the end of July, he had played with his new teammates. Or rather they had played with him.

Ricky Blanton, just back from the U.S. Olympic Trials, knew from first glance that he had never seen anyone like Jackson at his age. There was certainly no guard with his shooting ability at the Trials. Why wasn't he invited? Not many high school players are. The only high school player invited to these Trials was Alonzo Mourning, who had signed with Georgetown to play for Olympic coach John Thompson. As it turned out, the greatest flaw of the U.S. team was its poor outside shooting.

There were many times during the summer when Blanton wished he could have watched Jackson on video tape. C.J.'s hands were so quick that it was difficult even for his teammates to see what he was doing with the ball. Did he actually dribble it through his legs on the dead run? Or was it just a crossover dribble? No one could know for sure. But there would be plenty of opportunities to study him on tape once the season began.

His other teammates were equally impressed with his court creativity. Russell Grant stopped his own practice routine the first time he saw Jackson in the gym that summer. Jackson started working on his jump shot, and after he hit several in a row, Grant began counting to himself. He credited Jackson for making 50 out of 52, many from well beyond the three-point line. Most drew nothing but net. Then Jackson switched to practicing his dunks. He jumped so high that his head was almost at rim level, allowing him to slam the ball with one hand, then two and finally behind his head. It was a spectacular display of offensive power. Grant couldn't wait to tell his friends about the C.J. phenomenon.

When Jack Schalow visited LSU that fall, Brown tried to sell him on the merits of drafting Blanton. But Schalow spent most of his time watching Jackson. After one of C.J.'s more spectacular plays, on which he penetrated past two defenders, stopped on a dime and went up well above 7-foot Geert Hammink to hit a jump shot, Schalow remarked to Brown that there was nobody in the NBA who could do some of the things Jackson did routinely. Skill-wise, he could play at any level against anyone.

Brown was delighted to have Jackson at LSU and hoped he would provide four wonderful years of thrills. From watching C.J. in high school and in the All-America games, Brown knew Jackson was the best guard he had ever recruited. Once Dale actually saw Jackson practice, he began to appreciate just how superb he actually was.

The comparison he made was Jackson as a freshman and Isiah Thomas as a sophomore. Thomas led Indiana to the 1981 national championship as a sophomore and then turned pro, becoming an All-Star with the Detroit Pistons. Defensively, the edge went to Thomas. But offensively, Jackson had a definite advantage. It was exhilarating for Brown to think he had a player of that caliber.

Even though it went against everything he had done in the past, Brown quickly made up his mind that he was going to turn Jackson loose. There was no point in trying to bring him along slowly. He was already there. It would just be a matter of turning over the offensive reins and letting him freelance, whether on the fast break or in a set offense. There was no doubt in Brown's mind that Jackson could make a lot of things happen, and all of them were good.

Brown felt comfortable with this decision because of the type of person with whom he was dealing. Dale has said repeatedly the only thing he likes more than Jackson's basketball ability is his character. "I have already learned so much from him, and he is just a boy. He's not even half my age," he told Schalow. "I asked him once if he had one wish, what would it be? And he told me he wanted to be in a position to help other people some day. I think he is the most pure, kind-hearted person I've ever known, and I'm not saying that because he can play."

If it had been another player with equal ability but less character, Brown never could have trusted him enough to turn the offense over to him. But Dale was certain beyond all reasonable doubt that Jackson could handle the responsibility and would make the best of the situation, because it wouldn't go to his head. He would not become a selfish player, trying to get his points and then thinking about the team.

Jackson's childhood was much like Brown's. He was born March 9, 1969. He grew up in relative poverty in the small Gulf Coast city of Gulfport, never knowing his father, often going without the things his friends had, sometimes even going without food.

His mother, Jacqueline, spent little time at home. She was always busy working as a hospital attendant, trying to support her three sons. They lived in a small, poorly furnished rental house.

But instead of growing bitter toward society and trying to prove his worth—like Brown did—C.J. accepted his circumstances and developed a gentle, sweet personality. That is what Brown meant when he said he has learned from Jackson. He seems to genuinely appreciate everything that has come his way, mostly through basketball.

The C.J. File—The person who is most important in my life is my mom. She grew up hard. She didn't have much. She hasn't had a good life. She had to raise three kids and always had to work so hard. When we asked her for something, clothes or a toy, she didn't have the money, but she'd go out and get it anyway. I wish now that we hadn't asked her for anything. I guess kids think money grows on trees.

David, at 23, the oldest son, joined the Marines right out of high school. Omar, 12, is just starting junior high. David played some basketball, and Omar is starting to pick up the sport. But neither fell in love with it like their brother Chris.

The game became his closest friend and greatest joy in life when he was a toddler. His mother remembers him carrying around a basketball while he was still in diapers. "That boy never crawled," she once said. "He just started walking at seven months old. Somebody gave him a little basketball when he was a baby, and he was carrying it around with him before he was a year and a half."

Jackson grew up in an economically depressed neighborhood. But it is rich in basketball opportunities. His house is on the corner of 21st

Street and Thornton Avenue. On the other side of Thornton Avenue is Morning Star Baptist Church. It is a large, two-story brick structure that was built by a Reverend Jackson in the early 1900s. No one knows for sure if Chris is a distant relative of the preacher, although many of C.J.'s relatives are still active in the church. Chris has been a member since he was a little boy.

At the corner of Thornton and 20th is Oliver's Grocery. Jackson and his brothers went there to buy something to eat whenever they had spare change. Mrs. Oliver, an elderly white woman, still runs the store and proudly displays an autographed picture of Jackson on her counter.

From Oliver's, Jackson could walk to his choice of basketball courts in a few minutes. He turned left to get to the Old Center courts, turned right to get to the New Center courts or kept going straight down Thornton Avenue to his favorite court at Second Street Park. By walking several more blocks, he could arrive at Frank B. Brown Memorial Gymnasium, where the Gulfport school teams play their games. A block away is the white sand of the Gulfport beach.

By high school standards, Brown Gym is enormous, seating crowds of 2,500 or even 3,000 if extra chairs are brought in. Even before Jackson suited up, the old, poorly lighted gym had provided many dramatic moments, including four state championships in the '70s. There was no air conditioning, so the doors were left open to catch the Gulf breeze. It seems the wind always blows in Gulfport, but never enough to cool off a full house in the gym, which was nicknamed "The Home of Champions." It was about to become the home of a legend.

Before developing into a city-wide celebrity, Jackson was already an accomplished playground player. The basketball court became his domain. He couldn't wait to get out there and start shooting. Often, he would sleep with his basketball beside him in bed. Then he would be the first one up in his house, usually by 5:30 or 6. As soon as he could get dressed, he headed for one of the playgrounds. On most mornings, he was by himself. He didn't care. He had his ball and a goal to shoot at, and that was all he needed.

He favored Second Street Park, because he was often the only player on the court. The park is on the other side of the railroad tracks from Jackson's house. Like many Southern towns, Gulfport's black community lives on one side of the tracks and the white community on the other. This park is maintained better than most. New nets are put up regularly. The rims are double thick so they don't bend as easily and the court itself is small, a little more than half the size of regulation. The rest of the park is well-equipped with tennis courts, swing sets and other recreational equipment. Jackson didn't take any interest in other activities. The Gulfport beach, called the longest manmade beach in the world, is just a few hundred yards from the park, but C.J. rarely went there. He just wanted a place to work on his game, which he did tirelessly.

In the summer, he practiced all morning and well into the afternoon. Then he hurried home, got something to eat and went back to the court until it was too dark to see the basket. It didn't matter if it were scorching hot or pouring rain. He stayed out playing basketball. Friends invited him to go places and do other things kids like to do. He usually declined. He had pals like Van, Ronnie, Victor, Shrimp, Walk and Walter. They played ball with him several times a week. He liked to go up against the older boys. They bumped him and made him work for everything. But he always came back for more. He just wanted to play the game.

During the school year, he would get up early and shoot baskets for an hour. Then he would go home, take a shower and get ready for school. As soon as his classes ended, he returned to the court. His studies were a necessary evil. His heart was in the game.

The C.J. File—Most of my life is basketball. I've been playing since the fourth grade. If I didn't have basketball, I don't know what I would do. I met all my friends through basketball. I love to play ball. I just love it.

C.J. learned some things about basketball from watching older boys. Most of his knowledge came from studying the pros on television. He couldn't wait until Sunday afternoons to watch NBA games, especially if the Philadelphia 76ers were on. That meant he could see his idol, Julius Erving. Whatever "Doctor J" did, Chris tried to emulate. He worked continually on the spinning, twisting moves that only Doc could do. He tried to make his jump shot look just like Erving's. And he dreamed of being able to soar through the lane and slam dunk with one hand. That would come in just a few years. He was dunking in seventh grade and had mastered it by eighth grade, even though he was well under six feet tall.

Whenever he had to write a paper on somebody, he always chose Erving. Once, in junior high, he wrote a 24-page report on him. He went to see Erving's flop of a movie, "The Fish That Ate Pittsburgh," and loved every minute of it. The walls of his room were covered with posters, magazine pictures and newspaper clippings of Dr. J. And Erving's face was the last thing Chris saw before going to sleep and the first thing he saw when he woke up in the morning. Another connection was birthdays. Both are Pisces. Jackson told everyone that Dr. J was born on February 22 and he was born on March 9. And they both started playing organized basketball in fourth grade.

Jackson talked so incessantly about Dr. J that his friends started calling him Doc. It was a nickname he adored. He wanted to play like Doc, he wanted to grow up to be just like him. So he listened carefully to Erving's frequent plugs for getting an education and staying away from drugs. He followed every word of Erving's advice.

Even as a youngster, Jackson would not be satisfied until he executed to perfection. When shooting, he had to hit nothing but net. If the ball grazed the rim and still fell in, it didn't count as far as he was concerned. He had to hear the "swish." To make it tougher on himself, he imagined being guarded by the best defensive player in the world. He had to get past him to be able to shoot. Then his shot had to be perfect.

He developed his own shooting and ballhandling drills. He picked spots on the court where he wanted to be able to score from. Then he decided what kind of moves he would have to make to get open for those shots. To pass the test, he had to get every move right and hit all of the shots, without so much as nicking the rim.

If he had a perfect round, the drill took about 10 minutes. That rarely happened, because when he hit the rim or completely missed a shot, he went back to square one and started again. Usually, it took a half hour to complete. Sometimes, he was out there for hours. But he refused to quit, no matter if his arms and legs were aching, no matter if he needed to be somewhere else, no matter what.

It didn't take long for his dedication to start paying off. He became one of the best players in his neighborhood, even though he was younger and shorter than most of the boys he played against.

Still, he never considered playing for an organized team until one afternoon when he was in fourth grade. Like most days, he was out on the court playing ball, this time with his older brother. They were playing one-on-one at Central Elementary. Miss Cookie, one of the school's teachers, invited him into the gym to practice with the fourth-grade team. He had no idea how to play team basketball. All he had ever played was playground ball. He worried that he wasn't good enough to make the team. After he made it, he didn't think he could ever start. Then when the coach announced Chris was one of the starters, he didn't think he would be able to play well against other teams.

Before his first game, he was so nervous and sick to his stomach that he wondered if he should even play. But once the game started, he hit a couple shots and discovered it wasn't any different than being on the playgrounds. He could penetrate past his opponent, he could pinpoint passes between defenders to set up teammates for easy baskets, or he could put on a quick move and drill a jump shot. He scored 21 points in that first game, and his team won. It was the most wonderful feeling he had ever experienced. And he couldn't wait for more.

His career blossomed. He started every year, no matter how much older his teammates were. He was always the top scorer. His teams usually won. In sixth grade, his team's only loss was by a 43-42 score, and he scored 41 of the team's 42 points. He was one of the shortest boys on the team, but started at center or forward because of his jumping ability. From elementary school on, that little Jackson boy was a favorite topic of conversation in the city.

Gulfport High has one of the most successful basketball programs in the South. Bert Jenkins, a decorated soldier who fought in World War II under George S. Patton and was a prisoner of war for almost a year, turned out championship-caliber teams for 28 years. But never had he seen a player like Jackson. Jenkins first saw the whiz kid in a sixth-grade all-star game. Great jumper, great shooter, he thought. Then by eighth grade, Jackson had mastered the game like no one else who ever played in Gulfport.

"He could do things that my high school kids couldn't do," Jenkins said. "Of course, he was an unbelievable shooter. But he had everything else. He was tremendous at the look-away pass. I remember one time he was in the middle of a three-on-two fast break. He looked at the guy on the left and both defenders went that way. Then without turning his head, he hit the guy on the right for an uncontested layup."

Jenkins, who had already won five state championships and more than 700 games, was thinking about retiring in the mid-'80s. But Jackson changed those plans.

Jenkins knew he had an unusual talent on his hands. By then, Jackson was a self-made sensation. His reputation was already so great that he was picked for a preseason high school all-state team by the Jackson Clarion-Ledger/Daily News before ever playing a high school game. In Gulfport, players cannot compete on the high school team until their sophomore year. Otherwise, C.J. probably would have started in seventh grade. He needed only to be pointed in the right direction, and Jenkins made sure he was.

Everything changed when Jackson made it to the high school team. Jenkins had a free-throw shooting drill to start each practice. Everyone shot 10 times. If a player made all 10, he kept shooting until he missed. Practice did not begin until everyone was finished. But Jenkins had to change that policy after a few weeks. Jackson had consecutive streaks of 283, 267 and 246. So much for practice.

Jackson was equally impressive in games. He averaged about 30 points throughout his career and could have been well into the 40s, except that he seldom was needed to play a full game. He was all-state throughout his career. It took only a few games before Brown Gym was sold out every time he played.

"The whole city and the whole state had heard how good he was, and they all wanted to see for themselves," said Leon Theodore, an assistant coach at Central Junior High. "We all knew Chris was going to be a great player, because he wanted it so bad. He was a gym rat, always shooting after practice and at night. Whenever you'd see him, he had his ball. He'd dribble from one end of Gulfport to the other."

Even on the road, Jackson packed the gyms. During his senior year, Gulfport played in a tournament in Lake Charles, Louisiana, and as usual, the arena was jammed. But an unusual thing happened. C.J. was so spectacular that the home fans started rooting for him. In the second quarter, he drilled nine consecutive three-point baskets. It got to the point that the fans were standing and waving their hands to signal for a three-point shot whenever he crossed half court. He obliged with a career-high 55 points.

Along with Jackson's personal success, the Admirals dominated the state. They captured the state championship his last two years, compiling a record of 70-7. As a favor to a friend, whose son was still playing, Jenkins coached one season after Jackson graduated and finished with seven state titles and 866 victories.

Jenkins and his wife, Lil, took special interest in Jackson. They understood about his home life and took him under their wing, as did their friends Evans and Joe Walters. By then, C.J. had started to show signs of some kind of nervous disorder. Actually, it had begun with blackouts in elementary school. The twitches started in eighth grade. Nobody seemed to know what to do about it, including his doctor.

It got more severe in high school. Jackson would shake and flinch spasmodically. Lil, a registered nurse, suspected that it was a neurological condition and had C.J. examined by a specialist. It was diagnosed as Tourette Syndrome, a disorder that causes uncontrollable body twitches, facial tics and vocalizations that occur repeatedly in the same way. It can involve eye blinking, head jerking, shoulder shrugging, grimacing, throat clearing, barking noises and coprolalia—involuntarily vocalizing socially unacceptable words. All indications are that it is inherited.

The C.J. File—There were times when I didn't understand it, and I'd think, "Why me?" But you can't question the Lord. I just left it alone and accepted it. I just decided it was something I would have to deal with. It's life. I knew I had to stop worrying about people thinking things about me, because if they don't accept it, I can't do anything about it. That's just me. Father Bayhi has a prayer that says for every infirmity, there is a strength. I saw that in the prayer. Maybe for this Tourette, the Lord has given me basketball as my strength.

An estimated 100,000 Americans have Tourette Syndrome, which is called TS and was first described by French neurologist Dr. George Gilles de la Tourette in 1825. There is a national TS Association. There is no known cure, although some people grow out of it as adults. The only treatment is medication that reduces the severity of the spasms. Jackson started taking the drug called Haldol during his senior year. It helped a little.

But since junior high, he has had to deal with TS every day. Some days, it doesn't pose much of a problem. He can wait until he's alone and unwind from the tension that builds up inside him. On other days, he has trouble with the most routine functions. He can't hold a glass of water, has trouble eating and even struggles to comb his hair. He often takes up to an hour to get dressed. The only way he can manage is to stop whatever he is doing and concentrate on getting his body under control. It also prevents him from sleeping soundly. He often gets only a few hours of sleep.

Most of all, it greatly hampers his academic work. The twitches cause him to lose his place in a book and interrupt his train of thought. He has to read material two or three times to fully comprehend it. So he must study much longer than most other students. It is also difficult for him to finish tests in the allotted time. He got a medical waiver to take the ACT orally rather than in writing. But in college, he is tested with everyone else. He occasionally interrupts class by grunting involuntarily. Most students with TS must be given individualized instruction. Several doctors are amazed that Jackson does so well in a normal academic setting.

An athlete's schedule is not normal under any circumstances. Jackson's is typical of basketball players. That first semester, he and roommate Vernel Singleton got up at 7:30 or 8, depending on how late they stayed up or if they wanted to eat breakfast. Most days, they bypassed food for extra sleep. They usually had to hurry from Broussard Hall to get to their first class by 8:30. They had another one at 9:30. Then they took an early lunch at 10:30, followed by another class.

Around 1 o'clock they got back to their room for a short break before reporting to the Assembly Center. In the locker room, they changed into their practice uniforms and got their ankles taped. After that, they began stretching out to get loose for practice. They were out on the court about 2:30 to warm up. Then practice ran from 3:30 to 5:30. After showering and changing into their street clothes, they got back to the Broussard Hall dining area about 6:30 to eat dinner. Finally, they returned to their rooms by 7:15 or 7:30, exhausted from practice and a full day of activity, but still having to study. Their only free time was an hour or two late at night. On many days, Jackson's schedule was further compacted by interview requests.

Amazingly, he has been able to almost completely control the TS during practices and games, unlike Jim Eisenreich, whose professional baseball career was almost ruined by TS. Sometimes Jackson bats his eyes when under pressure. Otherwise, he shows no visible signs of the condition while on the court. It takes intense concentration to avoid a spasm. The constant motion of basketball helps.

He can usually hold off the twitches, jerky motions and vocalizations until he gets in the locker room. There, he unwinds from it all, sometimes swinging his arms and legs so much that he bumps his teammates sitting nearby. He is also effective at releasing this nervous energy at an appropriate time in a game. If he misses a shot or makes a bad play, he often shouts out loudly, occasionally cursing, which is a form of coprolalia and not intentional.

It is possible that TS contributed to Jackson becoming a basketball sensation. The condition sometimes causes obsessive-compulsive traits. The person feels something must be done over and over again. Children sometimes beg their parents to repeat a sentence until it "sounds right." Jackson seems to have applied that to basketball, repeating a drill or just shooting until it "feels right."

The medication he takes has a side effect that almost disrupted his basketball career. It produces a dramatic increase in appetite. His weight shot up from 150 to 165 pounds after he began taking it as a high school senior. Then he gained to 175 in his first three months at LSU. All the while, his height remained 6-1. His lean frame has started to get chunky, and his quickness and jumping ability have suffered.

But quick is still quick, and high is still high. He continued to dominate the competition. Twice he was chosen Mississippi Player of the Year. Parade Magazine selected him first team All-American as a junior and senior, which is a rare feat, especially for a guard. As a senior he was the consensus No. 1 point guard in the nation, and every major school with a basketball program wanted him.

By all rights, Jackson's senior year should have been the most enjoyable time of his life. On the contrary, it was by far the worst. He had to deal with the adjustment to TS, while trying to make a 2.0 grade point average and score high enough on the ACT to be eligible as a college freshman. His greatest challenge was trying to convince dozens of college coaches and representatives that he had already made up his mind about a choice of schools. It was a bitter recruiting struggle that tore apart a mother and son.

Letters and phone calls started pouring in from college recruiters during his junior year. By then, he already had LSU on his mind. It was close to home. It had a nationally recognized program and was always on television and in national tournaments. And it had Dale Brown.

The C.J. File—I had heard he was a great motivator. I'd seen his teams, and I liked the way they played. I saw him at games, and he didn't fuss at his players much. His players were really psyched up for games. I could tell it was something different. I really liked that. And they're like a family. They hug each other when they huddle. They really seem to care about each other. I really like that.

Initially, Jackson's mother agreed that he should pick his college, and it would be fine with her. But toward the end of his junior year, about a half dozen prominent residents of Gulfport started taking special interest in the Jackson family. They wanted to make sure he went to the *right* school. Each one seemed to have a stake in C.J.'s college future, and none wanted him to go to LSU. What followed was a nasty recruiting battle with Jackson caught in the middle. He went to LSU against everyone's wishes.

For more than a month, there was no communication between mother and son. He wanted to call her, but wasn't sure what to say. He started to write, but couldn't think of the right message. When he did call home, she was still angry and didn't have much to say at first. But she eventually warmed up to him again. He went home for a weekend, and before long, things were back to normal. She even told him that she and his little brother, Omar, would come to as many games as they could.

Jackson was glad to have everything resolved, but couldn't help feeling betrayed by those who had tried to steer him elsewhere. All he ever wanted was to be allowed to make up his own mind.

The C.J. File—I feel all the work that you've done, you should be able to go where you want to be. Of course, you want your family to be involved, but it's your decision, because you went through the sweat and pain. I don't think any kid should have to go through what I did, because it is rough. I think anybody should be able to enjoy his high school years and be able to choose where he wants to go to college. All that stuff wasn't called for. They tried to use me and my family.

At LSU, Jackson quickly found what he now calls his second home. He fell in love with the campus and was thrilled to be around Stanley Roberts, Harold Boudreaux, Ricky Blanton and his other new teammates. He was assigned a room with Singleton, another freshman from Mississippi. They immediately hit it off, developing a brotherly relationship. Rarely did one go anywhere without the other. Many of the freshmen had similar curriculums, so they went to class together, studied together and ate together.

Playing basketball every afternoon against some of the best players in the country, Jackson was in his glory. The competition was keen in their pickup games, but C.J. soon established himself as the best. Nobody could stop him. He and Maurice Williamson dominated from the backcourt; Roberts and Boudreaux were unstoppable inside. And Blanton was their wise, older leader. He often talked with Jackson and advised him how best to adjust to college basketball.

Even though Roberts, Boudreaux and Williamson had to sit out the season, Jackson knew there were enough quality players available to form a competitive team. He couldn't wait for the season to start.

While in most ways Jackson became another one of the boys, he didn't totally fit in. When the other players went out to their favorite bar on Friday and Saturday nights, he usually stayed in the dorm and studied or got someone to open up the Assembly Center so he could shoot. His social life was limited because he did not have a car. Since he spent only a few weeks of the summer in Baton Rouge, he didn't have much time to work and didn't earn enough money for a down payment on a car.

When everyone else went to home football games, C.J. was back in the gym working on his game. He had participated in the team's preseason conditioning program and played pickup games with the others, and had often gone back for more practice after dinner. That gave him time to work on the drills he had invented on the playgrounds. He just couldn't get enough basketball.

His adjustment to college academics was more difficult. He never had so much reading to do. It kept him up into the early hours of the morning, especially around test time. He got tutoring, which helped somewhat. But he was determined to make it academically. His sights were set on the degree that Erving talked about so much.

In many ways, Craig Carse tried to take some of the burden off Jackson. He and his wife, Leslie, a university tutor, help him with his studies. Carse initially sheltered him from the media and withheld public information on his TS condition, fearing the fans at other schools would taunt him. Sometimes his overprotectiveness bothered Jackson. But Carse offered encouragement and was someone to talk to when problems piled up on C.J.

The TS problem has created some awkward moments for Jackson's teammates. There are times when he can't control the twitches, and he goes into spasms. It flares up during team meetings, and there is nothing he can do about it.

There is something else unusual about Jackson. He is just as committed to his religious beliefs as he is to his basketball. He always wears a chain with a cross on it.

Throughout Jackson's childhood, Morning Star Baptist Church was a major part of his life. His family went to church on Sundays. That wasn't enough for many of his relatives, especially his grandmother. Myrtle Jackson made sure her grandchildren were taught the

Bible. She took them to Sunday school and to revivals, sometimes as far away as Slidell, Louisiana.

On Wednesday nights, the Jacksons would conduct their own worship services with Chris' uncle, Robert, doing the preaching. They sang hymns, prayed and listened to the sermon. Jackson remembered times when he ended up crying at the services. They had a profound impact on his life.

The C.J. File—They taught me to put my faith in God. They showed me right from wrong. I loved to go to church with them. They taught me how to pray. They taught me Jesus died for your sins and you need to believe in him to be saved. Without God, nothing is possible. With him, all things are possible. We just need to believe and keep our faith, and things will work out for the best.

Before every meal, Jackson says a blessing. Before every game, he pins into his shorts a small medallion with a picture of Christ on it. Then he pins a cross inside one of his socks. Before and after every game, he bows his head to pray in the crowded locker room.

He doesn't do these things in a showy manner, but his teammates, coaches and others around him can't help but notice his actions. They can't help but admire his faith, in light of everything he has encountered in his young life.

"This young man has amazing sensitivity and wonderful values," Father Jeff Bayhi says. "I really believe he is so very full of faith. He is very, very close to the Lord."

Vonnie Brown has been most impressed with C.J.'s character. She once told her husband, "Chris has so much purity. I just believe he has been touched by God."

Many wonder how such a harsh environment like the one he grew up in could produce such an extraordinary young man. In his book *Unto The Hills*, Billy Graham may have explained Chris Jackson in writing: "Comfort and prosperity have never enriched the world as adversity has done. Out of pain and problems have come the sweetest songs, the most poignant poems, the most gripping stories. Out of suffering and tears have come the greatest spirits and the most blessed lives."

Obviously, Brown hopes this unique young person and marvelous player stays at LSU for as long as possible. But even during Jackson's first few months on campus, there was talk he would stay only two years. His talent is already on the NBA level.

It is generally accepted, even among the school's most diehard fans, that such a tremendous talent will need only two seasons to sharpen up for the NBA. There is just too much money out there for him to stay the full four years. John Williams left LSU after two years and became a key player for the Washington Bullets, if not a star. Isiah Thomas left Indiana after two years, and certainly is a superstar. Almost everyone assumed Jackson will follow that same path.

Jackson doesn't. At first, he seemed genuinely surprised to be asked about his plans. From day one at LSU, he said it is his intention to get a college diploma. He learned that from Erving as a schoolboy, and he says he isn't going to forget it.

The C.J. File—The way I feel, I'm going to stay all four years. Doctor J is my idol. He talked so much about education. I understand how important it is. It is like a dream to be here, and I just want to follow my dream. I want to go to school and get my education, and then go on to do something else. I've dreamed about playing ball for a living, but that can wait. My degree is the most important thing now. You need your education. If something happens to you in basketball, you always have something to fall back on. The money isn't that important. You want to make a living. But I would do it for the love of the game.

Of course, Jackson gets positive reinforcement from his coach. Brown has stressed the value of maturing in a college environment before turning pro.

Jackson agrees that he needs time before he will be ready for the year-round grind of pro basketball. He has never been on his own. Going to LSU was the first time he had been away from home for more than a week.

The money isn't much of an attraction to him, either. He has already turned down so much to go to LSU. He knows he can get high-paying summer jobs to make enough for a car and entertainment. He has no reason to rush off.

His ambition is to keep his faith first in his life and keep playing basketball as long as he can. His personal goal is to play 30 years in the NBA. As unrealistic as it sounds, it wouldn't be enough for Chris. He has told Lil Jenkins that Gulfport will always be his home, and he will always want to go back to Second Street Park and shoot baskets.

When friends ask C.J. how long he wants to play the game, he says he'll play until he can't walk any more. Even then, he might play wheelchair ball. Basketball is his best friend—not that he doesn't have other friends.

The C.J. File—I'm shy. I don't talk much in groups. It's not that I think I'm this or that. It's just that I'm not good with conversations. I'm a hard worker. I believe the Lord is number one and most important in everything. I'm not the type to go out and party much. I don't drink. I don't smoke. I don't believe in doing those things. I just want to keep a healthy body. I'm just a down-to-earth person. I love people. I love talking to people. I wish I could communicate better than I do. I try. I just love people. I just love everybody.

9

Jamie's Season

Ricky's Diary, October 17—People don't expect us to do much. That's fine. That's really good for us. I know something good is going to come out of this season. I think we are going to win a lot of games and get back to the NCAA Tournament. I believe we can do it, and I know Coach Brown believes we can do it. Now we've got to make sure everybody else does.

Most years, Dale Brown devotes the last two weeks of October to teaching defense. That is the part of the game nearest and dearest to his heart. Defense is blue-collar work. It doesn't require great athletic skill, just great effort. This team was essentially made up of blue-collar workers. By all rights, it should become a solid defensive club.

To stress his players' work ethic, Brown came up with an idea of making a special team poster with all the players posing as ditch diggers. So one afternoon, they were all equipped with hard hats, shovels, picks, sledge hammers and power drills, and their poster was created. The title was "Hard Work Pays Off." It was also the theme of his program. The sports information department had 7,500 copies of the poster printed and the fans snatched them up as soon as they found out about them.

Despite his zeal for hard-nosed defense, Brown realized from the start that this team was a little different. Chris Jackson was the major difference. With him at the point, there was the possibility of developing a potent, high-scoring offense that could offset some major deficiencies, including lack of a defensive stopper, that one player who could shut down a top scorer.

So those early days of the season were committed to finding ways to best utilize the scoring abilities of Jackson, Ricky Blanton and Wayne Sims. Jackson gave new meaning to the transition game. LSU had not been blessed with that kind of running ability since Brown's first Final Four team in 1981. That team had a swift point guard in Ethan Martin, a walk-on from Baton Rouge who turned into a splendid floor leader, and two future NBA players, Rudy Macklin and Howard Carter. This team had three big scorers.

On the day after the Belle Rose excursion, Brown couldn't contain his excitement during the afternoon practice. He walked over to Ron Abernathy, a wide smile covering his face, and said: "Can these guys run or what? We need to run more. We're going to fast break on everything. We just need to get it in Chris' hands. He can penetrate, he can jump shoot, he can kick it to Ricky or Lyle on the wings. This will give us a new dimension."

The C.J. File—I had played with the guys so much in the summer that we were already getting used to each other. I'm starting to feel good about the team. We're getting to look pretty good. I feel comfortable with our offense. It's really a good feeling. I'm excited about the season.

Brown and Abernathy spent most of the two-hour practice working on fast-break strategy. Basically, they believed in getting a quick outlet pass to the point guard and trying to get a two-on-one or better situation with the wing players filling the left and right lanes. If they could get Jackson in the open court, just even with the defense, he would be difficult, if not impossible, to contain.

"You know what, Ron," Brown said. "If Kentucky changed its offense like this, they would call a press conference to announce it. We're not going to say a thing about it."

To run a fast-break offense, players must be able to get defensive rebounds. Otherwise, there won't be any outlet passes to the point guard. That could pose a problem for this team. Wayne Sims would be a solid rebounder, no question about that. Ricky Blanton could hold his own inside, but if he spent too much time rebounding, he couldn't get out on the break.

For their running game to be effective, there had to be someone else on the boards. Geert Hammink and Richard Krajewski had the size to handle it. But they were raw talents and might not be able to help this season. The only other candidate was Vernel Singleton. But he was slight of build and green as a freshman.

Brown reasoned he had to go with Hammink and Krajewski early. Their size was too tempting to pass up. Hopefully, they could develop some savvy and learn the system in the next month.

Hammink, recruited by Indiana, North Carolina and several other schools, had the most potential, simply because of his height. He would get the first look. But Brown didn't like what he was seeing. Once he caught Hammink standing around in the lane, arms at his side, watching Jackson dribble the ball.

"All right, hold up," Brown yelled. He was in a playful mood, so there would be no scolding. "Geert, have you ever heard of the Homestead Act?"

Hammink stared back with a puzzled look on his face. "What's that, Coach?"

"That's when the settlers came and staked out their land and settled here in the United States," he explained. "You look like you were settling there in the lane. You were homesteading, Geert. You've got to keep moving without the ball. Motion. Don't be homesteading on me."

Still a little perplexed, Hammink nodded that he understood. Shortly after that, he blocked a shot by Krajewski and almost retrieved the ball before it went out of bounds. Then he used Blanton's pick to get open on the other end and lofted a soft hook that rolled in the basket.

Delighted with the improvement, Brown walked over to see some of his friends seated in the stands. Only a select few were invited to practice. On this day, Al Guglielmo sat by himself in one section. Over by the railing, Jamie Roth and his mother, Debbie, were in their usual seats. On other days, the guests would include Tom Moran, Jim Talbot, George Eames or Joe Dean. Eames, a fiery radical, was president of the local chapter of the NAACP and a longtime friend of Brown's and all his players, black or white. A paraplegic, he always attracted attention when he came rolling into the arena in his wheelchair. Dean was another faithful friend of Brown's and had recommended him for the LSU job. When Dean expressed an interest in becoming LSU's athletic director in 1987, Brown rallied support for him on the Board of Supervisors and was instrumental in his hiring.

Brown sat beside Guglielmo and grabbed his arm. "I am telling you, Al, one year from now Geert won't be the same player. He is going to be a stud."

But the team needed him to perform right away. Next year would be too late. He might not play at all once Stanley Roberts and Harold Boudreaux stepped into the lineup. But Brown was convinced Hammink could play as a freshman. He kept calling him the next Rik Smits. Brown had been the first college coach to talk to Smits, having acted on the advice of a friend, Vladamir Haggar, a Czech who now coaches in Holland. At the time, Brown didn't have a scholarship to give. "That was one of the worst mistakes we've ever made, missing Smits," he admitted.

So when Haggar told him about a young center who was ahead of Smits in his development, Brown wanted him, sight unseen, even though he said he would never take another foreigner. He gave Hammink every possible opportunity. He placed him in a special program with strength coach Milt Williams. To help his basketball skills, he drilled with Craig Carse for a half hour before every practice.

That led to Brown putting the whole team through individual instruction at 3 o'clock with practice starting at 3:30 as usual. Primarily, each player concentrated on scoring from a certain spot, whether it be low on the block, as in Hammink's case, or out on the wing, as with Mouton.

Later that first week, Brown had another special event planned. He had already met with Blanton to discuss some distressing news. Jamie Roth, who was starting his third season as part of the LSU basketball family, had relapsed in his long fight with brain cancer. The tumors were multiplying, and he was not expected to live more than two or three months. The report hit Blanton hard. They had developed a unique brotherhood and shared each other's triumphs and setbacks. Losing Jamie would be a severe blow to Blanton, especially since it had seemed like Roth had recovered from the terrible illness that had threatened his life so many times.

During Blanton's second season at LSU, Brown had received a call from a basketball fan or an acquaintance—he couldn't remember which—who worked at a local hospital. She told him about a 10-year-old patient who had brain cancer and was expected to die any day. The boy was Jamie Roth, and all he talked about was LSU basketball. All he wanted to do was play with his purple-and-gold Nerf basketball set.

Brown was unable to get to the hospital that day because he had practice and then had to do his weekly radio show. So he called Debbie Roth, Jamie's mother, and told her to make sure her son listened to the show that night.

"It was January 17th, 1987, when we first talked to Coach Brown," Jamie's mother recalled. "He was on his radio show and said, 'I have something to tell Jamie Roth tonight. I want you to hang in there. I'm coming to see you tomorrow, and I've got a special surprise for you.' Jamie was so excited. He couldn't wait to meet Coach Brown. That was one of the best days of his life when Coach Brown came to see him."

The surprise was a basketball autographed by all the LSU players. Brown often brought gifts to patients in the hospital, most of whom he had never met. Usually, they wrote back to thank him, and that was the end of it. But with Jamie, it was only the beginning.

On this visit, Brown stayed more than an hour, talking with Jamie and his parents and shooting the Nerf ball with him. Brown promised him a seat on the team bench just as soon as he got out of the hospital. He did everything he could think of to cheer Jamie. And it worked, along with phone calls from Blanton, Nikita Wilson and Fess Irvin.

Within a few weeks, the skinny little boy had regained his strength and was released from the hospital. The next game, he was on the LSU bench, sitting beside Blanton, who was sidelined because of a knee injury. Jamie wore an LSU cap to cover his head that had been shaved for brain surgery. He and Blanton sat side-by-side the rest of the season, all the way to the Final Eight in Cincinnati. Often he would have to rush to the rest room in the middle of a game, and Blanton would hold his hand and take him there. Jamie came to practice daily and became as much a part of the program as any player.

"LSU basketball kept Jamie alive," his mother said during those winter months of 1987. Doctors said it was unlikely he would survive long enough to see Blanton play again the next season. Yet, somehow he did. He got stronger and kept coming to practice almost every day. He never missed a home game and made an occasional road trip. Blanton remained his hero, but he loved the other players like brothers.

Late in the 1987-88 season, he had a setback. His condition was worsening again. Doctors advised he would need chemotherapy. On the first day it was administered, Blanton was sitting beside him, holding his hand and telling him he would make it. Debbie Roth, not wanting to burden Blanton, asked him to leave. He would not. While Jamie shook, trembled and became violently ill, Blanton stayed by his side. Again, as improbable as it seemed, Jamie lived to see another season, Blanton's last at LSU.

Over the summer, Jamie gained weight and became almost too chubby. Brown teased that the boy had been drinking too much beer. Some of the players had trouble recognizing him, he looked so healthy. But the cancer was not gone. It came back stronger, just before the start of the season. Doctors told his parents that the only course was more chemo and even then his chances were slim. They decided against putting him through more pain. His final days, weeks and months would be spent with his two families.

"Coach, would it be all right if we did something special for Jamie?" Blanton asked after being told of the latest prognosis. They agreed he should be named honorary team captain. He and Blanton would be co-captains of the team.

Before practice that afternoon, Brown called the team together at center court. Jamie was sitting in the stands with his mother and sister. They were too far away to hear what was being said.

"We need to take care of some important business before we practice today," Brown told the players. "Ricky and I have already talked about it. Most of you know Jamie Roth. Well, they've found out he's only going to live another couple months. I personally don't believe he's going to die. I believe the Lord is going to intervene like he has so many times already. But what we thought we'd do is make him honorary team captain. That's up to you to decide."

Brown instructed everyone in favor of the idea to raise his hand. Immediately, all the players had their hands up. "OK, I guess that settles it. He's our honorary captain. Ricky, you go get him."

Blanton escorted all three of the Roths onto the court. They were clearly at a loss as to what was going on. Then Brown directed Blanton to break the news.

While holding Jamie's hand, Blanton said: "Jamie, we all got together and voted for an honorary team captain. He has to come to practice every day, sit on the bench at games, come in the locker room." Already, Jamie's face was beaming with excitement. "He has to be at the meetings. And he has to come on trips with us. We picked you. What do you say? Are you interested?"

Jamie was too emotional to respond. He just grasped Blanton, about waist high, and hugged him. There were tears in his mother's eyes as she kissed Brown on the cheek and thanked him. "That means you have to come to Hawaii with us, too," Brown added. "All of you have to come."

There was much to be done before the team's trip to Honolulu to play in the Chaminade New Year's Classic. Everyone hoped Jamie would be around to join them.

Later that afternoon, the players were working on the fast-break drills again when Brown suddenly halted practice for no apparent reason. "Look up at those," he said, pointing to the SEC championship and NCAA Tournament banners hanging from the ceiling. "We've got a mission just like we did those years. We can get another banner this year. Believe me, I have seen it happen too many times. This is our kind of year. Everybody has written us off. Just watch what happens now."

Regional and national publications had forecast a losing season for LSU. Even the local media had written off the team. Brown had already used some of the forecasts for mental ammunition. He had handed out practice T-shirts with an imprint of a scene depicting a column written by Baton Rouge sportswriter George Morris. It showed sharks swimming around the LSU team. The prediction was that, without its prize recruits, the team was doomed.

There had been other fateful forecasts, including one by Austin Wilson, sports editor of The Associated Press' New Orleans bureau. Wilson was talking to several reporters at an LSU football game earlier that month. He told them the basketball team was in serious trouble. Kevin Ford, a young assistant for the LSU Sports Network, said he thought they could still win 20 games. "If those guys can win 20 games," Wilson said, "I will kiss Dale Brown's ass at center court at the Southeastern Conference Tournament." The story got back to Brown, and he had it typed up and placed on the bulletin board in the locker room.

But it wasn't only the media. Even LSU's fans didn't take these players seriously.

Brown also shared that information with them. "Some of our best fans, who really mean well, are saying that we just need to get this year over with. They don't really mean anything bad. They're not critics. They're great fans. But they're still saying, 'We know everything will be all right next year, Coach. Don't worry if we don't win many games this season. We can wait.' Let me tell you something, everything is going to be all right. But we're not going to wait until next year. I don't want any of you to be thinking about next year. *This* is going to be our year!''

The players got a chance to meet some of their most ardent fans at a booster club dinner in the L Club Room. Everyone on the team was invited. They signed autographs, posed for pictures with children and ate lots of jambalaya. Then Brown was asked to speak. He invited Blanton and Abernathy to open for him. They spoke briefly, knowing that Brown might go 15 minutes or an hour and 15 minutes, depending on his mood.

Abernathy, supportive of Brown's philosophy as always, stressed that the team was going to be better than anyone expected them to be. Then Blanton really set the tone for Brown. ''A lot of people are counting us out already. That's fine. We don't feel that way, though. If you've seen us practice, you know we don't practice that way. We have a chance to do something good here. I think the more people talk bad about us, the more motivation we have to work harder. We have an opportunity to do something really special this year. This is our year.''

That was all Brown needed to hear. But first, he addressed some other subjects that were on his mind. He defended the hiring of Jim Childers, who was seated at one of the tables in the front of the room. He criticized the media for labeling athletes as stupid just because they hadn't met Prop 48 guidelines.

Ten minutes into his speech, he moved into a discussion of the season. ''I don't mean to be brazen by this at all, but these guys are going to shock the daylights out of everybody. You just watch us!'' He didn't need the microphone to amplify his voice. But he used it anyway, which made his voice carry even more.

''We are not going to sound the trumpet publicly. But I will let you people know we are going to have a great year. When it is all over, we will be back in a national tournament for the eleventh straight year. I guarantee you we will do better than everybody has picked us to do.''

After giving a brief overview of the players and schedule, Brown answered questions from the audience. They wanted to know about Jackson, recruiting and the investigation of Kentucky.

Brown said Jackson would be everything expected of him and more. Recruiting was going unbelievably well. There would be another major class coming in, although he declined to give specifics.

Most everyone already knew that Shaquille O'Neal of San Antonio, Texas, had visited LSU in September and was expected to sign with the Tigers during the early signing period in November.

They didn't know that he had grown two inches and gained 20 pounds and was now 7-0, 245. Brown had a personal pledge from O'Neal's father that he was going to send his son to LSU. Brown also had commitments from 6-8 forward Lenear Burns and 6-7 forward Shawn Griggs, two of Louisiana's top prospects. The team was going to be loaded with size and talent for years to come.

"If you don't have season tickets now, this is your last chance," Brown warned. "There won't be any left next season."

As for the Kentucky investigation, he was uncharacteristically guarded about his response. To him, Kentucky had always stood for the aristocracy of college basketball. The Big Blue represented everything bad in basketball and athletics in general, he thought. He had recruited against Kentucky for 16 years and had first-hand knowledge of major recruiting violations. But he also knew what it was like to be subjected to an NCAA investigation.

"I don't want to say much about Kentucky," he said, disappointing the fans who shared his dislike of the UK program. "I am sure we will all know soon." But after reflecting a moment, he added, "I don't want to say they cheat. But if they are guilty, I hope they get the guillotine." The crowd broke up in laughter.

Brown didn't reveal what he knew about the investigation, either. He had been told through friends at other schools and in the league office that Kentucky would be placed on probation and would have to forfeit all games in which Eric Manuel played during the 1987-88 season. Should that happen, LSU would get two more victories and would share the league championship with Auburn and Florida. Titles don't come easy. Brown would be glad to get one any way he could. As for this team, it would need to make a lot of progress and get some breaks along the way to compete for a league championship.

On Saturday, LSU made its first scheduled public appearance, playing an intrasquad game in Cecilia. Brown uses such events as recruiting tools. They are almost always held in towns where LSU is recruiting a player. The Tigers had already gotten Harold Boudreaux out of Cecilia. Now they wanted to lock up his brother, Carroll, if he could make his grades.

The old gym was packed with nearly a thousand fans. Even several members of the University of Southwestern Louisiana basketball team made the 10-minute trip from Lafayette to watch the scrimmage. Once again, most of the crowd came to see Jackson.

In warmups, Jackson seemed to have trouble focusing in the dimly lighted building. Once the game started, he limited himself to running the break and penetrating for short shots or passing to a teammate. Blanton benefitted most from Jackson's passing, scoring almost every time he touched the ball. He had 21 points in the first half to lead the Purple to a 71-57 halftime lead.

"We are really looking good on offense," Brown told the players at halftime. "This is the second week in a row we've scored 70 points in a half. We're moving the ball well, and we're getting good shots. Let's keep it up."

They did that and more in the second half. Jackson and Blanton put on a two-man fast-break exhibition. The highlight came on an alley-oop pass from Blanton to Jackson, who caught the ball with his right hand two feet above the rim and slammed it through for a ferocious dunk that brought the fans to their feet.

With Blanton scoring 46, the Purple won handily, 132-107. Jackson scored 13 points, but had nine assists. For the Gold, Kyle McKenzie had the best performance of his college career, scoring 31 points and showing some ability at point guard.

The biggest surprise was walk-on Tony Doyley. He scored 20 points for the Gold, showing he could hit the three-pointer or go inside against taller opponents. Brown went up to Blanton after the game and told him, "I think we've found us a player." Blanton was excited for Doyley, his former high school teammate, especially when Brown mentioned Tony would be placed on full scholarship.

But Doyley never made his debut in the Assembly Center. He was practicing with the first team on a limited basis when it was discovered he had an eligibility problem. Associate Athletic Director Larry Jones, who is a stickler for checking every detail before granting eligibility to an athlete, found an inconsistency in Doyley's high school records. He had never actually graduated from high school, instead earning a diploma by taking an equivalency test. That was how he got into Miami-Dade Junior College. In fact, his equivalency test score was not high enough, and he never should have been allowed to attend junior college. Doyley later learned that somebody at Miami-Dade had altered his test score so he could play there. Until the matter could be resolved, he had to sit out.

Losing Doyley greatly weakened the second team during the

Lyle Mouton plays tough defense against Oral Roberts University, but not tough enough to avoid an LSU loss or a post game "Brownout."

ABOVE. *Freshmen phenoms: C.J. shows no fear as he flips one up and over Georgetown's Alonzo Mourning. Blanton has position in case of a miss.* RIGHT. *Jackson gathers himself for a layup against Georgetown in the Superdome.*

How sweet it is: Dale Brown celebrates the 82-80 victory over Georgetown with his wife Vonnie, daughter Robyn and son-in-law Chris.

Ricky escorts LSU's No. 1 fan, Jamie Roth, across the court during the 1986-87 season.

The LSU brain trust, assistant coaches Ron Abernathy (left) and Craig Carse (middle) look on with Coach Brown in disbelief at the official's latest call.

Stages of arguing a call: First, indignation. "What? No way." (Photo by Stephan Savoia)

(Photo by Stephan Savoia)

Second, advocacy. "Come on Ref, you're killing us here."

Finally, resolution. "He's got to give us a call soon."

(Photo by Stephan Savoia)

Before Ricky Blanton's final home game, Brown reads a tribute printed in the Morning Advocate. *Looking on are Ricky and his parents, LSU's athletic director Joe Dean (far left), and Louisiana Governor Buddy Roemer (far right).*

Brown protests a technical called against the LSU crowd for throwing tennis balls at Florida's Dwayne Schintzius.

BELOW. *C.J. Jackson goes baseline, using the basket to shield the ball from defender Ian Lockhart of Tennessee.* RIGHT. *Ricky Blanton, Wayne Sims and Dennis Tracey greet C.J. after 2 of his 50 points against Tennessee in the Assembly Center.*

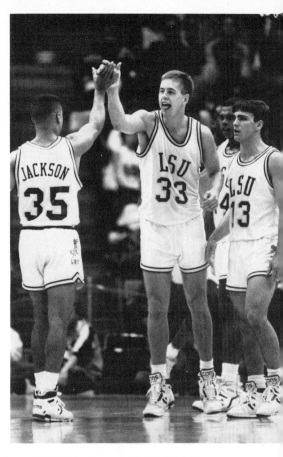

Interviewing Coach Brown and two star players, Ricky Blanton and Chris "C.J." Jackson, is an old adversary, former Kentucky coach turned TV analyst, Joe B. Hall.

Crunch time: Coach Dale Brown signals for his troops to put on the ''Freak Defense.'' (Photo by Stephan Savoia)

LSU's first round loss to Texas-El Paso in the 1989 NCAA tournament matched All-American Chris Jackson against future NBA first-round pick Tim Hardaway.

week leading up to the annual Purple-Gold Game. Brown pushed everyone a little harder in practice. He also called a team meeting to discuss some statements he had heard about Blanton.

He explained that people were joking about comments Blanton had made in a local newspaper. "Some people made fun of what Ricky said in the paper. He said we could win the national championship. Is that so ridiculous? I don't think so. How about you?"

For the next several minutes, Brown recounted the big games they had played in, the prominent teams they had beaten and the championships they had won just in the short time Blanton had been in the program.

"The only thing Ricky has not done is win an NCAA championship," he continued, speaking slowly but sharply. "That may be crazy to some people. They think Ricky is crazier than I am, because he's been here five years and he's catching the disease. And I think the disease is very simple: we so grossly underestimate what we can do. We don't achieve something because we don't expect it of ourselves. Well, I expect it of you. We demand great things from you, because we know that's the only way you're ever going to become great."

Turning to the three walk-ons, he said they should never feel inferior to anyone simply because they weren't heavily recruited. They had to believe they were as good as the scholarship players if they wanted to play as well as them.

Adding a personal perspective, Brown told how he was hired at LSU. He was an assistant at Washington State when the LSU job opened up in 1972. Several coaches were offered the position and turned it down. When it was finally offered to him, he jumped at the chance, giving no consideration to the fact he was not the first choice.

"That doesn't bother me one bit," he said. "They could have offered it to the whole Western Hemisphere, and I would have taken it and would have been just as confident that I could start something here. I believed in myself, and I want you to believe in yourself.

Another example he used was Don Redden. He related how Redden was a little slow of foot, not much of a jumper, just an "old plowhorse" who rose to the occasion and played the best basketball of his life in the 1986 NCAA Tournament. He was virtually unstoppable offensively in helping the Tigers advance to the Final Four.

Brown was trying to mold more Don Reddens out of this baby-faced, eager bunch of young men. He knew he had one in Blanton. He was fairly sure Sims had that kind of mettle. There was no question about Jackson's mental toughness after all he had been through. Russell Grant had a heart as big as Blanton's, but far less ability. The others really needed to be toughened mentally to survive the rigorous schedule they would soon face.

Brown challenged everyone to fight for a position and earn playing time. But he also reminded them to put the good of the team first. They could afford no infighting. This had to be a collaborative effort. He had to get the utmost contribution from every member of the team every time they stepped on the court.

He told them each practice presented an opportunity to improve individually and as a team, both physically and mentally. He would be sure to take care of the mental aspect. That was his talent. Every afternoon, without fail, he had some kind of stimulus—a thought for the day, passage from a book, letter from a fan, newspaper article.

One of the ways he kept the players' interest in practice was to chart every free throw they shot and post the results. They opened each practice by shooting two free throws and finished each workout by shooting 50. His challenge was to make the first two free throws every day. By the end of the season, each player would have shot about 180 times in the opening drill. If anyone made them all, he would get a reward. Usually, it would be a certificate or his name posted on the team record list.

This season, Brown wanted to make it even more significant. He knew every free throw would be important to this team. So on the Tuesday before the Purple-Gold Game, he gathered the players together in the locker room.

"I really want you to concentrate on your free throws," he said. "In fact, we will make it interesting. Ricky, what can we do for anybody who makes it through the rest of the season until the Final Four without missing his first two free throws every day?"

Blanton knew Brown was having some fun, but went along with it anyway. "I think we should treat that guy to dinner, Coach."

"All right, we'll do that," Brown said, struggling to hold back a smile. "We will send you to wherever you want to go in the state of Louisiana. It will be a beautiful dinner. You can bring a date and have a great time on us."

The plan sounded great to the players. They teased each other whenever they shot the first two free throws. "Come on, Chris, you're still in it," Mouton would tell Jackson. "The dinner is on the line. Don't miss now."

It was a nice way to break the monotony of practice and get the job done. Eventually, everyone had a shot hit the rim too hard or just rattle around and out. Jackson, as could be expected, would be one of the last to miss.

The next day, practice was delayed so the players could be interviewed on camera by media consultants. The video was reviewed by the consultants and players, and tips were given on how to improve for TV interviews. The players went in two groups, but in no particular order. Blanton was by far the most polished at this. But Jackson was surprisingly candid and smooth in his responses. Several of the other freshmen let their nerves get the best of them, especially Krajewski and Ussery.

Brown sat in on the second session. "These are pretty good, aren't they?" he remarked after watching Blanton and Mouton on tape.

"You've got some great guys, Coach Brown," said Sonia Forte, a former Baton Rouge TV reporter. "They're very expressive. They're honest. They come across really well. We've worked on a few things. There were a couple who were jumping around. Some of them were chewing gum while they talked. But they can correct that."

After watching more interviews, Blanton leaned forward and asked Forte, "Why does the media ask us questions that we can't answer? A lot of times it's like they're trying to get us to criticize each other. What should we do?"

Forte considered her answer, then told him, "If someone asks you an unfair question, you don't have to answer it directly. Just have a canned response ready. You're good at that, Ricky. You may say something like, 'We just have to keep playing hard and everything will work out for us.' That's the best way to handle it."

Brown couldn't wait to express his opinion on the subject. "Can I just add something?" he said. "Most of the media—now there are a few exceptions, but very few—want to get us. They'll say anything they can to rip us. So you have got to be careful about what you say. They'll do everything they can to try to trick you. They'll act like they're your buddy, and then they'll take whatever you say and use it against you. For instance, Jose Vargas is a prime example. They conned Jose into saying things he didn't want to say. So be careful when you talk to the media. Just tell them what you want to say, and that's all."

The second session concluded shortly after 4 o'clock. It was the first time practice had been late starting and would probably be the last, if Brown had his way. Before going over the practice plan, he talked about what they had just done.

"I would not have done this if I didn't think it was important," he said. "We took time away from practice for this, because this is one of the things you need to learn here. If all you learn from us is basketball, then we've been miserable failures. So it is very important what we've done today. It will help you communicate more clearly, whether it's on TV or just talking to a friend. So remember what you learned today."

The focus of practice was the offense against a fullcourt press. Few teams had been successful pressing the Tigers in recent years, primarily because they had good ballhandlers. This team was outstanding in that phase of the game.

"No one has been able to stop this press offense, not even Georgetown," he said while giving final instructions on its implementation. "They couldn't handle it. If we run it right, nobody will ever stop it. So let's concentrate and execute it right every time."

They practiced the regular two hours, which made the players late getting to dinner. But it was the final tuneup before the Purple-Gold Game, and Brown wanted to make sure everyone understood his assignments on offense.

Normally, the Purple-Gold Game is held on a Friday night before a home football game. That gives alumni and other fans a chance to see the basketball and football teams in one weekend. But the Assembly Center was booked for Friday, so the Purple-Gold Game had to be moved up to Thursday. No admission is charged for the scrimmage, which has attracted up to 10,000 fans. This year's crowd was closer to 5,000. But with the pep band, cheerleaders and Golden Girls dancers on hand, there was a game-like atmosphere.

This was the home-court debut for the nine new players on the squad. Nobody knew what to expect from eight of them. But everyone anticipated great things from Jackson. All that the fans had seen of him were video tapes of his high school games and brief appearances in high school All-America games on national television. Now he was live and in person. They couldn't wait to see him in action on the Assembly Center floor.

The other newcomers were of interest, too, particularly Hammink. The LSU fans had an affinity for foreign players, especially

Vargas. He had been a crowd favorite whether starting or riding the bench. They were certain to be fond of the tall, blond Dutchman as well.

Before tip-off, the tension in the locker room was thick. The players dressed quickly and waited for Brown to give final instructions. He told them to run two basic offenses and play strictly man-to-man defense. Then he went over some variations of the offense and closed with something to boost the young players' confidence.

"We've only had eleven practices, so we're just getting started," he said. "Our record is zero and zero. This game doesn't count, obviously. We've got a long season ahead of us. But fellas, I really think we can have a fun season. We can make something great out of this. We can win a lot of games, and we can enjoy ourselves along the way."

The early practices had been enjoyable to Brown. He liked the way the players were picking up the offense and how quickly they reacted to his instructions. Most of all, he could tell these young players were responding to his system. They listened attentively and absorbed his motivational material. If they continued to do that, they would develop the kind of attitude and drive that could push them over the top.

"I really believe this is our kind of team," he said, concluding with his short talk. "I feel better about this team than I have in a long time. This team has a lot of miracles in it. We can make miracles happen. I want you to remember something: you can have a great season. You can have any kind of season that you want, that you set your mind on. You just have to go out and play hard, play together, believe in each other and believe in yourself. Then anything can happen. We've proven that so many times. *Anything* can happen. We need a good start right now!"

After they went out for warmups, there was an introduction of all the players and coaches. Blanton received the loudest ovation, with many of the fans standing to honor the senior captain. But they also poured out their appreciation for the new leader, Jackson.

After the players were introduced, Brown took his turn at the microphone and told the fans to expect some surprises from this team. He also made a rare plug for season-ticket sales. LSU tickets were once a precious commodity, but with the decline of the Louisiana economy and some sub-par regular-season play in recent years, sales had dropped.

"I don't want to sound abrasive, but I'd get them now, because you ain't never going to get them after now,'' he said. The cheers nearly drowned him out before he could get out the last words. The reasons for his boldness were sitting on the bench beside Jamie Roth. Dressed in street clothes, impatiently waiting their turn to play, were Stanley Roberts, Harold Boudreaux and Maurice Williamson. All three would almost certainly have started on this team.

Without them, there was an obvious height and depth problem. There was no clear-cut choice for the center position. Hammink got the chance to play with Blanton, Jackson, Sims and Mouton on this night. They were the Gold team this time, and it was no contest from the start. Without Doyley's help, Singleton and Krajewski had more than they could handle.

Nobody could stay with Jackson. He glided down court on the break and created excitement on every possession for the Gold. Blanton was getting chip shots. Sims and Mouton were set up for some easy baskets. Every once in a while, Jackson would sky for a jump shot that more often than not sailed through the net.

Jackson and Co. built a 60-26 lead by halftime. To keep it from getting too far out of hand, Brown switched both teams to zone defense for the second half. Still, Jackson and Blanton were relentlessly on the attack before the Purple could get back on defense. Blanton put up a triple double with 49 points, 15 rebounds and 11 assists. Jackson was next in scoring with 26 points in the 134-80 victory.

The major question remained the center position. Hammink hit double figures in points and rebounds, but had been pushed around by Krajewski. He merely flashed a boyish smile whenever things didn't go right. Even Brown couldn't get mad at him. Krajewski fouled out with only five points and three rebounds. Both big men had faltered.

Sensing some disappointment from the two centers and all the members of the Purple team, Brown went to work in the locker room.

''I think the fact that we haven't put in any defense had a lot to do with the way things went,'' he said in a fatherly tone. ''The Purple team didn't play as well as they did in Cecilia, and that can happen, because we only had two veterans on the Purple team, Kyle and Russell. You two didn't play much last year, but you're leaders now. You've got to pick people up. And you will learn to do that. I think we really have a nice team. Coach Abernathy, tell them what I said on the bench.''

Abernathy hesitated. Brown had been his typical, chatterbox self, and it took Abernathy a moment to make sure they were on the same track. "That's right, Coach, you said we can win the conference this season. If we keep playing like this and improving, I know we can win it. You know how well we played tonight offensively."

"We've got better talent this year than we've had in quite a while," Brown chimed in. "We really didn't have much talent the last few years, and look at what we did: the Final Four, the Final Eight, beating No. 1 Oklahoma. We've got a better team this year. We've got more people who can play."

He cautioned the players not to tell the media any such thing. Seldom did he tell the media the same thing he told his players. It would be their secret. "We don't have to do any talking with our mouths. We can do it by participation on the court. We have great chemistry."

Finally, he explained that the starters had stayed on the same team so they could begin to blend, not to embarrass the reinforcements. There would be other combinations in practice, he assured them. Nothing was set yet.

Everyone had Friday off. The players needed to get their legs back after the game. The coaches needed to break, too. But they would return for a Saturday morning practice.

Brown had an unusual speaking engagement on Friday. He had agreed to talk to all the junior high students at Our Lady of Mercy School. Vonnie accompanied him. When they arrived, the auditorium was packed with hundreds of youngsters.

At schools, he usually relies on the same type of talks he gives his players. But he wanted to deliver a different message this time. His speech brought tears to Vonnie's eyes as he shared his faith in a most powerful way.

He opened with a question. "Do you know what a chicken is? A lot of people will call you a chicken. I was called a chicken. Some people call you that because you don't take drugs, you don't smoke, you don't want to steal. You know who's really a chicken? The person calling you that. They're a chicken because they don't want to stand up for anything."

His voice rang through the auditorium. "You've got a choice to make. You've got the greatest power in the world available to every one of you. Whose team do you want to be on? Do you want to be on God's team or do you want to be on the team with all the losers?"

This was a message he would not have shared two months earlier. He would have been too worried about being scoffed at. He might even have thought it to be "drippy," an expression he used to describe those he considered overzealous. But his new faith had changed that. He also shared some of his own frustrations as a boy growing up without a father. He focused most of his talk on his faith.

"God is a great coach," he said. "Some of you may be thinking, 'Well, I would like to be on God's team, but I don't think I can play for him.' You all know Ricky Blanton. What if Ricky went down and missed a layup, what kind of coach would I be if I yelled and screamed at him? I've got to lift him up. That's what God does.

"You can sin, you can make mistakes, you can have transgressions. God still loves you. You just need to ask him to help you, to forgive you. God is the greatest coach in the world. He is going to help you if you ask him. And God wants everyone on his team. He doesn't make any junk. You are all important. God wants you on his team."

Neither Dale nor Vonnie knew what kind of impact his words would have on these students. They prayed that the kids would respond. But they had no way of knowing how receptive these young people had been until the letters came pouring in. Dozens wrote, thanking Brown for his advice and telling him they would follow it.

One student thanked him for taking the time to visit. He also wrote: "Thanks a lot for your fantastic speech. I thoroughly enjoyed it to the maximum. After your speech, I went home and put a cross on the front of my cleats. I know how you felt as a child without a father. My father, who was a super dad, just left our family and moved to New York City. It was a big shock because he always coached me in everything. Thanks for your help." Most of the others wrote that they weren't going to be chickens or smoke or use drugs.

Brown hoped he would be able to influence his players like that. He believed this team would come around. Yet, there was no way of being certain. Some teenagers react differently than others, depending on their values, goals and dreams. He stressed the importance of dreaming and then doing everything within your power to fulfill those dreams.

On Saturday, the players got an early wakeup call. They had to be at the arena, dressed, taped and ready to practice at 8. The workout was set so early because it was homecoming weekend, and the football team was playing Ole Miss at 11:30 on national cable television. With practice starting at 8, fans could attend the two-hour session and still have plenty of time for tailgating before kickoff.

There were more than 100 spectators in the stands when the players and coaches began to appear on the court. Soon, the numbers would grow to several hundred and before practice ended, about 2,000 fans would have caught at least part of the workout.

Brown couldn't contain his pleasure over the large turnout. He mentioned to Abernathy several times that they should hold an open practice whenever there was a home football game. The fans didn't just sit back and passively watch. They were involved. They cheered every good play in the drills.

Although he had not planned to scrimmage, Brown decided to hold a short one for the fans' benefit. They roared when Jackson stole the ball from McKenzie and went in for a slam. The applause was even louder when Blanton got loose on the break and shook the rim with a crushing dunk.

The tempo of the practice picked up as more people arrived. The timing was even better than it had been in the Purple-Gold Game. Brown liked it so much that he extended practice 15 minutes. Before it was over, he asked the team managers to distribute copies of a motivational handout, "I Will Persist Until I Succeed." There were six sections to the message, each ending with the words of the title. The final lines read: "If I persist long enough, I will win. I will persist. I will win."

Many fans stayed after practice to get autographs from the players and coaches. They signed T-shirts, basketballs, copies of the team poster, schedule cards, hats and anything else available. Brown was kept busy autographing copies of his handout.

Brown and Abernathy were last to leave the court. Brown glanced at the upper deck of the arena and saw Russell Grant running the steps. He covered every step in the building every day after practice. Nobody told him to do it.

"Would you just look at him," Brown said. "Look at him up there. He's there every day. That's why he will play for us someday. He works so hard and wants to play so badly. I really notice that."

"He is our kind of player, Coach," Abernathy said. "That's what we are all about."

Brown leaned back in his seat and watched Grant run another aisle. Then he started to smile. "You know he's got no ability at all. No talent. But I wish everyone worked as hard as he does. Ron, I guarantee you something: he will do something good for us. He will win a game sometime. That's the kind of effort it takes."

Grant also worked out with Blanton and Sims after practice, doing sets of situps. After that, Grant and Blanton shot three-pointers for at least a half hour. They had to hit 10 from a certain spot before moving to another location. Blanton worked mainly on the left wing and top-of-the-key. Grant shot from the corner and wing. They might hit 60 or 70 percent, or they might make considerably more. Day by day, their percentages climbed, especially Blanton, who was not much of a shooter early in his career.

On Sunday, Brown celebrated his 53rd birthday. Tom Moran hosted a small dinner party at one of his Baton Rouge restaurants. There wasn't much said about basketball. Brown prefers to talk about other subjects when he's not coaching.

But as the final hours of October passed by, he had reason to feel good about his team. They had some flaws, but their many strengths more than made up for that. They were improving rapidly.

Meanwhile, recruiting couldn't be going better. O'Neal and Burns planned to sign national letters of intent with LSU on the first day of the early signing period. That was only a week away. Then Brown would officially have the second center of his dreams to complement Stanley Roberts. He had never been more certain of a player's intentions than he was of O'Neal's. In fact, he said that pursuing the San Antonio marvel was the most enjoyable recruiting experience in his 23 years of college coaching.

Brown made only one visit to San Antonio. It was a reunion of sorts, because he had first met the boy and his parents in Wildeflecken, West Germany, where he was speaking to American troops in 1985.

Their first meeting is an occasion Brown will never forget. While waiting to speak, he had felt a tap on his shoulder. When he turned around, there was a young man standing behind him. Brown had to glance up to look him in the eye and assumed he was one of the enlisted men. The man inquired about how to strengthen his legs because he wanted to jump higher.

As Brown described some exercises that would be beneficial, he looked down at the feet supporting this young hulk. They looked like water skis. Brown told him he would send more information on weight training and conditioning.

"By the way, how long have you been in the service, soldier?" he inquired.

The young man grinned and replied, "I'm not in the service, sir. I'm only 13 years old."

"You're only 13!" Then Brown studied him more carefully. He

had to be 6-8 or taller. He certainly still had to be growing. "What's your name, son?"

"Shaquille O'Neal."

"What size shoes do you wear?"

"Seventeen."

"I'd like to meet your dad."

They went to find the boy's father, Phillip Harrison, who is an Army sergeant. O'Neal uses his mother's maiden name, but Brown wasn't concerned about such details.

He introduced himself as the basketball coach at LSU. He said he would like to develop a relationship with the family in hopes that O'Neal could become a college player one day.

To Brown's surprise, Sergeant Harrison had no interest in his son becoming a basketball player.

"Coach, I really could care less about basketball," the sergeant said. "I want him to develop his intellect. I would like him to go on and be successful academically. I like sports. But my son is going to get an education. That's all I care about, thank you."

Once Brown finished explaining the advantages of going to college on a basketball scholarship, Sergeant Harrison began to come around.

"Sergeant, we're going to be good friends," Brown told him.

Over the next three years, Brown kept in touch with the family, especially after it moved from West Germany to San Antonio during O'Neal's junior year in high school. By then, Shaquille was approaching seven feet and already budding into a super talent. He agreed to make his first official visit to LSU in September of his senior year. Even then, he told several LSU players that he was going to play for Brown. But he also made visits to North Carolina, North Carolina State, Louisville and Illinois.

Brown never doubted O'Neal's intention to sign with LSU. Besides, Shaquille's father had personally guaranteed it during Brown's visit to their home.

It was an unusual visit for Brown and Craig Carse. As recruiting coordinator, Carse thought it was his responsibility to sell the family on Brown and the program. He kept lauding Brown's accomplishments and philosophy. Sergeant Harrison was not impressed.

Just the opposite, he got angry. "Coach Carse, I need to say something," Harrison said. "You talk too much. You sound like a used car salesman. You don't have to tell us about Coach Brown. We know more about him than you do. We've known him longer than you. We know what kind of man he is.''

Brown bailed out his assistant. ''Sergeant, let me apologize for Craig. I told him on the plane not to be pushy. I told him you are quality people and will make up your own mind. And I know Craig appreciates you being honest about how you feel.''

After that, Brown and the sergeant did most of the talking. When it was time for the coaches to leave, the sergeant walked them to the car. Then he pulled Brown aside.

''Coach Brown, don't worry, our boy is going to play for you,'' he said. ''We trust you and know what kind of person you are. He is not going anywhere else.''

On Wednesday, November 9, O'Neal signed with LSU, just like his father had promised. That same day, Burns also signed with the Tigers. Their other recruit, Griggs, decided to wait until April. He had pledged to sign with LSU, but wanted to take his time about making it official. Carse, a workaholic who calls his recruits several times a day, had done another solid job of organizing the recruiting. He credited Brown with finishing the job with his persuasiveness. Brown said Carse had given him a fresh start.

While all this was going on, the team's progress was delayed by two setbacks during the early days of November. First, Scott Guldseth told Brown he wanted to go back to North Dakota. He missed his family and was having trouble adjusting to the new environment. He was homesick and had made up his mind he could only be happy back in North Dakota.

Try as he might, Brown could not convince Guldseth to change his mind. It was agreed he would drop off the team, finish his courses for the fall semester and then transfer to the University of North Dakota.

About that same time, Larry Jones called to break the news that Doyley was a lost cause. His academic records had definitely been altered. They could not take a chance on playing him.

Neither Doyley nor Guldseth would have started. But they would have been ideal backups to Blanton and Mouton on the wings. They would have provided some greatly needed depth. Now help had to come from someone else. Grant and McKenzie were the logical choices. They weren't as tall, but offered more firepower.

Another possibility presented itself almost like a dream come true. One afternoon, the team was in the middle of practice when a towering young man walked into the arena and took a seat beside Jamie and Debbie Roth in the stands. Brown looked over at him a couple times, thinking he was a former player or perhaps a recruit brought in by Carse. But Carse didn't recognize him, either.

Finally, Brown asked Abernathy and found out that the mystery man was a friend of a friend of Abernathy. Abernathy had invited him to practice. He was 6-10 with stalk-like arms that seemed long enough to reach the rim without even stretching. His name was Ervin Johnson. The spelling was slightly different than that of the NBA star, but for a team lacking big men, there was magic in the name. Better yet, he was a high school graduate and wanted to enroll at LSU and play basketball right away.

After practice, Brown invited Johnson to stop by his office. He was immediately impressed with the soft-spoken, polite visitor.

"I just want to give it a try," Johnson told him. "I never stuck with basketball in high school. Now I just want to prove something to myself. I want to go for it and really accomplish something with my life. I know I can do it. I know I can do anything as long as I keep God first in my life. Nothing is too hard for God."

Brown asked a few questions about Johnson's high school career and what he had been doing since then. He kept looking at the long, thin arms and legs. With the proper diet and weight training, Ervin could fill out quickly. This seemed like an answer to a prayer. Brown had just lost two players and now this one turns up out of nowhere. He loved Johnson's attitude and beliefs. They couldn't have been any closer to his own.

Finally, he told Johnson that he would get a chance to join the team if he could get in school. No promises. But if he could handle it, he could play for LSU.

"That's all I need is a chance, Coach Brown," Johnson said. "That's all I want."

Because he had graduated from high school before Prop 48 took effect, he could be eligible to play starting the next semester. If he could get enrolled, he could begin practicing as early as December.

Johnson, who was working as a stock boy at night, didn't miss watching a practice the next two weeks. He worked out in the weight room and practiced basketball with Roberts, Boudreaux and Williamson. They were trying to get the most out of the year, even if they couldn't play or practice with the team.

Johnson and Roberts became friends, but it was soon apparent to

Johnson that he was out of his league. He couldn't compete with the massive Roberts. Finally, he decided to try another school and enrolled at the University of New Orleans, hoping to play there at a lower level.

Brown had not really counted on Johnson contributing much, anyway. It was more wishful thinking than anything else. He knew he had to get everything possible out of the available personnel. That meant pushing them a little more than they expected.

Part of that involved conditioning and discipline. Brown has been a task master in both areas since the day he took over the LSU program. He ran off more than half of the players he inherited in 1972. Collis Temple, one of the best players on that team, said everyone felt like quitting after going through Brown's regimented program. But they didn't. Instead, they won 14 of 24 games and were the surprise team of the Southeastern Conference.

This team would have to be in top shape to compete in the SEC, especially the starters, who would get little rest during games. To keep his players in shape and also in class, Brown put extra emphasis on his Breakfast Club. It was no treat for the players.

Any player who cut a class, missed an appointment with a tutor, missed a study hall, or even came a minute late to any team function, received an invitation to the Breakfast Club. That meant getting up at 5 o'clock in the morning and running sprints, climbing steps and jogging long distances for an hour. Johnny Jones was the coach assigned to the club. He was rarely in a cheery mood at that hour, so he ran them into the ground.

Most clubbers were freshmen. The veterans had already been through it and didn't want anything to do with it again. But the newcomers, including those who couldn't play, missed some early-morning classes and had to pay dearly. They begged and pleaded with Jones, but to no avail. Roberts and Williamson saw the most sunrises. But Jackson and the others eventually slipped up and joined the club. As the semester progressed, participation dropped dramatically. It usually took only one or two outings.

There were more strict penalties for serious offenses. Brown handed out a long list of team rules. If a major rule was violated, there would be no appeal. The player was automatically suspended. It could be for a game or two, a season or a career. Brown had not hesitated to boot some of his best players through the years. First-team All-SEC forward DeWayne Scales was kicked off the team just before the 1980

NCAA Tournament. Three starters were suspended early in the 1983-84 season. Each had violated a team rule. They were still eligible and could have continued playing, but not for Brown.

In one of his pre-practice talks, Brown warned that the same thing could happen to anyone on this team. "If you want to have a good year, you ain't going to be out at night running around and getting in trouble. Remember, I don't talk much about rules. But you're done if you break the rules. It's immediate, indefinite suspension. You are in training now and you have to take care of yourselves. You know how I expect you to act, and that's all I'm going to say about it."

These players never came close to getting in trouble. They went out together once or twice a week. They had dates like most other students. But they were focusing everything on basketball. Their first test was coming soon.

Meanwhile, Jamie Roth's condition had stabilized again. He was making the most of being a co-captain, coming to practice almost every afternoon. He shot during warmups, usually with his best friend, Blanton. But all the players were developing a close relationship with him, as well as with each other.

10

Gestapo, Communists and Apple Packers

Ricky's Diary, November 11—This is exciting. We get to put the uni-forms on for the first time. I don't know what to expect. I don't know what will happen tonight. I just know we're all anxious to play. I think the young guys are a little nervous, naturally. We've made some pro-gress, but we won't know how much until we've played somebody.

Assistant Coach Johnny Jones rushed into Dale Brown's office. He had season tickets in one hand and a stack of letters in the other. He also had several messages to relay on this Friday afternoon. It had already been a whirlwind day for Brown. He had spent hours on the phone and still had a stack of messages, not counting the new ones from Jones, that needed to be reviewed before he went downstairs for the first exhibition game of the season. Brown had no way of knowing how beautiful it was outside.

"See why I don't come into the office on game days," Brown said exasperated, peering over his glasses just long enough to see who was bringing him more work. "This is no way to get ready for a game." Ordinarily, he loves to be working on some project, while talk-ing on the phone and having a visitor or two waiting. In that sense, this was his kind of day.

But on game day, even if it were just an exhibition, he prefers to stay home by himself. He reads, watches television and takes a late-afternoon nap. But there was just too much that needed to be done today. He thumbed through the messages and then stopped to ask Jones, "Have you heard any more from Fess?"

Irvin had called that morning from his dorm room at James Madison University. He wanted to tell his former coaches that the NCAA was inquiring about his days at LSU. Actually, Irvin considered it more along the lines of harassment. NCAA investigator William S. Saum spent several hours Thursday on the JMU campus questioning Irvin on every subject from the clothes he wore at LSU to the food he ate. Irvin felt the NCAA was out to get LSU and thought the coaches should be aware of what was going on. He asked to talk to Brown, but Dale was tied up on the phone. Jones took the call and relayed the information.

Brown was furious. First, he tried to call Irvin, but couldn't reach him. Next, he put in calls for Dick Schultz and Saum at the NCAA office. Then he decided to inform the university's president, chancellor, athletic director and attorneys. He had broken no rules in dealing with Irvin. No one on his staff had done anything wrong.

Overall, Brown had a favorable opinion of the new regime at the NCAA. Since Schultz had taken over as executive director, Brown felt there was a sincere effort under way to adopt reasonable rules and establish integrity that Brown thought was lacking under Schultz's predecessor, Walter Byers. Brown communicated regularly with Schultz and was sure he would not approve of this kind of investigative effort.

"Dick Schultz does not believe he is a Stalin or a Himmler," Brown said about the new NCAA chief. "He approaches the job with the attitude that he wants to make athletics better for the athletes, not be the border patrol. He changed a philosophy within the office. He is now the one saying we need to pay a stipend to the players and make the road smoother for them. He plays no favorites. There is no crony system like there was in the past. If you're guilty, you'll get the maximum punishment. But by the same token, the NCAA isn't going on a witch hunt for four years like they did with us. He has been the beacon light to a new age. He has given me hope. He does not make the rules, but he can influence adopting more humanitarian standards, and he has done that already."

Earlier that year, NCAA officials gave Brown a recommendation about making Geert Hammink eligible. He had not graduated from the five-year Dutch high school system and couldn't enroll at LSU. But the NCAA has an obscure rule that allowed him to become eligible if he could exempt 24 hours of college work in placement tests. He passed 30 and was eligible. Brown was convinced the old regime never would have pointed out the rule.

"I think the NCAA is sending a clear message: We're not going to worry about an extra ticket given to a family or a T-shirt given to some kid or a ride to the dorm," Brown said. "But they're busting people for major violations. You don't need the Bible to enforce the rules. It's very simple: you don't change test scores, and you don't give them money or cars. All the changes I recommended years ago are slowly happening. I was never against the rules. I was for enforcing major rules and against rules that suppress athletes' rights."

What bothered Brown was the way Irvin said the investigator tried to intimidate him by acting skeptical when he said he didn't get anything from LSU. He also repeatedly told Irvin that he would not be penalized if he informed on LSU.

Shortly after Jones left the office, Brown got a call from LSU System President Allen Copping. Brown briefed him on the details of Irvin's call and demanded that something be done about it.

He told Copping, "The NCAA guy spent all that time with Fess and never asked about another program that had recruited him, never asked about James Madison. And he kept saying, 'This won't affect you at all. No matter what you say, you will be free.' Now let's stop there. What if Fess Irvin had been given a gold watch worth ten thousand dollars while he was here? Why should he be free? He committed a sin. He broke a rule. He should be penalized."

Copping agreed it was an unfair tactic. "There's more," Brown told him. "He asked Fess, 'Where did you get your car?' Fess told him that his father bought the car, which we know he did. His parents even called the NCAA when they bought it. The guy was real demeaning and said, 'OK, your parents bought you a 300ZX loaded, right?' Fess told him that was right. Then he asked, 'Why did you buy it in Baton Rouge? Isn't that where LSU is located?' Fess told him it is 20 miles from his house.

"Then there were more questions: 'Did your parents pay cash for it? Do you know any players at LSU who ever received money? Any clothes? Any grade changes? Any financial help? After all, the area is full of LSU alumni. When did you work? How much did you get paid? When did you eat? Who did you meet? How many visits did they make to your house?' He just kept grilling Fess. I mean it was just so unfair. And he kept telling him that nothing would be used against him.

"Finally, he says to Fess, 'You're not telling a tale are you? Is LSU really that clean? If everything you're telling me is true, LSU has the cleanest program in the country.' Fess told them, 'They are that clean.' Then the guy's final words to Fess were 'Take care of that car.' ''

Brown paused to let Copping respond. Copping suggested setting up a meeting to discuss the matter with university attorneys. Some kind of action needed to be taken.

Brown was encouraged by Copping's support. "They just investigated this program for four years and found nothing," Brown told him. "So what are they doing? I'll tell you what they're doing, they're using Gestapo tactics. That's just not right. I don't care if they check a guy. But they should check the guy, too, not just the program. They're telling the kids that it's legal for them to cheat. That isn't right. The NCAA has got to change. I really like Dick Schultz. I think they are changing things at the NCAA. But this is wrong. It is really wrong.

"Fess is a nice, little guy. I don't think he would lie. But Fess likes attention. He may embellish the truth. Nothing has happened here. So it doesn't make any difference if he lies. It's just inconvenient. It's just such a big headache dealing with it all the time. They just don't believe in human dignity."

Brown admitted that he had broken an NCAA rule in church that Sunday. He and his wife took Stanley Roberts and Maurice Williamson to Church Point, he told Copping. At one point in the church service, everyone went up front with offering envelopes. Brown glanced at Roberts and Williamson. He could tell by the look on their faces that they had brought no money. So he took four dollars out of his money clip and gave each player two bills. Technically, that was a rules violation.

"I dare the NCAA to come after me for taking two of my players to church," Brown told Copping. "But I'm not even going to do that any more. It's just not worth it."

Copping inquired about how Irvin was doing at James Madison, where he was sitting out a year and would be eligible to play for Coach Lefty Driesell next season.

"He told Johnny that he is really happy and doing well," Brown replied. "He told me before that he really appreciates me being honest. He said he more than ever realizes what I told him is true. I told him it would be better for him to get away. There was so much pressure on him here. There were too many people thinking he was a superstar. The poor kid couldn't lead his own life.''

Brown could have used Irvin, even if he weren't the super talent that many expected him to be coming out of high school. He would have started at off guard on this team, and Chris Jackson would have taken the pressure off him and made him a better player. But Brown had Irvin's best interests in mind when he advised him to transfer. Now he was glad Irvin was keeping him abreast of the NCAA's operations.

Most of the NCAA's investigative efforts at that time were being focused on the Kentucky program. The allegations kept piling up, and would spell the end for Eddie Sutton and his staff. Brown had undergone the same scrutiny for almost four years. So he thought he could offer some encouragement and advice to Sutton.

Brown had called him several times that week, but kept missing him. Finally, Brown's secretary, Wanda Thomas, got a call through to Sutton shortly after Dale got off the phone with Copping.

First, Sutton thanked Brown for publicly supporting him at the SEC Media Days in Atlanta. Most of the other coaches had refused to comment about the Kentucky investigation.

''I really appreciate your attitude, Dale,'' Sutton said. ''It's been a difficult time, as you can imagine. Some reporters came back and told me that you were straight forward and never once jabbed me. I've heard other coaches have. I appreciate your fairness. You've always been my friend. Now I know just how much of a friend you are.''

''Eddie, you know what the media wanted to talk about,'' Brown said. ''It wasn't about our teams. They were trying to get everyone to talk about Kentucky. I told them very simply that I feel for what you're going through and I think it's wrong the way the NCAA treats people. It's absolutely wrong. I also found out something I didn't know existed. I found out that most of those writers that I thought would die for the Blue and White have changed their colors now that they've got a little story. It was totally brutal.''

Brown was surprised at Sutton's openness and remorseful attitude regarding the investigation. He could tell there had been a dramatic change in his friend of more than 20 years.

But Brown wasn't ready for what he was about to hear. ''I know I've made mistakes in my profession,'' Sutton told him. ''I want to clean my life up. And I just realized that this isn't worth it. I know

wrong that has been done, and we're not going to refute that. And I
know wrong that has not been done, and they're making more of a
story out of that.

"I'm just changing. All the things that I thought were glorious
and beautiful, I've come to a rude awakening that they're not. I feel
now that I've got to step back and look at this whole thing again. I really need you as a friend."

Sutton extended a dinner invitation whenever Brown came to
Lexington. Then Sutton thanked him again.

Almost at a loss for words, Brown finally responded, "Eddie, I
really appreciate what you've said to me. Maybe all of us coaches can
really help each other. I really think we can. I am going to say a prayer
for you. OK, bye Eddie, and thank you."

Brown couldn't contain his happiness about Sutton's attitude. He
rushed out of the office to find someone with whom to share this secret. He looked in Jones' office, but Johnny was gone. Then he went a
few more steps down the hall and found Ron Abernathy in his office.

"Ron, God has touched Eddie Sutton," he said, drawing a puzzled look from his assistant. "I just got off the phone with Eddie, and
you wouldn't believe some of the things he said. That's the first time
he has ever talked like that. It made me feel good, man. That's the
best thing that's ever happened to him. He is really searching things
out. I know he is trying to find God. He is just a different person. I
think I can really help him."

Brown told Abernathy some of what Sutton had said. Abernathy
was amazed.

Meanwhile, Wanda Thomas was looking for Brown, because he
had a visitor. Jay Crow, who owns a Baton Rouge real estate firm, was
there to see Dale. They were old friends. Crow had handled some of
Brown's real estate investments and had often given him advice. He
was an ardent basketball fan, too.

Crow couldn't wait to tell Brown about what happened on a trip to
Raleigh, North Carolina. Crow was on a family vacation when he
bumped into Jim Valvano at the Raleigh airport. Valvano was talking to
an enormous teenager who was obviously someone he was recruiting
at North Carolina State. Crow's curiosity was peaked, thinking that
the recruit might be Shaquille O'Neal. So he introduced himself as an
LSU fan.

Valvano shook his hand and confirmed that the boy was O'Neal.
Not one to miss a chance for a joke, Valvano told Crow to give a mes-

sage to Brown. ''Tell Dale, he doesn't have to spend any more time on Shaquille. He doesn't need to visit him or call him, because he's coming here.''

Of course, O'Neal had already committed to LSU.

Brown couldn't wait to counter with his own humor. He picked up his Dictaphone and gave a message to Valvano. ''Jim, we did exactly what you asked us to do on Shaquille. We never called, sent him a letter or had any contact with Shaquille. We thank you for the advice. Obviously, I am joking. But Jay Crow relayed your message to me, and I thought I'd try to show some humor. Hope you have a great season.''

Brown had made the appointment with Crow because Dale wanted information on how to start the orphanage that he and Vonnie wanted so much to direct. Crow already knew of several potential locations, but suggested studying the market more closely to find the best site. He also offered some ideas on fund-raising.

Crow also had a business proposition of his own. He thought it would be a good idea to train some players as real estate agents. That would give them some excellent job experience and perhaps lead to a career after basketball. It also wouldn't hurt his business to have LSU athletes selling property for him. Brown agreed that it was a promising plan and asked Crow to follow up on it.

It was late in the afternoon. Brown had a few more calls to make and still needed to hand out season tickets to friends. He got Jones to do that.

Next he called John Wooden, whose scheduled visit to LSU the next week had to be canceled because Wooden wasn't feeling well. They discussed another date, but Wooden didn't want to travel for a while. They agreed to talk about it later in the season.

Much of Brown's coaching philosophy and strategy is based on what he picked up from Wooden. When Brown was first hired at LSU, he and Jack Schalow went to Los Angeles to study the Wooden system at UCLA. Brown inquired about every detail of Wooden's coaching genius. After that, Wooden visited Brown in Baton Rouge. After Wooden retired in 1975, Brown tried to get him to come every year.

''Coach Wooden is the biggest influence on me as a coach,'' Brown said. ''I value his simplicity in approaching the game. I have tried to follow his philosophy on handling players, media and fans. He taught me about organization. I have learned so much just from the man that he is.''

Finally, at about 6 o'clock, Brown got his mind on the game. There wasn't really much to contemplate. The opposition was the Brewster Heights Apple Packers, a team of former college players who were hoping to improve enough to make it to the NBA. They were based in Brewster Heights, Washington, and were the defending national champions of the Amateur Athletic Union. Nonetheless, such teams rarely offered any real competition. Tonight, LSU would focus on sharpening its all-around skills against outside competition. The season opener was only two weeks away, and there was still much to cover.

This was the first season that the NCAA would permit teams to play two exhibition games. Brown also had scheduled a game against the Yugoslavian national team, which had just won the bronze medal at the Olympics. If they brought their best players, it would be impossible for LSU to win. Of course, that was just the type of situation that energized Brown.

Actually, he was angry at himself for not finding out earlier that the Soviets were also touring the country. He had not learned of their tour until earlier that week, after LSU's exhibition commitments had been made. He still seethed about the Soviets' gold medal victory over the United States in September.

Brown had avenged the Soviets once before. LSU played them in an exhibition game in 1977, five years after the Soviets' controversial victory over the U.S. in the 1972 Olympics at Munich. But Brown approached it like the Olympic game had just been played. He rallied his players around an anti-Communism theme.

"Those damn Communists stole the gold medal from us," he told his players in a fiery pregame talk. "This is the greatest country on earth. There is no way we can let them win again." To help his cause, he brought his Soviet guests into a dark room and showed them basketball films for several hours before the game. They were squinting all night. The arena was packed with fans waving miniature American flags. LSU won 99-96 in double overtime. Brown was ecstatic for weeks.

Had he known earlier about the 1988 Soviet tour, he would have come up with more gimmicks. He believed anything was fair play when it came to the Soviets, even though he had recruited their best player. But they were playing at North Carolina that night, and LSU had to be content with the Apple Packers.

In past years, Brewster Heights had presented little trouble for

LSU. But these were no run-of-the-mill Apple Packers. They were in decent condition, they had some size, and they were surprisingly talented. And they caught LSU by surprise. Wayne Yearwood, a powerfully built 6-8 forward who had played at West Virginia and for the Canadian Olympic team, destroyed the Tigers' man-to-man and zone defenses. He made 11 of 12 shots and scored 22 points in the first half. The Tigers, trailing most of the half, were fortunate to pull even at 53-53 by halftime.

There was a hush over the arena, which was about two-thirds empty anyway. This was not supposed to be one of Brown's best teams, but surely it could beat an AAU team. If it couldn't, a long, long season lay ahead. The fans knew that, and so did the players. Nobody understood better than Brown.

What bothered him most was the unaggressive, almost lazy play on defense. His centers, Richard Krajewski and Geert Hammink, had looked like statues standing with their feet planted in the lane. Yearwood cut past them and to the basket with the greatest of ease. It was a defensive embarrassment for Brown, who prided himself on that part of the game. He was fuming and wanted to vent his anger on the guilty players.

Brown met first with his assistant coaches in a spare training room across the hall from the players' locker room. He roared his disapproval of the way the team was giving up layups and putbacks. After a few minutes, he got his temper under control and began to discuss with Ron Abernathy how to change things in the second half. They decided to use a man-to-man with Ricky Blanton guarding Yearwood.

While that was going on, Blanton tried to awaken his teammates with a scathing talk. "We looked terrible out there," he screamed. "We have got to play harder. What's the use of practicing like we do unless we're going to play hard? Let's get out there and play like we practice."

Still steaming, Blanton took his seat and waited for Brown to enter, fully expecting him to deliver a more fierce critique of the first half. He was sure Brown would snap them out of their doldrums. He had seen it happen so many times in the previous four seasons. Even the first-year players expected a tongue-lashing. Brown had not raised his voice very often in practice. But when he did, he brought everything but thunder and lightning. That was the kind of response that the players anticipated. They hung their heads and waited apprehensively.

When Brown entered the room, the look of dismay was gone from his face. Blanton noticed it right away. Jackson and the others avoided looking him in the eye. If they had, they would have seen how calm and low-keyed he appeared. Brown gave his assessment in a loud, but otherwise non-threatening tone of voice: "All right fellas, there is nothing to worry about. I am not surprised by this."

The players looked up in surprise.

"This is a good team we are playing," Brown continued. "These guys can play. But we can play a lot better than this. We came in here tied. We personally didn't play a good first half. We didn't play an intelligent first half. We didn't communicate well with one another. Our defense wasn't very good. Maybe that can be expected. But if we can tie the first half playing that bad, let's go out and cut them apart in the second half."

Brown would not have been so easy on a veteran team. But these were not only young players, they were unusually sensitive, too. He realized he couldn't be too harsh or it might break their spirits. But he knew he still had to push them.

Brown began to write on the drawing board and talk at the same time. "There are three things that summarize our program," he said, having already written the first. "One is family. The next is perseverance." He abbreviated the word at pers., because spelling is not one of his strengths. "Perseverance means never, never, never giving up. And we will not give up tonight. Number three is what we call aggressive second effort." He jotted down hustle, and then put down the marker. "I am not worried about the first two. But boy, are we lacking in number three. Not everybody. But overall, we are. And I would like to send a quiet message tonight. You really can't play for us or play much if you can't do that."

He picked up the marker and circled the last word. That was the only way he had ever played or coached basketball. He would accept nothing less from his players.

"You really can't do much for us unless you hustle," he said. "We're not asking you to win. We're not asking you to be flawless. When you get beaten, we will pick you up. But you guys have to give everything you've got the whole time you're in there. Your guts have got to be spilled. That's what we're all about. I am really proud to be a coach at LSU. And I will be proud of you if you play like that. If you do that, winning will take care of itself."

At that, he was finished. He motioned to Blanton to form the huddle. The players circled in the middle of the room, hands clasped together over their heads. Blanton led a cheer of "Get 'em!" They all shouted as they broke the huddle and started toward the door.

The defensive adjustment worked well. Blanton hawked Yearwood and took away the easy shots he had been getting. The Tigers kept clicking on offense and pulled away for a 103-94 victory. Jackson had not shot well, but still scored 25 points. Not wanting to upstage his older teammates, he had been cautious about asserting himself.

This wasn't against the Soviets. Or even the Yugoslavs. It was just a meaningless exhibition, but still a valuable lesson for everyone. Brown had kept his temper from flaring, just as he had resolved to do. His players had listened to his advice and responded to his motivation. They had won.

Beating the Yugoslavs would take more of a combined effort, especially if they brought their Olympic team. Brown had a little more than a week to prepare his young players to take on a group of physically superior, veteran athletes who had played together for as many as 10 years.

During the week, LSU spent most of its time working on defense. Brown would not be satisfied until it improved. It was the first time in his career that he didn't have at least one player who excelled at the defensive end. Typically, he had more defensive specialists than scorers. Somehow he had to develop aggressiveness on this team.

There was some good news. The Yugoslavs had opened their tour in Miami and lost. Obviously, they had not brought their best team.

Brown learned that former LSU center Zoran Jovanovich was playing on the Yugoslav team. He told his players that under no circumstances was Jovanovich to score a basket, even if it meant crashing into him. He didn't have to tell Blanton, who was eager to go up against his former roommate. He felt Jovanovich had deserted the team by returning to Yugoslavia the previous year. He couldn't wait to face him.

The game was to be part of an international double-header on Sunday afternoon in the Assembly Center. LSU's women's team was scheduled to play the Canadian national team at 1, and the men's game would follow at 4. There were few fans in the arena for the women's game, but the crowd began to arrive during the final minutes and grew to about half capacity. The LSU women set a bad precedent by getting soundly beaten.

When the late-arriving Yugoslavs finally showed up, a sweep for the visitors looked highly probable. These weren't their Olympians, but they were giants. Jovanovich was listed three inches shorter than his actual height of 7-1. Four of his teammates were as tall or taller than him.

LSU's only chance was to outrun their larger opponents. They did that for the first 10 minutes of the game. Jackson was more assertive leading the fast break and either scoring himself or getting it to Blanton in the left lane. They pushed the lead to 28-15 and appeared on the verge of breaking the game open. Brown began to pull his starters to rest them and give the others some playing time. The move backfired. Jovanovich led a rally that helped the Yugoslavs pull within 42-41 at halftime.

Brown was more emphatic during this halftime break than he had been against Brewster Heights. But he held his tongue. There was no ranting. He gave instructions and encouragement. But LSU couldn't handle the Yugoslavs inside and wasn't shooting well enough to outgun them.

Even though the Tigers continued to lead most of the second half, they couldn't put away the Yugoslavs. Jackson hit a 3-pointer to put LSU ahead by five with less than five minutes left. But the lead slipped to a point before Lyle Mouton made a jump shot with just under three minutes to play. The rest of the way, the Yugoslavs powered the ball inside. They scored nine points in a row and took the lead for good on a tip-in by Jovanovich.

In the closing seconds, Brown leaned over to Abernathy and whispered, "I'm glad we're going to lose. This is going to teach us an important lesson. We can't take anyone for granted. We'll be better for this." The 92-84 loss was a painful blow for everyone on the team, including Brown.

But again, this was no time to chastise the players. Brown sensed they needed more positive reinforcement. "It is very simple," he told them. "For us to be successful, we have to do the extraordinary. That's not whining. That's not complaining. Forget your girlfriends and everything else. Go think about this game. They are a better team than we are right now, but we should have won this game. If we had participated as hard as we can, we would have won. This can be a blessing in disguise if you understand that. We can win a lot of games if you play your heart out. Now put this one behind you. We have to get ready for a game that counts."

The season opener was five days away. The team was months away from where it had to be to satisfy Brown.

11

The Process Begins

Ricky's Diary, November 25—This is what we've been working for for six weeks. We've got to win. It's very important that the young guys get in their minds that LSU wins. We play to win, no matter who it is. They need to get the feeling that they're supposed to win, rather than just coming out to play. We have to establish ourselves right away.

When the day for the season opener finally arrived, Dale Brown knew the crowd would be sparse and the enthusiasm lacking for basketball. The next night, there would be about 80,000 football fans in Tiger Stadium for the regular-season finale between LSU and Tulane.

Only the most ardent basketball enthusiasts attend the early nonconference games at LSU. It would be an uninspiring setting for a young team that needed every boost it could get. The opposition, Marist College of Poughkeepsie, New York, certainly would not generate any special interest. Brown didn't mind. He would try to make it seem like an important game.

To prepare for it, Brown stayed home that Friday, breaking his usual game-day routine by taking Vonnie out for some early Christmas shopping. Although he normally didn't enjoy such activities, he had a wonderful time with his wife and was in a cheerful mood all day. Part of the time he thought about what he would say to his players. Like with most non-conference games, he had not bothered to send an assistant to scout Marist. His only concern was his own team.

His objective was not so much winning this game, or the next. Not even winning the Southeastern Conference title. He didn't really care how many games his team won, as long as it was enough to get them into the NCAA Tournament. The previous season, LSU had received an NCAA bid with only 16 victories, the fewest ever for an at-large team. LSU would play 30 regular-season games this season, so Brown was sure they would have to go at least 17-13 to make the NCAA field. But whether they were 17-13 or 22-8 didn't really matter to him. His season was the NCAA Tournament. But to get into it, his team had to play reasonably well in November, December, January and February.

During those months, he would give hundreds of pregame, half-time, postgame and off-day talks about how to believe in him, in the LSU system and in themselves. His players are so brainwashed with his positive attitude, in good times and bad, that before long they begin to think like him. Ultimately, he wants them to play that way, too.

But Brown spends much more time telling his players they can become a great team and accomplish any goal than he does teaching them how to become great basketball players. By this time every year, he is bored with fundamentals, drills and the X's and O's of coaching. Often he spends only a few minutes of the day on basketball. Everything else is focused on motivating his players. He is eager to start building the character and attitude that he believes are so much more important.

That afternoon, while Brown was out shopping, the players met for the pregame meal. It is always four-and-a-half hours before tip-off. Ron Abernathy, Johnny Jones, Jim Childers and Father Bayhi ate with them this time. Often, only Abernathy attends pregame meals. Brown never joins them, preferring to keep to himself all day.

Abernathy usually goes over the scouting report, showing video tape and reviewing how to best handle each opponent. There was no scouting report for Marist, so everyone ate and began to prepare himself on his own. It was a typical high-carbohydrate meal consisting of broiled chicken, pasta, carrots, bread and honey, and peaches and ice cream for dessert. The new players followed the example of Ricky Blanton, sitting at a table in the back of the dining hall, near the television set. Blanton was in his usual seat for dinner. He also had special seats for breakfast and lunch.

Blanton followed the same routine before each game. He takes a certain sidewalk on the short walk to the arena from Broussard Hall. Then he always gets Jay Magee, and no other trainer, to tape his ankles. After that, he goes out on the court and stretches out in the middle of the floor. During Brown's talk, he has to roll up the pant legs on his warmup. And when he goes to the restroom, he routinely uses the same toilet. If it is occupied, he waits. Many of his teammates have adopted their own routines. Roommates Chris Jackson and Vernel Singleton do everything together while they prepare to leave for the arena, even to the point of combing their hair in unison.

The opening-night meal took only 20 minutes to finish for everyone except Abernathy, who is among the slowest eaters on campus. He has to rush to finish a meal in less than an hour. He was still working on his plate of chicken when the players returned to their rooms to rest. Blanton has another ritual of listening to a special song. This season, it would be the theme song from "Rocky." Jackson, Singleton and most of the freshmen watched television or took a nap for two hours. Then at 6 o'clock, an hour and a half before tip-off, they began to walk to the arena, where they put on their uniforms, got taped and warmed up.

Brown usually follows his own routine. He takes a nap in the late afternoon, gets a light snack and then changes into a suit or sports coat and slacks. He leaves his house precisely at 6. About 15 minutes later, he arrives at the arena and goes either to his office or downstairs to the locker room. He discusses the game plan briefly with Abernathy and then chats with Doc Broussard or one of his many friends who stop by before games. Exactly 45 minutes before tip-off, he sends one of the team managers out on the court to call the players into the locker room for the pregame talk. That is the first time they see him on game days.

On this night, Brown was wearing a blue blazer and gray slacks, relatively casual attire for him. He generally saves his best suits for televised games or particularly important nights. Blanton was the first player to enter the locker room, soon followed by his 12 teammates. Brown and Blanton exchanged greetings, and it was business as usual. Jackson entered without saying a word. There was a challenging season ahead, and no time for pleasantries.

Brown was ready to go to work at his specialty. Some say his teams win many of their games in these moments. He speaks only 20 minutes, sometimes not that long. But he drives home his points, always raising his players' spirits and expectations to the point that they perform above other's expectations.

He continued to stand as the players filed in and sat down on chairs in front of their lockers, along two walls of the rectangular room. The assistant coaches and Father Bayhi had already made themselves comfortable on the couches at each end of the drawing board. It was not a large room. All the players could reach out and come close to touching Brown once he started his regular pacing. That could be good, when Brown was speaking eloquently and inspirationally, or bad, when he fell victim to his temper and raged ferociously.

When Sims came through the door, Brown was already counting to make sure everyone was there. Satisfied, he motioned for the door to be closed and paused briefly before beginning his talk. Already, he was pacing. If he were calm and relaxed, his pacing would be confined to a five-to eight-foot area in front of the drawing board. Should he get excited or upset, he would pace the length of the 20-foot room. Since this was just the opener, he stayed at his end of the room and spoke about as softly as he can, which really isn't all that soft. His voice can always be heard in the hall, even with the heavy door closed.

LSU's regular season really started when Brown opened his first address with a bold prediction and stiff challenge, but one he believed, truly believed, would be met by this team. "If you will follow us, I know where we will go. I've been here 17 years. It doesn't make any difference what the opponent is like. It's just that the system will work. So if you will adjust to the system, you can do anything you want. You can make it to a national tournament. You can play in the NCAA Tournament. And if we get into the NCAA Tournament, you know what can happen. I am telling you that you can do anything you want. Tonight is a good chance. We played two exhibitions. Now you get your first college team."

All eyes were focused on Brown. All ears were tuned into the speech. No other sound could be heard, except an occasional rumbling noise in the hall. The only movement in the room was being made by Blanton, who had pulled up the pant legs on his warmup suit and was swaying to release nervous energy.

Brown was getting warmed up himself. He picked up the tempo of his talk and pace. "The game is not a whole bunch of chemical formulas. The game really starts inside you. How you feel about yourself. Now if you have talent and you feel good about it, you're really in a good position. And we have a lot more talent than anyone is giving us credit for.

"Tonight is the first little step to getting where we want to go, which is Seattle for the Final Four. Everybody says that's a joke. It's a joke to try to win this league. We've heard all that. But we don't believe it. Follow us. Believe in us. Believe in each other. And we will walk through the hard times. We will get where we want to be. We will do so much more than they said we could. But we're going to do it for ourselves. We're going to do it starting tonight, gentlemen."

For the next several minutes, he went over the defensive assignments. Abernathy had gotten a copy of Marist's press release that detailed its performance in an exhibition game and described its starters. Brown matched up their starters with his—Blanton, Sims, Jackson, Singleton and Lyle Mouton. His plan was simple and wouldn't change no matter who played for Marist. When the Tigers made a basket or free throw, they would go into a full-court man-to-man press and fall back into a helping man-to-man defense. Offensively, they wanted to get the ball to Jackson and push it up the court. If the shot wasn't there, they were told to go into the pressure release, a basic offense using passing and screening.

After clarifying a few details with the players, he was about 15 minutes into his talk and ready to wrap it up. As he often will do, Brown closed with a personal touch. "You guys aren't any different than me. For 32 years, I've been dragging my butt out on the court. Every night now I say to myself, 'OK, Denny the Dimwit, here's what you're going to do: you're going to be intelligent, you're going to watch Ricky, you're going to watch Lyle, you're going to talk to the coaches and stay on top of things.' Then pretty soon I get emotional or my mind blanks out, and I go home practically every night of my career and say to myself, 'What am I doing? How come I wasn't more conscious of things?'

"It's the same way with you guys. Just don't go out and play the game. Read what's going on out there. Study the guy you're playing. You have to help us. We can't play in your bodies. We can guide you. We can call timeouts and coach you. We can keep the discipline and the mentality of this team. But you have got to do it! Gentlemen, you have got to do it! Now let's have a nice one."

Ordinarily, that would have ended the pregame message, and the players would have headed back upstairs to conclude their warmups. Blanton was almost out of his seat to huddle the players for a final cheer that the captain always leads before the team goes on the court. But Brown held them up. He had forgotten about Father Bayhi. This season, he had someone to complement and enhance his messages.

Father Bayhi, whose voice is truly soft and gentle, leaned forward and said he wanted to share some thoughts with them. Then he read from a photo copy of a section of First Corinthians. He read the passage and summarized it. "Guys, all members are part of one body. The body cannot function without all of its parts. This applies to all mankind. You can have a winning season. You can reach any goal you set. But you've got to do it together. Everyone on this team is important. Everyone must contribute. Everyone will share in the honors. We need everybody to be at his best. And we need to keep God first in everything we do."

Father Bayhi stood up and reached out to clasp hands with Brown on his left and Childers on his right. He led a short prayer and closed with the Lord's Prayer. Then Blanton moved to the center of the room and put his hands above his head. His teammates circled him, joining their hands together above their heads. "All right, let's get it done," he shouted. They broke the huddle with a resounding yell.

In the early minutes of the game, the players and the fans had little to cheer about. It was a dull affair. Nothing was going right for LSU, and Marist was playing only slightly better, just well enough to take an early seven-point lead, which quieted the crowd even more. At the first official timeout, LSU was down 15-9 and Brown could not hold in his anger. He was most upset at the defense under the basket. Blanton and Sims drew his wrath, but not as much as Singleton, who was pulled out of the game for Richard Krajewski. Moments later, Brown yanked Mouton and replaced him with Russell Grant.

To the amazement of most everyone in the building, two of LSU's most awkward, unathletic players turned around the game in a matter of minutes. Krajewski, four inches taller than Singleton, put a larger body on Marist's big men. That blocked the path for any easy baskets. Then Grant, who was heckled by the LSU students when he didn't take a wide open shot, responded by shredding Marist's zone defense. He didn't shoot the first time he touched the ball because he had been ordered by Brown not to shoot on the first possession after coming off the bench.

In fact, Brown had drawn a cross in red ink on Grant's shoes, just to remind him. Grant looked down once and passed. But the next time he touched the ball, he didn't hesitate, shooting a 3-pointer right through the net. Before halftime, he had swished three consecutive 3-pointers and two free throws for 11 points, helping LSU build a 47-23 lead. The students who had taunted him earlier were now chanting, "Rus-sell, Rus-sell, Rus-sell."

Brown, though, was still upset when he got to the locker room for the 15-minute intermission. All that he could think of was the way Marist had abused LSU's defense in the early going. He went directly to one of the training rooms, where he met with his assistants. The players went to their dressing area and waited.

"Ricky, our damn best player, was asleep out there, and we're still 20 points ahead," Brown fumed to his coaches. "He didn't do anything. He was in a daze." Johnny Jones tried to offer an alibi for Blanton, but Brown cut him off. "I don't want any excuses for him. And Lyle was lazy out there. He looked like Mr. Country Club again." This was just the beginning of what would become a long struggle between Brown and his captain and a season-long confrontation with Mouton. In both cases, Brown felt compelled to demand more from them than they asked of themselves. He thought that was the only way this team could win consistently and achieve the type of season he wanted.

If he had gone to speak to the players right then, it would have been the season's first Brownout. Blanton and the other returning players had seen many of them, especially the previous season when the team had so many ups and downs. A Brownout occurs when Dale loses control of his powers of reason and lets his emotions take over. Through the years, it has happened occasionally on the court, but regularly off the court. Once Brown goes into such a rage, he becomes a frightening intimidator. No one moves a muscle. Most players don't dare to breath. They only listen carefully and usually respond with improved performances. But there had been no Brownouts so far and there would be none tonight. He had changed his demeanor as well as his faith.

"He just understands things so much better and knows what he believes now," Blanton had said earlier that week.

After discussing second-half strategy with his coaches, Brown regained his composure. In other years, he would have been hyped for the rest of the night. Instead of dwelling on Blanton and Mouton, he fixed his thoughts on the splendid performance of Grant and Krajewski. They had combined for the most spectacular play of the night. It started with Krajewski tipping the ball and diving for an attempted steal. He couldn't quite get his hands on it, so Grant plunged to the hardwood in a daring effort to get the loose ball. Finally, Krajewski scrambled to his feet and took the ball away. He turned and threw a pass to Blanton for an easy layup. The crowd finally had something to be excited about and roared its approval. Most pleased by the effort was Brown. He loved to see players dive on the floor for the ball, much more than watching them slam it through the net or hit a 20-foot jump shot.

With that play in mind, he took a positive approach to his halftime talk. "You had them so rattled in a short period of time, just from being physical and aggressive. It got contagious. You have now got to keep that aggressiveness up. We have got that big lead, and we don't want to be passive. Let's cut them apart. They've got to take us man-to-man, so let's run our offense and get some layups and good shots. Look it over. Be patient and we will win this one."

Brown was right on two counts. LSU won the game easily. And Grant, who seemed destined for a career on the bench, had delivered a victory. His offensive spark and all-around hustle had turned it around. Even with Jackson scoring only 13 points in his debut, LSU went on to a 94-58 victory. Brown was jovial and had long since forgotten about his disappointment with Blanton and Mouton, although it would come up again.

"This was a culmination of hard work," he told the players. "Russell and Richard turned that whole game around with their hard work and defense. Russell is a living example of flat ass never giving up. He never gives up. We tried to persuade him into transferring. We thought it might be best for him to go somewhere he could play more. That shows how smart we are. He would not give up. He just hung in there. If we do that, we can win a lot more games and do everything you want to do."

Satisfied with the overall effort, Brown gave the team Saturday off and scheduled a Sunday afternoon practice. They had to get ready to play Oral Roberts University on Wednesday. It was another opponent that Brown had not bothered to scout. It was only November, and his full attention was on improving his team's defense. He was still sold on a full-court press, backed up by man-to-man and was convinced he could always call on the Freak Defense against stronger opponents.

Brown, who has always made up his teams' schedules, agreed to play ORU as a favor to the school's president, Oral Roberts, the evangelist. They had been friends for years and had almost joined forces.

Shortly after Brown coached LSU to the 1981 Final Four, Roberts contacted him and wanted him to coach at ORU. He made an offer that Brown had to consider, $1 million over four years. That was many times what Dale was making at LSU, even after a hefty raise. In the final analysis, Brown determined he was closer to a national championship at LSU than he would ever be at ORU. That didn't detract from his friendship with Roberts.

It was thought that Roberts might come to Baton Rouge to visit with Brown and watch the game. But Roberts was on a crusade. He had visited with Brown during the summer. Brown had gone to Tulsa for a basketball clinic and needed to get back to Baton Rouge in a hurry. He returned on Roberts' private jet.

Another reason Brown scheduled ORU was for an easy victory, just like Marist—or so he thought. The Titans had won only eight games the previous season and weren't expected to give LSU any trouble.

Brown did expect ORU to run and gun and score its share of points. So he stressed defense in his pregame talk and demanded they play fearlessly, following the example of Grant. ''I don't want you to play dirty or anything like that. We don't want cheap shots. But I'll tell you what, I wouldn't let my man get the ball. If I had to pin myself to him, he wouldn't touch that damn ball. So be aggressive. I want you to play with reckless abandon. That means dive on the floor for the ball. Sacrifice your body. Spill your guts. When you play with reckless abandon, you're tough to beat. I'll be proud of you if you play like that, and you'll be proud of yourself.''

About half of the players followed his orders. The half that didn't spent most of the first 20 minutes sitting beside him, instead of playing. He was most distressed with Mouton. Either Mouton would conform to Brown's standards of selfless, tireless play, or he simply would not play.

Fortunately for Mouton, LSU was having little trouble with the undisciplined ORU team, which shot the ball about every 10 seconds, whether anyone was open or not. The Tigers, with reserves playing much of the first half, led 58-48 at halftime and appeared headed toward their second easy victory.

In the coaches' meeting at halftime, Brown blasted Mouton. He made up his mind Mouton would be benched for the second half. Singleton also caught Brown's wrath for failing to be tough on defense, even though he had scored the first two baskets for LSU and seemed to have a hot hand.

Having blown off some steam, Brown was ready to give the players their instructions. He looked over at Ricky Blanton and asked him who was playing the hardest. "We'll start whoever you say," Brown told him. Blanton called out the same five that Brown had picked out: Jackson, Sims, Grant, Kyle McKenzie and Blanton.

The decision was made. Those would be the second-half starters. If Grant and McKenzie had a good half, they might even become permanent starters. The only problem was that LSU couldn't win with that lineup. If Brown had been planning just for that game, he would have realized it, too. But he was thinking beyond Oral Roberts. This was a statement to Mouton and Singleton. There was a possibility ORU could come back against such a small lineup. But even if LSU lost, Brown felt it would gain in the long run. This was the time of year he molded his players into the roles he had chosen for them.

Ironically, his final words before halftime ended were: "Don't let it get close and go down to a last shot." It got close in a hurry, because ORU killed LSU on the boards, getting second and third shots. When Mouton and Singleton finally got back in the game, LSU's lead was down to one point, and the game was headed to the wire. Jackson, who was beginning to take charge and would finish with 25 points, hit a 3-point shot to tie the game at 96 with only six seconds left.

ORU point guard Greg Sutton, guarded tightly by Jackson, brought the ball down for a final shot. He was at the top of the key when he realized he had to get off a shot, so he jumped toward the basket and shot off-balance. It didn't come close, but he crashed into Jackson and a call had to be made.

Harrell Allen, the official closest to the play, blew his whistle and started to put his arm up to make a call. But he delayed. Mac Chauvin, who had not even gotten to halfcourt, also blew his whistle. As the referee, Chauvin had to make the call.

It was not an easy one for Chauvin, who is a friend of Brown's and lives in Baton Rouge. For that reason, he had asked not to be assigned to the game. But here it was, the deciding call, and he had to make it. Brown thought it would be a charge, as did the LSU players and the 8,000 fans. If it had been a charge, the game would have gone into overtime.

Chauvin called a blocking foul on Jackson. The fans roared their disapproval. Brown protested vehemently. Sutton went to the free-throw line for two shots. With no time left, he had to make only one to win the game. His first shot went in, clinching the upset. Brown came out on the court, just to make a point. He walked slowly toward Allen, demanding that he tell Brown what his call was. Allen didn't answer. Chauvin did, giving Brown a technical foul and then another. Eventually, Sutton got six free-throw chances and made four, giving ORU a 100-96 victory.

Heartbroken, the LSU players and assistant coaches walked toward their locker room. Brown was right behind them until he detoured through a hallway and headed back toward the officials' dressing room. He would not be satisfied until Allen told him what his call was. To prevent coaches and fans from confronting the officials, a security guard is always posted outside their locker room. Brown, with a full head of steam, was going to walk right past the guard. The guard stuck out his arm to block the hallway, but Brown pushed it aside and proceeded into the locker room. He told Allen that he was not going to leave until he heard the call. Allen would only say: "I saw a foul." No matter what Brown said, Allen was not going to tell him. Finally, Brown left the room—no less angry than before.

On the other side of the arena, the LSU players had their heads down and were fighting back tears while they waited for Brown to show up. The assistant coaches were looking for Brown. They weren't sure whether to talk to the team themselves or to continue waiting. By then, Brown was already late for his radio show.

About 15 minutes passed before he finally appeared. He had his coat draped over his shoulder and was shaking his head. He stood in front of the players for several minutes, and then started talking in a dejected tone of voice. "Apparently, you didn't listen to what we said. I told you we do not win games like this. What did I tell you at half? A last-second shot could beat you."

Then he noticed how distraught Jackson was and tried briefly to comfort him. "It was a horseshit call, Chris. At best, it was a no-call. And probably it was without question a charge. But that doesn't have anything to do with it. We should not have been in that position."

For the next several minutes, Brown pointed out the breakdowns that put them in a position to lose on a last-second play. He was beginning to get more intense when he looked in the corner. There sat Mouton, anxious to get to the showers. He had taken seven shots and missed them all. If he had made just one, LSU might have won. Mouton's offense, however, didn't bother Brown as much as his sloppy defense and lack of hustle. If a player exhausted himself chasing after his man and running down loose balls, it didn't matter to Brown how many shots that player made. He knew that kind of effort would win in the long run. But Mouton would not put out that kind of effort. Brown would ride Mouton until he did, or kick him out of the program.

"Lyle, you might as well not have suited up tonight," Brown said, now beginning to boom. "You might as well have stayed and looked at yourself in a mirror or gone to a dance. All the talent that you've got and you shit in your pants tonight. You didn't do a damn thing. We need you, Lyle. We need you. We can't expect guys to come off the bench all the time. We need you!"

Switching to other players, Brown remained critical, but wasn't as scathing. Singleton got almost as much attention. "I think we have more confidence in you than you have in yourself," Brown told him. He reminded him that few freshmen had ever started at LSU, and he expected bigger things from him. But he didn't come down on Singleton too hard, fearing he might rattle him. It was just the opposite with Mouton. He knew Mouton had enough self-confidence to handle criticism. He sensed that Mouton was arrogant and needed to be shaken up in order to perform at his maximum level.

Brown moved close to his target. "Lyle, I need to know, and so do your teammates, if you're going to play hard for us or not. Is there a barometer or something to measure if you're going to come to play? What's your problem, Lyle? We sure as hell can't figure it. We never know when you're going to play."

He stopped and stared at Mouton. It was a deep, piercing stare. In moments like these, Brown can be the ultimate intimidator. No other player dared to look at him or Mouton. They all felt sorry for Mouton and wanted to make sure they never got in that position.

As a freshman, Blanton had been the fall guy, the player on whom Brown vents his frustration. He sympathized with Mouton. But he also knew Mouton needed that kind of stimulus. Everyone on the team knew Mouton was dogging it on defense.

After a short pause, Brown asked, "What's the problem, Lyle?"

"I don't know, Coach," Mouton muttered, hanging his head.

Brown went back to the "We need you" refrain. He repeated it three times, each one louder. "If somebody told me they needed me, I'd crawl to the end of the earth for them." But that was not the way Mouton had been raised. For him to play for Brown, he had to change everything about his very makeup. It wouldn't be easy. But LSU could not be successful without him. Brown knew that. So did Mouton.

That night, Brown met with Mouton. Brown rarely meets with players individually after a game. He usually waits until the next day. But this couldn't be delayed. Although he had cooled off, Brown was still firm and demanded more effort. "If you don't start playing hard, you are going to sit beside me the rest of the season," he said matter-of-factly. Mouton made a mistake by trying to defend himself. That merely set off Brown's temper.

"Lyle, what is wrong with you? It's like you're always looking at yourself when you're playing. Are you ashamed to be black or something?"

At first, Mouton didn't answer. But he knew he had to. "I know you're the coach, but I don't have to take that from anybody." He considered getting up and leaving—the office and the team. But he stayed and listened.

Blanton went to see Mouton in his dorm room to tell him everyone, including Brown, was behind him and wanted him to succeed. But that could only happen if he played the way Brown told him.

On Thursday, Brown reviewed the game tape over and over. In slow motion, it clearly showed that Jackson had set himself before Sutton took the final step into him. It was a charge. But the game had not been played in slow motion, and there was no recourse. Chauvin, who came by Brown's office to see the tape, admitted he had missed the call.

Even though LSU held a two-hour practice that afternoon, Brown was occupied with other thoughts. His daughter's wedding was scheduled for the next night. Early in the practice, Brown interrupted his pacing to talk to Abernathy. "Ron, my heart really hurts. I can't believe my little girl is getting married." It didn't matter that Robyn was 25, or that Brown truly liked her fiancee, Chris Prudhomme. She would be moving to New Orleans, and their relationship would never be quite the same. He was thankful that he had rekindled the closeness with his wife.

Brown gave the team a break by cancelling practice on the wedding day. Only the assistant coaches, Doc Broussard and a few close friends were invited to the wedding, which was held at St. Thomas More Catholic Church in Baton Rouge. To ensure it remained a private affair, there was no announcement in the newspaper. Father Bayhi helped conduct the service. Dale and Vonnie sat in a pew by themselves. None of Brown's relatives attended. Some of Vonnie's family made the trip from North Dakota. Afterward, there was a lavish reception at the Country Club of Louisiana.

Once he got over that emotional day, Brown put everything into basketball again. He held practices on Saturday, Sunday and Monday to get ready for Louisiana Tech, which had an up-and-coming program and had just taken third-ranked Syracuse to overtime on the road.

Brown was relaxed. He knew these players needed more building than they did scolding. He called them together for a long talk before Monday's practice and tried to make sure no one was discouraged, especially Mouton.

"I am more determined than ever," he said, squatting in front of the bench. "In the midst of giving away a game to Oral Roberts, in the midst of despair, I have a good feeling. We are going to find some way to get back to a national tournament. I don't know how many times I've said that to Ricky. And every year we've done it."

Based on what LSU had shown so far, even Brown would have gladly settled for an NIT bid. But having been to five NCAA tournaments in a row and eight of the last 10, he knew there was still a chance to make it to the big party. It would take victories over teams like Louisiana Tech.

It was only the first Tuesday in December, but the game was being built up as a war between north Louisiana and south Louisiana. Despite playing on the road, Louisiana Tech was favored to win.

Brown pulled out all the stops to get his players psychologically prepared. He changed the starting lineup, inserting Krajewski for Singleton and Grant for Mouton. He went overtime in his pregame talk, which lasted almost 30 minutes. He talked about the early days when he was building the program. "I'll tell you nobody thought we could do it." Then he described how he and his assistants barnstormed the state, putting up purple-and-gold nets on every backyard goal, handing out LSU key chains and motivational literature, kissing babies and promising a winner.

After that, he showed a tape of a local sportscast by Rich Lenz. In his preview of the game, Lenz said Krajewski had no chance against Louisiana Tech center Randy White, rated one of the nation's premier big men. That got Krajewski's attention.

Brown also read newspaper reports that quoted Louisiana Tech players making boastful statements about the game. Even Joe Dean was part of Brown's arsenal. Dean had informed Craig Carse that he thought all the coaches should get a bonus if they could get 12 victories out of this team. That immediately became the team's first goal.

"Finally, I hope that you will see tonight that the impossible is what nobody can do until somebody does it," he said, clapping his hands to accentuate the message. "This Randy White is rated one of the toughest centers in the country. He is a first-round draft pick. They say he is Tech's next Karl Malone. I am tired of hearing all the crap. We are the kings of Louisiana."

LSU came out and played by far its best basketball of the season. Krajewski held off White with some body language under the basket. Jackson was smooth with his jump shot, scoring almost at will. LSU scored 11 consecutive points to go ahead 18-8. Louisiana Tech got untracked and regained the lead, but it was nip-and-tuck throughout the half and the score was tied at 45 at halftime.

Brown was disappointed at losing a 10-point lead, but sensed that his players needed to be patted on the back this time. They were close to pulling off their first upset of the season. "You guys are really doing a good job," he said enthusiastically during the halftime break. "It looks like you're playing intelligent and having fun. You really look good. It's a big improvement over last game. We've improved so much. Now what we do in the second half has to be better than the first. And if you do that, we'll come down here happy."

With Jackson displaying his extraordinary scoring ability for the first time, LSU regained control and went ahead by nine points. Jackson overwhelmed Tech guard Brett Guillory, repeatedly faking him out for easy jump shots.

The C.J. File—I was just on. I felt like I was back in high school. I couldn't miss. It really boosted my confidence. I'm on track now.

But White began to beat Krajewski with power moves inside, and Tech pulled even. LSU had a chance to win in regulation, but Jackson was trapped and the officials inexplicably refused to give Blanton a timeout, even though he signaled for it with three seconds left.

The overtime period was a shootout between Jackson and White. Jackson, who had 35 in regulation, was brilliant from long range and scored 13 of LSU's 19 overtime points. But White kept Tech close, and Guillory finished off the Tigers with six consecutive free throws for a 111-109 victory.

It was another agonizing defeat for a group of young LSU players who for the most part had known only victory as high school players. Jackson set an Assembly Center scoring record and drew national attention with his 48-point performance, but was emotionally crushed by the loss.

Once again, Brown had to raise their spirits. This was no time to criticize anyone, even though there were several prime candidates. Mouton had played better, but still not at the level expected of him. Krajewski had done a respectable job of defending White, but had missed all five of his shots. Geert Hammink had also thrown a shutout, missing four times.

What they needed more than anything was to be reminded that there were three months left in the season and they were headed in the right direction. Their 1-2 record wasn't a good start, but they could turn it around.

"It was a big improvement tonight," Brown told them in a consoling tone. "They're a good basketball team. We can play better. We have to play better defense. There's no reason to pout about this game. It's off the schedule. We've now got to come back in two days and play McNeese State. Then we have to go to Florida. I'll tell you this was a hell of a lot better job than Oral Roberts. Your improvement has been phenomenal. That's all that counts."

For the next 10 minutes, he pointed out exactly what they had done better than in previous games. He saved the corrections for later. In closing, he turned their thoughts to March. "This game ain't going to have any effect on us going to the NCAA. It's over, it's done. Forget about it."

That night, he had trouble falling asleep. It wasn't so much the loss that bothered him as it was how they had lost. His teams rarely blew large leads, because their strength was always defense. This group didn't play good defense, for which he blamed himself. He finally got out of bed at about 3 in the morning and started to read. First, he read the Bible for about an hour. Then he skimmed several Christian books. Finally, he came to the conclusion that the two losses were just a trial for everyone on the team. They would all be stronger for it.

Practice went well the next day and by Thursday night, Brown was eager to play somebody. The opponent would be McNeese State, a Southland Conference school in Lake Charles, Louisiana.

In preparing his players to go out against McNeese, Brown spoke with absolute confidence. "I am so positive if you don't quit, the results will come. There have been some impossible things happening here. I should just let Ricky talk. He was a sophomore when we lost to Georgia. We had the ball and a one-point lead with a second to go, and we lost. What place were we in, Ricky?"

"Sixth place, I think, Coach," Blanton replied.

"Sixth place, that's right. Remember what the papers said? LSU couldn't win. But we won the SEC championship. The next year, the Final Four trip to Dallas was impossible. The next year, the Final Eight trip was impossible. Last year, beating Oklahoma was impossible. This year, getting to a national tournament is impossible. You can't play for other people's expectations. I don't want to be known as a miracle worker. I ain't no miracle worker. I just happen to have people who believe in themselves. I know what kind of people you are. And I know we're going to do the so-called impossible again."

But LSU was still troubled by poor defense. Krajewski and Hammink couldn't stop anyone. Sims seemed to be following their example. To make matters worse, Jackson couldn't find his shooting range.

McNeese built a 43-39 lead in a sloppily played first half. Brown was furious. He blasted everyone at halftime. Because Sims was a veteran, he caught most of the wrath. Finally, Brown warned if they weren't careful, they would lose to a small Louisiana school just like Kentucky had done on Wednesday when Northwestern State beat the Wildcats at Rupp Arena. Brown couldn't stomach the thought of losing back-to-back games to in-state schools. Finally, he stormed out of the locker room, and Blanton dished out a tongue-lashing of his own.

In the second half, they were sharper offensively. But their defense couldn't put the game away. Jackson saved them with some clutch free throws, and they limped in with a 91-89 victory. That evened their record at 2-2. But it didn't do anything for Brown. He tried to keep his emotions under control. He knew he could correct without screaming. He wanted to be composed. But he was incensed by the poor play, and his temper flared.

Only Blanton, Sims, Mouton, Grant and McKenzie had seen him in a full-blown rage. The new players were in for a shocking surprise. It would turn into the first Brownout of the season. Blanton could see it coming as soon as Brown took off his sportscoat during his postgame talk.

What really set him off was the postgame feedback from his coaching staff. Abernathy was hot and shouting. Johnny Jones, Craig

Carse and Jim Childers were more mild in their evaluations, although Jones brought up a valid point. He suggested that everyone on the team follow Grant's example. In the first four games, Grant had spent almost as much time diving after loose balls as he had standing erect.

That was how he got to LSU in the first place. Brown had agreed to let Grant walk on the team the previous season after seeing a high school tape of him diving for a loose ball, opening a gash on his cheek and breaking off a tooth. Brown fell in love with him. Grant had also developed an adept outside shot that had actually become one of the team's best offensive weapons.

"I spent a half hour this summer on the phone doing everything in my power to try to convince Russell to transfer," Carse told the team. "I feel like an asshole. I apologize to Russell right now. You have all got to play like Russell."

Talk of Grant giving more effort than anyone else set off an alarm in Brown's mind. Abernathy responded the same way and was first to say something.

"Guys, if you don't start playing hard and being aggressive, you are not going to play here." Abernathy rarely loses his temper, but this time he stood up and screamed. "We won't let you wear that LSU jersey if you don't play hard. We will run your ass off. LSU means too much to me. It wasn't always that way. I remember when you'd say you coached at LSU, and they would laugh at you. Now LSU has a program that everyone respects. We won't let you put on that LSU uniform unless it means a lot to you, too."

That was all Brown needed to hear. Someone might as well have thrown a bucket of gasoline onto a bonfire. The time bomb was ticking, and an explosion was inevitable.

First, Brown repeated some of Abernathy's comments, threatening to run off anyone who didn't want to win badly enough. "You have to be special to play here!" he fumed. "Not every psycho guy in the country can play here at LSU. We picked you because we know what kind of people you are. But if you haven't got the spirit, get out of my face. I can't stand it! I just can't stand it!"

Suddenly, he edged toward Blanton. None of the other players could believe what was happening. They didn't think Brown would ever tear into the team captain. But Blanton knew better. He realized it was only a matter of time before a poor performance ignited a Brownout. This one would seem devastating to the new players.

The C.J. File—I was surprised. It was scary. I could tell he was angry, because we didn't play well. I always try to do everything right so I don't get fussed at. I don't want to give anybody a reason to get mad at me. He was really mad at everyone. But I knew he was only trying to help us. He was just letting us know we can't play like that.

Blanton actually considered the incident relatively minor. In a way, he was glad to catch Brown's anger to show everyone there were no favorites on the team. They were all in it together.

Brown was slamming his right fist into his left hand, creating an intimidating popping sound. He was yelling so loudly that the veins on the side of this head were popping out. His forehead was crinkled and his cheeks were flushed.

Leaning over to get right into Blanton's face, he roared his displeasure. "Ricky, you have got to be our leader. Remember what you did in Atlanta. This stuff." Then he mimicked "The Blanton," the gestures of celebration Blanton flashed after making his game-winning basket against Kentucky that sent LSU to the 1986 Final Four. "All of a sudden, you're a fifth-year guy, and you lost your spark. You lost your damn spark! I need you!" He put his hands on Blanton's shoulders and shook him. "I need the Ricky Blanton that was in Atlanta! That's who we need. I will be your captain if I have to."

With almost every word, Brown became louder and more threatening. He turned away from Blanton and looked to his left where Sims sat timidly. He had never caught the brunt of a Brownout. But that was about to change.

Brown was almost nose to nose with the powerfully built Sims. His 17 points and 10 rebounds were long forgotten. Brown was only thinking about some key mistakes Sims had made.

"Damn it, Wayne! You have got to get in there and do like you're supposed to!" he yelled. "There was a loose ball tonight and Wayne, you looked at it. In a crucial part of the game!" The word crucial was further emphasized with a resounding clap of his hands. "You are the strongest guy on the team. But all those weightlifting records don't mean a damn thing unless you use your strength. You can't stand around like that. I just can't believe you would do that." Brown paced away from Sims and returned to his usual spot in front of the drawing board. At the height of his scolding, he smashed his fist into one of the wooden cabinets, never flinching, not even stopping his line of attack.

Looking to his left again, he peered at Mouton, who had not started the game. The only thing that saved Lyle was the fact he played only sparingly and had not committed any glaring errors.

For his grand finale, Brown lashed out at the entire team. "Listen to me! You strap your damn jock on your mouth and listen to me. We leave for Florida tomorrow. Don't get on that bus tomorrow unless you want to play! If you think it's silly to do what Russell did, that's bullshit. I am not tolerating it. Ricky, I want you to be one emotional guy out there. I want you out there huddling those guys and pushing them. Wayne, you have got to do your job. We are not going to lose. And if we lose, I am going to knock somebody on the ground and step on his mouth.

"We are going to win. And we are going to do it just exactly how we have in the past. And I am going to have more damn energy than I have ever had before. And if you don't want to win, don't get your ass on that bus tomorrow. I am serious. I don't want your ass on that bus unless you are going to play it our way! Our way! You guys were so unemotional. I don't ever want to see another game like this."

Finally, he stormed toward the door. On his way, he asked Father Bayhi to lead a prayer. "I'd feel like a hypocrite if I prayed right now," Brown said, opening the door to leave.

Though his face never showed it, Sims was angry, too. He didn't understand why Brown was being so hostile toward him. He thought he had played a good game, and they had won. The younger players didn't move. They were in a mild state of shock. Blanton called a players meeting that night to explain the situation.

"We needed that to wake us up," he told his teammates. "We deserved that. We needed that. There's something you have to understand about Coach Brown, he isn't going to tolerate you not giving it everything. Absolutely everything."

Blanton expected more eruptions like that. The freshmen and sophomores hoped it would be the last. Jackson knew he had never seen anything like it before.

The blowup affected Brown as well. He quickly regretted getting so angry. That was the way he would have handled such a situation in the past. He was caught at crossroads. He wanted to lead this team according to the standards he had been studying, but it was difficult to rid himself of his old patterns—especially since they had been so successful.

Later that night, he talked with Vonnie. "How many people have truly demanded excellence out of you?'' he asked. She just listened to him. ''There are five billion people in the world,'' he continued. ''How many of them demand excellence? Looking back, I wish somebody had pushed me harder. I want to be their friend for life. But I want to be their leader before I want to be their friend. If you're always stroking people, then you're a politician. I've got to be honest. If I brag about Ricky, shouldn't I tell the truth when he doesn't play up to par? The truth is brutally honest.''

Deep inside, Brown knew he no longer wanted to coach like that. He didn't want to live like that, either.

He considered apologizing to the players. But he was concerned that might take away their edge for Florida. To have any chance in this game and other major tests, these players had to go beyond themselves. And it was his job to get them there.

12

The Freak

Ricky's Diary, December 9—We're all in the doghouse. Coach Brown kind of pissed me off and got me ready to play Florida. It doesn't bother me. I know he's doing it for a purpose. This is a big game for us, and he has us ready to play.

Every player showed up to board the team bus Friday afternoon. Brown, like always, drove by himself to Metro Airport and met the team there for a two-hour charter flight to Gainesville.

There wasn't much said on the trip, but Brown could tell by the intense look on their faces that his players were eager to play. He just wasn't sure they were ready to go against a team like Florida. The Gators had a devastating front line of 7-2 center Dwayne Schintzius and tight end-like forwards Livingston Chatman and Dwayne Davis. LSU's only chance was to keep them away from the basket and put pressure on Florida's inexperienced guards.

This was an important game, but one LSU wasn't expected to win. It required something extra. Whenever Brown needs an edge, he usually falls back on defense, particularly his Freak Defense.

He has used the Freak throughout his career at LSU, but never so much as in the mid-80s. That was when his teams were short on talent and outmanned in virtually every big game. The Freak became his great equalizer and led to the postseason success of 1986 and 1987.

If he had put together a Freak highlight film, it would have focused on the 1987 stretch drive that produced improbable victories over Georgia Tech, Temple and DePaul. More so than in any other game, LSU almost certainly would not have beaten DePaul in the Midwest Regional semifinal without the Freak. It negated a gross mismatch in talent and was particularly effective against Dallas Comegys and Rod Strickland.

Brown and Strickland had met again that following summer. They had been selected to the Playboy preseason All-America team, Brown as the coach and Strickland as the point guard. All the team members were flown to Disney World for a weekend, during which Brown and Strickland got a chance to talk about the tournament game. Strickland still wasn't sure what kind of defense he had faced. He told Brown that DePaul coach Joey Meyer said there was no such thing as the Freak Defense and that LSU was just playing a 2-3 zone.

Strickland, however, knew differently. He asked Brown if LSU had used a triangle-and-two or diamond-and-one in the final minutes of the game. Strickland said he had argued with Comegys over which offense to run, because they couldn't agree what kind of defense LSU was playing. Brown explained that LSU had used those two defenses and several others, all part of the Freak. Then he went into some details. Strickland seemed a little overwhelmed and finally said, "Coach, I really like the way you play defense."

Brown says the Freak really isn't complicated. He came up with the concept as a high school coach in North Dakota in the late 1950s. After it proved so successful at LSU, coaching friends and associates encouraged him to write a book on his defense, which he eventually did. He was tired of having to explain the defense wherever LSU played.

Basically, the Freak is a combination of just about every form of defense played in basketball: man-to-man, straight zone, traps, matchup zones, changing zones, combinations of zone and man-to-man, and presses. What it does is change constantly, often during a single possession, thereby confusing the opposition and keeping it off balance. The defensive alignment can be switched by a signal given by the coach or defensive captain, or it can be based on the area of the court in which the ball is entered. Brown calls these variations his Visual Clue Freak and Entry Pass Freak.

In essence, it is a way of disguising defenses much like football teams try to keep the opposing quarterback in doubt by changing coverages, or a pitcher tries to keep a batter guessing by mixing pitches.

To attack the Freak Defense, the opponent must first recognize what it is. But if the defenders are switching from one alignment to another, that can be extremely difficult. Just ask Strickland.

The Freak also works because Brown believes in it so completely. And whatever he believes in, his players believe in. That gives them a psychological edge that may be more vital than the tactical advantage of confusing the opponent. Whatever the case, the Freak works. It was the first thing Brown thought of when he started planning for Saturday's game with Florida.

Up to this point of the season, he had not called on the Freak. The quality of opponents didn't dictate the need for it. But the Tigers had spent several practices working on it to prepare for the day when it would be needed.

When he introduced the Freak to this team in early November, he worried that it would be too much for the young players to absorb at once. So he called on a friend for help. He picked Al Guglielmo to be his straight man.

He wanted Guglielmo to try to explain the defense, and fail. Then Brown would bail him out and show the players just how simple it was. But Dale was fooled. Guglielmo went on for about 10 minutes rattling off every aspect of the Freak as if he had invented it. It just so happened that he had paid close attention to Brown at practices and games and had a thorough understanding of it. He even knew the dozen signals that are given on the Visual Clue Freak.

By the time he finished, the players were so impressed they gave him an ovation. Brown couldn't contain his surprise. Then he used it to his advantage, telling the players, "Now there's an example of an ex-LSU football player—the guy couldn't play basketball because he wasn't smart enough—understanding the Freak Defense. If he can learn it, anybody can. That should be motivation for you guys. So let's really pay attention because this can help us down the road. It can help us a lot."

He went over some of the finer points as well as some theory behind the Freak. It took more than a half hour to cover every possible situation so they could begin practicing it. Brown was sure they could all master this defense. He could visualize it working against some of the powers they would have to play later on.

The C.J. File—I had heard about the Freak Defense when they went to the Final Four. When we got into it, there was so much to remember. When the ball goes here, you do this. And when the ball goes over there, you do that. I was confused. I guess I was freaked out. I know it must freak out the other team. It's got to keep them guessing all the time.

At pregame meal Saturday afternoon, Ron Abernathy showed the players video tapes of Florida. There was not much difference from the previous season, except the big men were even better and the backcourt was weaker without Vernon Maxwell. Abernathy stressed the importance of being physical inside.

Later, Abernathy met with Brown to make final decisions on the game plan. Brown thought they should play Schintzius like they did Will Perdue in their first victory over Vanderbilt the previous season. They held the league's most valuable player to eight points in that game, using a version of Brown's defense that he calls the Freak Zone. Abernathy agreed. It should work just as well against Schintzius.

The players learned of the defensive plan 45 minutes before tip-off. Brown explained that the defense would be effective against a big center with limited mobility like Schintzius. The plan called for Russell Grant to line up behind Chris Jackson, just above the free-throw line. That would set up a 1-1-3 zone with Ricky Blanton, Richard Krajewski and Wayne Sims low.

When Florida brought the ball down court, Jackson had to pick up the ballhandler and Grant was to front Schintzius on the high post, allowing Krajewski to play behind him. Blanton and Sims had to guard Chatman and Davis on the baseline. It left somebody open on the perimeter, but Florida was such a poor shooting team from outside, hitting only 25 percent from three-point range, that Brown thought LSU could get away with letting the guards shoot from outside.

If Schintzius set up at the low post, the defense would automatically change. Either Blanton or Sims would front him and Krajewski would play behind him. Again, it was designed to keep the ball away from him.

Brown hoped it would confuse Florida for a few minutes and give LSU a chance to get off to a good start. This was his team's first road game of the season, and there were still lingering memories of the Louisiana Tech loss and McNeese State blowup. He didn't want his players to get behind early and get flustered.

Offensively, they were told to fast break. There would be no walking the ball down court. On every possession, they were to force the action. Brown and Abernathy had seen on the tapes that the Florida players didn't hustle back on defense. That was how Illinois and Florida State got to them. That was LSU's best chance.

To complement his game plan, Brown had plenty of motivational material. He started by writing "20-5" on the board with a long, squeaky piece of chalk.

Then he told them what it meant. "After tonight, you will have beaten Florida 20 out of the last 25 times that we played them. We won 15 straight against them at one stretch. Many times, we didn't have good matchups, supposedly. We weren't supposed to be able to match up physically, but we matched up mentally with a team attitude that we knew we would win. And I feel that same way now. Ratings don't mean anything. Throw those out the window. This team was rated number one in the country by SPORT magazine. They've been in the Top 20 in every poll."

Actually, SPORT magazine and many other publications ranked Florida number one in the SEC. The Gators had been picked from 12th to 18th in the national polls. Brown was known to exaggerate in order to help his own cause. The point was well taken by his players. Florida had a quality team.

"We weren't ranked by anybody, but we know where we're headed," he continued. "But we are going to beat this team tonight. I am so sure of it." Then he wrote "1-0" on the board. "That's going to be our record after tonight in the Southeastern Conference."

Then he closed with more encouragement. "Guys, this is the most important thing: let's send a message to the league. They think we're dead. They think we're buried. Let's show them tonight we are not dead! We can win this league. Now let's go out and show it!"

After the players went out for their final warmups, Brown remained in the locker room. He doesn't like to go out early at road games, because the fans often taunt him or even throw debris at him. He doesn't like any distractions.

During warmups, Grant discovered he couldn't bend his left knee. An old injury had been aggravated by all the spills he had been taking. He was in pain, but told no one. Nothing would keep him from playing.

Jackson was a little tense about playing his first road game, especially after ESPN announcer Bill Rafftery came up to him and said,

"You're going to get 50 tonight, Chris." Jackson just shook his head and continued warming up.

Meanwhile, Brown spent the final minutes chatting with his friend Curry Kirkpatrick, who was gathering information for a feature story on Schintzius to appear in Sports Illustrated. They discussed some of the crazy antics Schintzius had staged during his three years at Florida. The latest incident had occurred that fall when he attacked another student with a tennis racket outside a Gainesville bar. Schintzius was suspended and missed the team's opening trip to the Great Alaska Shootout, but was now back in top form.

"I am really worried about Schintzius tonight," Brown told Kirkpatrick. "He could absolutely destroy us. How big is he anyway? He looks 7-4. We don't have anybody who can guard him. All we have is Richard Krajewski, and he's not really very good yet. But we've got a special little defense to use against him. It's got to work."

The Freak Zone worked even better than Brown had hoped. Schintzius, corralled at the high post by Grant and Krajewski and occasionally Jackson, was not a factor in the first half. The Florida guards were chunking wide-open shots off the rim. Blanton and Jackson were putting on a tremendous show of fast-break basketball for the ESPN audience and an astonished Florida crowd.

Blanton made nine of his first 10 shots. Jackson was warming up for his finest hour, scoring 22 points in the first half. They kept beating the Gators down the floor. In one stretch, they scored 12 unanswered points. Florida finally got a basket. Then LSU ran off another streak of 10 consecutive points. The lead bulged to as many as 26, and the Tigers never got out of the Freak Zone. Just before halftime, Florida made a brief run, but LSU still was in control at 54-37.

Blanton gathered his teammates in the locker room before the coaches arrived and urged them not to let up. "We had a great half, but we've got to keep it going. Let's have 20 more minutes. Twenty more minutes!" Several others joined in, chanting "Twenty more minutes! Twenty more minutes!"

Jackson shook his fist and shouted out to no one in particular. "Man, we've got them. We've got them. Now let's finish it! We've come too far and we've worked too hard. We've come too far to let it get away now."

Just then, Brown walked in. He had nothing to be angry about on this night. The team had performed splendidly and was on the verge of a major upset.

He told them he wanted the same effort in the second half. "We cannot let up. They can't possibly win this game if you play as hard as you did in the first half. And maybe we can give an ounce more. They got timid in the first half. We didn't. We played well. But we can play better."

He stressed the importance of the first few minutes of the second half. It was their chance to knock out the Gators and put the game out of reach. But on the other side of the arena, Norm Sloan was giving one of his more emotional halftime speeches. Schintzius later said the talk changed their attitude in a hurry. "Coach got on us pretty good," he said. "He really got our attention. We knew what we had to do to get back in it."

Getting the ball low on offense and getting back on defense was the only way the Gators could come back, and they began to do it. Schintzius led a strong comeback. LSU held them off for a few minutes, but eventually Florida's size began to take its toll. The Tigers got into foul trouble and had to abandon the Freak, instead going with a 2-3 matchup zone. Krajewski fouled out with more than 14 minutes left. His replacement, Vernel Singleton, soon got into trouble and joined him on the bench with five fouls. That left Geert Hammink as their only chance to hold off Schintzius and Co.

Hammink did a respectable job against the Florida center, even though Schintzius capped a 9-0 streak by driving past him for a layup to pull Florida within three points just before the midway point of the half.

On the next break in the action, Brown called Jackson to the bench and gave him some simple, but timely instructions. "We need you to take more shots. Just keep shooting," Brown told him.

In the final 10 minutes, Jackson put on an exquisite show. He either shook himself free for a three-pointer from the top of the key or drove for a shorter jumper. In the process, he fouled out three different defenders, hit eight of 10 shots and even drew applause from the Florida fans. By the time the smoke cleared, he had established an NCAA freshman scoring record and arena record with 53 points.

The C.J. File—I was shocked. I never thought I'd be able to come out and play like this. Of course, I dreamed about things like this. But I didn't really think it would happen so fast.

Jackson had led LSU to a 111-101 victory that sent several messages. First, it told the conference and the nation that the Tigers weren't dead. Also, it told everyone that LSU had a phenomenal freshman. Finally, it reassured those 13 players and their never-say-die coach that their dreams could come true.

With the Freak Defense, some magnificent play from Jackson, lots of hard work and belief in themselves, they showed they could beat a team like Florida on the road. From that night on, they were convinced they could win anywhere against anybody.

Why did the Freak work so well against Florida? There were two major reasons: the element of surprise and the fact that the Gators were not a balanced team. Since LSU had not used any form of the Freak in its first four games, Florida was expecting a matchup zone, man-to-man and fullcourt press. The Florida guards wanted to work the ball inside in the first half, but everywhere they looked, there were two defenders. The outside shot was wide open. They just couldn't hit it, which was what LSU had expected.

After the game, Jackson went back on the court with Brown and Blanton for an ESPN interview. Strangely enough, several hundred Florida fans, primarily students, had remained in the stands hoping to catch another glimpse of the young phenom. When he walked over to the ESPN cameras, the fans started applauding.

The C.J. File—I thought they were going to boo me at first. Then when they started cheering, I didn't know what to do. I wasn't sure if I should wave to them or not. It was a good feeling, especially because we won.

The enthusiasm generated by the victory over Florida lasted through a 10-day break for final exams. There was an upbeat mood as the Tigers practiced intermittently between exams. Their next basketball test would come against unbeaten, fifth-ranked Illinois. Before that, they had a pop quiz against Tennessee-Martin that figured to be solved in a hurry.

During that week, Jackson was besieged with interview requests. While he was trying to study for his first finals as a college student, he was being sought by newspapers, television and radio stations and magazines. Sports Illustrated named him national Player of the Week. He had scored 124 points in three games and set scoring records in the only two college arenas in which he had played. Kirkpatrick and the rest of the SI staff were keeping an eye on him for a major feature story. But they were beaten to the punch by NBC, ABC, CBS and

ESPN, which taped in-depth reports on him. Kirkpatrick, doubling as a network sportscaster, did the Jackson report for CBS.

Jackson immediately moved into the race for the national scoring title. After five games, he was averaging 32.4 points, two points behind national leader Hank Gathers of Loyola-Marymount. But a scoring title and all the media attention didn't really interest Jackson. He was tuned in on the team goals.

The C.J. File—It's great people are interested in me. But it takes up so much of my time. I guess you have to do it. It's a part of playing basketball. I'm dealing with it pretty well. I try not to get to the point I'm fed up with it. When I was a kid, I dreamed about being interviewed by TV stations. Now it's part of my life.

Part of the excitement of witnessing a new superstar was trying to give him a nickname. Maravich would not have been quite the same without Pistol Pete. Earvin never would have been a household word, but Magic worked perfectly for Johnson.

The possibilities for Jackson were endless. Many liked Action Jackson. Others preferred Maravich-like nicknames such as Re-Pete and the Chris-tal Pistol. His teammates still called him C.J., and he remained Doc to his Gulfport friends. But if it were up to him, Chris would do just fine.

Meanwhile, local interest in the team surged. The school was selling thousands of dollars worth of tickets every day. The Illinois game was nearly sold out. There had not been this much interest in LSU basketball so early in the schedule since the 1980-81 season.

Brown's bold prediction about season tickets was on target. Fans were snatching them up for next season. There were indications that the Assembly Center would fill up this season as well.

Even tickets for the Tennessee-Martin game were selling quickly. Three days before the game, there was some major excitement in the Assembly Center that the fans never heard about.

It was Saturday afternoon. Exams were finally over. Now Brown had to get his players concentrating on basketball again, so they had an hour-long scrimmage. With Grant out, Mouton was back working with the first team. He was having one of his better offensive days, hitting several long jumpers in a row. But defensively, things weren't going well for him. Brown had yelled at him several times.

About midway through the practice, the breaking point came. Mouton was supposed to be guarding Kyle McKenzie, but McKenzie pulled what it is known as a "snowbird." That occurs when one player stays back on defense, so if there is a missed shot he will be wide open for a layup at the other end of the court. Brown didn't see McKenzie sloughing off on defense. All he saw was an easy layup against the first team, and in particular against Mouton.

That was the last straw. "Get out of here, Lyle," Brown screamed. "You're done for the day. You haven't done anything all day anyway. Just get out of here. Go take a shower. I don't want to see you again today."

Everyone stopped in his tracks. Brown had often disciplined his players by making them run sprints, but he had never kicked a player out of practice. Mouton didn't know what to do. He thought about trying to explain what had happened, but he knew that would only make Brown more furious. So he walked off the court and went to the locker room. But had he done the right thing? Should he go back upstairs and tell Brown he wouldn't let it happen again?

Mouton made another mistake. Several of the assistant managers were in the locker room, and he asked for their advice. One of them suggested that Mouton would be better off trying to return to practice. So he did.

When Brown saw him, he abruptly halted practice and told him face-to-face: "Lyle, if you're not out of here in exactly one minute, you will never play here again." Mouton turned and left the court. This time, he went to call his parents and tell them he was coming home to Lafayette. He wasn't sure if he would ever come back. At that moment, he didn't think he would.

When Mouton got home and discussed the situation, he reconsidered his decision. His father, Lyle Sr., convinced him that it was always easier to run away from problems in life. He encouraged his son to face up to this one.

On Monday, Mouton's parents went to see Brown and reaffirmed what they had told him during their son's recruitment, that "he's your boy now, and we know you're going to make him a man." Later, Mouton met with Brown and said he was ready to play Dale's style of basketball. Brown agreed to let him back on the team, but with the understanding he was now the 13th man and had to work his way back up the roster.

So with Grant limping and Mouton demoted, LSU was short-handed for Tennessee-Martin. It got even worse when Jackson and several reserves came down with the flu. Brown considered resting Jackson to make sure he would be ready for Illinois in two days. But Jackson insisted he felt well enough to play. So he went out and spear-headed a transition game that cut apart Tennessee-Martin and set several school and arena records.

Even though Jackson scored only 13 points in the first half, the Tigers raced to a 65-36 lead and the victory was assured. He played briefly in the second half and finished with 21 points. Blanton and Singleton had career-high totals of 37 and 25 points, and the Tigers scored on almost every possession on their way to a 128-89 victory. Tennessee-Martin stayed somewhat close on the excellent shooting of point guard Mike Hansen, a freshman from Madrid, Spain.

Jackson, Grant and Dennis Tracey took turns trying to contain Hansen, but to no avail. All he needed was a half step to free himself for long jump shots. He easily outgunned Jackson, scoring 31 of his game-high 40 points in the second half.

Brown never thought about going to the Freak to contain Hansen. He didn't like to give up that many points to anybody, but the game was well in hand. Besides, the Freak works best when used sparingly. He would save it for days when it was really needed. One of those was right around the corner.

13

Blood Bath

Ricky's Diary, December 22—This one is really big for us. We're pretty fired up right now. We had the win over Florida. Now we've got finals out of the way. We really want to play a team like Illinois. The guys are really eager. They took it personally when people counted us out. I think they want to prove something.

Everyone's spirits were high for the Illinois game. After all, they had won three in a row, beaten a quality opponent in Florida and shown just how good they could be. Maybe even good enough to beat a major power.

Illinois was unbeaten and ranked fifth in the country. But even Coach Lou Henson admitted his team had not been tested on the road. There was reason to believe, especially for Dale Brown, that the LSU Tigers could pull the upset. This was his kind of game.

On Wednesday, LSU and Illinois had to practice in the basement gym, because the arena was being set up for graduation exercises.

LSU had the court first. Brown didn't want to practice long, since the Tigers had played the night before. So he used most of the practice time to talk about Illinois. He had been mulling this game since the victory over Florida. The Tigers were 4-2, and an upset of Illinois would be a major step. He compared it to playing Oklahoma the previous year when the Sooners were unbeaten, ranked third in the nation by The Associated Press and ranked number one by The Sporting News. But the unranked Tigers had knocked them off. They could do the same thing to Illinois, Brown assured his players.

His words echoed in the small gym. He had letters to share with the players. He read most of a Sports Illustrated article detailing the rags-to-riches story of Orel Hershiser. This team was just like the Dodger pitcher.

"If you play hard and do exactly what we tell you, we will beat Illinois," Brown told his players. "We can't match up with them man-to-man, but our team can match up with them. Our team has a lot of heart. They've got the All-Americans, but we've got something more important than that. I feel an upset coming on. I just feel it. We're really relaxed. We're going to play hard, and we're going to beat this team."

The date was December 21. Brown pointed out that beating Illinois would be a wonderful Christmas present and great way to get ready for LSU's trip to Hawaii that would begin the day after Christmas.

Because there were 12 days between the Florida and Illinois games, the LSU coaches were treating the latter like an NCAA Tournament contest. Not only did Brown design a special defense to use against the Fighting Illini, but he also actually worked on it in practice. In most situations, he would have just gone over it on game day and reviewed it in his pregame talk. But he wanted to make sure his young team was well prepared to execute another variation of the Freak Defense. The Tigers would press fullcourt and fall back into a combination of zone and man-to-man.

Ricky Blanton, Wayne Sims and Richard Krajewski would play a triangular zone low, and Chris Jackson and Dennis Tracey would play man-to-man on the perimeter. The intent was to neutralize Illinois' powerful inside game. The Illini often started a lineup of five players 6-6 or taller. They didn't have a true big man, but all of their starters "played big." LSU would be giving away several inches of height and many more inches of jumping ability to Marcus Liberty, Kenny Battle, Nick Anderson, Lowell Hamilton and Kendall Gill.

Yet, Illinois wasn't taking LSU lightly. Henson had known Brown for almost 30 years and respected his flare for the unexpected. After watching a tape of the LSU-Florida game, Henson had no idea what kind of defense Brown might try on his team.

Henson was also concerned about the momentum LSU seemed to be building. "We have a veteran team, and Dale's team is so young," he said before taking his team through Wednesday's practice. "He has done a tremendous job with this team. I have always respected the job he has done down here. I think many people in this part of the country take him for granted and don't appreciate the great job he has done. He is a tremendous coach, and everyone in the country realizes that. This team is a very good example. Look what they did against Florida. This is a young team, and he has them playing like a veteran team."

The two coaches chatted while the Tigers left the court and the Illini began their warmups. Brown didn't tell Henson, but the size and conditioning of the Illinois players caught Dale's attention immediately. They were a sleek, powerfully built group of athletes who seemed almost interchangeable. Later, in his office with Ron Abernathy, Brown said he couldn't remember seeing such impressive-looking players. But he still expected to beat them.

The next night, he came armed with more letters, some newspaper clippings and lots of inspirational thoughts. This was serious business. He had to get his players to rise to the occasion, or they would be in trouble.

One columnist had written that Illinois would beat LSU by the same margin that LSU had defeated Tennessee-Martin two days earlier. Brown, in his locker room speech, tried to convince his players that could not happen. "This game will not be decided on talent. It's what is in here." He pounded his right hand over his heart. "That is why you're on this team, and they're on their team. The game will be decided by who plays the hardest for 40 minutes. I don't gamble. But if I were betting on this game, I'd bet whoever plays the hardest on that 94 by 50 court for 40 solid minutes will win this game. I think we all know who that will be."

With Russell Grant out, most likely for the rest of the season, Tracey got the first start of his career. His assignment was to guard Nick Anderson, a slick, 6-6 guard-forward. It was the perfect example of what a physical mismatch LSU faced. Anderson could take the 6-1 Tracey inside or just shoot over him. There was nothing Tracey could do to stop him.

Illinois had similar height or quickness advantages at every position. LSU's only chance was to bother the Illini with the Freak Defense and try to out-run them on offense.

Jackson carried the Tigers early, despite being guarded by Gill, one of the best defensive guards in the country. Often, Gill needed help on the flashy freshman. LSU was running on offense and took the lead in the first half, which ignited the near-sellout crowd of more than 14,000. It looked like the Tigers might go into the locker room with an advantage. But Illinois, which shot 69 percent in the half, mainly on layups and slam dunks, surged in the final minutes to take a 61-51 lead.

Brown knew he had to make a defensive change. But what? His team had already given up 100 points or more to Oral Roberts, Louisiana Tech and Florida. They just weren't a very good defensive team. Their only chance was to fall back into a zone and try to eliminate the easy baskets inside.

Brown knew his players could sense the game slipping away. So he did his best to recharge them at halftime. He showed little emotion, other than raising his fist a few times. His objective was to calm his inexperienced team and regroup them for a second-half run.

"They can't play defense against you. You guys scored 51 points," Brown said, trying to turn the situation around. "This game will be won in the second half, not the first. If you get this team down to the last four minutes, I promise you they are going to choke. They're undefeated. They're nationally ranked. They're playing us, and we're not supposed to be worth a damn. They will break in the clutch."

Close was the operative word. They had to be within striking distance to put any pressure on Illinois. That never happened. The Illini ran away in the first five minutes of the second half. Mercifully, Henson pulled his starters just past the midway mark. Jackson had fouled out by then, sealing the Tigers' fate.

Brown left most of his starters in until the end, trying to salvage something. They did manage to score 100 points. But the Illini set a school record with 127.

If there had been another game to play that week, Brown would not have been too hard on the team. But the Tigers would not play again until their Hawaii trip. For that reason, he wanted to give them something to think about. He was also disturbed, because they seemed to let down once Illinois went ahead by 20. That was one thing Brown would not tolerate. He stomped into the locker room and sat down with his right hand over his face.

The C.J. File—When he just sat there, I started to worry. I could tell everyone was worried. Then when he finally got up, I thought, "Boy, we're in big trouble now." He started talking real calm. But I knew he was going to start fussing. My heart was pounding.

It wasn't a Brownout, but it was close. He roared his dissatisfaction. "Guys, you quit out there. You gave up! You could have won that game. But you didn't have the guts to keep fighting for it. We didn't have five guys who wanted to win. But we're going to find them, if our coaches have to put on uniforms."

He stopped in his tracks and began to slam his hands together. He thought about what winning this game could have meant to this young team. He considered what might happen down the road if they didn't play better. Finally, he decided they needed something to think about over the holidays.

"When you go home," he said, slowly looking around at each player, "I want you guys to have the worst night you've ever had in your life. I hope you can't sleep at all. I hope your night is terrible. Just keep thinking about this game." Again, he paused to reflect. "I do hope you have a nice Christmas. But when you come back Christmas night, we're going to strap on our jocks and practice harder than you've ever practiced in your life. It's going to be a blood bath. Be prepared. It will be a blood bath!"

Even the younger players knew what was in store for them. Brown would make them practice non-stop for at least two hours, and then Ron Abernathy would make them run wind sprints until they could no longer get up and down the court. It was not the Christmas present they had wanted.

After Brown was finished, the team joined hands and recited the Lord's Prayer. There were some private prayers said as well. Brown left the locker room by himself, refusing to take anyone to the press conference. He asked the media not to interview any of the players, because they were in a hurry to catch flights or drive home for their two-day Christmas break.

At the press conference, Brown painted a much different picture. He shouldered most of the blame himself. He called it an architectural problem, saying, "When you see these buildings fall down in Mexico City, I don't think you can blame the workers that put those suckers up. This is the first time I've ever felt like a failure at LSU. I've been disappointed in myself a lot of times. I don't think I was as smart as I should have been. I made a mistake, or just wasn't in the game like I should or was immature and concentrated on the officials. I felt like a failure tonight.''

Brown said there was a five-minute stretch in the second half when his team seemed to throw in the towel. He accepted responsibility for that and said his players would never give up again.

Later that night, he finally simmered down. He stayed up until 4:30, replaying the game in his mind. His conclusion was that Illinois, with all its experience, talent and depth, was almost unbeatable, especially for a tenderfoot of a team like his own. He realized he had been too hard on his players after the game. He also decided a brutal practice would serve no purpose, other than to tire them before the long flight to Hawaii, where they would play Morehead State, Chaminade and Nebraska in the Chaminade New Year's Classic. All three were beatable if LSU was rested and ready to play. Then the Tigers had to make another long trip to Maryland for a fourth game in six days.

Of course, none of the players knew what Brown was thinking. They expected him to come back as angry as he had been after the Illinois game.

Jackson went home to Gulfport to spend Christmas with his family and visit some friends. Brown's warning was lodged in C.J.'s thoughts.

The C.J. File—I wasn't going to enjoy the time off anyway, because we had lost. But after he told us it would be a blood bath, I really couldn't enjoy it. I'd be home doing something fun, and then I'd think about what he told us. I knew we were in for it. Our practices can get pretty tough anyway.

In Miami, Blanton experienced the same difficulty. He was sure Brown would carry out his threat and run everyone into the ground. In previous years, he had always followed through on threats of punishment.

Blanton told friends, ''We're going to have three-hour practices every day when we go to Hawaii.'' He didn't do much over the holiday, choosing to rest for the task ahead.

It was even tougher for Mouton. He didn't know if he would ever get another chance for some significant playing time. He might be buried on the bench for the rest of the season.

Most of the players returned to campus late in the afternoon on Christmas day. The practice wasn't scheduled until 9, so Blanton had a late flight into Baton Rouge and was the last one to get back, about a half hour before practice. He carefully watched Brown and was relieved to see his cheery mood. But even Blanton didn't anticipate what was about to happen.

A team meeting was called in the locker room. There was nothing unusual about that. Brown varied the routine, holding meetings just about anywhere. The players fully expected to get blasted again. Instead, they got an apology.

"First of all, we're not going to kill you in practice tonight," Brown said. The players were relieved and amazed. "I made a mistake the other night. And when you make a mistake, you should be man enough to admit it. I overreacted, no question about it. I apologize to everyone of you. I should not have lost my temper like I did. And I said some things on the bench that I regret. We should never use that kind of language. I promise you that I won't any more. We're going to practice for an hour, and that will be it."

Blanton had never seen Brown make such a change in attitude. He was elated, his younger teammates even more so. Now they could actually look forward to going to Hawaii.

Brown also announced there would be changes in the lineup, changes in the offense and changes in the defense. He was, in effect, starting over. The Illinois game had demonstrated that LSU had to have more athletes in the lineup. That meant Mouton and Vernel Singleton would replace Krajewski and Tracey.

Offensively, there were times when the players had looked confused. Now they would run only two offenses: the regular pressure release against man-to-man defense and a spread against zone defenses. On defense, they would play either a man-to-man or matchup zone. The Freak was abandoned, at least for the time being. They just weren't experienced enough to make the split-second adjustments.

After going over the new plans, Brown offered some encouragement. He pointed out that the 1986-87 team was also 4-3 at this point of the season and went all the way to the Final Eight. He told them they could do the same thing.

"First, we're going to win all four of these games on the road. We want to have a good time. It will be good to spend time together, and we will be a better team because of it. But we're also going to win four games and come back here 8-3.''

Throughout practice that night, Blanton kept reminding his teammates of just that, that they could be 8-3 by the end of the week. They were having a crisp, productive workout until there was a mishap on a loose ball. Blanton and Singleton dove for it, and Singleton's elbow rammed into Blanton's face, breaking his nose. It wasn't bad enough to require immediate surgery. That could be taken care of after the season. But it would impede his breathing until the swelling went down, which would take about a week.

So LSU left on its road trip with a different lineup, new offensive and defensive schemes and their captain injured. There was reason to doubt that Brown could pull this one off.

On Monday morning, they boarded a commercial flight just after sunrise and spent most of the day on planes and in airports. Because of that, they didn't practice when they finally arrived in Honolulu.

In addition to the team, there was a large traveling party. Brown believes such trips are valuable as an opportunity for the team to grow closer. To further emphasize the family nature of the program, he invited more than a dozen friends of LSU basketball. As promised, Jamie Roth and his family were special guests. Jamie was feeling fairly strong, and the excitement of going to Hawaii with the team perked him up even more. This was designated as the wives' trip, which meant the school would pay for the coaches' wives to join them. Vonnie still wasn't feeling quite up to traveling, but Cynthia Abernathy, Leslie Carse and Cindy Childers gladly accepted the invitation. Former athletic director Carl Maddox also made the trip, along with Father Bayhi and George Eames.

They had a free day on Tuesday. That gave everyone time for sightseeing and fun on the beach. They were staying at the Turtle Bay Hilton, one of the more exclusive hotels on Honolulu's north shore. Late in the afternoon, they took time out to practice.

The C.J. File—It's beautiful in Hawaii. I like the beach and the ocean. But the best thing is being together like this for a whole week. We've been on a lot of walks. We're just a lot closer. It's good to have everyone with us. It's like a big family.

On Wednesday, their first-round opponent was Morehead State, which is Abernathy's alma mater. He had seen them practice in the fall when he went there to receive a distinguished alumnus award. He wasn't impressed with what he saw.

Nonetheless, Morehead hung close for much of the game. The tournament was being played in the old Bloch Arena on the Pearl Harbor base. Only a few hundred fans, mostly naval personnel, were in the stands. It wasn't an atmosphere conducive to playing great basketball. Brown took a low-key approach as well, deciding that the coaching staff would wear warmup outfits, rather than suits.

But the Tigers' new lineup performed exceptionally well together and got solid support from Geert Hammink. But they didn't put the game away until the final minutes. Mouton and Singleton combined to hit 10 of 15 shots and score 21 points in the 101-88 victory. Jackson led with 30 points, and Blanton got 15, despite the broken nose.

In other years, Brown would have chastised his players for letting Morehead stay in it so long. Not this time. "You gave it some real effort," he said afterward. Then he wrote the word on the chalkboard. "E-F-F-O-R-T. That is what won this game for you," he said. "You really fought hard on the boards. Vernel and Geert, I thought you really did a good job. Lyle, you helped us. We can turn this thing around with that kind of effort. I love each one of you guys. You are great guys. But you've got to play like that every night, not just when you feel like it."

Next on LSU's agenda was a meeting with Chaminade, the giant-killer of the islands. The Silverswords have staged many major upsets, most notably knocking off Virginia when it had Ralph Sampson and was ranked number one. This Chaminade team was capable of such feats and had the added incentive of coach Merv Lopes announcing he would retire at the end of the season. The game had been rescheduled for 8 p.m. to accommodate Chaminade fans. And because of delays in the first two games of the day, it didn't actually start until after 9.

Some players were uptight in the locker room because of the delay. But Brown went to work to relax them. "We are going to play well tonight. I can just feel it. We didn't have a good game last night. We can play much better than that. Let's start it tonight." Then he reviewed some adjustments on offense and defense.

When the game finally started, Jackson showed early that he didn't have his usual rhythm. But Blanton and Wayne Sims picked up the scoring slack, and Singleton and Mouton had another good game. They stretched the lead to 47-38 at halftime and again overcame a second-half challenge to win comfortably. Blanton scored 34 points to lead the 94-79 victory.

Once again, Brown was pleased with their intensity. They could have played better. They also could have crumbled in the second half. Overall, it was a step in the right direction.

Brown spoke briefly because it was late and they had to play Nebraska at 1 p.m. Friday. They had a long drive back to the north shore and had to get some rest. "That was a good job tonight," he told them. "But we're going to have to play even harder. I mean we can win 12 or 13 games like that. But that ain't enough. Nobody here wants to settle for that. We've got to turn it up even more, starting tomorrow. Nebraska is a darn good team. We have to turn it up a notch."

Maddox was even more impressed with the team by this time. "Here, we were in an old gym at Pearl Harbor, there weren't 200 people in the stands, and these boys were playing like they were in Madison Square Garden in front of 20,000 fans," he said. "Dale's teams have always hustled, but I really like this team. They're so much fun to watch. And they're just a well-behaved, happy group. They really made little Jamie feel like part of the team."

Since Nebraska had also beaten Chaminade and Morehead, this game would be for the tournament championship. The Cornhuskers had an inside game that could hurt LSU. They had 7-2 sophomore Rich King at center and two strong forwards in Pete Manning and Richard Van Poelgeest. They lacked only speed and consistent backcourt play.

But Eric Johnson, the younger brother of the Detroit Pistons' Vinnie Johnson, and Ray Richardson both played well against LSU. The Tigers used their transition game and some hot shooting by Blanton to take a 16-point lead midway through the first half. But they couldn't hold it, and Nebraska pulled within 56-51 at halftime.

Just before the half ended, the Cornhuskers got an easy breakaway basket because Hammink didn't get back on defense. Brown blasted him on the way to the locker room. Dale was angry primarily because they had blown a big lead. After he gathered himself and talked to his assistants, he realized his mistake.

"Geert, I apologize for talking to you the way I did," he said in the locker room. "I embarrassed you, and I was wrong. We're a family, and we're going to keep everything to ourselves. We are going to win this game, but it's going to take some better defense. We gave them 51 points. We need to cut that in half."

That didn't happen. Nebraska began to jam the ball inside to King and Manning for layups and short jumpers. Before long, the Cornhuskers had taken the lead and LSU seemingly could do nothing to stop them. The game was slipping away in a hurry. Nebraska built the lead to 86-80 and had the ball with less than three minutes left. Then LSU came up with the play of the season, scoring six points in one second.

LSU went to a fullcourt press, Tracey running step-for-step with Johnson. Tracey reached in and tipped the ball away. Then he tried to break away for a layup. Johnson grabbed him by the arm to try to stop him, but Tracey switched to his left hand and layed the ball in. An intentional foul was called, giving LSU the basket, two free throws and possession of the ball. Tracey sank one of the two free throws to make it 86-83 with 2:09 left. On the inbounds play, Blanton passed to Jackson, who hit a baseline jumper and was fouled by Johnson. C.J. converted the three-point play to tie the game at 86 with 2:08 left and give LSU its sixth point in one second. Moments later, Jackson hit a 15-foot jumper that proved to be the game-winner. Nebraska scored one point in the final three minutes of the 90-87 loss.

The LSU players celebrated wildly, but only briefly. They had to get dressed for a flight back to the states. Brown even kept it short. "I would like to compliment you for the way you played today. We just ran out of gas late in the first half. But what we did at the end was almost impossible. Dennis, that was a tremendous play you made. Chris, you came through for us again. We've won three. Now we need to get the fourth at Maryland."

Tracey had become the defensive stopper that Brown needed so desperately. And to think Brown wasn't going to have tryouts for walk-ons until Tracey changed his mind with a gripping letter:

"Dear Coach Brown, I realize that I am not a first team All-American wanting to be on your team. But I do feel that I possess something that many players really don't care about. Two of those most important things are defense and intensity, something your teams have always had much pride in.

"Even with intensity, I may not be able to score 30 points or win games for you. But I can promise you that I will contribute every day with effort and intensity. Coach, I learned back in high school that with desire, effort, heart, and God, that you can accomplish anything.

With this attitude, I have been able to accomplish many things. However, it seems now that I have come to the end of the road.

"Coach, I am not asking you for a handout, rather I am asking you for a chance. A chance to prove to you that I can contribute and help your team be successful. I feel that with a chance I can show you what you're looking for. I thank you for your time and would appreciate it if you would contact me with an answer. Thank you and may God bless you and your family. Sincerely, Dennis Tracey. P.S. Coach, my strong will and intense desire can make a difference. If you give me a chance, I'll prove it to you.''

Tracey had certainly done that. Now the team had an overnight flight to Dallas and then changed planes to go on to Washington, D.C. It was New Year's Eve, but everyone was too tired for any festivities. Besides, Brown gave them an 11 p.m. curfew, so they had to bring in the new year in their rooms. On Sunday, they spent New Year's Day practicing at Georgetown University and taking a tour of the nation's capital.

On game day Monday, both LSU and Maryland were travel-weary. The Terrapins had just finished runner-up to host Texas-El Paso in the Sun Bowl Tournament. Also, both LSU and Maryland were trying to get ready for a conference game on Wednesday. It would be survival of the fittest. This was the major bowl day for college football and a scant crowd of 6,819 showed up in Cole Field House for the early afternoon game.

The Tigers had another handicap to overcome. More than half of the team had diarrhea after eating Chinese food Sunday night. They were anxious to get the road trip over with and return home. But they were even more intent on completing their mission of four victories. Brown chose for the coaches to wear warmups again since they had been successful with them in Hawaii.

Jackson, coming off back-to-back sub-par games, was one of the players feeling ill. But he showed right away that he was ready to play. He scored 15 points in the first 18 minutes, leading LSU to a 39-26 halftime lead. Then he went almost 16 minutes without a field goal, and Maryland got back in the game. But C.J. picked it back up in the final minutes, scoring 15 of LSU's final 17 points, including the biggest basket of the game.

After Maryland's John Johnson tied the score at 77 with 18 seconds left, there was no doubt who would take the final shot for LSU. With Johnson in his face, Jackson hit a 17-foot jump shot to give LSU the final margin of victory. Maryland had a chance to tie in the final seconds, but Jackson closely guarded Greg Nared and forced him to shoot an air ball at the buzzer. The entire Maryland bench cried foul, but the officials made no call.

Exhausted from four games and weak from diarrhea, the Tigers were fortunate to pick up their fourth victory. They were even more fortunate to leave their locker room before one of the hot water pipes burst. One of the managers heard the noise and went back to find the steamy water spraying all over the place. They had escaped just in time.

There was yet another flight to catch, so Brown had made his points in a hurry. "I would just like to thank the Lord for somehow allowing us to get out of here with four wins. We're not done yet. We've won four. Now we're going to get the Southeastern Conference."

14

Contenders

Ricky's Diary, January 3—I'm really pleased with what we've done. We beat a couple of good teams in Nebraska and Maryland. Our goal was to win all four games, and we did it. That was a lot of traveling, and we're tired right now. But we finally did something we set out to do. That's really satisfying.

Everyone needed a day off after returning from the Maryland game and their 12,000-mile adventure. Dale Brown knew that, but he couldn't do anything about it. This was the day before their SEC home opener with Mississippi State. The travel-weary players went through a light workout Tuesday afternoon and turned their full attention to the SEC. They were 8-3. With a little more improvement, perhaps they could make a run at the league title.

If there were a good team for LSU to play after such a long trip, it would have to be Mississippi State. Brown had no trouble finding motivational angles for this game. Foremost on his list was last season. Mississippi State had won both regular-season games.

Also, Brown wasn't fond of the Bulldogs' coach, Richard Williams. They had engaged in a dispute at a summer basketball camp in the early '80s. Since then, their relationship was cool at best. Williams would not talk about Brown.

Another factor in what could be described as a tense rivalry was Chris Jackson. Mississippi State had continued to recruit him long after he made his intentions clear that he was going to LSU. Many people in Gulfport let Jackson know that he should have gone to Mississippi State. So he wanted to play well in this game. Vernel Singleton also had been recruited by Mississippi State.

In his pregame address, Brown assured his players that Mississippi State did not have their number. "Last year, going into the Mississippi State games, we had beaten them 17 out of the last 21 times. And for some reason, we just did not play well against them. We lost two games to them last year, the same way. They were games we should have won. And the one we lost here, 49-47, was one of the worst games we've ever played. We didn't get up for those two games."

That was a fatal mistake in the SEC. There are 10 teams in the league. It was once Kentucky and nine weak sisters. But in recent years, there has been great balance. Any team can win on a given night. Brown tried to make certain his players weren't going to fall victim to a third consecutive letdown against Mississippi State. This was undoubtedly the most dangerous position they had been in against the Bulldogs, because of the long road trip, fatigue and illness.

"What it comes down to is game preparation, teamwork, effort and getting yourself psychologically ready to play," Brown said. "We need to go out there and assert ourselves immediately. Immediately!"

What happened immediately was Brown lost his composure. On the first possession of the game, Mississippi State's Cameron Burns, a high-scoring forward who had been recruited by LSU, knocked Singleton out of the game with an elbow to the mouth. On his way down, Singleton heard Burns say, "Take that!" It took seven stitches to repair Singleton's lip.

Brown didn't hear Burns' comment. If he had, there would have been no telling what he might have done. Even so, he was in a rage and screamed for a flagrant foul. When he didn't get the call, he turned his attention to Burns, yelling that it was a cheap shot. His fury never wavered.

Meanwhile, Jackson and Blanton got off to a miserable start. Blanton was scoreless for the half. Jackson was on his way to a career-high 17 missed shots.

The C.J. File—I was so excited. I wanted this game so bad. I started rushing myself. I was trying to do too much at once. I knew I was doing that. But being so excited, I couldn't help it.

Mississippi State's fast start complicated the problem. The Bulldogs were hot, especially sophomore guard Doug Hartsfield, who went on to score a career-high 25 points, missing only three times all night.

Still, LSU trailed by only six points going into the final minutes of the first half. But Brown was so enraged that he pulled all of his starters except Wayne Sims. In a matter of minutes, the deficit grew to sixteen, and the Tigers were in serious trouble.

During the outburst, Brown went down the bench to shout at Blanton. "Ricky, you got beat back down the court. I can't believe that. If you don't start playing defense, if you don't start helping us, you're going to be here for the rest of the night. I don't care what happens."

At halftime, Mississippi State led 54-39, and Brown didn't hold much back. He was careful not to shake up Jackson or Singleton. That meant he had to vent his anger on Blanton, Sims and Mouton. "You guys might as well have stayed home tonight," he bellowed. "You didn't do a thing out there. We're going to find five players. I don't know who they are. But we are going to find them."

All the makings of a Brownout were there. Blanton was determined to do everything he could to prevent it. His teammates could sense the urgency to play well in the second half, and they did just that.

Despite falling behind by 19 in the early minutes, they dominated the second half just like Mississippi State had dictated the first. Jackson, though still not hitting from outside, began penetrating for layups and close-in shots. He was on his way to a game-high 30 points. Blanton heated up offensively and scored 10.

LSU kept chipping into the lead, getting closer and closer as the final minutes ticked away. Finally, the Tigers moved within a point of the lead in the last minute and worked the ball around for a potential game-winning basket. They wanted a high-percentage shot from 15 feet or closer. Brown had just reminded them of that during a timeout. But when Blanton got the ball on the wing, 20 feet away from the basket, he felt confident of making a three-pointer. The ball bounced off the rim. LSU had to foul, and Mississippi State won 87-84.

The players were aching from the defeat. It was their third last-second loss at home.

As usual, Brown was last to enter the locker room. But instead of standing, he took a seat next to Abernathy on the larger of the two couches. He crossed his legs and sat perfectly still, staring at the carpet for about five minutes—what seemed like an eternity to the players.

When he finally got up to talk, he crossed the room to where Blanton was sitting. Blanton had barely glanced up at him before Brown began his harsh commentary. "Ricky, I can't believe you took that shot. I told everyone in the huddle not to take a three-pointer. You let us down!" His voice was already booming and he was almost nose-to-nose with his captain. "They call you Rambo. Shit, you ain't no Rambo."

A local publication had nicknamed him "Rambeau Blanton" for his courageous play over the course of four years. He had been featured on the cover of that publication, dressed in military fatigues, looking like he was ready to take Sylvester Stallone's role in the next "Rambo" movie. Blanton was proud of the picture, because he felt it stood for everything he believed in. It hurt him to hear Brown belittle that image.

Brown paced over by the drawing board. "See this damn poster on the wall?" He slammed his fist on the "Hard Work Pays Off" poster. Then he turned back to face Blanton. "You don't deserve to be on that poster. You haven't worked hard all night. How can you let yourself be on that poster if you aren't going to bust your ass? You ain't no Rambo. You're Cinderella. That's all you are. A damn Cinderella."

It didn't get any better for Blanton. The criticism continued right into the postgame press conference and radio show. Many of the LSU fans listening to the radio couldn't believe their ears. That couldn't really be Dale Brown berating Ricky Blanton. Blanton could do no wrong in the eyes of LSU fans. They never expected to hear Brown criticize his captain, the player who had been the heart and soul of the Tigers for so long. But he did.

Since Blanton took all the heat, the outburst couldn't really be considered a Brownout. Maybe a partial one. The other players were impressed, though. They knew if the captain got that kind of treatment, anyone could get it.

Even before he got home, Brown was feeling guilty for being so harsh. Then Vonnie and Robyn reminded him how much Blanton had done for LSU. "Are you expecting too much out of this team?" Vonnie asked. So often when he blew up, it took his wife's insight to bring him back to reality.

Suddenly, he came to grips with the fact that they had simply played a bad game. They were tired and sick. Those things can and will happen over the course of a long season. This was not one of his most talented teams. And Blanton was not his most talented player.

"I wish I hadn't used such demonstrative words," he told Vonnie. "I wish I would have been more reserved in the way I said things. I didn't mean to be a smart aleck. I shouldn't have said anything about Rambo. There's a difference between disagreeing and being disagreeable."

The next day, Brown called Blanton into his office for a personal meeting. He offered an apology and explained that he had lost his temper after Singleton got hurt. "I'm trying to do better, but I messed up this time," he said. Then they discussed how to correct the mistakes made against Mississippi State, particularly the lackluster start.

Later, at a team meeting, Brown said he had reviewed everything and realized he had made several mistakes. He should have set an earlier curfew the night before the game. But he had wanted to give the players a chance to see their families and friends, because they had been gone so long. He also planned to tighten up the visitation rules in the dorm on game days. The players were being distracted by too many visitors.

After that, Brown apologized to all the players. "Last night, I was not pleased with my performance in many ways," he said. "I was a smart ass to Ricky last night, and I apologize. I was angry at Ricky, because he didn't play hard at all in the first half. Not hard at all. But I recognize there are ways to be critical without being a smart ass. I got emotionally involved when Burns hit you, Vernel. You responded better as a teen-ager than I did as an adult. I wanted to punch his damn lights out. That is an immature attitude. So I lost a little bit of my responsibility."

Hearing their coach shoulder some of the blame made the loss a little more bearable for the players. They could have extended their winning streak to five games. They could have stayed in first place in the SEC with a 2-0 record. But they didn't. Now it was time to look ahead to Saturday's game against Auburn.

Brown expected to beat Auburn, but it was too early to tell just how bad Sonny Smith's team would be. Just ahead for LSU was its first major road trip, to Tennessee and Kentucky. It would be easy to look past Auburn. Brown wanted to make sure that didn't happen. LSU couldn't afford to lose another home game.

After resting on Thursday, the team came back for a light workout Friday afternoon. They were eager to make amends for the defeat. And Brown had refueled his motivational tanks. He called a meeting before practice and attempted to regroup the team.

His first topic was team goals. They were closing in on their first goal of 12 victories and halfway to their second goal of 16, which would clinch a winning season and an NIT bid. He reminded them how much they had already achieved and how good they could become. "We're an unselfish team. We have good chemistry. And we work hard. Those are the three most important assets that a team can have."

He also encouraged his players to set personal goals, particularly on defense. He challenged each of them to hold his man below his scoring average. If they could do that, they could beat any team. Certainly, Auburn would be no match.

Jackson and Blanton exploited Auburn's man-to-man defense in the early going and were both on their way to 30-point games. They put the game away in a matter of minutes, just like Brown wanted. But LSU's defense distressed him again. Despite a 22-point lead at halftime, they were giving up easy baskets to Matt Geiger, a slow, physically weak center.

When Johnny Jones informed Brown that they had given up nine put-backs in the lane, Dale almost slipped back into a shouting mode. But he caught himself and offered instruction instead of criticism.

They responded well, even though Geiger finished with 21 points. Their defense picked up significantly, and the offense continued to click. They broke the game open in short order and stretched the lead into the 30s before settling for a 104-77 victory. Brown was delighted, even with the defense.

Smith was even more impressed. He was amazed at how well LSU was playing.

"It doesn't matter what type of player Dale has, he puts them into a position that he is comfortable in," Smith said. "I think that is the key to his success. Whatever it takes to make that player good, he puts him into that position. It's just like a year ago he had Blanton flashing up into the high post, because that was needed on that team.

They don't need that on this team, so he put him on the wing, and Blanton responded unbelievably. He is just the master of putting people where they need to be.''

All of his players were beginning to find their spots on offense. Blanton got most of his points by running the left lane and getting lay-ups or short bank shots. Sims had developed two favorites: a turn-around jumper from the left baseline and a straight-on jumper from just to the left of the free-throw line. Singleton had developed a nice spin move in the lane and usually shot a bank shot from the right side. Mouton's favorite area was a long jumper from the right wing. Jackson got most of his baskets from the top of the key, particularly just to the right side.

Brown's theory evolved from his association with John Wooden, who believed in keeping things basic and honing those skills through repetition. Now that LSU's offense was almost where he wanted it, Brown focused on defense. It would be crucial to play good defense at Tennessee and Kentucky.

But while Tennessee coach Don DeVoe was busy getting his team ready for LSU, Brown took some time off. He relaxed around the house on Sunday. On Monday, he left practice early to fly to Pensacola, Florida, for a speaking engagement.

Most of Brown's speaking dates are in the offseason. He doesn't like to interrupt his schedule during the heart of the season, but this appointment fit well. In fact, the Pensacola Sports Association had re-scheduled its annual awards banquet from May to January to accommodate Brown. He planned to be traveling in May.

This appearance was arranged by Jerry Brown, a Pensacola attorney, LSU graduate and faithful Dale Brown fan (but no relation). He had heard Dale speak at another dinner and couldn't wait to get him for the PSA.

Upon his arrival, Brown went right to work trying to find out detailed information on the city's history, economy, environment, recreational interests and sports association. Within a half hour, he had assimilated enough data to personalize his speech. At the convention hall, he carefully noted some of the top award-winners so they could be included in his talk.

"I couldn't help but be impressed by all the awards given out tonight," Brown began. "But your final reward will be heartache and tears if you've cheated the man in the glass." His theme was looking into the mirror and learning to like what you see.

After getting the audience's attention, by mentioning all the positive things he had learned about the city, he shifted into the heart of his speech. "What I'd like to talk about tonight is something that has not changed in the 430 years since the Spanish first came to this shore. It never will change. There is no pill, prayer or magic prescription that you can go buy, beg, steal or borrow. It's the journey that we're on on this earth. And the journey is really no different for any of us. It doesn't make any difference if you've ever been to the Olympics. It doesn't make any difference if you're black, white, Jewish, Baptist, Catholic, female, male, 5-8 or 6-8. It's the journey that all of us don't need to get into a spaceship to find. It's our journey on earth. How to find peace, love, happiness and success.

"Now that rolls off the tongue easier than it's found. There's all kinds of talk shows. There's all kinds of books. How to do this, and how to do that. And yet almost none of those books, with the exception of one, has the answers in it."

Although he didn't name the book, most of the principles that he used in explaining how to find peace, love, happiness and success were taken from the Bible. For the next half hour, he went into detail on how to go about getting these things.

Many coaches offer similar speeches, but Brown is in great demand as a speaker for several reasons. His message, mixed with timely anecdotes, is thought-provoking, inspirational and entertaining. He knows how to relate it to his audience. His delivery is polished and powerful. Just like on a basketball court or in a crowded locker room, he takes charge and drives his points home. He is a showman, philosopher and psychologist. Over the course of his speech, most listeners are invigorated by his positive outlook and challenging theme.

The Pensacola audience of about 500 listened attentively and applauded enthusiastically throughout the 50-minute speech. Brown got so enthusiastic that he was shouting and waving his arms. He hit the light on the podium and knocked it out, but he never lost his train of thought or even slowed down. This was his element. He loved to stimulate others, and he was doing just that. He closed with some personal philosophy.

"I believe that the strongest power that we have is called belief faith. Belief faith begins with yourself. In the mirror, you're looking at your best friend or your worst enemy. Our world revolves around us. It starts and ends in your heart. What you are and hope to be begins with belief in yourself.

"You believed you could walk when you took your first step. You believed you could talk when you said your first word. You believed you could learn when you started school. You succeeded because you believed you could, or you failed because you didn't believe. Our whole life is based on belief faith of one kind or another. You make America great when you believe in democracy. You make your community better when you believe in growth and progress. And finally, belief faith begins and ends with belief in yourself. There's nothing you can't do if you believe in yourself."

Brown's next mission was to make his team believe it could beat Tennessee and Kentucky, the only teams left with unbeaten SEC records. If LSU, 9-4 overall and 2-1 in the league, could beat Tennessee, it could tie the Volunteers for first place. A sweep of the two road games would be a major coup.

To get it done, LSU would have to make strides on the defensive end. For that reason, Brown had his assistants put together a defensive highlight film. It was 15 minutes of steals, blocked shots, drawing charges and constant man-to-man pressure. All of the sequences were taken from video tapes of their first 13 games. Brown reasoned if they could see themselves playing great defense, perhaps they would respond with even more.

What also concerned him was Tennessee's experience. The Volunteers started an all-senior lineup, led by Dyron Nix, a quick-leaping, 6-7 forward who was the preseason choice as MVP in the league. DeVoe's team also had a strong supporting cast, lots of depth and more than 20,000 fans.

At Knoxville, Brown went over the game plan, spending extra time on a new twist to the Freak Defense—a diamond-and-one with Sims guarding Nix. They went over it in practice Tuesday and again before the game Wednesday night. An added motivation for the Tigers was the presence of Doc Broussard, who was feeling stronger and had made his first road trip of the season.

Then Brown started building the team's confidence, which was even more crucial. "It will just come down to making a commitment," he told the players. "It takes effort. Once you give it effort, you will feel so good about yourself. You really will feel good, even if you don't win. Now it's not fun to ever lose a game. Now look at Chris. He's only 19 years old. I've been at this almost two times as long as you've been alive, and I still go out there with the same emotion. And I have never, maybe I will before I die, God willing, done my best job. But

I've given my best effort. I'm going to get better. And you're going to get better."

In the final minutes before tip-off, Brown stayed in the locker room with his assistants. He noticed a worried look on Craig Carse's face. "Craig, you don't have anything to worry about. I just read a great book by Hal Lindsey, and he made a wonderful point. We should never worry, because when we're worrying, we take our mind off God. We're not listening to what he tells us to do. There is really no need to worry."

Tennessee went ahead by as many as 14 in the first half, but Brown remained relaxed and kept a clear head on the bench. During timeouts, he stressed the importance of running the offense and playing under control. Things began to click. Even though Jackson's only basket came on the last shot of the half, LSU trailed by just six. At halftime, Brown suggested how to better attack the Tennessee man-to-man defense. Then he reminded the team what was at stake in the league race.

Before returning to the court, Blanton took Jackson aside to offer some encouragement. "It's all right, C.J. Don't worry about the first half. You'll get 20 in the second half, and we'll win it."

Blanton was almost right on the money. Jackson scored 24 points in the second half. LSU got Nix in foul trouble and made several runs at the Volunteers. But nobody could deliver the knockout punch. Ironically, Dennis Tracey, a poor shooter, came the closest to putting the Tigers ahead. They trailed by a point when his three-point shot went in and out. They had similar results on several other chances to take the lead, and Tennessee held on for a 100-96 victory.

It was a game won by experience. Tennessee's senior starting lineup had held together under pressure. LSU had played hard, the Freak Defense had been effective, and Brown had not blown up. That kind of performance normally would have meant a victory.

Brown, though, couldn't contain himself any longer. Instead of continuing to emphasize the positive steps they had made, he singled out everything that had gone wrong. Sims took the brunt of his anger. Mouton got his share, too.

"Wayne, we've got a decision to make about you," Brown said, stalking in front of his players in the locker room. "I like you, Wayne. But I can't get you to play hard. You're like Lyle was at the beginning of the season. So if you don't play hard, I'll put your ass on the bench. You've started every game, haven't you?" Sims, who had scored 20 points but taken down only five rebounds, nodded timidly. "Fourteen games. If you don't play for us at the end, we haven't got a prayer. At a crucial time, you let them get rebounds on us. Damn, I never know what to expect from you. I never know!"

At that, he slammed his fist into the chalkboard, which was attached to a cinderblock wall. The impact gave out a loud thud; it had to have hurt his hand. But he never showed it, immediately returning to his criticism of Sims' rebounding. He threatened to make Sims the 13th player on the team, just like he had done with Mouton.

For the next 10 minutes, he vented more of his disappointment. He pleaded for five players to rise to the test and develop some chemistry. Once he got that out of his system, he settled down and tried to put the pieces together again.

"That loss doesn't mean anything," he said in closing. "Hell, that loss isn't going to decide this league. We've got to give them some credit for not cracking. It's going to be a long year, and we're only going to get better. Forget that game. It's over. Let's get ready for Kentucky."

LSU was still on semester break, so the team flew to Lexington on Thursday and had two days to rest and get ready for Kentucky. The Wildcats, meanwhile, had to play at Florida on Thursday in a late game on ESPN. They beat Florida to improve to 3-0 in the league, but had to fly home in the early hours Friday.

Another matter occupied Brown that week. The NCAA had just approved Proposition 42, which would prevent schools from giving athletic scholarships to partial qualifiers under Prop 48. They would have to pay their own way to school and still sit out the first year or they had to go to junior college. Brown banded with Georgetown's John Thompson and Temple's Don Chaney to lead a national campaign against the measure. Thompson would walk off the court at two games in protest of the new rule. If Brown had thought of it first, he likely would have done the same thing.

Instead of talking basketball, Brown spoke of the new proposition when he was interviewed by ESPN on Saturday. "I am totally disappointed in our organization. They take away a year from the kids. That's bad enough. But not giving them any aid, that is not what this country stands for. Martin Luther King said it very clearly, 'When one man is in captivity, no man is free.' Why not be honest? The NCAA hasn't done it yet. And all of us—coaches, presidents, chancellors, faculty reps and athletic directors—we'd better go home and examine our consciences.

"I think we should just declare all freshmen ineligible, but let them be on scholarship for four years. It's a tremendous setback for racial relations in this country and also a tremendous setback for people who are stamped with some test that says you've got a brain or you don't have a brain. That's not what the Statue of Liberty stands for out in the harbor in New Jersey. It's a major mistake, and it should be rescinded."

ESPN was televising the LSU-Kentucky game, and Brown had agreed to be wired. He was ready to put on a show for the national cable audience. He wanted his team to do the same. After reflecting on the Tennessee loss, he came to the conclusion that he had spent too much time on defensive preparations, which took away from the offense. Knowing that Kentucky would try to slow the tempo, he instructed his players to fast-break on every chance.

To be effective at that, LSU had to do two things: get some rebounds and get Jackson into the flow. Neither happened early Saturday night in Rupp Arena, and Kentucky seemed to be well on its way to 4-0 in the league. The Tigers cut a 14-point deficit to 33-26 at halftime, even though Jackson was struggling. But they were in serious danger of being swept on the road trip.

Brown dug into his motivational bag and came out with something to relax his players and get them to believe they could win. "Let me explain something to you guys making your first trip to Lexington. There was no question we were going to catch them, even though we had no offensive rhythm whatsoever. What you have to understand is in Rupp Arena, if you keep putting pressure on this team, the crowd will turn on their own team. Now I am telling you if you take the game to the wire, they will lose at home because of the tension. They are supposed to win everything, they think. But you will beat them if you play hard."

Maybe it was just coincidence, but LSU fought to the very end and somehow managed to extract a victory. It didn't hurt that Jackson loosened up and scored LSU's final 16 points. It certainly didn't hurt that coach Eddie Sutton received a technical foul while Kentucky had possession.

With the score tied and just six seconds left, Jackson drew a foul and went to the line for a one-and-one opportunity. He looked calm as he toed the line and prepared to shoot. Inwardly, he was about to explode with nervousness, excitement and anticipation. If his first shot missed, Kentucky would have a golden opportunity to win.

The C.J. File—I wasn't having a good shooting night at all. I stepped back from the line and said a little prayer. It was a tough situation. When I shot it, I didn't know if it would go in. I was so off. Nothing felt right.

His shot was slightly off target and spun on the rim. C.J. bent his knees and tried to coax it in with body English, jerking his right arm backward. The ball fell into the net, and Jackson raised a clenched fist. The second attempt was much easier. It went straight in to make it 64-62.

Still, Kentucky had a chance to win on a three-pointer. Brown ordered his players to play tight man-to-man. He also went to a full-court press to try to take time off the clock. The press worked to perfection. Chris Mills had to rush up the left side of the court, dribbling between Jackson and Dennis Tracey. As he neared halfcourt and prepared to launch a desperation shot, Tracey stole the ball. It was over. LSU had gained a split of the difficult road trip. The month of January was half over, and the Tigers were very much in the race.

None of the LSU players had ever won in Rupp Arena. It was a night to be cherished. And these 13 young men made sure they didn't leave any emotion behind. They sprinted down the hallway to their locker room, shouting as loud as they possibly could. Brown was busy with ESPN, so the players had their own postgame meeting. Everyone rushed over to slap Jackson on the back or hug him. Joe Dean rushed in and gave out high-fives to all the players. Then Blanton started everyone clapping rhythmically. The sound echoed loudly in the locker room and continued for several minutes.

Before Brown arrived, most of the players undressed and headed for the showers. Jackson sat by himself and draped a towel over his head. It was quite a moment for any player, much less a freshman. He bowed his head and prayed silently. Everyone left him alone until he raised his head several minutes later.

LSU returned to Baton Rouge a winner, but had two difficult home games ahead, against Vanderbilt and Alabama. The race was on.

Brown needed something special for these next two home games. LSU was just 4-4 at home and 6-1 away from the Assembly

Center. To put extra emphasis on the home games, he came up with a theme of "Win Eight for Ricky," dedicating the final eight home games of the season to Blanton.

A collage of Blanton photos from high school through his five LSU years was displayed on one of the locker room walls, along with a poster listing the eight home games and the "Win Eight for Ricky" slogan. Brown was sure the players would respond, even if he couldn't be certain they would win all of those games, which included visits from Vandy, Alabama, Ole Miss, Tennessee, Kentucky, Georgia, Nevada-Las Vegas and Florida. Realistically, they could lose any of those games, perhaps all eight.

On the night before the Vandy game, Brown carried his anti-Proposition 42 campaign on to a national cable audience. He appeared on "Crossfire" as an opponent of the measure. The proponent, Ira Berkow, a columnist for the New York Times, said he was actually against Prop 42 as well. He supported Prop 48. So it wasn't much of a crossfire.

Vandy coach C.M. Newton, meanwhile, advocated other ways of dealing with such controversial issues. He and Brown rarely saw eye-to-eye on issues. Their philosophies are about as diametrically opposed as they could possibly be. Newton, about to be named athletic director at Kentucky, has always been the conservative, diplomatic type.

"Sometimes Dale uses the media as his forum instead of dealing one-on-one," Newton said. "I think that was the case with him and Bobby Knight. I think that is again the case with him on Proposition 42. I think if you really sincerely have a problem or an issue with a person, you should go to that person and you work it out."

Their teams contrasted just as much. Vandy had size, but limited athletic skill. LSU lacked size, but possessed plenty of athletic ability. On Saturday, they would both be battling to put some heat on league leader Tennessee.

Early on, LSU's athleticism, combined with the "Win Eight for Ricky" goal, proved too much for Vandy. The Jackson-Blanton combo was clicking and the Tigers' lead grew to eight. But Vandy stayed in it long enough to make a determined run just before halftime. Barry Goheen scored three baskets and Vandy scored the last 10 points of the half to take a two-point lead. Goheen made the play of the half, stealing a pass from Singleton and hitting a three-point shot at the buzzer.

Brown pulled off his coat as he walked into the locker room and was already snapping. He went right for Singleton. "Vernel, maybe that will wake you up! You haven't been awake out there. We've had two guys who are playing, Ricky and Chris. The rest of you might as well be somewhere else."

He went down the line, pointing his finger at the other players and shouting, "You haven't done anything." He was so angry his veins were showing on the side of his face.

Then he walked over to the Blanton poster. "Does this mean anything? Win eight for Ricky. Hell almighty." Finally, he paused to catch his breath and get his mind back on the game. They had to do something different to combat Vandy's 1-2-2 zone. He decided to rotate the off guard, either Mouton or Tracey, to the point and put Jackson on the wing. Defensively, they just needed to be more intense.

It got worse before it got better. Goheen kept scoring against Blanton, and Vandy seemed to be taking control. Then Brown made a costly mistake. He had spent too much time riding the officials. LSU had the ball, and trailed by nine when Brown drew a technical for disputing an earlier call. Vandy got two free throws and a basket out of the possession, stretching its lead to 13.

LSU was in a giant hole, but had enough time to climb out if everything worked right. Jackson and Tracey made several steals that led to baskets. The outside shooting of Jackson and Blanton took care of the rest, and the Tigers came roaring back.

The game went to the wire with Vandy leading by a point. If LSU lost, it would be its fifth home defeat of the season. That would be disastrous. Jackson tried to work for a go-ahead basket, but Vandy had committed only three team fouls and could afford to keep fouling and forcing LSU to take the ball out of bounds.

With four seconds left, Blanton inbounded to Jackson and moved quickly to set a pick for him in the right corner. Jackson dribbled away from the basket, but suddenly sprang up and twisted around for an 18-foot jump shot. It zipped through the net with a second to spare. The arena erupted. LSU had won, 85-84. Jackson was mobbed by teammates.

After the excitement died down and the players were able to get to the locker room, Brown apologized to them for the technical. "It would have been my fault if we lost that game," he said. "I shouldn't have lost my temper. Thanks for bailing me out, Chris."

The C.J. File—I just got in a rhythm. I've been in a good rhythm lately. When you're in a rhythm, you get a lot of confidence. I feel I can get the job done. Everything is going right for us. It just seems like nothing can go wrong.

Brown could now envision his young team making a real challenge for the title. They had won consecutive games that were imminently losable. There was something extraordinary about these players. They were attentive to his instructions and responsive to his motivation. Better yet, they knew how to win.

Determined to keep them winning, Brown took home tapes of their last few games to study before the Alabama game on Saturday at home. It was a task that he usually left to Abernathy. But this game was important enough to require extra preparation.

On game day, he shared some of the things he picked up from studying the tapes. "When we don't move our bodies, we're not a very good team," he said. "When we move, when we're cutting and slashing and using our own individual characteristics, we're pretty hard to handle. And the reason is we've got guys who can put the ball in the hole. But you can't stand around. You have to keep moving."

He anticipated that they would need one of their best offensive performances. Alabama was the hottest team in the SEC, having won four in a row to tie LSU for second place at 4-2.

For the time being, Brown still stressed the team goals of 16 victories to clinch a tournament berth and eight home victories for Blanton. Brown wrote the numbers five and seven in the corner of the drawing board. They needed five victories to get to 16 and seven more at home to meet the Blanton goal. By then, everyone assumed they would easily win 12 games to reach the Joe Dean goal.

Brown spent extra time talking about the importance of striving for goals. "I think Ricky would get up here and tell you that the worst feeling in the world is to end something and think I didn't do my best. That is a terrible feeling. And the best feeling is to say I gave it all I've got. We don't want to go to bed tonight thinking we didn't do everything we possibly could to beat Alabama."

Strategically, the focus was on defensive rebounding because of Alabama's inside strength, particularly in the person of 6-7 senior forward Michael Ansley. He had collected 67 rebounds in his last four games against LSU. This season, he was shooting a remarkable 67 percent from the field and averaging 21 points.

When Brown finished talking about the game plan, he turned the meeting over to Father Bayhi, who had just returned from a trip to Medjugorie. Father Bayhi shared a story about visiting St. Peter's in Rome, where he went to a newsstand and bought a paper. "There, it was in big headlines in USA Today: Tennessee topples Tigers by 4. And I read the whole account. It dawned on me that I was in Rome and I was reading all about the LSU basketball team. That shows me what you guys can do, what influence you have. You can really make an impact.

"I just pray tonight that you do your best and give it everything you've got and that you seek God's strength in it all." Then they all joined hands for the Lord's Prayer.

In the arena, they were greeted by a huge crowd. Interest had been steadily building in the team, but this was easily the largest crowd of the season. The count would reach 15,242, the second-largest crowd in the arena's history. Hundreds of fans had to sit in the aisles or stand in an overflow area between the lower and upper sections.

LSU and Alabama put on a memorable show. It quickly became clear that this would be a hard-fought battle, probably right to the end. Alabama showed why it had gone on a winning streak. Ansley was getting help inside from David Benoit and Melvin Cheatum, both Louisiana natives. When LSU tried to sag inside, Alvin Lee tossed in jumpers.

But with Jackson getting off to a good start and Sims and Blanton contributing, the Tigers kept pace. They just couldn't quite break through for the lead. At halftime, Alabama was up 45-41.

Being close didn't satisfy Brown. "That was a lousy first half for us and we're only down four. That shows what we can do in the second half if we play well. We just have to play the way we know we can. Now let's analyze how we can win the game. If we can take away five baskets—five times they dunked on us—we will win this game. We stayed close, but close isn't what it's all about. Now we are going to put up another win right at this spot. Right here. Right here." He tapped on the Blanton poster.

"We have got to pick up the intensity. We have a full house here, and you haven't even got the crowd in the game. You let Alabama intimidate you. Get in there and get the crowd in the game. They're cockier than hell. They're like Mississippi State. Establish yourself and put your brain in the game, and you will come down with a win."

Brown walked over to the drawing board and wrote a capital E. "Guys, it's the big E. How many times have I said it? Effort. Don't be soft. Get out there and bust your ass and we will win this game! It takes *effort!*"

It also required a defensive adjustment. LSU switched to man-to-man with Sims drawing the assignment of guarding Ansley. He had the strength and size to match up with the powerful Crimson Tide forward. Now it was a matter of mustering the will to do it.

LSU fell behind by six near the halfway mark of the second half. At that point, Brown did something he has never done before during a game—and he has done just about everything imaginable. He stood up and walked to the end of the bench to see Father Bayhi. He bent over and whispered to the priest, "I realize now I've got to turn this over to God's hands." Then he turned and walked back to his seat.

Shortly afterward, Sims began giving his best all-around effort up to that point of the season. When Ansley tried to power his way inside, he bumped into a 240-pound obstacle that was determined to keep him away from the basket. Ansley fouled out with five minutes left.

That opened the door for LSU. Jackson and Blanton made certain it was not a wasted opportunity and hit key free throws down the stretch. Jackson led all scorers with 30 points, marking his seventh game with 30 points or more. But the most important plays were steals by Mouton and Tracey. LSU held an 11-4 advantage in steals and won 80-76.

After the buzzer sounded, there was more excitement, although it was not quite as exuberant as after the Vandy game. The players ran out of the arena to the roaring approval of the crowd.

Downstairs, Brown was ecstatic, shouting across the room to Blanton as he prepared to change the numbers on the board. "Ricky, we've got a four and a six left." Everyone was slapping Blanton on the back. Then Brown yelled out, "Coaches, we get our pay raise. We won 12 games. Thanks, guys. We've got one goal out of the way. I'll go tell Joe Dean."

When the excitement began to ebb, Brown looked over at Mouton. There were so many times when he thought Mouton would never put out the kind of effort needed of him. But in this game, he had showed his teammates, and especially Brown, that he was committed to the team. Mouton sacrificed his offensive game, played superb defense and was instrumental in the win.

"Lyle, you've proven tonight you can play defense," Brown announced. "That was the best defense you have ever played. You made a hell of a difference in the second half. I am really proud of you. You didn't give up when I got on you. You have shown a lot of class."

He doled out compliments to everyone else who had played and closed with praise for the whole team. "Again tonight you demonstrated what can happen when you play hard and listen to what we tell you. That was a good basketball team you just beat. They are going to the NCAA Tournament. You grinded it out. You just grinded it out. That was wonderful what you did, Lyle. It was a heck of a win. I am really, really, really proud of you."

To stress how important defense had been, Brown took Mouton, Tracey and Sims to the press conference. He devoted most of his time there and on his radio show to lauding their defensive contributions.

LSU got some help that night when Kentucky upset Tennessee at Knoxville, handing the Volunteers their first SEC loss. Tennessee still led the league at 5-1, but LSU was right behind at 5-2.

After taking Sunday off, the Tigers had two days to get ready for a road game at Georgia, where they had not won in four years. It was an outstanding chance to break that string. Georgia, picked by most to win the league, had fallen on hard times with a 2-5 conference record.

The danger now was looking past Georgia to Georgetown. Most of the sports talk around the LSU campus focused on the game against second-ranked Georgetown on Saturday afternoon at the Louisiana Superdome in New Orleans. It would be nationally televised by CBS. Brown was doing everything humanly possible to ensure all the tickets were sold. That would mean setting an all-time NCAA attendance record of 65,000-plus.

Even though Brown spent much time talking up the Georgetown game publicly, he was careful to speak only about Georgia to his players. Still, they would have to have their heads buried in the sand not to know what was about to occur in New Orleans.

On Wednesday night in the Georgia Coliseum, Brown anticipated some problems, so he spent extra time on his preparation of the team. "Tonight marks almost the halfway mark of the Southeastern Conference season. When you get on that plane tonight and leave here, you can be all alone in first place, all alone. And everybody thought you were going to be all alone at the bottom."

He had obtained some extra ammunition for this game. An LSU fan had called that week to inform him of comments made by Georgia's Litterial Green during a radio interview. Green, a highly touted freshman from Moss Point, Mississippi, and the chief rival of Jackson throughout their high school careers, had made some derogatory remarks about the LSU players.

Brown read a transcript of the interview to his players. "Question: Do you feel you could accomplish what Chris Jackson has done if you were on the LSU team? Green's answer: 'He surprised Florida, plus I had a 40 game in high school, he only had 20. Plus, he's on a weak team. We wouldn't even recruit some of their starters.'

"Question two: What do you feel about the matchups with your team and LSU? Answer: 'Get serious, Patrick (Hamilton) is All-SEC and me, too. Not to take anything away from LSU. They do what they can, but they're a weak team. Singleton and the two heavy guys flatten out and all they do is watch Chris. My team is full of All-SEC players like I said. In fact, we wouldn't even recruit those three or at least they wouldn't be in our top eight or 10.'"

This went on for several minutes, Brown reading more slights. When he finished, Brown cautioned them to use this stimulus the right way. Athletes of any kind don't appreciate being taken lightly. This was a competitive group, and Brown knew it would get them going.

But for the first 20 minutes, Green's words came true. He didn't miss a shot in the entire half, and his teammates were nearly as effective. They had LSU on the ropes and were headed toward a rout. Their lead went as high as 18 points. It was 50-33 at halftime.

Brown was upset, but in a sensible way as he gathered the team in the locker room. "I cannot believe how dumb we are playing offensively. We're averaging 95 points and we've got 30 on the board at halftime." He explained how to attack Georgia's defensive plan of doubling Jackson and leaving the off guard open.

The second-half plan was for Jackson to pass off to Mouton on the wing whenever Georgia went to the double team. Defensively, Jackson was switched to guard Green.

Despite the dire circumstances, Brown was convinced they could get back in it. "One of their main problems is they can't hold a lead late in the game. They've lost a lot of leads. We've got to get close going into the last four or five minutes. If we can do that, they will fold in the end. Now they can have that half. When we play as horseshit as we did, why can't we have this half? It is going to test your character tonight. If you believe you can win it, as bad off as you are, you will surprise the heck out of yourself. You will win.''

Abernathy encouraged them to dive on the floor like Blanton had been doing and to hustle back on defense. Johnny Jones had the final word, saying, ''We can win this, fellas. Just believe in yourselves and don't let down. We can win this!''

The offensive strategy worked perfectly. Georgia continued to double on Jackson, so he dished off to Mouton on almost every possession for the first five minutes of the half. Mouton hit three consecutive three-point baskets and then added a two-point shot. Just like that, LSU was back in the game. It went to the final seconds. Sims hit two free throws to put LSU ahead 80-79. Georgia had a chance to pull it out, but Singleton deflected a 22-foot shot by Green to preserve a most improbable win.

There was some big-time rejoicing going on in the visitors' tiny locker room. On the way there, Brown had his arm around Doc Broussard and whispered to him, ''God was really with us tonight. What a night! I have never been around a greater bunch of guys, and I can never remember a greater comeback.''

Then he shared his feelings with the rest of the team. ''You have proven without a doubt that you can play defense.'' He turned toward Mouton and grinned at him. ''Lyle, I have humiliated you. I have been on your ass. I kicked you off the floor. You didn't quit. And I want to compliment you. You shot us back in the game and you played excellent defense. I am so proud of you.''

Next, Blanton drew his praise. ''Ricky, you'd better not graduate. I don't know how I can coach without somebody like you to holler at out there and you never talk back. You did a great job tonight. You all just wouldn't quit. You got them tight just like we said, and you won it. We're going home, and what we're going to do, men, is break the record in the Superdome. We've got Georgetown. So the number two team in the country has got the number one team in the Southeastern Conference. If I were a betting man, I'd bet on LSU.'' He went around the room shaking hands with everyone.

At courtside, Georgia coach Hugh Durham was telling reporters that he hoped he had seen the last of Jackson, who scored 23 despite Georgia's double teaming. He said Jackson would be a high first-round NBA pick if he went out as a freshmen. ''I'd like to see him go,'' Durham said, smiling but revealing his true feelings.

Brown and Durham later met on the court. They discussed the

game. Brown complimented Durham on the defense he had used against Jackson.

"Well, the critical thing was when Mouton started to hit after halftime," Durham said. "I knew at halftime you were over there saying, 'Don't worry about it, Mouton, they don't guard you, so you bury the shot.' You've got to build up their confidence. I knew you would be doing that."

"That's exactly what I said. I told him to shoot us back in the game."

"You can't be in there saying if it's there, take it. You're telling him he's going to make them. I know how you do that. You're telling him, 'Hey, I don't care what happens, just shoot it. I believe in you.'"

"When you're 18 down, you'll do anything."

"But Dale, if he misses those shots, what you did in the locker room doesn't work. Now you've got to come down to Plan B. But you didn't have to do that. But boy, that's frustrating for us to lose like this."

Brown tried to cheer his friend. "Hugh, keep your chin up. You've been in it long enough. You know it's going to turn around."

That night, LSU flew out of Athens with a four-game winning streak that boosted the Tigers' record to 13-5 overall and 6-2 in the SEC. Now everyone could start thinking ahead to Georgetown.

15

Hoya Hullabaloo

Ricky's Diary, January 26—It's a great feeling to be in first place. This means so much to us, because we're such a young team. We talked so much about getting here, and we did it. Now we've got to stay here. Georgia was the big win. We needed that for the SEC. Now we don't have anything to lose against Georgetown. That's a good position to be in.

As fate would have it, LSU's charter flight home from Georgia was somewhere over the state of Alabama at the time the Crimson Tide was finishing off Tennessee in overtime. That moved the Tigers into first place in the SEC. They found out after landing in Baton Rouge just before midnight.

For the next several days, they could take their minds off the league race and focus on Georgetown. Actually, Dale Brown's attention was more on the attendance than the game itself. All day Thursday and much of Friday, he committed his time to giving interviews to hype the game and making calls to promote it. He also scrambled to open several sky boxes and more than a hundred courtside seats. This was one of those times when he simply did not have time to think about coaching basketball. The Superdome just had to be sold out.

The game was officially declared a sellout Thursday afternoon when Superdome officials reported that 65,913 tickets had been sold. About half of those had been purchased by two major sponsors and distributed to their customers. Not satisfied, Brown kept trying to get as many extra tickets as possible. He pleaded with Superdome officials to oversell the general admission area to make sure attendance would surpass the crowd of nearly 58,000 that actually attended the Indiana-Syracuse national championship game in 1987, also held in the Superdome. Officially, the LSU-Georgetown game had already broken the all-time NCAA attendance record, because the NCAA bases its figures on tickets sold plus media in attendance.

"I don't want to just break the NCAA record," Brown told Russ Potts, the game's promoter. "I want to get everyone in there. I want to break the turnstile record. That is what really counts."

Of course, playing Georgetown counted for something, too. The Hoyas had everything they needed to make a run for the national championship. Charles Smith was the veteran floor leader, and Alonzo Mourning was a shot-blocking freshman star. They also had the New Orleans connection of Dwayne Bryant, Jaren Jackson and Johnathan Edwards. Personnel-wise, it was one of John Thompson's finest teams, rivaling the quality of the Patrick Ewing era.

Georgetown had won six consecutive games to improve to 15-1 and No. 2 in the nation and would become heir apparent to No. 1, following Illinois' loss to Minnesota on Thursday night. The only thing preventing the Hoyas from moving to the top of the rankings was LSU, a surprise leader in the SEC, but hardly a team capable of pulling such an upset. Still, CBS was eager to match the nation's top two freshmen, Chris Jackson and Mourning. The network's top crew of Brent Musburger and Billy Packer was coming in to handle the national telecast.

Taking a break from his promotional activities, Brown called a team meeting Thursday afternoon. They would meet for 15 minutes and then practice for 45 minutes. He gave them the rest of the day to rest.

Brown chose the locker room for privacy. He had statistics, letters and praise waiting to hand out. His voice still reflected the excitement of the monumental comeback in Athens.

He went around the room and pointed out what each player had done to pull out the victory. For a change, every starter and all five reserves who played drew a favorable review.

"I don't know if you saw the coach's comments after the game,"
he said, pulling out a page of quotes by Hugh Durham that had been
distributed to reporters. "They asked Coach Durham to comment
about Litterial Green. What did you think of his play? Here is what he
said: 'He played well, but when I looked at the scoreboard, it says
Home and Guest, not Green vs. Jackson or Cole vs. Blanton. All that
matters is the team score.' I think that pretty well tells you some
things. We beat them as a team. That is the only way we could have
come back from 18 points down. That is the only way we can beat
Georgetown."

Then he read parts of several letters before talking about the
Georgetown game. He wrote the figure 65,913 on the board and explained that it would be the largest crowd in the history of college basketball. But the game itself was not a pressure situation. The Tigers
had taken care of Georgia. They were in first place, a spot that few
outside the program thought they had a chance to attain. Sure, Brown
wanted to pull off a great upset in front of the huge crowd. But it
wasn't essential.

What he didn't want to happen was for LSU to get wiped out.
That was a distinct possibility if the Tigers didn't play well. But his
primary concern was making steady improvement, regardless of the
score on Saturday. So he told his players there was no reason to be
uptight about playing the Hoyas.

"I want you to have fun in New Orleans," he said. "But you
guys, please don't be content with what you have already done. On
April 4th, when the Final Four is all over, then you can be content.

"Here are some things I think will help us. I don't want it to
sound like a Bible class, because I don't want anybody sticking anything down my throat. I really think we're getting some spiritual help
and the kind of people you are is helping us. I really believe that. I
have found that I can do things that I didn't expect to do when I am
unselfish and I try to involve God in it. So I sat down and took some
things out of the Bible to read to you and for myself. I took things out
of three areas, brotherhood, positive thinking and love."

At a time when almost any other coach would have been discussing how to defend against Mourning inside and Smith outside and
how to break the vaunted Georgetown press, Brown was busy reading
scripture. He had done his share of preaching as a coach, but not actual Bible-toting preaching. Somehow, though, it didn't seem to catch
anyone off guard. The players and assistant coaches, most of whom

went to church regularly anyway, paid attention to Psalms, Proverbs and the gospels like they would a new version of the Freak Defense or a different way to run the pressure release offense.

He stopped reading and looked quickly over to Ron Abernathy, seated to his left. "I am embarrassed, guys," he said. "I am embarrassed to say I don't even know how to pronounce this book. Ron, you are a Baptist, so you better know how to say it." Abernathy glanced at it and told him how to pronounce *i-klee-zi-as-teez*. Brown got it right after several tries.

"This one from Ecclesiastes is really good," he continued. "Listen to what it says, 'I looked throughout the earth and saw the swiftest person does not always win the race, nor the strongest man the battle.' Boy, oh boy, how we've proven that. Isn't that a beautiful message for us?"

What Brown had done was read the entire Bible and underline verses that fell into the three categories he considered most important. Then he had Wanda Thomas type them up, so that he could share some with the team from time to time.

"This isn't Dale Brown's big mouth talking. This is Biblical passages. This is God's word, which I believe in totally," he told his players. "And I know that you guys believe in it. I don't know if you know what you're ready to do. I think you're more aware of it now. You're making history. How can a team that was laughed at and scoffed at and said, 'We're not worth a crap'—how could we sell 65,913 seats? You know why? There are a hell of a lot of people who would like to be in your tennis shoes, and they come and watch and say, 'Gee, they're not supermen. How in the hell are they doing it?' I do not have a doubt in my mind that Georgetown will not win the game. I don't have a doubt. Last night at halftime, as badly as we had performed, I could tell in your eyes, by the way you were listening, that you were going to do what we told you. I knew you were going to win."

He looked around the room at each player. "Now let's not be content with first place!" he pleaded. "Let's go down there and have some fun. But let's play hard and let's beat them!"

The next time they met was in the Superdome, just before a short workout Friday afternoon. Georgetown, meanwhile, flew into New Orleans unannounced and went directly to a hotel on the other side of the Mississippi River. John Thompson didn't bring his team to the Superdome to practice, and no one was available to the media.

Thompson, who has a history of not cooperating with the media, did participate in a teleconference to promote the game earlier in January. He was uncharacteristically candid, even in regard to Brown.

"Dale, even when he has not had good talent, has been able to upset good teams," Thompson said. "I think he gets up for those kind of games, and he likes that. And that's what I like about him. He's flamboyant, colorful, and I think he is direct. I like that about Dale, too. You don't have to wonder what he's thinking about. He will tell you."

With Georgetown incommunicado Friday, all of the media coverage focused on LSU. There were reporters from all over the country covering the game, almost to the extent of a tournament game. Brown had to shoulder the brunt of the media onslaught, which he was only too happy to accommodate.

He came prepared to talk about more than basketball. Prop 42 was still very much on his mind. He cornered Musburger and Packer, trying to gain their support. He also had a surprise for them.

To demonstrate the difficulty of the admission tests, Brown had obtained sample questions from the English section of the SAT. He gave six questions each to Musburger and Packer. "Since you're journalists, you should be able to get them all right," he told them.

As Brown had hoped, neither sportscaster could get all six right. "See what I mean," he said. "How is a kid from Thibodaux, Louisiana, supposed to answer these if two of the nation's best communicators can't?"

On the day of the Superdome showdown, Brown took his wife, daughter and son-in-law to Commander's Palace for an early lunch and then on to the arena. There were already hundreds of cars circling the place and thousands of fans making their way to their seats. It was a carnival atmosphere, coinciding with the second day of Mardis Gras parades.

Brown and Thompson had agreed to release a joint statement concerning Prop 42 that was issued to the media covering the game. The statement read: "Louisiana State University and Georgetown University wish to commemorate this very special day with a salute to the meaning of America. These young men participating in this game today—black and white—are from every socio-economic background. They come together for four years to learn from each other. Out of this learning experience comes an understanding of one's fellow man. And out of this comes brotherhood. Surely, this is one of life's most meaningful lessons. We are proud to be part of a game that is more than a game. Sure, we want to win. But we also want to deliver a clear message: America works because Americans, like these young men on the basketball court, have put aside the terrible anchor of prejudice and embraced the glory of brotherhood.''

Inside the LSU locker room, Brown sat quietly, reviewing some notes on the game plan and motivation, interrupted occasionally by one of his assistants. About an hour before tip-off, he went into the main section of the huge locker room. Then he asked for a manager to call the players off the court. When they arrived, he started talking and pacing.

"We have been involved in so many monumental games like this over the last few years," he said. "I have found that our team has a passion inside of itself, without being wild or smart or arrogant or pointing fingers. I'm talking about a silent confidence. That confidence is almost a spiritualism. You feel good about yourself. You don't have to go talk to anybody or point your finger at anybody or get a dunk. You've already got that. That is why you have been a successful team. This game today is a tribute to you. No promoter made this game happen. People like the way you play, the team that wasn't supposed to do anything. They appreciate that you have a family. They appreciate that you rose above the odds. And remember a prediction is just somebody's opinion of you. It's nothing else.

"So today I just hope you go out there and have fun and play hard. You have no obligation. You've got to do nothing. I told my wife on the way over here that we sat here in this very room in 1981 for the NCAA regional championship and I felt like a teenager, compared to what I feel now. I am not what I want to be, but I am getting there. If you sincerely put it in the hands of the Lord, it is going to come out all right. That is the way it is. No matter what happens. So you don't have to get butterflies or feel tight or anything else. You have got to play hard and relaxed."

Then he went over the game plan. The defensive emphasis was on getting back and denying fast-break baskets. He told them the Hoyas probably would not shoot well early, because they hadn't practiced in the Superdome. On offense, his plan was to be patient and execute. He spent extra time on inbounds plays against the zone press, which Georgetown traditionally relies on. Jackson would be the key to breaking the press, because he had enough quickness to attack it on the sidelines.

The matchup was compared to LSU playing Oklahoma in 1988.

That game was played in New Orleans, too, but it was in the Lakefront Arena, a smaller facility on the University of New Orleans campus. Oklahoma was undefeated and averaging 115 points a game. LSU handled the press and was in front all the way.

"I feel the same way today that I did against Oklahoma," Brown said in closing. "I can see the headline. I know what it is going to say. This Georgetown team is not as good as the Oklahoma team that we played last year. And I think our team is better than the team that beat Oklahoma!" By then he was pounding his fist into his hand and beginning to raise the roof. Finally, he said, "I guess we should go win this game." His players jumped out of their seats and huddled in the middle of the room. Then they headed out to the court to meet Georgetown.

They were greeted by a partisan crowd that grew to 54,321, just short of the all-time turnstile record, but still a regular-season record. The Superdome was rocking like one huge Mardi Gras party. The cheers came pouring down on the Tigers when they went out on the floor; a chorus of boos was showered on Georgetown. The Hoyas, dressed in black warmups, looked the part of the bad guys. The gold-clad Tigers were ideally outfitted for their role of the hometown favorite.

The C.J. File—It was great to know all those people were for us. They were LSU people. We really appreciated them all coming to see us. That got us even more fired up. When you're out there in front of all those people, you just want to do your best. Plus, it was Georgetown we were playing, and we wanted to beat them.

Most of the millions of basketball fans watching on TV and probably even the majority of the LSU fans in the arena did not expect the Tigers to win. They were hoping for a close game, at best.

At the outset of the telecast, Musburger made it clear that he didn't anticipate an upset. His opening words were: "It could be a special Saturday afternoon for the Hoyas of the Big East who travel down to take on the LSU Tigers of the Southeastern Conference, because a win will move Georgetown to No. 1 in all the polls."

The Hoyas opened with some inspired play. Smith, who was Thompson's point guard on the U.S. Olympic team, shredded the Tigers' matchup zone. He nailed his first six shots, including three three-pointers, staking Georgetown to a 20-14 lead. But the Tigers weren't rattled. They played just the way Brown had directed them, calm and determined.

The next time the officials stopped play, Brown sent Dennis Tracey in for Lyle Mouton and switched to a man-to-man defense. What resulted was incredible pressure defense by LSU, highlighted by a blocked shot by Wayne Sims, two air balls and then Tracey blocking Smith's jumper in the lane. Tracey, playing in his hometown and competing against Bryant, a former high school teammate, was all over the court on defense. He even hustled to collect several rebounds.

The Tigers, meanwhile, scored five unanswered points and the deficit was all but gone. Bryant, Smith, Jaren Jackson and Mark Tillman took turns trying to guard Jackson. Even though the Hoyas kept putting fresh players on him and double-teamed him whenever possible, Jackson would not be denied.

C.J. made the play of the half. Working against Bryant, he started going right, then dribbled through his legs to cut to his left. In the same motion, he changed directions again by dribbling through his legs. Finally, with Bryant faked out, Jackson sprung up for a jump shot from well outside the three-point line and threaded it through the net.

His masterful displays of ballhandling even stunned the veteran announcers. "One of the things you wonder," Packer said, "is how a kid from Mississippi could have these moves. TV was Jackson's coach." Without meaning to, Packer offended many basketball coaches in Mississippi and throughout the South. His comments were considered a slight to the coaches and many lashed out at Packer in what developed into a national story.

Later, Packer explained he was only trying to illustrate the impact of TV. In fact, he was correct in Jackson's case. C.J. had learned most of his tricks from watching Julius Erving and Michael Jordan on television.

As for the game, the Tigers were beginning to take control. Jackson was not having his best offensive game, but Wayne Sims was. His soft one-handers and rainbow jumpers were floating over Mourning's outstretched arms and falling into the basket. Sims scored 18 of LSU's first 39 points before picking up his third foul and going to the bench.

That slowed the Tigers only temporarily. They still managed to secure a 44-41 halftime lead amid almost non-stop cheering in the Superdome.

"I'm amazed that LSU has been able to tempo the game the way they have," Packer said during the halftime break. "They've done just an incredible job. They shot 54 percent against one of the best defensive teams in the country."

Brown was delighted, not so much with the lead as with the confidence and composure his team was showing. The Tigers had come so far since their December beating at the hands of Illinois.

"The game is ours," Brown declared in the locker room. "If the game works down to the final minutes, the more tight they're going to get, the more involved this crowd is going to get and the better we're going to play. They came in here No. 2 ranked, and this thing wasn't even supposed to be close. Now every shot they take, they're going to be thinking, 'Gee, they're hanging with us. We were supposed to knock them out.'

"It's just like last year against Oklahoma. The closer you get to the end, they will not stay with you in the end. Their national ranking and the Big East pride is on the line. Here we are, we just kind of wandered in from the swamps, and we're ahead of them."

He stressed that they could play better both offensively and defensively, that they could knock out Georgetown. He complimented Blanton for his defense on Mourning, who had scored one point. "He doesn't know where he is right now," Brown said. "He is totally screwed up. He is half mad. He is hitting you in the back. I would guess he will get thrown out of the game. Keep him in that same posture."

Before sending them back to the floor, Brown reminded everyone how important the first four minutes would be. They had turned the Georgia game around in those four minutes.

"I'll tell you guys," he concluded. "If you pick up the pace, you will have beaten the team that the media ranked No. 2. I guess we're number one. Let's go prove it."

Both teams raised their level of play in the second half. They went at each other like league leaders should. LSU switched back and forth from zone to man-to-man, Tracey again doing a good job on Smith.

The Tigers pushed their lead to 50-45, and Thompson took a timeout. During the break, the CBS cameras were in the LSU huddle and Brown was miked for sound. It was a fascinating scene as he improvised to come up with the best possible defense to combat Georgetown's height advantage.

"Dennis and Chris play man to man, and you three play zone," he said, pointing to Blanton, Sims and Vernel Singleton. Then he changed his mind. "Chris, you play off number 12. Dennis, you play man-to-man on Smith."

In a way, it was similar to what they had done against Florida, so the players understood what Brown was asking them to do. The announcers and likely most of the audience had no idea.

"It's incredible how this guy gets it done," Packer said. "It started out as a box-and-one and he comes up with a new defense during a timeout."

"What a democratic coach," Musburger interjected.

"It will be interesting to see what they actually play at the other end," Packer remarked just before Blanton inbounded the ball.

Once it became evident the LSU players knew what they were doing defensively, Musburger commented, "I've seen this happen before. Dale was miked for a game against Kentucky, and the same thing happened. If you play for him, you understand it. There's something magical about his communication."

The defensive adjustment allowed Tracey to take away Smith's jumpers and put three men sagging inside against Mourning. It bothered the Hoyas.

Ultimately, Jackson was the difference. He began to heat up from long range and thrilled the crowd with a spectacular four-point play, the first of his career. It occurred when he was dribbling at the top of the key and moved toward Sims' pick. But instead, he pulled up and shot before Tillman could try for a block. He hit the three-pointer and drew enough contact from Tillman for a foul to be called. He calmly sank the free throw for a 61-53 lead. The Tigers stretched it to 10 points just past the 10-minute mark.

But their youth caught up with them. Tracey and Jackson both missed the front end of one-and-one free throws, then Singleton missed two more free throws. Thompson switched to a spread offense that opened things up for Mourning and Jaren Jackson, and the Hoyas came back.

After Jaren Jackson sank a three-pointer to put Georgetown ahead by a point, Brown signaled for a timeout with 4:37 left. Once again, the cameras zoomed in on him.

"We're going man-to-man," he said, speaking softly in an effort to relax the players. "Hang in there. We have one timeout left."

Then in an emotional moment, he looked to his left at Blanton.

He pointed his finger at him and raised his voice, "Are we going to win?" It was more of a command than a question.

"Yes," Blanton replied.

Brown went down the line, pointing at each player who was in the game and saying the same thing, "Are we going to win?" Tracey, Jackson, Singleton and Sims each responded in the affirmative.

As they clasped hands to break the huddle, Brown had one more order. "Take over, baby. Come on, Chris!"

Musburger summarized what Brown had just done. "Norman Vincent Peale never ran a huddle any better," he said. "The power of positive thinking."

It couldn't have worked out better for Brown and his believers. Blanton hit two free throws to put LSU ahead, 80-79, in the final minute. With 24 seconds left, LSU had to find a way to stop Georgetown, which had the ball and a chance for a game-winning shot. Smith took the ball straight down the court against Tracey and went up for a shot. He missed, but Tracey was called for a two-shot foul with 20 seconds left. Brown took his final timeout to try to ice Smith.

During the timeout, Brown explained what he wanted done offensively after the free throws. That was obvious. Jackson would get the ball again. Then Brown offered more positive thoughts. "Hey, I've got a feeling he's going to miss. I've got a feeling. I've got a feeling."

Smith missed. His first shot rolled off the front of the rim. His second one went in to tie the game. But LSU had the final shot.

Lyle Mouton inbounded to Blanton against the press. Blanton threw back to Mouton, who finally got the ball to Jackson. C.J. streaked down the left sideline and drew a triple-team from the Hoyas. Somehow, he escaped.

The C.J. File—I got the ball and just started dribbling. I didn't know how many seconds were left. They had people all over me. When I spun around, they almost stole it. I just jumped up and threw it when I saw Russell.

Russell Grant, playing in his first game since the knee injury, had replaced Tracey in case LSU needed someone to take the last shot. He caught Jackson's pass on the right wing and fired a 20-footer. It was headed in the right direction, but Mourning leaped up to deflect it.

The shot missed the rim, but Sims reached out to tip it toward Blanton on the other side of the basket. Blanton, fearing the buzzer was about to sound, was caught underneath the backboard when he controlled the ball. He had to jump back into the lane to bank a shot off the glass. Somehow, it went in as the final seconds ticked off.

The Superdome exploded into a wild frenzy. On the floor, Blanton felt numb and couldn't move for several seconds. Then he was mugged, first by Tracey, who flew off the bench, and then by the rest of his teammates.

Brown raised his arms and screamed in jubilation. Then he looked down the sideline at the solemn Thompson. Dale lowered his arms and walked over to see him. It appeared he might hug his coaching rival and friend, but they just shook hands. Thompson walked off with his disappointed players, and Brown joined the midcourt hysteria.

The locker room was flooded with well-wishers. Joe Dean was as excited as any of the players. Tom Moran wheeled in George Eames, who wanted to hug each player, starting with Jackson, who had scored 26 points and was picked for MVP for LSU. Mourning had finished with nine points.

Even Harvey Schiller went around shaking hands. He told Brown how important this victory was to the conference. It could mean an extra SEC team getting into the NCAA Tournament, Schiller said, in thanking the whole team. The victory would also move the Tigers into the national rankings. But it meant even more to the players. They had come so far in such a short time. Anything was possible.

Once the noise began to die down, Brown huddled the players in the middle of the room. He got down on a knee and told them in an emotion-filled voice, ''I just want to say something before Father says the prayer. I have never, as long as I've been a coach, been more proud of a team, win or lose, win or lose. The win was fine. But the lesson was more important. I just thank God for guiding us. I love you all. We are not done yet. It was a wonderful day. You should be so proud of yourself and this team. We are not done yet.''

The celebration resumed after Father Bayhi concluded his prayer. This group of castoffs had just upset what would have been the number one team in the nation. There was much reason for merriment.

The C.J. File—This was the most exciting game I've ever played in. Everything just feels so good right now. It seems like we improve every time we step on the floor together. If the game is close, we feel like we're going

*to win. We have that confidence. We play harder when we're down. We
really played hard today. Ricky won it for us. He's our leader. We can
always count on him.*

The danger now was obvious. They had somehow managed to
pull off the great upset. A letdown was inevitable. Gerald "World
Class" Glass, a smooth, streak-shooting small forward, and his Ole
Miss teammates were coming to the Assembly Center. If LSU stumbled, the victory over Georgetown would be diminished.

On Monday, the national rankings came out and LSU was in the
Top 20 for the first time since the 1984-85 season. The Tigers were
ranked 19th. Now they really had something to defend.

But a problem presented itself on the day of the Ole Miss game.
Singleton became ill and vomited at the pregame meal. Jackson felt
like he was coming down with something, too. The flu was all over
town, and Brown worried the entire team might get sick. His greatest
fear was losing to Ole Miss.

In the final minutes before the game, Brown did his best to get
their minds off the sickness and on Ole Miss. "How did we get to be
first in the Southeastern Conference? How did we get to be 6-2 in the
league? How did we get to be 14-5? You did it. You did it because you
believed in what you were doing. Now there are times you are going to
get knocked off the path. Something like this sickness is going to hit. I
know, because I've been sick for two days."

He stopped talking and looked around the room. When he saw
Doc Broussard wasn't there, he asked team manager Tom Cherry to
get him. "I've watched this man go through a heart surgery. They
took a saw, and they cut him right down here. They thought he was
dead. I knew he wasn't going to die. He's tough. Tonight, some of you
are sick and aren't feeling well. Sometimes you have to play with an
injury, play in pain. Tonight you have to do that."

Brown read an inspirational message about controlling fear. Before he finished, Broussard arrived.

Brown beckoned him to the drawing board. "Doc, why can some
guys handle injury and sickness better than others?"

"We're not trying to give you a sales pitch at all," Doc said, his
head down and a grim look on his face. "You all are in good condition.
But when you get to feeling bad, it's just natural that you want to slow
down. Everybody does that. But believe me, the little thing that we
had happen this afternoon is absolutely minor when you're getting

ready for a major ballgame. Coach Brown would never bullshit you. I would never bullshit you. It is absolutely minor. This is too important of a ballgame to allow this to affect us. Don't even think about it.''

Once the game began, there were no signs of fatigue or sickness on the team. Ole Miss appeared to be feeling worse. At least, the Rebels played that way, all except Glass and Tim Jumper. But they couldn't carry the team. LSU built a 48-34 halftime lead and was pulling away.

Brown cautioned about slacking up. ''We've got to remember what happened against Georgetown. We had a 10-point lead in the Dome and we thought we had it won. But Georgetown went ahead of us. This sucker is not over. We need to put a team away to send a message to the SEC. We need to knockout punch somebody. We need to knock them out!''

There was more of the same in the second half. Singleton, showing no side effects, had a marvelous game. He posted up inside against Glass and scored over him repeatedly. He led the team with 23 points and had 10 rebounds. It was never close, even though Glass scored 31 points. The only thing left was to get 100 points, which the Tigers accomplished with time to spare. They finished with a 105-75 rout of what was supposed to be a league contender.

The celebration was mild. They had won their sixth in a row, but this was one the players expected to win.

Brown, though, was thrilled that his team had played so well coming off the Georgetown game and with the bug hitting them. ''Coach Abernathy and I sat there on the bench and talked about this,'' he told them. ''I'll be honest. You guys are almost surprising to me sometimes. That was one of the best efforts I've seen. You sucked it up. You were sick. You were hurt. I am so proud of you.''

Then he started talking about Saturday's long-awaited rematch at Mississippi State. ''If there's ever a game we should get up for, it's Mississippi State.'' He certainly would be. It had been in the back of his mind since their first meeting.

But there were other matters to attend to that week. Brown had decided to limit access to the players, particularly Jackson. C.J. was being swarmed by the media. He had enjoyed the attention at first. Now, with the pressures of basketball and school, he didn't need his time to be monopolized by the media. Brown arranged for a weekly press conference for Jackson on Thursdays. C.J. was off limits at all other times, except after a game.

With the flu nagging almost everyone on the team, Brown looked for some extra stimulation. He turned to the media. On Thursday, he read the players a column in a local publication that quoted Curry Kirkpatrick at the Georgetown game. Brown read an excerpt: ''I was talking to Billy Packer before the Georgetown-LSU game and we both said there was no way LSU could beat Georgetown.'' Brown grinned at the players, not needing to say any more.

He did have a comment about Packer's colleague. ''Here's how the media operates. I gave a copy of Dennis' letter to CBS before the game. What Brent Musburger read on the air wasn't what he wrote. Dennis was saying you can improve yourself with hard work and God. He left the word God off the air. We could stick 'dammit' in there, and they would have read it. But we can't put God's name on the air. So what I'm trying to tell you is don't get too involved with the media. Remember what got us here. We got us here. Not the media. And I'm not trying to develop a Georgetown paranoia. But stick together.''

Brown didn't tell them that he had been on the phone all week trying to get in touch with Musburger. When his call was finally returned, Dale voiced strong displeasure.

On Friday, the team stayed home because Brown wanted to fly to Mississippi State the morning of the game. The flight would take less than an hour. Besides, he was busy getting them pumped up. Maybe too pumped.

Brown didn't like Mississippi State, and it showed in his pregame talk. ''If you let hot dogs like that stay with you, then they think they have a chance and play harder.'' He reminded his team it could reach the goal of 16 victories and widen its lead in the SEC, which was a game over Vandy and Kentucky.

Otherwise, he was positive in his speech in the cramped, steamy locker room. ''There are only two ways that you can approach life. You can approach it either as a victim or as a gallant fighter. You've got to decide then if you're going to act or react. If you're a victim, you're going to react. If you're a gallant fighter, you're going to act. Most of the time when you act, you're guided pretty well. You're guided by some incredible things that God has given us.

''One, God has given us this awesome ability that we have inside of us—mentally, physically and spiritually. And he has given us the freedom of choice. The tragedy is most of us refuse these. We don't utilize the ability we've got. We don't think we have a freedom of choice. We say, 'Well, I was a victim of circumstances. I had a cold, or we were on the road, or that teacher didn't like me, or I was born to a poor family.' What you have to do is take advantage of these things that God has given us. We really do have awesome ability. We haven't peaked yet. And there's two things you can do: act or react. Don't let luck have anything to do with it. If you act, good things will happen to you and you will win tonight."

In the early going, Jackson and Blanton had trouble offensively. But the Tigers were still playing well enough to handle Mississippi State, which had lost six in a row. Jackson was pressing too hard in front of a sellout crowd, which had come to watch and taunt him.

The C.J. File—I knew what their reaction was going to be. But it bothered me when they started booing and cursing at me. It was hard to play there anyway, because the lights are so bad. That's really the only place I don't like to play.

Since the Tigers weren't shooting well from outside, they took the ball to the basket and forced the action. Mississippi State was fouling its way into trouble and LSU took a 38-34 halftime lead.

Brown cautioned about playing tight. "You have to eliminate any emotions that you have. Relax on your shots. They've missed several calls, but that's all right. They all catch up. We will win this game if you keep playing hard."

Offensively, LSU had to be more patient, especially Jackson. He had been pulled out twice already. "We were on the brink of putting them away," Brown said. "We had a nine-point lead, and we went down and took a shot. It wasn't really a good shot. I had just said to Ron, 'If we hit here, she's over.' It would have been 11 or 12. And we didn't do it. So use better judgment. We just haven't gotten into a good rhythm on offense. Come on down, relax, move the ball a little better and we'll get out of here fine."

Again in the second half, they had a chance to put the game away, leading by nine. But the offensive flow just wasn't there. Jackson was bothered by the close defensive play of Greg Lockhart, who admitted after the game that he was tapping C.J. on the elbow every time he went up for a shot. But Lockhart was called for only one foul.

Singleton was so sick that he had to come out of the game and take medication. Lockhart led Mississippi State's comeback with 24 points, and the Bulldogs delighted the home crowd with a 96-79 upset, their fourth consecutive victory over LSU.

The LSU players were deflated. They hung their heads as they trudged off the court to the sound of hecklers. Brown walked around the locker room patting each player on the back and consoling him. Then he asked for their attention.

"You've got to be ready to take the bad with the good," he said softly. "We will bounce back from this. This Mississippi State team is probably the team with the most depth in the Southeastern Conference. But they're 3-7, and they're done. They'll finish in the second division. We got a good ass kicking. We did not play well. Our shots did not drop. It was a terribly officiated game. It was just a bad night. There's no sense in hitting any lockers. We are going to be all right."

He reminded them the worst they could do would be tied for first place. That wouldn't happen. Vandy had lost earlier that night, and Georgia would beat Kentucky on Sunday.

Brown offered more encouragement. "These are the times when this program rises," he said. "Most programs are going to find somebody to bitch at. That LSU jersey has won. It has dominated this league. We will win again." He turned to Abernathy and asked him to tell the team what he had said late in the game. Abernathy responded, "The Lord has a way of making all things work for good."

"Boy, we've been praying during victory and thanking God," Brown continued. "We've been spoon fed. It just wasn't in the plan. It's a nice little test. But we're not going to change what got us here. Now let's pray and thank God for everything he has enabled us to do." They joined hands and closed with the Lord's prayer.

On Monday, they had a team meeting to begin preparations for a trip to Auburn. They were still alone in first place, but had fallen out of the national rankings.

Brown told them to forget the loss. He pointed out Oklahoma's loss on Saturday. Illinois had lost twice; Duke had lost four out of five. Finally, he complimented them for not getting on each other.

Later, they scrimmaged hard for 45 minutes. Then Brown talked to them again, this time at courtside.

"That game will win us the Southeastern Conference championship," he said. "It was a long time since we lost. Now we will make a stretch run. We always rise from the ashes."

Auburn could help any team bounce back from a loss. Sonny Smith had by far his worst team and one of the weakest SEC teams of the decade. It had lost its first 10 conference games and showed no signs of improvement.

The Auburn crowd was small and not a factor. Brown chose to play man-to-man defense the entire game to make his players more aggressive. Jackson and Blanton were both on, and it was soon apparent that the matchup of the league leader and cellar dweller would be no contest.

LSU led by double figures most of the game. The only thing going for Auburn was the shooting of Keenan Carpenter, who launched rockets from well beyond the three-point line and scored a career-high 44 points. LSU led by as many as 21 and settled for a 104-91 victory.

Brown erased the number one on the chalkboard at Auburn. The victory had assured them of a winning season and trip to a national tournament. So he set a new goal of winning the SEC championship. If they won their next five SEC games, they would clinch at least a share of the title.

"Right now there are two things that we must improve upon to go where nobody thinks we belong," he said. "This is what we have to do to win this league. This is what we have to do to go to the Final Four." He wrote on the board: clean up your defense and keep people from getting cheap baskets on the board.

"What kind of work is that? That's blue collar work. That's dirty work. That is not your talented athletes. That is not your gifted stars. That is exactly what you are. Hard workers. With that kind of effort, we can make it!"

Before the first drill of October, Brown had committed this season to the "Hard Work Pays Off" theme. It had carried them to the top of the SEC. Now it would have to keep them there.

16

The Ring

Ricky's Diary, February 9—We're really playing well. The confidence is there, especially after beating Georgetown. That's one I'll never forget. Now we're on a roll. We've got to keep it going. Everyone has to understand it's not over yet. We can't let this affect us. This is when we really have to pick it up. We've come too far to let it get away.

Once lightly regarded, LSU now had its sights set squarely on the SEC title. To emphasize the point, Dale Brown collected all four of his SEC championship rings and made photocopies of them. He taped a copy to each locker before the players reported for Thursday's practice.

"You guys can order the rings. It is up to you," he told them. "To win this league all you have to do is win the next five SEC games, and the ring is yours. I think we're going to be playing in April, and I think you're going to accomplish something that I've never seen accomplished. I've never seen a team improve as much as you have."

Tennessee was the next opponent. There was an extended letter-reading session Friday. Brown read the words of fans, friends, university officials and even a nun. He wanted this game. His talk lasted as long as the practice.

"Who's the oldest person in here?" he asked the players. Before anyone could answer, he did. "Ricky, you're 23, right?" Blanton was actually 22.

"When I was 23, I was just beginning not to be a punk. About 20, I started to change. At 52, I changed again. Now I'm 53, and I remember everything my mother said to me. She had an eighth-grade education. She didn't own nothing. When she died she had a rocking chair, three dresses and some cheap costume jewelry. She died in an old folks home. But my mother had something special. She always told me the truth. And I think what a dumb shit I was. I thought I knew everything. I'd think, 'OK, Mom, sure. That's bullshit.'

"But everything she said happened to me. After she died, I wished I could get her back in front of me and say, 'Mom, gee, I really love you. I wish I'd listened to you.' No, I had all the answers. She had a wisdom and a love. She maybe didn't have any better intelligence than I did. She didn't have a degree. She was poor. But that woman saw things very plain."

It was an emotional speech for Brown to recall those childhood memories. He didn't even pace, and his players were tuned in to every word, waiting for the bottom line. "If you will understand what I'm telling you, you will be better for it. There's a word called expectations."

Pausing, he wrote it on the board. "Every guy in this room has an expectation for himself. Sometimes your expectations don't match our expectations for you. That's because you ain't 53 years old, and you haven't been coaching 32 years. We know more about your limitations than you know about your limitations. What we want is for you to leave here fulfilling all your capacities. What we told you, you must have believed, because you've gone so far. Now don't shut us off. I know how far each of you can go. Further than any of you think you can go. If you will trust our expectations, you can do what I'm telling you. You can win the conference and go to the Final Four."

In the early months of the season, contending for the league championship was a long shot. Making it to the Final Four seemed like an impossible dream. Brown was drilling it into their heads that it could be a reality if they continued to follow his directions. And they were beginning to conceptualize it.

By this time, the grind of the long season was starting to take its toll. The starters were playing 35-40 minutes a game. Staying fresh became a priority, even more than improving aspects of the game.

Brown cut the practices to the bare minimum. They usually worked out for 45 minutes, sometimes just a half hour, other times not at all. They would run just enough to break a sweat and practice enough drills just to maintain the offensive rhythm.

Saturday morning, Ron Abernathy set up a game plan that called for the players to be more aggressive than they had been in the first meeting with Tennessee. They had played the Freak Defense at Knoxville, trying to neutralize the inside game of Dyron Nix. They abandoned the Freak because only Blanton had a true grasp of it. This time they would go man-to-man against the Volunteers with Blanton—as usual—getting the toughest assignment. He had that Rambo glaze in his eyes in the final minutes before tipoff of the regionally televised game in the Assembly Center.

Brown came up with something extra just before sending the team out on the court. Donald Ray Kennard had picked up Los Angeles Dodgers manager Tommy Lasorda in Lafayette, where he had given a speech on Friday night. Brown, an ardent Lasorda fan, had arranged for him to talk to the players. Brown and Lasorda met briefly before the game.

"Tommy, I got so excited when you won the championship," Brown told him outside the locker room. "That was wonderful. I was so happy for you. And you are so animated. You enjoy it so much."

"Dale, let me tell you, you made me the happiest man in the world when you beat Georgetown," Lasorda said. "I watched the whole game and loved it. You're having another great year."

Right after that, Brown informed the players they were going to meet the manager of baseball's world champions. Lasorda came in with Kennard and went around shaking hands with the players, talking as he went.

"I'll tell you guys something, you're really a great team," he said. "I was really happy when we won the world championship. But you guys made me very, very happy when I saw you guys beat Georgetown." Everyone burst out in laughter.

"I guarantee you what a great game it was. And you guys are really fortunate to have a coach who is interested not only in your basketball achievements, but for your personal achievements. And he's very, very proud of each and every one of you."

By then, he had shaken everyone's hand and was back beside the door. "You represent a great institution. The LSU tradition is wonderful. I tell our players, 'Wherever you go, you represent a great organization like the Dodgers.' And you guys do the same thing. Everyone who goes to LSU is proud of what you have accomplished. And when the guys come in behind you, you leave a legacy that they must follow. Leave it good. And good luck. I want to see a win today."

LSU took control in a hurry. Blanton's physical play bothered Nix. He cut off Nix's drives and stayed close enough to prevent him from shooting long jumpers. Nix hit two of eight shots in the first half. Chris Jackson, meanwhile, was in sync—and Tennessee was in trouble. He scored 21 points and helped LSU build a nine-point halftime lead.

Brown stressed giving Blanton more help on Nix. If they continued to hold him in check, there was no way Tennessee could win. "Don't feel comfortable just because we scored 56 points in the first half. That doesn't mean we're going to score 56 more in the second half and win by 18 points. We have to go to work on defense. Let's play this last 20 minutes at 110 percent and put this away. Let's attack, attack, attack. It's going to be real hard for them if we're the aggressor."

He pointed to the goal on the drawing board of five SEC victories, pointed to Ricky's board, and started pounding his fist into his hand. "Keep it going! Keep it going! Keep it going!" he bellowed.

In the second half, Jackson destroyed Tennessee's man-to-man defense, hitting his usual long jumpers and running the fast break like a colt. His points were piling up, but his most spectacular plays were passes. On one fast break, he crossed half court and on the dead run threw a one-handed bounce pass 40 feet to hit Blanton in stride for an easy layup. Another time, he got into a two-on-one situation and when Tennessee guard Clarence Swearengen came out to take him, C.J. scooped an underhand lob to Vernel Singleton who slammed the alley-oop. The Assembly Center exploded with applause, and Jackson trotted back down court smiling and waving his fist.

Jackson scored 50 points to break his own arena scoring record. Brown took him out of the game to a standing ovation. Jackson walked to the end of the bench. Before sitting down, he hugged Jamie Roth, who seemed more excited than Jackson. The 122-106 final was like an NBA game. But LSU had played solid man-to-man defense. It was the team's ninth 100-point game of the season, tying a school record set during Pistol Pete's senior year.

The C.J. File—I was just hyped up for this game because they beat us earlier. We had it at our place, and we really wanted to win bad. It was

an early game, and I slept real good, so I was real fresh. I could have
played another game I felt so good.

In the locker room, Brown complimented Blanton and Sims on
their defense. "I'm really proud of you. That was a good basketball
team. Again, I think we're a special group of guys." He changed the
SEC goal to four and wrote the score on Ricky's board. "I'm just so
proud of you, so really proud of you. You gave it a great effort for everything but about a minute-and-a-half stretch. That was a really
hard-played game. What more can I say?"

Brown took Blanton, Jackson and Sims to the press conference.
Johnny Jones began to laugh, then everyone cracked up because Sims
had played a horrendous offensive game. But Brown chose him because of his defense.

After the game, Jackson got a call from Lil Jenkins. She congratulated him on his accomplishment, but that was not the reason for the
call. A young Gulfport boy had a brain tumor. Just like Jamie Roth, little Tavaris Woods wasn't expected to live long. Tavaris wanted to meet
his hero. It was a busy time for him, but Jackson immediately agreed
to come.

Sunday afternoon, Evans and Joe Walters picked up C.J. and took
him back to his hometown to visit with Tavaris. They spent about a
half hour together in the hospital. The boy wanted to know everything
about Jackson and the LSU team. He wore an LSU sweatshirt and
clearly adored Jackson. After the visit, the Walters took Jackson back
to LSU so he could study.

The C.J. File—I guess we don't realize how fortunate we are to have our
health. We really need to be thankful for what the Lord has given us. It
hurts to see a little boy suffering like that. But it makes you feel good if
you can help some way. It's the same with Jamie. But he's so strong he
makes you feel strong. He knows he's dying, but he's so happy all the
time. He's just real special.

Coincidentally, Jamie Roth was to be the honorary coach and
Blanton's special guest for the home game with Kentucky on Wednesday. He wrote a poem that was passed out to all the players on the
night of the game.

Jamie stood up and moved into the center of the room and motioned for Blanton to join him there. He came up to just above Blanton's waist. Blanton put his arm around the boy.

Jamie said it was a night he would never forget. Then, with a big smile, he read his poem:

"Ricky and all you guys, I love you so.

"You have done more for me than you will ever know.

"But if I had just one wish, it would be simple for me.

"A ring on my finger forever to see."

The players and coaches broke out in laughter and clapped for Jamie. Brown stepped in and said, "I can tell you one thing, Jamie, that is going to happen."

Preparations for this Kentucky game were unusual. There was nothing on the bulletin board, which normally would be covered with stories on how great Kentucky was. LSU was expected to win easily. Brown knew that would happen if the Tigers dictated the tempo and didn't allow Kentucky to make it a 60-point game, like in Lexington.

"Don't get too emotional out there, because it's Kentucky, it's on TV, there's a sellout," he cautioned. "This is just one step toward what we want to do. You've got the rings pinned up on your locker. Jamie just said it. We want that ring. And we can move closer to it tonight."

The crowd was at a fever pitch from the moment the players came out for warmups. It grew to a peak when the Tiger mascot came out of a trap door in the ceiling and slid down a rope upside down. To further charge the electric atmosphere, the live bengal tiger mascot was also brought into the arena—in his cage, fortunately. Some of the students, though, behaved like they had just been let out of a cage. But such a response was expected when Kentucky came to town.

The young LSU players got caught up in the excitement and their performance suffered.

Ordinarily, they would have been in trouble. But this Kentucky team had a losing record and, more significant, a losing attitude. They knew their season was all but over, because of the NCAA investigation.

Jackson wasn't shooting well. But like few players can, he still scored in a big way by changing his game. He drove past Derrick Miller for closer jumpers and set up everyone else for better shots. LSU built the lead to 45-37 at halftime but hadn't played well. The fans didn't seem to care. LSU was ahead. That was all that mattered.

But not to Brown. He tried to calm his players at the half. "We did not play hard. We tried too hard, and we played tense. We can't think about losing a game. Forget about it. You've got to go play the game. What you've got to do is play intense, not tense. You've got to relax and let the game come to you. We want this too badly.

"I am no longer impressed with Kentucky written across their jersey. They should be impressed with us. We're in first place. But we're acting like this is an upset or something. They have not been to the Final Four or the Final Eight four times in the '80s. We have. What you have to do is quit TRYING to play hard. Just PLAY hard. You have to quit being TENSE. Be INTENSE. That's what we must do."

With a delivery that sounded like his friend Jesse Jackson, Brown kept emphasizing the need to relax and play naturally. He reminded them of his HIT theory of playing hard, intelligent and together.

It took longer than Brown would have liked, but they eventually loosened up and began playing in that determined, but almost effortless manner that had carried them this far. Kentucky actually took the lead for 40 seconds. Then LSU picked up its defense and turned on its offense. All five starters got into the act. Each reeled off double figures.

Not only did LSU win, but it routed the Wildcats like never before in front of the home fans. The only thing the Tigers didn't accomplish was the tenth 100-point game of the season. But nobody in Deaf Dome would dare complain about this 99-80 pounding of Kentucky.

Jackson finished with 34 points for his ninth game of 30 or more. His scoring average was 28.5, second in the nation. Defensively, Mouton had made several key plays to spark the rout.

Brown showered Mouton with compliments for his defensive effort. "Lyle, I am really proud of you. You got more steals and interceptions than anyone. You really came through for us when we weren't playing a very good game. I am really proud of what you did tonight."

In evaluating the overall performance, Brown was slightly critical but in a constructive way. "I am not going to tell the press about it, but we did not play real well almost two-thirds of the game. That is why it is so important that you love each other. When things are going wrong, you didn't get on each other. We really had a horseshit first half. But we hung in there together and we got a victory. I think we were too psyched up. I know Ricky wanted this one for Jamie, and he tried so damn hard he played tight. But you kept your cool. It all happened again on what?''

The players responded in unison, ''Defense.'' Brown again complimented Mouton and told everyone that Lyle was the only player going to the press conference. Then he reminded them that an important road game at Vanderbilt was coming up Saturday.

He also put in a word for a future trip. ''Guys, do you realize we can be in Seattle? Do you realize that? Honest to God. Don't think, please don't think that this is some Jimmy Swaggart speech trying to get your money or trying to suck you into something. I've got such a good feeling about this team. You can walk into Seattle, Washington. You can play in the Final Four.''

Finally, he let them know what referee John Clougherty had told him. Clougherty had officiated the LSU-Illinois game and said afterward, ''You may get to play them again.'' He repeated those words after the Kentucky victory. Brown suggested that rematch could happen in Seattle.

The next day, Sports Illustrated subscribers began receiving their February 20th edition, and LSU had a cover boy. Looking surrealistic in his deep purple warmup suit against the dark purple, overcast evening sky, Jackson stood alone on a playground holding a basketball. The title on the cover read, ''He's A Pistol: LSU Super Frosh Chris Jackson Evokes Memories of Pete Maravich.'' In the coming days, C.J. would also appear on the cover of The Sporting News and Basketball Weekly. In those articles, he talked publicly about his Tourette Syndrome condition for the first time. He was relieved to get it out in the open.

The LSU staff had known for weeks that Curry Kirkpatrick was working on a feature story on Jackson, and that he probably would be on the cover. When word got out, it was the talk of the town. It was the most sought after issue of SI ever in Baton Rouge. Fans made midnight dashes to convenience stores all over town in quest of Chris. Bookstores and newsstands sold the magazines by the hundreds.

All this was going on while Jackson and his teammates were trying to prepare for Vanderbilt. Brown called Chris into his office to offer some advice on how to handle being on the cover of SI. ''When you walk into the store and see yourself on the cover of Sports Illustrated, then all of a sudden you won't think Sports Illustrated is all that big of a magazine anymore. You think, 'Hey, I'm on the cover of that. It doesn't take much to get on the cover.' I think you will find Sports Illustrated isn't all that big of a deal.''

Jackson didn't even read the article until Friday. He spent Thursday taking a makeup test and missed his regular Thursday afternoon press conference.

The C.J. File—When I was a kid, I would dream about being on the cover of Sports Illustrated. But that was just a dream. I never thought I'd be in Sports Illustrated, and I really didn't think I'd be on the cover. It's an honor. It's exciting. But it's not going to make me overconfident or anything.

Although Louisiana still had a football-first mentality, the people of the state went absolutely bonkers over Jackson. Perhaps it was his cute, puppy-dog look, or maybe his soft, gentle personality. Of course, his captivating floor shows had something to do with it, too. Like Pistol Pete before him, Jackson had turned into a folk hero. Even LSU quarterback Tommy Hodson, on whom the school had spent thousands of dollars to promote as a Heisman Trophy candidate, had nowhere near the appeal of Jackson, especially among children. C.J.'s child-like qualities endeared him to the younger generation.

If some entrepreneur had come up with a line of Air Jackson shoes for boys and C.J. dolls for girls, they would have sold out in a hurry. One Baton Rouge businessman did capitalize on the craze. The owner of Fred's bar started ''Action Jackson Night'' after every home game. The price of drinks was based on how many points Jackson scored. If he had 20-29 points, drinks cost a dollar; 30-39, 75 cents; 40-49, 50 cents; and 50 or over, 25 cents. After Jackson's 50-point game against Tennessee, the owner had to raise prices.

Two days after the victory over Kentucky, the team took a commercial flight to Nashville. Early in the evening, snow flurries were falling as they went out to dinner.

Just before the 11 o'clock curfew, Brown held a team meeting in his suite to discuss Vanderbilt. ''They aren't a super defensive team. They aren't super quick. They aren't a super rebounding team. You have done it three out of the last four years up here and beaten them. So the same thing will apply tomorrow night, and you will beat them again.''

The city was abuzz with talk of the showdown that could move Vanderbilt into a tie for the league lead with LSU. Many in town called it the biggest game in Vanderbilt history. ESPN was televising it nationally.

On Saturday, Brown was confident. He knew the key matchup would be Blanton on Barry Goheen. Blanton's instructions were to shadow Goheen wherever he went on the court.

Blanton was able to contain Goheen, but his concentration on defense took away from his scoring. In fact, he didn't score in the first half, which left a huge void in LSU's offense. Barry Booker smothered Blanton just like Blanton was doing to Goheen. Thus Jackson had to generate some offense. He kept LSU within five points at halftime. But there was a sense of desperation in the locker room at halftime. Doc Broussard remained outside. He told a friend that it didn't look good.

Brown didn't see it that way. He never does. "We can win this game if we just get our offense working a little better and keep up the intensity on defense," he said, speaking confidently. "The key will be the first four minutes. If we can get it going, we can knock them out then. They had their chance early, but you guys held your ground and got right back in it. We will put ourselves in a wonderful position when we win this game. Just give us a little more effort and this baby is ours."

It sounded reasonable. But it didn't work this time. Goheen ignited the Commodores' running game and every time they scored, Memorial Gymnasium sounded like a power keg exploding. Vandy kept pouring it on and turned the game into a 108-74 massacre, even though Jackson scored 38 points. The big difference was Blanton. He had seven points, breaking a streak of 29 games in double figures.

The loss knocked the Tigers out of the Top 20 again and out of sole possession of the league lead. They had been embarrassed on national TV. They now shared the lead with Vanderbilt and Florida. It shattered their confidence, making the visitors' locker room seem like a morgue.

Brown sat on an equipment case between the two benches where the players were seated, heads down and spirits shaken. First, he talked about the Auburn game of 1987, when LSU had been blown out by 38 points. The Tigers went on to reach the Final Eight.

"There are nights like these," he said in a gentle way. "They just did a good job. We could have played better, but we didn't. Now we have to forget about it."

Only a few minutes were spent reviewing the game. Everything was channeled into reviving their morale. "I have never been more proud of you guys than I am right now," Brown said. Everyone froze and stared at him. "I am proud of you for this reason: you didn't quit. Also, you didn't turn on each other. Those are two positive signs. We can do nothing about today. That is over. But we can do a lot about Monday. Just remember this, we are still in first place in the conference. You have won 10 out of your last 12 games. I don't think the world is falling apart. We will bounce back.

"Let's bow our heads and pray. We always are so elated when we win. Let's not forget to thank God for everything he has given us. We just lost one game. We have so much to be thankful for."

Later, he gave the media a similar spiel. When he said he had never been more proud of this team, Baton Rouge State-Times sportswriter George Morris raised his eyebrows and smirked. Brown saw Morris' reaction and snapped, "That's why I'm a coach and you're a sportswriter." He recounted the story on his radio show after the game and again on his television show to emphasize how important unity is to any team, especially this one.

Since their next game was Monday against Georgia at home, they practiced Sunday at the Assembly Center, right after flying home from Nashville. It was a light workout. The attitude was good, and the players seemed eager to make amends for the embarrassing loss.

Just to make sure, Brown looked for an emotional lift. Late Monday afternoon, he called Gus Weill and asked him to speak to the team just before tip-off.

Weill prepared a fiery speech like he has done through the years for four Louisiana governors and dozens of other politicians and officials. He started by describing how Brown had told him in October that this team would win the conference. Weill admitted he thought Brown had flipped out. But now he knew Brown had been right, that he had seen something unique in this team.

Then Weill added a personal touch. He detailed an experience he had in the hospital two months earlier. "They stuck tubes in every hole in my body. And when they were through with the tests, I was laying in the bed waiting for my surgery. And the doctor came in and clapped his hands. He said, 'Mr. Weill, we really know you now.' He had tested everything on my body. But he didn't know ME.

"No man knows another man. We know *ourselves*. But you guys have an advantage that the rest of us don't have. For 40 minutes tonight, you have an opportunity to say who you are. You can show everyone, 'this is what I'm made of, this is why I'm better than the man I'm playing against.' So go tell them. Go tell everybody. Go show everyone who YOU are. And beat them!''

Weill turned and walked out before Brown could thank him. Brown closed by saying, ''Let's go show them that 34-point ass whipping has our attention. Let's go out and beat their ass.''

In a reversal of the first game with Georgia, LSU controlled the first half. There were no signs of the Vanderbilt loss in these players. They had another large crowd behind them and were doing almost everything right.

With the Tigers playing so well, victory seemed out of reach for Georgia, which was struggling to avoid a losing season. The Tigers built a 43-26 halftime lead, the same margin by which they had trailed in Athens a month earlier.

The fast start pleased Brown, but he wanted more. ''If you turn it up just a notch or two, you can really have a good game. We've got 20 more minutes, just like Gus said, to show who we are. It's us versus them, and me versus you. We can put another W up there and get closer to that ring. Let's keep it going. We can win it on defense.''

But it was Georgia that picked up the intensity by going to a full-court press in the late going. Litterial Green, Patrick Hamilton and Rod Cole combined for seven steals, and the Bulldogs closed quickly.

After a timeout, LSU adjusted to the press and got the ball to Jackson. Soon they were back in command and on their way to an easy 97-83 victory.

There was another victory etched on the Blanton board, and a mild celebration followed. No one got carried away. They realized a major test awaited them at Alabama on Wednesday. They were back in sole possession of first place at 11-4, a half game in front of Vanderbilt and Florida. Alabama was a game and a half off the pace. With games remaining against Alabama and Florida, LSU controlled its own destiny.

The next afternoon, the Tigers flew on a charter flight to Tuscaloosa. It was their second road trip and third game in five days. They were tired, but eager. Brown decided not to practice Tuesday and there was only a short shooting practice on the morning of the game.

On most road trips, Brown had time to read at the hotel. He often found material to share with his players. In his final talk before the Alabama game, he read part of an article on the late Ray Kroc, founder of McDonald's.

His respect for the man was clear as he read a quote from Kroc: "If you believe in something, you've got to be in it to the very ends of your toes. Persistence and determination are what make winners. Nothing can take their place. Talent alone will not. Unsuccessful men of great talent are common in this world. But persistence and determination and dedication make winners."

Brown put extra emphasis on the conclusion of the article. "Finally Ray Kroc says, 'Why do I do it? Because of all the money? My greatest satisfaction comes in being able to say thank you, God, for my success and by helping other people not as lucky as I've been.' That is a pretty simple philosophy, isn't it? I think you all recognize that is our philosophy."

There was a sellout of more than 15,000 in Coleman Coliseum for the important league game. Alabama had won seven in a row over LSU at home and had not lost a home game all season. An added attraction was "Wimp-Alike Night" with all fans receiving masks in the likeness of Alabama coach Wimp Sanderson. Many of the students had scowls on their faces and wore plaid sports jackets, just like the kind Sanderson wears. It was a festive night in the old gym, which looks more like a huge airplane hangar than a basketball arena.

Before the Tigers headed out to the court, Brown reminded them of the SEC rings that could be theirs. The managers had taped pictures of the championship rings all over the visitors' locker room.

His final words were about Alabama's home winning streak of 15 games. "I can just see the headlines now: 'LSU Breaks Tide Streak.' That is what we are going to do tonight. We have not won many over here, but that is going to change tonight."

The Tigers got off to a good start and the big crowd was no factor. Even after Jackson injured his left ankle and had to sit briefly, they kept up their offensive consistency and kept Michael Ansley off the boards. Their halftime lead was 39-33 and could have been larger if Jackson had been close to his normal self.

Someone had accidentally stepped on C.J.'s ankle, causing a slight sprain and deep bruise. He couldn't push off on his long jump shots and had to gingerly walk the ball down court. Defensively, he even had trouble guarding Gary Waites, who is not much of a scorer. Still, Brown kept C.J. in the game, hoping his mere presence would help.

During the break, Brown urged his players to pick it up even more, while Doc Broussard worked on Jackson's ankle.

C.J. held his left ankle and squirmed with discomfort. Doc took him into an adjoining training room to retape the ankle and get him away from the other players. They didn't need to see him in pain. Yet, they all sensed the inevitable.

With Jackson slowed, Brown realized LSU wasn't going to score many points in the second half. So he stressed defense and making good decisions. "If you play smart the second half, you will bury them. They will panic. They will throw everything up. They can't possibly beat us if we go out and play intelligently."

Finally, he reminded them that there were only 20 minutes left in this game and 100 minutes remaining in the SEC season. "I can see that headline, 'Tigers Break Tide Streak.' It is going to happen."

It didn't. Jackson continued to play on the gimpy ankle, but was ineffective. If anything, he hurt the team. The offense crumbled around him. There was no ball movement, no screening, and not much scoring.

Ansley, also bothered by a sore ankle, became inspired and took over inside. He scored a game-high 24 points and helped Alabama dominate the boards 51-28. Alabama rolled to an 87-72 victory, and the headlines would be more along the lines of "Tide Turns Tigers Again." Jackson scored 16 points, breaking a string of 17 consecutive games with at least 20. He was limping badly. He and his teammates were exhausted from having played three games in five days. They were disheartened by the loss. They were out of first place; Florida and Vanderbilt had taken the lead that LSU had held most of the season.

After the game, Brown made sure he was last to enter the locker room. He started pacing right away, but didn't say anything. The suspense was building as each second passed. His coat was already off, not a good sign for the players. There was no doubt he was agitated. They had fallen out of first place and lost a golden opportunity to move into position for an outright championship. Now a tie appeared to be their best hope.

There would be no soothing talk like in Nashville. It was going to be a Brownout, and every team member, whether he played or not, was going to catch Brown's fury.

His voice boomed when he started talking. "I have told you guys from the very beginning you have got to have five guys playing together. Five guys! One freshman and one senior cannot carry this team every damn game!"

He commanded the managers to take down the pictures of the

championship rings. ''We don't want to embarrass ourselves and let Alabama see them,'' he snapped.

Brown began pounding his hands together, swinging his arms and screaming at the top of his lungs. If there was anything he despised, it was lack of emotion, especially in a big game. He thought they had been flat in the second half.

''Ricky, what did you tell me at the timeout? What did you say to the guys?'' Brown asked.

''Quit feeling sorry for yourselves,'' Blanton answered.

As usual, someone else's criticism stoked Brown's anger. He had not lost his temper like this since the Illinois game in December. There was no stopping him now. He grew more fierce.

''You were all walking around like this,'' he said, hanging his head and walking toward the door. Then he turned and continued to blast away. ''Can't you guys see you've got to pick it up? That's bullshit! I don't mind losing. But I hate like hell to lose like this. You gave them that game. You GAVE them that game!''

There was a knock on the door, but Brown was too involved to answer. About 30 seconds later, there was another knock. He responded this time, shouting, ''The door is locked, and it's going to stay locked!''

Outside was Alabama senior Alvin Lee. He had been told by Sanderson to apologize to Brown for a gesture he had made at the LSU bench. Lee didn't dare knock the third time. He eventually caught up with Brown before LSU left the arena and offered an apology.

That wouldn't do for the LSU players. They had to answer for their listless play. Mouton drew the early fire; Sims and Dennis Tracey got theirs later. Blanton was the only one to be complimented, and briefly at that.

Near the end of his 20-minute rage, Brown scolded Geert Hammink and Kyle McKenzie, neither of whom had played in a week. He slammed his fist onto the portable drawing board. Then hit it again. The third time, he knocked it over. It would have crashed to the floor, but manager Greg Polk moved over and caught it.

Finally, Brown took a break to collect his thoughts. His volume dropped to almost normal. ''Well, we've got to win them both now. And we will. We will still win the championship. But I am sure disappointed in the way we played tonight. Doc, tape their ankles, because we are going to practice hard tomorrow. We are going to win this SEC championship if I have to spill my guts to do it.''

Players and coaches alike were upset. No one wanted to talk. They just wanted to get on the bus, go to the airport and get out of town. But by then, the media and fans were lined up in front of the locker room. Brown went grudgingly to the press room. He waited for Sanderson to finish his comments. After five minutes, Brown turned and walked out, saying, "I can't wait all night for him to finish."

Meanwhile, the players had found a way to slip out of the locker room through the training room, thereby avoiding the media. They were on their way to the bus when Brown returned, leaving angry reporters and disappointed autograph-seekers behind.

On the bus, Doc Broussard spoke to Brown and convinced him to back off a hard practice for Thursday. The players were hurting and exhausted from the grind of three games. They needed rest, not more work. Brown got the point and scheduled individual meetings with the players, but no practice.

On Thursday, Brown stayed home and relaxed most of the day before the meetings. That gave him time to realize he had gotten carried away again and lost his temper unwisely. He didn't apologize to the team, because the players didn't meet collectively. But his individual talks were upbeat.

After meeting with Brown, even Mouton felt better about his situation. "I know I'm really close to playing the way he wants me to play," he said. "We understand each other better. I don't think he was necessarily fair with me last night. But I know what he was trying to do."

They all knew what they had to do now.

Eight Days Left

Ricky's Diary, February 22—We've never played well at Alabama, and nothing changed this time. We were ahead at halftime, and we just threw it away. Everything just fell apart. Chris getting hurt had a lot to do with it. We're all a little down right now. But this is when we usually rise up.

Once LSU began to get the Alabama loss out of its system, it was time to prepare for the final eight days of the regular season. Almost certainly the Tigers had locked up an NCAA bid. They were 19-8 overall, including the victory over Georgetown. But there was much to gain in the final three games.

First, they would play Nevada-Las Vegas in a nationally televised non-conference game on Saturday at the Assembly Center. Then they would close the SEC season with a home game against Florida on Wednesday and a trip to Ole Miss next Saturday. With a little help, they could still win at least a share of the championship.

Of greatest concern was the condition of Chris Jackson. His left ankle was tender. He was getting whirlpool baths and hot-and-cold treatment continually on Thursday and Friday. He could walk with a slight limp, but wasn't ready to play. Doc Broussard thought he could get C.J. ready for UNLV, but Brown didn't want to take any chances, especially for a non-conference game. "I don't think Chris can play," he told Ron Abernathy before they discussed the game plan Friday afternoon. "Doc says he should be ready, but you'd have to step on a land mine before he'd say you're hurt." Abernathy agreed that Jackson should sit unless he showed signs of improvement.

After a half-hour practice Friday, the other players were starting to get the spring back in their legs, just in time for the visit from the Runnin' Rebels, ranked 18th and on a roll. UNLV had won five in a row, including a near-blowout of North Carolina State at Raleigh. But Jerry Tarkanian's team was also weary from playing three times that week.

This game had been scheduled for December, but was moved to accommodate CBS-TV. Brent Musburger and Billy Packer were in town again.

Just hours before the 1 p.m. tip-off, Brown decided to start Jackson and see how he responded. Dale planned to keep a close watch and at the least sign of pain, C.J. was coming out.

In the pregame meeting, Brown rattled off the positions that UNLV was picked to finish by national publications. Most ranked Vegas in the top 10.

Then he reminded them where LSU had been picked. "We were not even ranked in the top 100. I think this game will point out vividly, just like the Georgetown game, that is just somebody's expectation. If you spend your life listening to what others say about where you're going, they'll live in the mansion on top of the hill and you'll live in the shack at the bottom, because they'll convince you that's where you should live. They'll say you're stupid and you don't belong up there. This game today is perfect for us. They're good. Jerry Tarkanian said this is the most talented team he has ever had. They played Oklahoma twice and lost to them by two points both times. They whipped North Carolina State at North Carolina State. They are a darn good team. But they haven't played us. We are going to beat them today."

Jackson got off to a slow start. He was showing signs of the injury and Greg Anthony was turning in the best defensive job against Jackson of anyone all season. Jackson couldn't push the ball down court and didn't shoot his normal 20-footers. Brown considered taking him out. But midway through the half, C.J. warmed up and began to penetrate, either scoring in the lane or setting up Blanton, Sims or Singleton. LSU took control and finished the half with a one-point lead.

LSU had to contend with a diamond-and-one defense that UNLV

was occasionally using against Jackson. At halftime, Brown dia-grammed several variations of LSU's regular zone offense that would work against that defense.

"Guys, I don't see how they can beat us if we have a good second half," he said. "We're going to win this game today, and then we'll go home and watch the rest of the league struggle." Vandy was playing at Florida later that afternoon in a matchup of the league leaders. LSU needed Florida to beat Vandy, and then the Tigers would play Florida at home. But there were more pressing matters on hand.

It turned out to be UNLV's offense that gave the Tigers fits in the second half. The Rebels worked the ball in to David Butler and George Ackles, both active 6-10 post players, and began to carve up LSU's zone defense. They took the lead and stretched it to nine points on several occasions and had chances to go even farther ahead.

Urged on by the home crowd, the Tigers rallied in the closing minutes, They pulled within a point on a long jumper by Jackson that was close to a three-point shot. Brown argued vehemently, but to no avail. LSU trailed 86-85 with 20 seconds left and had to put the Rebels on the free-throw line. Anthony made his first attempt, but missed the second and Sims cleared the rebound.

Tarkanian made a good decision by going with a full-court press. Sims threw an errant pass, and Jackson had to lunge after it to prevent the ball from going out of bounds. It was right in front of the Vegas bench, and Tarkanian argued that Jackson had gone out of bounds. But the officials didn't see it that way. Jackson's pass went back to Sims, who passed to Mouton near midcourt. Then Mouton fired a pass to Blanton in the right corner.

Making sure he was outside the three-point line, Blanton went up for the shot and threaded it through the net with four seconds left. Tarkanian didn't want a timeout, and all the Rebels could get was a desperation half-court shot by Anthony that hit the backboard well to the left of the goal. The arena burst into delirious celebration of the 88-87 victory.

Blanton, mobbed again by his teammates, just like against Georgetown, was named CBS player of the game and appeared on the wrap-up with Jackson and Brown. Jackson summed up the moment best. "I just thank God for giving me the opportunity to play today." Without Jackson, who scored a game-high 29 points, LSU would not have been in any position to win.

Downstairs, the locker room was filled with overjoyed players, coaches, school officials and Brown's friends. Lester Scott wrote on the drawing board, "Twenty wins." Everyone took turns hugging Blanton. Blanton picked up Jackson and gave him a bear hug.

An ecstatic Brown was clapping and patting everyone on the back. Then he introduced a first-time guest to the locker room. "My wife wanted to come down here and say something to you last game, but she was afraid she would cry. I got her to come down for this one."

Beaming with emotion, Vonnie went around squeezing the players' hands and hugging some of the older players. She kissed Mouton. "All I can say is thank you. Thank you all so much. You were wonderful." Then she left, fighting back tears.

Brown handed out his own compliments and then reminded everyone that they had a mission left, beginning with Florida. "We're going to win this last home game for Ricky. Then we're going to get this ring for Jamie. We're going to get that ring, even if I have to cut somebody's finger off. It was a great comeback. But we are not through!"

Another victory was filled in on Blanton's poster. How unlikely it had seemed a month ago that they could win even most of those eight remaining home games. Now they had won seven in a row, and the eighth would be for the championship.

Later that afternoon, LSU got the help it needed when Florida rallied to beat Vandy in overtime and claim sole possession of first place in the SEC. LSU was a game behind. By beating Florida on Wednesday, it could tie for the lead. The order blanks for championship rings could then be filled out.

The team took Sunday off like it normally does, and Brown scheduled only light workouts to get ready for Florida. But on Monday, Blanton suggested that they hold a short scrimmage to make sure everyone was sharp. Florida would be his final game in the Assembly Center, and he wanted to do everything he could to make it successful.

So they went a half hour of controlled scrimmaging and closed with 10 minutes of game-situation play. It was their first regular scrimmage since December, and the intensity level was sky high. Among the handful of observers in the stands was a pro scout, who kept count of the number of times a player dove for a loose ball. He was well into the 30s before it ended and told Brown that an NBA team wouldn't have that many in a season.

Everyone on the team was eager to play Florida, which had become the hottest team in the SEC. The Gators had progressed markedly since their December loss to LSU and poor start in January. They had won 10 consecutive conference games. Florida had never led the league this late in the season. The school had never won an SEC title, and the Tigers didn't want to help it make history.

Later that afternoon, the finalists were announced for The Associated Press' player and coach of the year awards. Jackson was the only underclassman among the 10 finalists for Player of the Year. Brown was the only coach of an unranked team to be named a finalist for Coach of the Year. They had come so far in just a few months. The nation took notice.

Tuesday's practice was a typical walk-through, shooting workout that LSU uses the day before a game. The only thing different was the audience. LSU President Allen Copping had invited all members of the state legislature to visit practice. It is an annual event for the politicians. In some years, only six or seven show up. But with the team doing so well, there were dozens who stopped by to greet Brown and his players and wish them well.

Precisely at 3:30, Brown called the team together at midcourt. He could tell they were ready to play, so he offered only a light dose of incentive. "I don't like to be in a situation where I have to bid someone farewell. And even though it's only one person, that person means a lot to me. We have never lost and we are not going to lose the last game of the year in this gym." He was overstating his case again. LSU had lost five home finales under Brown.

"We are going to win this game for Ricky," he continued, "even if we have to get down on our hands and knees and scrub the floor. Our first goal is to win this SEC championship. Then I'm telling you we can go a long, long way. I really believe we can win the national championship. But first, let's take care of Florida."

Before they started the first shooting drill, all the players went over to meet the legislators. Brown didn't join with them. He sat on the bench and began to joke with Doc Broussard. He teased him about supporting David Duke, the former Ku Klux Klan grand wizard, who had just won a seat in the state House of Representatives.

Brown wanted to know why Duke wasn't at practice. It would have made for some interesting conversation, because George Eames of the NAACP showed up just minutes later.

"You know, Doc, there were times when I would have run over

there," Brown said, looking at the legislators in the stands. "It's nice of them to come, but we don't need them any more."

Broussard held back a smile until Brown had walked away. Within a half hour, Brown had spotted a familiar face in the stands and was hobnobbing with the legislators. He shook hands or spoke with most of them before they left.

Not even the legislators could have gotten extra tickets to the Florida game. It had been sold out since Saturday. The whole city of Baton Rouge seemed to be caught up in bidding Blanton farewell. The TV and radio stations and newspapers all had special stories on him. A full-page cutout of his jersey was on the back of the Morning Advocate sports section. No one wanted to see him play his final home game. But nobody wanted to miss it.

In a pregame ceremony, Governor Buddy Roemer congratulated Blanton on his career achievements and proclaimed it "Ricky Blanton Day" in Louisiana. With the crowd standing and applauding loudly, Roemer read the proclamation to Blanton and his parents. "I'll tell you what it says Ricky. It says, 'Thank you for your guts. Thank you for your teamwork. Thank you for the miracles. Thank you for making Louisiana a better place.'"

Brown also paid tribute to his captain. He chose to read the message on the newspaper cutout. "Thanks Ricky Blanton for a thousand thrills, for your dignity, for your class, for being the man you are, for being a part of us. We will never forget you. And we are going to remember you all the way to Seattle."

When Blanton was introduced, his mother and father standing at either side, the thunderous ovation lasted several minutes. He kept his composure until he could finally talk. Then he thanked the fans for their years of support.

"Hopefully, we can bring you an SEC title," he said before trotting back to the locker room to the sound of more cheers. It got even louder when he was the final player introduced and came running out of the locker room to break through a six-foot picture of himself.

This game belonged to Ricky Blanton. There seemed to be no way LSU would lose. Brown would try his best to make sure of that. But he didn't figure on two things: LSU was extremely tight and Florida played superbly to the end. The combination created problems.

In the first five minutes, the only player to score for LSU was Lyle Mouton. Everyone else was hitting the rim, rattling in and out, or missing everything. Florida had built a 15-4 lead with just over five minutes gone, and LSU had dug a huge hole for itself.

Brown kept looking at the clock and wondering if he should call timeout or wait until a television timeout. He chose the latter, then told them to relax and run their offense and everything else would work out. Jackson made up his mind to get them out of it. And he did.

His first basket of the half came at 14:38, his last at the buzzer. In between, he hit eight shots and finished the half with 26 points. His 15-foot jump shot put the Tigers ahead with 1:30 left in the half and took the roof off the Assembly Center.

Every person in the arena, except those on the Florida bench, press row and the scorer's table, was standing and screeching at the top of his lungs. They never got a chance to sit until the half ended, because LSU scored nine points to take a 50-44 lead. Dwayne Schintzius, the 7-2 Florida center, didn't even make a move down court on two LSU possessions. Jackson scored easily both times and Florida looked dead in its tracks.

In the locker room, Brown came across a small boy who had somehow wandered into their midst. This was no ordinary child. His face was disfigured, apparently from severe burns. When Brown went to shake his hand, he found only a stub.

For the next few minutes, Brown forgot about the game. He talked to the boy, then brought him into the room to sit on the couch beside Father Bayhi. Finally, he patted him on the head and turned around to face the players.

Confident of victory, he instructed them on how they could finish off the Gators. ''We're going to stay in the press. They can't handle pressure. They start panicking. So we're going to press them these first five minutes. I would really like to stagger them. If they would have been in the situation we were early, they would have tossed it in.'' Then he pointed one last time to Ricky's poster, reminding them they had one more to go.

To start the second half, Brown went with Richard Krajewski and Dennis Tracey, whose defense had been instrumental in LSU's comeback. Krajewski had been playing hard in practice since his meeting with Brown in the aftermath of the Alabama loss. His fiery effort seemed to bother Schintzius.

Krajewski, subbing for Vernel Singleton, had a game-high three steals and was shutting down Schintzius. Krajewski got winded midway through the second half, but his defense, coupled with Jackson's firepower, enabled LSU to build a 60-48 lead.

Whenever LSU had been in this position in the past, somebody—usually Jackson or Blanton—made sure the Tigers didn't give up the lead. Whenever Florida had been in this predicament, the Gators folded like an umbrella in a hurricane. Neither occurred on this night.

Schintzius and Livingston Chatman began to pick apart LSU's man-to-man defense. The Gators went on an 11-2 run and took the lead on back-to-back layups by Schintzius and Chatman. They edged in front by as many as six points, and even a four-point play by Jackson wasn't enough to regain the lead.

Jackson had a chance to tie it with a three-pointer in the final seconds. But knowing Florida would give a foul before letting him shoot an open three-pointer, he rushed his shot and missed badly. Krajewski, not realizing that the ball had been last touched by Florida, dove for it and knocked it out of bounds.

LSU had to give a foul to stop the clock, and Clifford Lett went to the line for a one-and-one with one second left. The LSU fans went wild in protest of no foul called on Jackson's shot. They began to throw paper debris on the court. Not wanting a technical, Brown rushed to the microphone and demanded that it stop. Even before the game started, a student had thrown a tennis ball at Schintzius. Brown climbed into the stands to find the culprit, who was ejected from the arena.

Because of his tennis racket incident in the fall, Schintzius had been pelted with tennis balls wherever the Gators played. In a crucial game at Vanderbilt, the Commodores had the ball and a two-point lead with two seconds left when fans started lobbing tennis balls at him, resulting in a technical foul. Schintzius made two free throws to force overtime, and the Gators came away winners. If that had not happened, Vanderbilt would have been in first place now instead of Florida.

This time, the tennis balls were pointless. The game was wrapped up for the Gators, who taunted the fans, daring them to throw something at them. The students couldn't resist. They threw more tennis balls at Schintzius. They hurled ice, paper cups, beer cans, pens, coins and anything else that wasn't bolted down.

Finally, the officials called a technical foul. Brown stormed on to the court, going nose-to-nose with Don Ferguson, usually one of his favorite officials. He heatedly explained that he had done everything he could to prevent such fan behavior and it served no purpose to prolong the game.

Brown was about to be ejected when Joe Dean came out of the stands to his rescue. Dean pulled Brown off the court and let the game end. Lett, undeterred by the pelting of trash, made six out of seven free throws. He was supposed to get only six attempts, but the officials lost count. Instead of winning a close game, Florida finished a 104-95 victor, clinched a share of the SEC title and eliminated LSU from contention.

The C.J. File—It really hurt to lose this game. We wanted it so bad. At the end, they were getting cocky, and that made me more mad. I can't stand that.

Arguing with the officials had given Brown a chance to let off steam before he met with his emotionally wounded players. They had wanted so desperately to win the last home game for Blanton. That was even more important than the lost title.

Brown tried to comfort and lift them back up. "It was a terrible call. Chris got fouled. They knocked the ball out of bounds. That was the only way they could have beaten us. It hurts, but oh, how much we've got to be thankful for."

He paced the floor slowly and chose his words carefully. Remembering the little boy who had joined them in the locker room at halftime, he asked his players to think about how that boy must feel every day. "He's got so much to overcome. I guess we take a lot for granted. This hurts, but there's always a reason for things. To be honest with you, I think this prepares us better for the NCAA Tournament.

"We are going to the NCAA Tournament. That did not win the NCAA championship. We are going to get a ring. We are going to have a ring for Jamie. It may be a ring for winning the SEC Tournament. It may be a Final Four ring. But we are going to get a ring, I promise you that."

For the first time that season, Brown directed all 13 players to get dressed and come to the press conference. He complimented them for their comeback, offered special praise for Krajewski and Tracey, and stressed that LSU would bounce back from this. "I'll tell you what, they haven't built an elephant gun big enough to knock my ass down. We will be back. Everything works out for those who understand things.''

Turning to Blanton, he said, ''We've got nothing to be ashamed of. Ricky, we didn't win this one. But we're going to be playing for another month. Let's not think the good Lord let us down. I'll tell you, without divine intervention we had almost no chance of being as successful as we have. We are not done. We have a month left. There's a little pain now. But we've got a heck of a lot to be thankful for. We're going to the NCAA. We're going to Seattle.''

Brown asked Rabbi Barry Weinstein, one of several guests in the locker room, to lead the closing prayer. Weinstein remained standing by the door as he prayed. ''It is written in the Bible that we're supposed to turn to God day by day. Rabbis often wondered what that meant, and the answer that they got is that each day is a gift from God. There is so much in this room for which to be thankful, for each one of you men who play basketball and make us so proud in Baton Rouge, for Coach Brown, for his staff, for this building, for the people who were here tonight. You are our inspiration. You are our blessing. You give us in Louisiana so much hope, so much pride. You give us reason to thank God day by day. I pray for your strength, health, well-being, safety. I pray that all of us can play the game of life the way that you played it tonight with courage, with stamina, with honesty, with faith. I pray that God will bless you and your families until we gather again.''

Brown had the final word. ''We're proud of you. We're thankful for what you've done. Remember, no excuses. Forget about it. We're going to get a ring.''

Wiping it out of his own mind was easier said than done for Brown. It was not so much that they had lost a title shot, it was how they lost it. The championship was theirs. All they had to do was finish the game the way they had started.

Never had Brown's team at LSU been so close to a title and let it slip through their fingers. It was an indication of fatigue. It was also a sign of inexperience. Brown stayed up all night contemplating every detail of the game. Did he make a mistake? Should they have pressed the entire second half? Was Krajewski in too long? How about Tracey?

By daybreak, he had resolved most of the questions. They were beaten by a bigger, more experienced team that was on a roll. It was time to look ahead to Ole Miss and then the SEC Tournament. He prayed for the wisdom to handle this defeat and grow from it.

Another problem arose Thursday. Marvin Willett, the dorm supervisor, was having trouble with a few basketball players and other athletes. Willett believed in strict discipline, and Brown backed him completely. He invited Willett to the team meeting that afternoon and assured him the rules would be followed.

All the young players already had been treated to the Breakfast Club, the 5 a.m. running session given by Johnny Jones. The most recent morning runners were Jackson and Singleton, who had gone out for hamburgers and missed curfew by half an hour. On game nights, the players had an 11 o'clock curfew. Brown changed that to 11 on all nights until the season ended.

Anyone who broke dorm rules faced more serious measures. Brown made that clear at the team meeting. "If you mess up, you're suspended. It's that simple. I don't care who you are, the first man or the thirteenth man."

In this case, girls had been visiting the players' dorm after hours. So Willett limited the dorm visitation hours to four hours a night, 7 to 11, Sunday through Thursday. There would be no visitation on Friday and Saturday. On some weekends, there had been girls in the athletic dorm all night. That was about to stop.

Brown wanted to end LSU's late-season slide as well. At 20-9 overall and 11-6 in the SEC, the Tigers could still finish second in the SEC or fall back into a tie for fourth. It would be crucial to the pairings in the SEC Tournament the following week at Knoxville, Tennessee. If LSU beat Ole Miss, it would play in the quarterfinals against Kentucky or the winner of Ole Miss and Auburn. But if it lost to Ole Miss, it could slip into the fourth seed and have to play Tennessee in the quarterfinals. The Volunteers would be on their home court.

Brown wanted to make sure his players understood the importance of the Ole Miss game. He believed they had already clinched an NCAA bid. But those things are never certain, especially if they wound up losing to Florida, Ole Miss and then to their first SEC Tournament opponent. The NCAA invitations would be given out a week from Sunday, and Brown didn't want to miss the grand ball of March.

Brown decided to keep the team at home Friday and fly to Ole Miss the next morning. It was a short flight, and he wanted to keep the players relaxed. He also liked to spend as little time as possible in small towns like Oxford and Starkville.

On Friday afternoon, a short practice was held in the Assembly Center. To liven things up, Brown came prepared with a story to tell the players. He called them together on the sideline and waited for Doc Broussard to come across the court. Then he proceeded to tell about seeing Doc with a beautiful blond, blue-eyed young lady at a local restaurant the night before. The players were overcome by laughter. But Doc cut off Brown, saying he was going to tell the story.

Doc explained that the woman was the daughter of an old friend and that he had recruited her to play golf at LSU. She had just completed her playing career and was finishing her degree. Doc said he was taking her to dinner as a favor to his friend. "Some of you know her," he said. "Her name is Cissye Meeks. She's in a class with you, isn't she, Chris?" Jackson looked surprised and shrugged. So Doc asked Singleton and again got a surprised look.

Now nobody believed him. Brown and Abernathy were taking turns poking fun at him. None of the players dared say anything, but they couldn't hold back smiles and more laughter. It delighted Brown and served his purpose well.

After that, he reviewed their team goals. They had set nine goals for the season, some from the outset, some that were added. They had accomplished five out of a possible six with three to be determined.

The goals already accomplished included a winning season, playing in front of the largest crowd in college basketball history, beating Georgetown, winning at least 16 games to secure an NIT invitation and in Brown's opinion, clinching an NCAA bid by winning 20 games. The only goal they missed was the Southeastern Conference title. But they still had three major goals left: winning the SEC Tournament, getting to the Final Four and winning the national championship.

"Are those last three impossible?" Brown asked. "We know they aren't. Ricky has been there. We were in a lot worse position in 1986, and we played in the Final Four. It will happen again."

Then he pointed to the 1980 SEC Tournament championship flag that was hanging from the ceiling of the Assembly Center. "We can get another one of those, starting next week. That flag belongs here. So in the midst of what you call failing, you're not failures."

As extra incentive, Brown announced the United Press International All-SEC team. Jackson made the first team and was Player of the Year. Brown was selected Coach of the Year. But Blanton didn't make the first team. Brown called it "one of the great injustices of all time.'' Then he announced that Blanton was assigned to guard Ole Miss star Gerald Glass, who was selected on the first team.

Brown had more to say about the all-conference team. ''A guy called me today and asked me what I thought about being Coach of the Year. I told him, 'I want to know why Ricky Blanton wasn't selected to the first team.' He didn't have an answer, but I do. And Ricky, you keep this in your mind. Years ago, John Wooden told me in sports, you're going to be in the public eye, and being in the public eye, you're going to receive a great deal of unjustified criticism and undeserved praise, and you should not be unduly affected by either. Ricky, don't you show that externally, but I hope that helps you. I'm not doing that just to stimulate you. You don't need that. But we need to whip them.''

Blanton would need plenty of help-side assistance to stop Glass, who had been rated among the top three shooting guards in the country by most pro scouting services. Glass was quick off the dribble and could hit any kind of shot inside 18 feet. LSU would try to double him whenever possible and force some of the Rebels' weaker players to take shots they didn't want. That strategy had enabled LSU to rout the Rebels in Baton Rouge.

This game looked like it might be over quickly, too. But it was Ole Miss that came out in a blaze. Glass was almost unconscious, hitting everything he put up. He overwhelmed Blanton with his speedy first step and quick release on his jumper. Glass scored 14 points before the first official timeout, just over four minutes into the game. Brown put Singleton on Glass. He also tried Tracey and Krajewski before the half was over.

Nobody was going to stop Glass on this night. He was barely grazing the net on his gorgeous jump shots from about 10 to 12 feet. The Rebels stretched their lead into double figures, and the sellout crowd of 8,000 was wild.

Jackson was not without offensive fireworks of his own. No one could contain him, either. Most of his shots were farther out; he scored 19 points. But the first half belonged to Glass. He had 28 points in the first 15 minutes. Then LSU switched to a matchup zone and Glass scored one basket the rest of the half. LSU pulled within seven points.

It was still anybody's game. But the Tigers had to find a way to contain Glass. At halftime, Brown decided they would switch to a box-and-one with Singleton guarding Glass.

Then Brown had to make sure everyone wanted this victory as much as he did. Most of his criticism was directed at Blanton and Mouton, who had contributed little at either end. He kept his composure and tried to instruct. If it happened in the second half, he wouldn't be so nice. No one was thinking about the SEC Tournament any more. All their thoughts were on Ole Miss.

"You're far from being out of it," Brown said. "But you've got to put more enthusiasm into it." He stopped momentarily to take a stat sheet from Johnny Jones. "Glass has 30 points. He's hit 13 out of 18 shots. Rebounds, they're killing us. They're the smallest damn team in the league, and they've got 20 rebounds to our 11. That's a hell of a job Ricky, Wayne, Vernel and Lyle. They shot 64 percent from the field. You played that game like you're proud to have won 20 games. Bullshit, you have got to play hard and with enthusiasm if you want to win this game!"

Their spark was rekindled in the second half. Mouton and Blanton began to get into sync, and Jackson put on one of his finest shooting displays. But Ole Miss shattered the box-and-one defense with three-pointers, building its lead back into double figures. LSU went back to man-to-man, and Singleton managed to limit Glass somewhat before fouling out in the final minutes.

Even though Ole Miss led by eight with just a minute and a half left, LSU wasn't out of it. The Tigers extended the game by fouling, and Jackson scored three times from three-point range and was fouled once. He hit the free throw for a four-point play that tied the score at 106 with 17 seconds left, capping an incredible comeback. The Tigers had set a school record of ten 100-point games in a season. But this game was far from over.

Glass had a chance to put Ole Miss ahead after Kyle McKenzie fouled him with 14 seconds left. He missed the front end of a one-and-one and Sims rebounded. Sims got the ball to Jackson, who drove for an off-balance 20-footer that hit the side of the rim and fell off. Sims again pulled down the rebound, and his six-foot shot rolled around the rim and skipped out of the basket at the buzzer. They went into overtime. Jackson already had 52 points. Glass had 49.

The C.J. File—It was really exciting. I'd come down and make it. Then he'd come down and make it. Then I'd score, and he'd score. I was thinking, "Man, it's not supposed to be like this." He couldn't miss.

He'd be leaning in and somebody would put a hand in his face, but swoosh, it went in.

Russell Grant was sitting on the bench, oblivious to anyone on the court except Jackson and Glass. "Nobody was paying attention to the game," Grant said. "Everyone sat back and watched Chris and Glass shoot. It was some of the most incredible shooting I've ever seen. I loved it."

In overtime, LSU took the early lead, even without Singleton, Sims and Mouton, who had all fouled out. Krajewski, Geert Hammink and Tracey came on to replace them. LSU had a chance to go ahead by six, but Jackson's three-pointer rattled in and out. Ole Miss tied the game at 112 on a three-pointer by Glass from the left corner.

Jackson missed an opportunity to push the LSU lead back to three, just missing another long jumper. That gave Ole Miss the ball with less than a minute left. Glass drew a two-shot foul and went to the line with 12 seconds left. He made the first, but was strong on the second try. LSU had another chance to win.

Jackson took the ball the length of the court, dribbled through three defenders and shot a 22-foot jumper from the right wing. It hit the back of the rim and bounced high with three seconds left. Blanton got the rebound, but before he could shoot, Hammink mistakenly tipped it away. The Ole Miss team and fans broke loose in celebration. LSU retreated to its locker room in dejection.

Jackson had outscored Glass, 55-53, in one of the great shootouts of all time. He broke his NCAA freshman scoring record and finished the regular season with 895 points. But his personal achievement was of little consolation.

The C.J. File—I didn't have any idea how many points I scored. All I knew was we lost. The only shot I remember was the last one, and I missed it.

Brown went right to the chalkboard. All eyes were on him as he slowly wrote three lines: 1. Season one—20-10; 2. Season two—SEC Tournament; 3. Season three—NCAA Tournament.

The tension mounted. Still, Brown didn't say anything.

Finally, he began shaking his head and turned to address the team. "In just a moment, I am going to erase season one, and we are going to erase it completely from our memory. I want to make a few comments before I erase it.'' He praised Singleton and Mouton for their second-half performances. He called it a marvelous comeback. But the compliments ended there.

Once again, Blanton caught the most flak. ''Ricky, Glass literally cut the heart right out of you. That wasn't you out there. He ate you alive, and you just backed off. That wasn't you out there.''

The he addressed the whole team. ''You backed yourself into a corner. You literally blew a chance to be second in the league. You put yourself in the toughest bracket in the SEC Tournament. And you wind up tied for fourth. We should have won the league, and we finish fourth.''

Brown was getting worked up, but he wasn't out of control. The rally had lifted his spirits, even though they didn't pull it out. Abernathy added some stern words, then Brown finished the session.

''Ricky, I don't know what happened to you. You get all those honors in the paper and those plaques. I don't know what was the matter with you. Maybe you just decided you're an NBA player, so you don't have to play for us any more. You didn't do anything for us. You didn't do anything.'' At last, he erased season one. Then he concluded, ''We've got season two now. We had better get our damn jocks laced up and be ready to play and especially our captain. Let's shower and get the hell out of here.''

No one was in the mood to talk to the media. Brown had to do his radio show and speak briefly at the press conference. The media requested Jackson and Blanton for interviews. Jackson got up to go outside, but Craig Carse told him he didn't have to do it. Carse told an Ole Miss official ''they aren't interested in talking.'' Both players were glad, especially Blanton. Jones, though, asked Carse why he wouldn't let them talk, and they wound up arguing in the locker room.

Blanton was among the first players to board the team bus. But Brown sent a manager to get him. Then he took him into a side room and resumed scolding for 15 minutes. After that, Brown had to film his television show, which took almost half an hour. Then he fulfilled a promise for an interview with a Baton Rouge television station and finally signed about a dozen autographs. Meanwhile, the players had waited on the bus.

Brown usually enjoys doing his television show. Most often, show host Jim Hawthorne has to be careful not to let Brown talk too long. But on this night, Brown held his hands over his face between segments and had to invent a smile. It was difficult to give positive responses. But he managed.

His first assignment was to talk about Blanton. "Well, I'm going to miss Ricky. He's an overachiever of the highest degree. He's also a wonderful person. And we wouldn't have gotten close to 20 wins without his leadership. This year was tough for Ricky. I love him like a son. But I have no one else to go after. There aren't any other juniors and seniors. There's only one Ricky. And as a result, he got all the aggression. I asked him to do everything. I am going to miss him. He is a remarkable human being."

Doc Broussard was angry, because Brown had let the players wait too long. Brown was still fuming. Jones and Carse remained angry at each other. It was not a fun night in Oxford.

If that weren't enough, their charter airplane had to carry a light load of fuel so that it could get up enough speed to take off on the short runway. The plane had to land in nearby Greenville to take on more fuel. Then it had to contend with high winds on the way home.

The wind tossed the plane around like a bottle on the open sea. Blanton was one of several players who threw up. Almost everyone felt ill by the time the plane reached Metro Airport. They unloaded at almost 2 a.m., tired, queazy, distraught, but thankful there were two seasons left.

18

Season Two

Ricky's Diary, March 6—It's tough to lose two games like we just did. The Florida loss was really hard for me to take. I don't think I've ever been more hurt and flat disappointed. It took the air out of me. I was just deflated. It was so painful. It's something I'll look back on, and there will always be a pain there for that game. I think we're playing not to lose. We forgot what it took to get on top. There is a problem. I think the publicity got to us. It's nothing you can put your finger on. Just an invisible problem.

On the way home from Oxford, Dale Brown caught wind of the flare-up between Craig Carse and Johnny Jones. He called them aside at the airport and tried to resolve the issue. He explained to Jones that he had instructed Carse to make all decisions about granting interviews for Jackson, because of his Tourette Syndrome. Jones relented. That was one problem solved.

Getting ready for Tennessee would be quite another. The players had to concentrate on midterms all week, leaving no time to practice in Knoxville. Brown gave them Sunday and Monday off to study and rest up for postseason play.

Brown was troubled by a nagging chest cold, disappointed with the way the team was playing and upset with himself again for the blowup in Oxford. But on the way home from his office Monday night, everything changed. It was below freezing, the wind was gusting, and suddenly his car ran out of gas. He grew more angry by the minute as he walked to find a gas station.

When Brown finally arrived at one, the startled attendant began screaming, "It's Coach Brown! It's Coach Brown!" The young man explained how much LSU basketball meant to him and how much he had enjoyed the season. He said he had told his friends that the Tigers were going to end up in Seattle. That caused Brown to think about what the team had already accomplished. It gave him a shot in the arm. "You don't know how much you helped me," he told the attendant.

The next day, there was a press conference at LSU. Naturally, the media wanted to know if Brown thought the Tigers had another miracle left in them, particularly for the SEC Tournament. Dale was cautious in his reply. "I don't see the field in any way except it's tougher than heck the bracket we're in. And I think we've put ourselves in a tough situation. I just know any team can win it, except Auburn. I don't think Sonny Smith has a possibility of winning it. If he does, he should be crowned king of this country, instead of president. I don't think he can win it, otherwise anybody can."

Brown did say he expected Florida, Vandy, LSU, Alabama and Tennessee to be in the NCAA field. "Based on the power formula which the NCAA has, I would say we are locked. But I don't know that. We have got to try to win the 21st game."

Asked about Jackson being SEC player of the year, Brown was reluctant to praise him too much. "I made a mistake by saying he's the greatest individual player I've ever coached. But he is. And now what you do is insult everybody else. I shouldn't have said that. That puts a lot of pressure on him. And what does John Williams think about it? What does Rudy Macklin think about it?

"And I don't want Chris' career always being about who's the best. Most insane asylums are filled with delusions of grandeur and persecutions. And so I think when you start comparing yourself and having to live up to other people's expectations, it's very, very difficult, and he is a team player. I would bet, and I'm not going to ask and embarrass him, that he has not read the Sports Illustrated article. For me to push that, I think would be an injustice to him."

Later that afternoon, the players gathered for their first practice of the week. They were told to meet Brown in the locker room at 3:30. As was becoming customary, he wanted to apologize.

"I was so mad at myself when I got home and realized what I had done the other night. It just took me awhile to realize what I did. I was so mad at myself I could have kicked myself in the teeth. What happened was we got so high and then the Florida game and the Ole Miss game got me down. You have to be careful not to burn yourself out.

"One reason we continue to win is we have good people in this program. Damn good people. You get into misunderstandings, but we work them out. And that's the difference in good people and a good program. I have never had a team in 32 years of doing this that I've been more proud of. I was so disgusted with the way we played against Ole Miss. But I feel so good about this team. I feel so good about what we're about ready to do. What we've done is wonderful. But it's not over. We've got some great things ahead of us.''

He talked briefly about the challenge of playing Tennessee on its home floor. Then he read from a fan's letter. "My heart bled purple and gold Saturday night, but by Sunday, the optimism I've learned from you reassured me. First, the odds are definitely in our favor against Tennessee. After all, after three wins, they're due for a loss. And after two losses, we're due for a win.

"Second, we're better off in that bracket, even though what you said, because we're in the same bracket with Florida and they just don't seem to have the character to maintain their intensity. Their first goal was reached, an SEC championship, which they backed into. I think we can beat them. Third, if we don't, God forbid, win another game, who can complain about a season that brought wins over Georgetown and Nevada-Las Vegas and two wins over Kentucky. All this in a supposedly rebuilding year. Yes, this is a team of destiny.''

They practiced for only 45 minutes, but there was plenty of running. All the players worked up a good sweat, and the timing seemed to be there on offense.

Brown called the team to the bench for a short talk. "We put a great big mountain in front of us. It's in Knoxville. We've got midterms. We're not going to leave early. But we need mountains. We like to climb mountains. Georgetown was a mountain. Las Vegas was a mountain. This is right up our alley. And selfishly, I would love to have another opportunity to play Florida in the semifinals.

"Now I don't want to put too much emphasis on this one game. And I told Ricky this: We want to go up there and play well. Remember this, it isn't important that you're the best, it's important that you do your best. Put that in your mind. Lyle, you don't have to be the best. Vernel, you don't have to be the best. Chris, you don't have to be the best. No way. What's important is you do your best. If everybody does their best, everything will fall into place. Believe me.

"We're going to take it easy tonight and tomorrow and get ready to play Tennessee. You need to rest. You need to pray. You need to psychologically get ready. And you need to wipe out sorrow. Don't keep it in your mind. We have 27 days left to the Final Four. We need to approach it this way: 'I just want to do my best.'"

Everyone on the team understood it would take one of their best efforts to beat Tennessee on its home court. The players had tests to take on Wednesday and Thursday before departing on a commercial flight to Knoxville. LSU was the last team to arrive at the tournament site and the only team that didn't practice.

The rest had been long overdue. Blanton was starting to feel like his old self again. Jackson couldn't wait to play. The other players were fresh physically and emotionally. The only concern was their offensive slump. If it had just been caused by fatigue, they should be able to bounce back. But the cause might be something more serious. Nobody was really sure.

Brown had left on an earlier flight so that he could take his turn at the tournament's press conferences. Each head coach is required to address the media. Brown was given the noon slot and had to rush from the Knoxville airport to make his appointment. He surely wouldn't be late to one of his favorite activities. Most of the reporters who covered the conference were there. Brown was their best bet for colorful quotes, and he didn't let them down.

Tennessee coach Don DeVoe was finishing while Brown was talking to several reporters. He didn't hear DeVoe pay him a strong compliment. "Dale Brown does do a magnificent job with his basketball team. They've had tremendous success against us. He's out-coached me, out-recruited me, he's beat me at just about every turn of the corner and I recognize that. He's a great motivator and I think he does a great job."

Brown had little to say about Tennessee. His concentration was on his team, now more than ever. He touched on most of the same things he said in Baton Rouge. Then he answered questions. The first concerned the factors contributing to LSU losing four if its last five SEC games. The question caught Brown by surprise.

"We lost four of our last five SEC games?" he asked the reporter. He admitted that he didn't realize that. Of course, mixed in with those four league losses was the dramatic win over UNLV. That had tempered the late slide in conference play. Brown cited several reasons for the skid: limited talent, depth and size. Also, he pointed out that the SEC had some of the nation's leading players and teams in scoring, rebounding, field-goal percentage and free-throw percentage. LSU was fifth in the nation in both scoring (93.8) and free-throw percentage (77.5).

Brown wanted to finish the interview with a funny line. The target was Florida coach Norm Sloan, who had twisted Brown's comments from another press conference to motivate his team before the LSU-Florida game a week earlier. Brown had been asked which contenders had the most favorable schedule in the last week of the SEC season. He responded that LSU and Alabama did, because they both had a home game and Florida did not. Sloan used the comments as if Brown had said Florida had no chance to win the league.

Brown considered it an unfair tactic and wanted to make his point in a good-natured way. "If Norm Sloan has got his tape recorder on, I think that Florida should win the NCAA championship," Brown said. "They've got the greatest talent, the greatest coach, the greatest cheerleaders, the greatest athletic director, the greatest academic counselors." His drollery had the media rolling with laughter. At the suggestion of a sportswriter, he added that Sloan's wife is the greatest singer of the national anthem, too. That brought more laughter.

When Sloan heard about it later that day, he showed why he has been nicknamed "Stormin' Norman." As far as Sloan was concerned, this was no joke. He wanted to go for Brown's jugular, whether it be on or off the court. If LSU defeated Tennessee and Florida survived its quarterfinal game, they would be matched in the semifinals.

Sloan tried to do battle Thursday night. He was sitting at press row preparing to watch a first-round game between Georgia and Mississippi State and hoping to run into Brown. He didn't have to wait long. Brown was assigned the seat to Sloan's left.

When Brown sat down, he tried to make small talk. But Sloan turned red and began blurting obscenities that could be heard by everyone within shouting distance. All around them, reporters and officials were stretching their necks to hear exactly what was being said. Many expected a physical confrontation between two of the most fiery coaches in the conference. Brown had toned down his act in recent months, but would it be enough? Could he restrain himself?

At first, he thought Sloan was trying to return the practical joke. Surely, he was just pretending to act unruly to make some fun. After several minutes, Brown realized it was no laughing matter.

Sloan's best shot came in the early moments when he told Brown, "We kicked your ass in Baton Rouge, because you were so stupid. You didn't even mention us being in the race. That was really stupid. You're an asshole. I used to like you, but you're an asshole. You're one of the good ol' boys in the conference, who never give Florida any credit."

Astonished, Brown couldn't make up his mind what to do. In other years, there would have been no question. He would have grabbed Sloan by the throat and choked him or punched him in the mouth. Part of him wanted to do that now. But he didn't.

Brown never stopped smiling. He remained calm and took his time before speaking. There was no Brownout. Finally, he explained that he had only answered a question about the league's schedule in the final week. He tried to convince Sloan that no slight was intended.

Brown thought about something he had just read in a Christian book called "Our Daily Bread." It addressed how to handle undue criticism and insults. He reflected on the example of Jesus accepting the insults of Pontius Pilate. He came to the conclusion that Sloan's outburst was not worth losing his temper over. Instead, he let Sloan continue.

It took about 15 minutes before Sloan ran out of steam. He hadn't anticipated Brown's reaction. He sat another 10 minutes without saying a word. He stared at the players on the court with an icy glare, while Brown watched with a happy, content look.

Brown considered leaving to find someone more friendly to converse with. He chose to stay and force Sloan to understand him. He also felt great triumph in dealing with such a hot-head reaction. He thought it might even help Sloan. It did.

Sloan started talking about Reginald Boykin, one of the Mississippi State players. Both coaches remarked about what a talented player Boykin was and neither could figure out why he didn't get more minutes. That led to other basketball talk and soon it was halftime. Brown had to leave to do a television interview. Before he left, Sloan wished him good luck against Tennessee.

Another chance for Brown to lose his cool presented itself Friday morning. Since he had stayed up until 3 in the morning, he slept in and didn't come out of his hotel room until the team bus was loading at 11. By then, every member of the LSU traveling party, except Brown, had read the lead story in the Knoxville News-Sentinel. The headline read, "LSU gives Vols ample reason to be motivated."

Joe Dean had fueled the fire by making some derogatory remarks about Tennessee and in particular Dyron Nix. The comments were made at the Birmingham Tipoff Club the previous week.

The LSU players had a copy of the story and passed it around during the pregame meal. Ron Abernathy made several remarks about it while going over the scouting report and showing video tapes of Tennessee. Even Father Bayhi seemed perturbed after reading it.

Nix was quoted as saying, "He (Dean) said I didn't have a big heart. I read it. He was referring to our chances of getting into the NCAA Tournament and the comment was made. Now I'm going to respond to it. If you don't know me, don't speak of me. I'm going to prove differently tomorrow and there's not a thing they can do about it. I have a tendency to get more things done when someone speaks about me."

Tennessee had every advantage it needed already. Something like this could ignite the whole team. Nobody likes to be insulted, especially athletes. In coaching, there is a cardinal rule that you never give the opponent any kind of verbal ammunition or "bulletin board material." This story was sure to be plastered all over the Tennessee locker room.

No one on the LSU staff had dared show the article to Brown. They feared he would get on the phone and lash into Dean and then lose track of everything else. Finally, as the coaches were boarding the bus, Abernathy mentioned the story to him. There was no immediate reaction. Abernathy held his breath. The other assistants did, too. But Brown's only response was to shrug his shoulders and say, "I wish he hadn't said that." Everyone was amazed.

Brown was in a cheerful mood when he entered the arena with the team. The first person he bumped into was John Guthrie, the former Georgia coach, now associate commissioner of the Southeastern Conference. Brown and Guthrie were old coaching pals. Guthrie was also the supervisor of officials for the SEC, so he got many late-night calls from Brown when Dale had a complaint about an official. That didn't seem to shake their friendship.

Guthrie's 10-year-old daughter, Dana, was particularly fond of

Brown. She ran up and hugged him. Then she showed him some good-luck posters she had made for him and told him that she was wearing an LSU T-shirt under her blouse. Her father winced at that, and told Brown that he had to be impartial, even if his daughter were not.

Also greeting Brown was Austin Wilson, who was covering the tournament for The Associated Press. Wilson joked that he had brought some Chapstick and was ready to pay up on his bet that he would kiss Brown's other side if LSU won 20 games. Brown appreciated the humor and told Wilson to save his kisses for his wife.

During pregame warmups, Brown walked over to the Tennessee bench to speak with Nix. He offered an apology and told him he was a class player. Nix appreciated the gesture, but didn't forget what prompted it.

Brown knew he was going to have to be at his best, motivationally speaking, to pull this one off. He covered the chalkboard with inspirational messages, statistics, records and scores in previous SEC Tournaments.

"Everybody must contribute," he stressed in his pregame talk. "When it comes to tournament time, that's when you have to mesh. And that's why we've played so well this time of year. Hey, I could put a list up here of all the things we've done in March and it would go all the way down to China." He stopped to point to some of the big tournament victories that he had written on the board.

"When you look at this list, what happened then was because five people were playing together and the people coming off the bench meshed. I still think that 75 percent of this game is mental. We think we have an NCAA bid, but we're not going to think about that. This game today is for the Southeastern Conference championship. If you win today, you will go on to win the championship."

After discussing the defensive matchups, he sent the team out for final warmups. He hoped to get a shot at Florida in the semifinals, but there was enough to worry about in this game. Nix was a dangerous player even when he didn't have extra incentive. Blanton drew the task of guarding him, just like he did in Baton Rouge. Ian Lockhart and Doug Roth also posed problems for LSU inside. Wayne Sims and Vernel Singleton would have their hands full.

Just before tipoff, LSU learned that Nix would not start. DeVoe had been bringing him off the bench and would continue to do that. Lockhart, Roth and Mark Griffin would be Tennessee's frontcourt.

One thing did work to LSU's advantage. Since it was an early afternoon game, the huge Thompson-Boling Arena was only about two-thirds full, and the fans weren't overly enthusiastic.

If the Tigers could get off to a good start, Brown figured they could take the fans completely out of the game.

Singleton controlled the opening tip, and LSU went on offense. Jackson drove straight down against Clarence Swearengen and missed badly, barely grazing the rim on an off-balance jumper in the lane. It was a sign of things to come for LSU.

Tennessee was having no trouble scoring against LSU's man-to-man. Griffin hit a 3-pointer. Roth followed with a tip-in. It was quickly 5-0, and the crowd was very much in the game. Brown didn't want to use a timeout this early, so he tried to settle his players from the sideline. Jackson finally got on the board with two short jumpers, but at the first break, Tennessee was ahead 9-4. The Tigers were ice cold, and their offense was stagnant.

In the huddle, Brown wanted to calm his players and get their minds off the poor start. Looking at Singleton, he said, "It looks like you're really uptight. You've just got to relax. There's no reason to be uptight about this game. It's no different than any other. Now take your time on offense. Move the ball around. We're all right."

Two minutes later, Nix made his first appearance with Tennessee already leading 13-4. If he sparked the Volunteers, it could be over in a hurry. Instead, it was obvious he wanted this game too badly. He missed his first shot and was called for traveling on the next possession. Finally, somebody other than Jackson scored for LSU when Mouton hit a jumper to make it 15-6.

The next time down, Blanton charged into Griffin and picked up his second foul. Tennessee continued to spurt, building a 21-10 lead. Brown made a decision at the next official timeout to switch to a 2-3 zone, because Nix, Roth and Lockhart were starting to heat up inside. The move slowed Tennessee offensively and enabled LSU to make a run.

Even with Blanton sitting out, LSU managed to put together a late streak, cutting the big deficit to four. The key play was a steal by Singleton, who assisted Jackson for a layup. The Tigers had a chance for the final shot to pull within two or three, but Mouton stepped out of bounds with the ball. Griffin drilled his third three-point shot just before the buzzer to push it back to 41-33.

Brown was livid. He couldn't believe that Mouton would step out of bounds on a crucial possession. But he was much more upset with Singleton, who had not gotten out quick enough to cover Griffin in the corner. His voice echoed through the halls as he screamed at Singleton all the way to the locker room. It didn't get much better inside.

"I have tried to be calm and patient with you the whole damn half," Brown continued, already speaking in a threatening tone. "Vernel, that's THREE damn times you've let that guy hit a three-point shot from the corner. Will you wake up!"

Brown slammed his fist against the chalkboard and stomped to the other side of the room. Mouton was his next target, and Brown took him to task for a lackluster effort. Sims hadn't hit the boards enough and was chastised for it. Even Jackson heard some cross words for not coming to get the ball more on offense. Blanton, scoreless in the half, somehow escaped Brown's tirade.

Despite the poor first half, LSU was still very much in the game. Brown wanted everyone to understand that. "That was the worst first half we've played all year long, and we're only eight points down. We didn't do anything intelligently. They don't think they can beat you. They're substituting people in and out of the game. They were confused when we changed defense. Now if you use your brain on offense, we can win this game. We are averaging 109 points off them. You've got 33. All you have to do is concentrate and get into a rhythm, and we will get this game. Then we will win the championship."

His halftime talk was cut short so the players could have more time to warm up for the second half. They went out with seven minutes left on the clock, but the halftime entertainment wasn't over, and the players had to wait several minutes. Brown complained to tournament officials, but to no avail. He realized then that the team should have practiced the day before the game. They had shot 37 percent in the first half, about 13 percent off their season average. Part of that could be attributed to Tennessee's aggressive man-to-man, particularly Griffin's hustle in denying Blanton the ball. "I couldn't get it to Ricky," Jackson said later. "Griffin did a good job on him."

Even after shooting around for five minutes and listening to Brown stress offensive movement, the Tigers weren't much more effective. Blanton opened the second half by missing a 10-footer in the lane. At the other end, Jackson fouled Swearengen in the act of shooting. Swearengen made one free throw to stretch the lead to nine. Jackson answered with a three-pointer to cut it to six. But Griffin countered with a tip-in and three-pointer, and the margin was back to 10 at the first official timeout.

It didn't get any better. Tennessee's Greg Bell sank a three-pointer from the top of the key. Then Griffin delivered his fifth bomb of the game to build the lead to 54-39. Brown used his first timeout with 14:07 left.

The C.J. File—We were all pretty tired. Ricky was even tired. I've never seen him like that. I remember looking over at him and he had his head down and was trying to suck in some air. I was thinking, "Oh my goodness, this can't be happening." My legs were real weak, too. I knew we were in trouble.

LSU went back to man-to-man, hoping to get some steals. But Jackson became too aggressive, fouling Swearengen and giving up a three-point play that built the lead to 18 points. Soon it was 20 and all but over.

LSU fought hard, but there was too much ground to make up. Tennessee made its free throws down the stretch and won 95-77.

The loss bothered Brown, but he knew they had gone down fighting for everything they could get. There would be no more yelling. No temper flaring. He was disappointed, but satisfied with the second-half effort. Now his task was to rebuild their confidence and get ready for the NCAA Tournament. Dean had been told by a friend on the NCAA selection committee that LSU was assured of a spot in the tournament. Brown hoped he was right.

In the locker room, the mood was somber. The loss hurt. Blanton had a wounded look on his face. Jackson was bellowing loudly and shaking his fist. Singleton held his head in dejection. What troubled everyone even more than losing this game was that the season seemed to be slipping away from them. Their hopes of a championship of any kind were fading. There was every reason to believe they would lose their first game in the NCAA Tournament and finish the season having lost their final four games.

The first thing Brown did was go around the room and shake every player's hand, whether he had played or not. Singleton and Mouton received compliments. Brown thanked everyone else for not giving up and for putting out until the buzzer.

Even with the door closed, the Tennessee pep band could be heard in the background playing the school fight song. But Brown spoke as softly as he had all season. "I don't know what went wrong. We're such a good offensive team, but we didn't have it today. The rhythm just wasn't there. That's all right. Season two is over.

"That's a quick season. Now we have to get ready for season three. Just a couple comments before we forget about this game. You didn't listen to us early in the game. You're not going anywhere without us. We're not going anywhere without you. And we're sure not going anywhere without each other. Remember that."

There wasn't much else to say. Brown announced they would fly home in the morning and meet Sunday night after CBS announced the NCAA field. Then they would practice to get ready for a tournament game. Father Bayhi closed with the Lord's Prayer. Brown prayed that he could find a way to turn this team around in a hurry.

Before going to the press conference, he remembered something Vonnie had told him that morning on the telephone. He shared it with the team. It was a passage from a daily devotional, and it was about discouragement. Vonnie had been beset by more illness and was worried about the possibility of another tumor. Doctors ruled that out, but she had remained sick in bed for most of the week. The message had helped her immensely, and it seemed to be the right thing to tell the team.

"Now I've never quit one thing in my whole life," Brown said in finishing his talk. "As disappointed as I am right now, I am not discouraged. We've had worse situations and come back. The *first* guy I see with his head down, I am going to grab you right by the hair. Forget about it. We've won 20 games. We are not through yet. So don't anybody be discouraged. We are going to come back."

Fighting discouragement was nothing new to Dale Brown. He had spent a lifetime overcoming long odds. Within a few minutes, he had put the game behind him and was looking ahead. It helped him to be at a tournament, because he had plenty of friends there. He could talk and get his mind off his team for a while. There would be time later to analyze and make adjustments.

On the way back from the press conference, he ran into John and Dana Guthrie again. He graciously accepted their condolences. When he noticed how disappointed Dana looked, he took her by the hand and led her to the locker room to meet Blanton and Jackson. Blanton talked with her in the hall, where he was still answering reporters' questions. Then Brown took her into the locker room to see Jackson, who was sitting beside his locker, still dressed in his uniform. His glum look immediately turned to a smile when he saw the little girl.

"This is one of your biggest fans, Chris," Brown said. "Meet Dana Guthrie. Her dad is head of officials."

Jackson put his arm around her and hugged her. He told her how glad he was to have a fan like her. She wouldn't say much, but Jackson kept talking to her anyway. After several minutes, Brown took her by the hand again and led her to the door. He asked Craig Carse to stand with her while he talked to Jackson and Singleton alone.

While Brown was telling his two freshmen how proud he was of them, someone called for him in the front section of the locker room. He went out and found Dana in tears. Jackson came out, too, and walked up to the girl and hugged her again.

"It's all right, honey," he whispered. "Everything is going to be fine. Now what's bothering you? You shouldn't be crying like that."

In her tiny voice, muffled by sobs, she answered, "Chris, I wanted you to win. I wanted Coach Brown to win."

Jackson pulled her closer and tried to comfort her. "Don't worry about this one, sweetie. We're going to win our next game. Don't cry now. We'll win the next one for you."

Tears running down her face, Dana tried to smile. Brown took her by the hand and led her back to her father at the other end of the arena. Dale was touched by her reaction as well as the tenderness displayed by Jackson. After all, C.J. was right. It was just a game. If they didn't win again that season, they still would have gained so much.

Instead of returning to the hotel with the team, Brown stayed to watch the second quarterfinal game between Kentucky and Vanderbilt. He hoped Kentucky would find a way to win for Eddie Sutton. He feared it would be Sutton's last game at Kentucky, perhaps in major college basketball. The Wildcats led early, but Vanderbilt came back and put them away.

The loss sealed Kentucky's first losing season in 62 years and ended any chance of Sutton surviving as its coach. He would resign on March 19, and two months later Kentucky would be put on three years probation by the NCAA.

Sutton and his players were deflated. Brown went to their locker room to see if he could offer some encouragement. He had intended to speak only to Sutton, but was invited to address the players, all of whom were in tears. Sutton introduced him as a dear friend.

"I just want to say a few things to you," he said. Then he walked around the room shaking hands. "I want to shake each one of your hands. You showed a lot of class this season. You have learned more from this than you could have ever learned from winning a championship. You were never hot dogs. You didn't quit. You showed a lot of class. I am proud of you all."

Brown turned and left the locker room. He spoke briefly to Sutton in the hall and then headed toward the exits. He had to go back to the hotel, tape his TV show and then talk to the team again. He had called a midnight meeting.

In the hotel lobby, he happened to see Jacqueline Jackson waiting for Chris to come downstairs. She had driven 12 hours to get to the game and had brought along her youngest son, Omar. They had arrived early that morning, but got lost trying to find the arena and missed the game. But they had heard all about it and were naturally disappointed. Brown wanted to cheer them, so he told Chris to invite his mother and brother to be on the TV show, which was going to be filmed in the hotel lounge.

When Jacqueline Jackson arrived for the show, Brown walked up to her and gave her a hug. They had resolved their differences and both seemed to agree LSU was the best place for Chris. On the show, Dale asked her about everything from her son's first experience with basketball as a toddler to her views on the season. Her replies were short but thoughtful. It was clear they had bridged the gap. Omar, meanwhile, sat on Brown's knee and pledged to follow in his brother's footsteps and play at LSU. The show gave Brown another lift.

The team meeting went just as well. He spoke for only 10 minutes, but delivered one of his more positive talks, even though he felt miserable from the effects of his cold.

He pointed out that Arizona and Oklahoma had narrowly escaped upsets to lightly regarded teams that day. LSU had nothing to be ashamed of losing to Tennessee at Knoxville.

"I guarantee you, if you keep on playing hard, we're going to make something very special happen this season," he told them. "We ain't through yet. We can still get to Seattle."

19

Hoosiers in the Desert

*Ricky's Diary, March 11—I can't figure out this season. We had those
big wins over Georgetown and UNLV. But the two losses to Mississippi
State are haunting us. I keep looking back to the first game with Mississippi State, and I could have hit the shot to win it for us. And then in the
Georgetown and UNLV games, I did hit the shot to win it for us. I wonder why it couldn't be reversed. With two wins over Mississippi State, we
would have still won the league. I just wonder why it's like that. But I
guess that's the name of the game.*

Exhausted, ill and feeling a little sorry for himself, Dale Brown
slept late Sunday morning. It was a gorgeous day in Baton Rouge with
the temperature climbing into the 70s, but he couldn't get going. He
finally read a little in bed and spent the early afternoon sunning himself by his pool. Gradually, he began to revive.

Father Bayhi, Craig Carse and Jim Childers were on their way
over to watch the announcement of the NCAA Tournament field. Father Bayhi brought a large casserole dish of crawfish stew and everyone ate before the show came on. By then, Brown was starting to feel
better. There was still some apprehension over the bids. Where
would they go? Who would they play? Who would be in their bracket?

Brown passed out copies of the tournament bracket, and all four men were poised to fill in the blanks.

Only moments before the CBS telecast commenced, Brown leaned over to Childers and said, "This is the most exciting time of the year. I love this." Childers nodded his agreement, although this was his first time going through it as part of a college team.

The players watched it on their own, some at the athletic dorm, others at friends' houses, all waiting to hear their assignment. Ron Abernathy and Johnny Jones were at home. They would meet with Brown later, and then attend a press conference in the L Club Room. The players would participate in the press conference and then go to practice.

If LSU got in, there would be high hopes, talk of another miraculous March. If the NCAA passed up LSU, it would be a depressing night, especially since the team was going to practice.

When LSU was announced as a 10th seed and matched with seventh-seeded Texas-El Paso in the West Regional at Tucson, Arizona, nobody reacted. Brown just stared blankly at the TV screen. He still didn't show any emotion when it was revealed that Indiana was in the same bracket. If LSU beat UTEP and Indiana beat George Mason, it would be rematch time in Tucson. Dale Brown vs. Bobby Knight. The media would have a ball with this one.

As expected, LSU was scheduled to play in the late game Friday. Kent Lowe, assistant sports information director, had heard reports that CBS wanted to showcase Chris Jackson in a nationally televised first-round game. No one was surprised that LSU was playing in Tucson. And UTEP was one of the teams that the LSU coaches had suspected could be their first-round opponent. They didn't know much about the Miners, except they had won a lot of games and were a quality team with a highly accomplished coach in Don Haskins.

At a commercial break, Brown finally said something. "I wonder why we got a lower seed than Vanderbilt?" Everyone seemed puzzled by that. Vandy, with a 19-13 record, was seeded eighth and would play Notre Dame. Brown had predicted LSU might play Notre Dame. He also thought LSU would be seeded seventh or eighth. But quickly, he turned it around, remembering how well they had done the last time they were seeded so low. They also played Indiana in that 1987 tournament.

Carse suggested that the NCAA wanted to match Indiana and LSU. Both CBS and ESPN pointed to that possibility. In Louisiana, everyone remotely interested in college basketball was chomping at the bit to get at Indiana.

Soon, Robyn called her father to say she believed this was their chance to finally beat Indiana. Then Jones called and told him, "I know we're going to win two games anyway." The phone continued to ring every few minutes.

Any other time, Brown would have been delighted to have Indiana in his bracket. He would have focused everything on avenging his two losses to Knight. And this was the ideal circumstance. Indiana had won the Big Ten and was seeded second in the West. Many thought the Hoosiers should have been a number one seed. As for LSU, what chance did a tenth seed have? It was just the kind of situation that was perfect for a Brown upset. Oh, how wonderful it would be to crush Knight at his best.

Those thoughts flickered through his mind, but for only a few moments. Then he got a grasp on himself. The feud with Knight was part of the old self that Brown was struggling to overcome. His disdain for Knight's tactics would not get in his way this time. There would be no talk of wrestling him naked. In fact, there wouldn't be anything said about Knight or Indiana from then on.

"Let's make one thing clear," he said to his assistants, "we are not going to talk about Bobby Knight and we are not going to talk about Indiana. We have got a hard enough problem with Texas-El Paso. I've played them twice before and they're always good."

Brown discussed with Carse about how to get information and video tapes of UTEP, a member of the Western Athletic Conference. Brown had a variety of contacts in the WAC, including his first college boss, Ladell Andersen, who had just concluded what would be his last season at Brigham Young University and final year as a coach. There was also Benny Dees at Wyoming, who had been an assistant at Alabama and head coach at the University of New Orleans. They would be sure to help with a general scouting report. Unfortunately, neither was home that afternoon and would have to be contacted after practice.

The only thing Brown knew about his opponent was based on two previous meetings with Haskins' teams. Both had been physical games that went to the final possession, LSU winning each time. That was precisely the type of contest Brown wanted to play this time.

To do that, he had to get this team back on track. There was no time to waste. He wanted to practice that night and use every other available time. This would not be a week like the last. The team was going to be well-drilled, emotionally charged and hungry. Brown pledged to himself to work harder than he had all season and to demand the same of his players. There would be plenty of time to rest in April.

He got his message across to the players with a lively pep talk in the conference room that night. His mind was focused on one thing: recharging these players. Somehow, because of mental or physical fatigue or poor strategy on his part, they had peaked too early and run out of steam in March. It was up to him to get them back. His first order was to attack, always be on the attack. In practice. In preparing mentally for the game. Then on the court against UTEP.

As Brown stood at the head of the long conference table, every player knew it was going to be a demanding week, win or lose in Tucson. "Listen up and look me in the eye," he began, waiting for everyone to look his way. "We are going for one thing and one thing only. We started the season out with all kinds of goals. We accomplished most of them. There's no goal left now but the national title. There ain't no win this game or win that game. If we lose, we are done. But we are not going to lose."

All their concentration and motivation had to be channeled toward UTEP, he stressed. No other game mattered if they lost that one. He told them it didn't make any difference that they could play Indiana. No one on this team played against the Hoosiers in 1987, anyway.

Then he reminded them how much they had to be thankful for. He said they needed to give thanks to God for all the blessings of the season, especially getting into the NCAA Tournament. "I'm not very good at making up prayers, but I would like to thank God for making us stay together and doing what everybody said was impossible. I think—and I'm not trying to stick anything down your throat—if we had not been close to God, we would not have won 10 games this year. We would have been lucky to win 10 games."

On that note, he asked everyone to stand and bow his head. They all grasped hands, and he led a prayer. "Dear God, I would like to thank you for another opportunity to do something good here. I would like to thank you for staying with this basketball team all year long. I pray that you will give us the strength to do good during this NCAA Tournament, to follow what you want us to do. Make our goals correct, that we may honor you. We'd like to thank you by saying an Our Father." They all said the Lord's Prayer together for the umpteenth time. Everyone had it down pat by now, even if they had not known it on October 15th.

Brown couldn't know at the time, but this would be the last prayer he would lead with this team. He had it set in his mind that they were going to get past UTEP and then get past a second-round game against that team from Bloomington. After that, it would be on to Denver for the regional semifinals and final, and the Final Four trip to Seattle would be next. There would be plenty of opportunities for team prayers along the way, and Father Bayhi wouldn't always be there. So Brown fully expected to be leading many more prayers.

Certainly, the way they practiced over the next three days would not indicate the season was coming to a close. Brown was ferocious with his pleas and brutal with his physical demands. He thought they were soft in Knoxville. He made up his mind it would not happen in Tucson.

But before entering the battle ground of practice Sunday night, the players got to visit the demilitarized zone. They had to join Brown for a short press conference in the L Club Room. All of the beat reporters from Baton Rouge and New Orleans were there. The bright lights from the TV cameras were glowing, but there would not be much to report on this night. Brown had no comment on Knight and had little to say about UTEP.

About halfway through the press conference, Jamie Roth and his family slipped into the back of the room, sat down on a couch and waited. They had just come back from Houston, where doctors determined Jamie's condition had worsened. He had been given six more weeks to live. But that would be long enough for LSU to get to the Final Four. Despite being in severe pain and barely able to walk, Jamie had come to be with his team on this night, to try to offer some encouragement after the Tennessee loss and to wish them well in Tucson. He would not be able to travel with them any more.

Brown had seen them come in and joined them as soon as his interviews were concluded. They talked about the season, while the players finished their individual interviews.

"We're going to get you that ring, just wait and see," Brown told him.

"Don't worry about that ring, Coach," Jamie said, his gentle voice barely audible. "It would have been nice. But that don't mean nothing. Just being with the team, that's what really mattered."

Merely trying to talk seemed to make Jamie hurt even more.

Brown remained cheery outside, but it tore him up to see the boy like this. He knew it would take a miracle to save Jamie now. But he also knew if they could pull off another March miracle, it would bring such joy to their little captain.

The "Road to Seattle" began in a remote location for the Tigers. The main floor of the Assembly Center was still set up for a gymnastics meet that had been held that afternoon. So they had to retreat to the basement gym for what would be an hour and a half of the most grueling basketball of the season.

As soon as Brown stepped on the court, he shifted into overdrive and didn't let up until the workout ended shortly after 9. He ran through shooting drills with Wayne Sims, who was in an offensive slump. Sims had to complement Chris Jackson and Ricky Blanton for LSU to be effective offensively. With Brown throwing him crisp passes to the high post and then down on the block, Sims was keenly aware that he had better start hitting. He made almost every shot he took in the drill.

Once everyone had warmed up, Brown called them to midcourt for a quick huddle. "We've got one thing on our mind now—winning a national championship. We are going to work hard enough to win a championship. Everyone is zero and zero now. We are going to win this game. We are going to bust our ass and win this game!"

If anyone needed an extra push, Blanton was ready to deliver it. He had that cold, fearless look on his face, like he was ready to fight for his life. He glared at Brown during the talk, absorbing every word and getting more and more eager to do battle. Then he let it all explode on the court.

They started with shooting drills and moved right into a controlled scrimmage. Actually, the only thing controlled about it was that Brown stopped play from time to time to make corrections or scream for more aggressiveness. The players had already made up their minds to play out of control, with no regard for their own safety.

The intensity was tremendous. The sound of squeaking shoes and grunts of exertion echoed off the cinderblock walls. Bodies were flying everywhere. On the first possession, Lyle Mouton and Kyle McKenzie plunged to the floor after a loose ball and were quickly joined by three teammates. Shortly after that, Russell Grant leaped for a mishandled pass and crashed onto the deck. He grabbed his bad knee and flinched in pain, but was back on his feet before anyone could help him up.

Offensively, they got back into the kind of flow they had developed midway through the season. Jackson brought the ball up, Blanton popped out and took the pass on the wing, and either penetrated himself or hit Sims on the low post or Singleton cutting across the middle. When Sims got the ball, he took his soft turnaround jumper or passed back outside to Jackson or Mouton. Everyone was involved in the offense. Everything was clicking.

Brown wanted more. His voice got louder, his pace grew quicker. He was all over the court. He praised the good plays, but was never quite satisfied. His displeasure found a familiar target—Mouton.

The hard running caused all the players to gasp for air and ease up whenever they could get away with it. Brown caught Mouton sloughing off on defense and ripped into him. "Lyle, you're a sissy. You're a damn sissy. Everyone else is killing themselves and you're loafing. Let's get going."

The players picked it up another notch. There was more reaching for steals, more contact under the basket, more effort everywhere. Blanton clenched his fist after hitting his fourth consecutive jumper. While running back on defense, Jackson shouted, "We've got to work hard. Let's do it. Harder!"

Finally, Mouton hit a bomb from the right corner and sprinted into defensive position. He tipped the ball away from Dennis Tracey and slammed into him trying to get possession. It was an obvious foul.

Brown screamed his approval. "That's it, Lyle! I'll take that foul. I'll take it. That's what we have to have from you. Way to go, Lyle!"

In 90 minutes, they had put it all back together. They were tired and sore, but eager to get after somebody. Their offense was flowing again. Nobody was standing around waiting for Jackson to take over. There was a steady blend of passing, screening, dribbling, cutting, shooting and boxing out. It was the best they had looked all season. It was by far the hardest they had worked.

Brown left the gym thrilled about the step they had just taken. He couldn't wait to get home to call for information on UTEP. It was one of those times when he felt like he had enough energy to fuel an entire team. And maybe he did.

Now it was a matter of maintaining the enthusiasm and building on it until game time. Brown got to the office early Monday morning and set out to get more reports on UTEP and fill his mind with more ways to rev this team.

There was conflicting information on UTEP. Andersen reported that the Miners were on a roll and would be almost impossible to beat in Tucson, which is a relatively short drive from El Paso. Dees and one of his assistants offered slightly different opinions and weren't sure about what kind of offense UTEP would use. Brown needed to see video tapes to make up his own mind. None would be available until Tuesday.

That afternoon, Debbie Roth called and asked if she could stop by to see Brown. She was having a hard time dealing with Jamie's worsening condition and needed someone to talk to about it. Brown did his best to pick up her spirits, but wasn't sure how much help he had been. His mind was so tuned in on the game. He had trouble focusing on anything else.

There was some good news, too. A reporter called to get comments about Jackson receiving yet another award. A big award. He was selected first team All-American by The Associated Press. Only one other freshman had ever received such recognition. Wayman Tisdale of Oklahoma had made first-team All-American as a freshman in 1983.

Jackson was joined on the team by four seniors: Sean Elliott of Arizona, Stacey King of Oklahoma, Danny Ferry of Duke and Sherman Douglas of Syracuse.

Brown told the reporter the first story about Jackson that popped into his mind. "Chris got 36 points off somebody, and I read the next day in the paper that his coach thought his player really did a good job on Chris. So that's a lot of pressure. I don't want to add any more pressure. But he is by far the best player I've ever coached. He's just a very unique player, and he's going to get better. That may be hard to believe, but he will."

At practice, Brown's first command was to remove all the chairs and tables from the arena. Anything that wasn't nailed down had to go. Then he announced that nobody—players, coaches, managers, trainers or guests—would sit down at practice. "We can sit down when the season is over," he said.

Practice was nearly as intense as it had been Sunday night. They went at each other with a passion. It seemed they were practicing too hard at times, possibly risking an injury. But Brown kept asking for more. And they gave it.

The only break came near the end of the hour-and-a-half workout. Standing beside Jim Childers near the stands was Mike Hansen, the hot-shot point guard from Tennessee-Martin. He had decided to transfer to a Division I program. Arizona, UCLA and North Carolina were interested, but Brown had persuaded him to commit to LSU. Hansen was making an official visit and wanted to enroll at LSU in the summer. He would have to sit out a year, but would be a valuable asset for the 1990-91 season.

Brown called the players together at center court and motioned for Hansen to join them. "I'd like to introduce Mike Hansen to you guys. This is the closest any of you have come to him. He scored like a hundred points against us." All the players shook hands with him. After practice, Jackson sat and visited with Hansen for half an hour. Hansen liked C.J. right away and said he hoped to get a chance to play with him before he turned pro.

Rumors had been circulating for weeks that Jackson had decided to leave LSU for the NBA. His selection to the All-America team fanned the flames. LSU had a press conference scheduled on Tuesday to discuss the NCAA Tournament. Brown decided this would also be the best time to end the speculation about Jackson.

That morning, Brown asked Gus Weill to help Jackson prepare a statement. Jackson told him what he wanted to say and Weill scripted it. Then they rehearsed. When Jackson got in front of the media, he showed his usual poise. There was a hush in the room, many thinking he was turning pro, just like John Williams had done in a similar press conference three years earlier. Jackson had other plans, saying, "I want to make it unmistakably clear that I came here to get an education and to play basketball, in that order."

He explained that he intended to stay the full four years. His goal was to join the NBA with a degree in hand.

Brown again had few comments for the media. He informed everyone that he and his team would not talk about UTEP. They didn't want to give out any more motivational material for the opponents. Brown would only discuss LSU.

And he was very open about that. "I've been kind of abusive this week in practice. I'm driving these kids harder than I've ever driven them. Now I'm not talking about grabbing their jerseys, and that kind of abuse. But the truth about attacking on the boards."

The battle cry was sounded again that afternoon. The workout involved another hour and a half of running and contact. It was their final tuneup at home before playing UTEP. They hoped it would not be their last home practice of the year. If they played the way they had practiced, it would not be.

The C.J. File—We're really ready to play. It's the NCAA Tournament and that's special. This is what we've worked for all year. Plus, Coach Brown is really fired up. He's making our practices tough. They say if you practice hard, you play hard. We haven't practiced this hard all season.

The team spent most of Wednesday traveling. They had a late-afternoon commercial flight to Dallas from Baton Rouge and after an hour layover, they caught a flight to Tucson. By the time they finally got to the Hotel Park Tucson, it was late in the evening.

Before everyone got off the bus, Brown stood up and reminded them that they were there to win a national title and that was the only thing they should be thinking about. There was time only to get something to eat and then head back to their rooms to get some sleep. The players ate by themselves. The coaches were at another table, along with Vonnie, Robyn and Chris Prudhomme.

There wasn't much to do on Thursday. Their 8 o'clock practice was the last one scheduled. To pass the time, the team took a sight-seeing trip to Old Tucson, a desert location used regularly to film Westerns.

Brown and Abernathy continued to study tapes of UTEP. After a couple hours, Brown said, "We've seen all we need to see. We know what they're going to do." He was concerned about the quickness of UTEP's three-guard lineup. Tim Hardaway was particularly impressive driving to the basket. But the guards weren't great shooters and didn't work the ball well to their big men. A matchup zone would work well against them, he decided.

The rest of the day, the coaches and players relaxed in their rooms and watched the day-long ESPN coverage of the tournament. Brown had to leave early with Jackson and Blanton to attend a press conference. He held a short team meeting before practice, so they didn't get on the court until 8:10. That left 50 minutes before they had to be finished.

There were a few dozen UTEP fans still in the stands, having just watched their team practice. Carse and Jones had spent much of the day at the McKale Center watching all the teams in LSU's bracket work out. These practices are simple, used primarily as a chance to get a feel for the court, baskets and environment.

Since LSU had not practiced since Tuesday, Brown pushed the team extremely hard for the first 15 minutes. They ran one-man fast break drills and then three-on-two drills. Everything was at full speed. Attack. Attack. Attack.

After they broke a sweat, the rest of the time was devoted to shooting. Jackson was sent to one basket to shoot nothing but three-pointers from the top of the key. Blanton and Mouton worked on three-pointers at the other end. Sims and Singleton went to one of the portable baskets at the far side of the arena, and the other players shot together at another goal. Everyone was shooting well. Jackson and Blanton hit more than 75 percent of their shots.

Brown huddled the team as time was about to expire on the arena clock. "This night is just like the one when we practiced in the Super-dome for Georgetown. They're going to toss it up here tomorrow night, and it's going to be a war. We are going to attack and we will beat Texas-El Paso, just like we beat Georgetown."

He was into his hand-slapping, arm-waving routine. "We have got to be the aggressor. I am going to roam the sideline. I ain't going to be asleep on the bench like I was at Tennessee. They think they're aggressive. Man, they ain't seen us yet. Georgetown is picked to win the national championship. We beat Georgetown. There is no reason why we can't win the national championship."

Blanton had the final word before they left the floor. As the players locked their hands together over their heads, he shouted, "We worked too hard this week to come here and lose. This one is ours!"

They thought the Hotel Park was theirs, too. Seton Hall also had been assigned to it, but for some reason—nobody at the hotel seemed to know why—the Big East team pulled out and found its own accommodations.

On the morning of the game, however, the place turned into the Hotel Hoosier. There were Indiana fans—red blazers, red hats, red skirts—swarming all over the place. They arrived by the busload, talking up the impending matchup with LSU, which already was the major story of the regional. When some of the fans began to bump into LSU players, coaches and other officials, the desert party really kicked into high gear.

The Hoosier invasion didn't hit home with Brown until later in the day. He had stayed in his suite with his wife most of the morning, relaxing and reading newspapers. There weren't many Indiana fans in that section of the hotel, so he didn't think much about it. When he went to the team brunch, several IU fans came up to shake his hand.

One jolly, gray-haired gentlemen, wearing a Hoosier jacket, told him, "Dale, we're pulling for you to beat UTEP. We want to play you." Brown thanked him, smiled politely and walked away, not giving it a second thought.

That afternoon, his attitude toward sharing the hotel with Indiana fans changed in a hurry. After the team had gone to a nearby high school gym for a short shooting practice, the players were in their rooms resting before the pregame meal. Many of them were trying to take a nap. But that became impossible when the IU band, cheerleaders and two hundred fans converged at the pool area in the middle of the complex for a pep rally. The drummer had been pounding away for almost an hour before Brown found out about it. He had been in the restaurant with his guests and didn't hear the commotion. When it was called to his attention, he hit the roof.

Ignoring catcalls from the IU fans, Brown walked swiftly toward the hotel offices and demanded to see the owner. A desk clerk directed him to the executive office, where he found only a secretary. She told him that the director of marketing was the man in charge. Brown demanded to talk to him immediately or, he said, the entire LSU party was pulling out. She scrambled out of the office to find her boss.

Bo Bahnsen, one of the LSU officials, was already there trying to get somebody to stop the pep rally. "This is absolutely ridiculous," Brown told him. "We're trying to get ready for a game, and they pull this on us."

As the minutes passed, Brown grew more upset. Then the unsuspecting marketing director, Jim Wright, showed up. He was greeted by a five-minute tongue-lashing. Somehow he never flinched and convinced Brown not to leave the hotel. Wright left for the pool and came back with a relieved look on his face. The band would be finished by 4:30. It was already 4:22.

Brown was somewhat mollified, but had a little more fury to vent. "Jim, I cannot believe you let this happen. You must have known about how we get along with Indiana." Wright acknowledged he had read about Brown's clashes with Knight. If Brown had known at the time what Johnny Jones found out later, that Wright was an IU alumnus, there's no telling what might have happened.

"This is really uncalled for," Brown snapped. "I'll tell you what, if that band plays another song after 4:30, I am going to take that tuba player and throw him in the pool." He hadn't forgotten about Knight throwing an LSU fan into a trash can. The joke was lost on Wright, who had a worried look on his face again.

Actually, the music ended before 4:30. Brown was still angry, but he returned to the restaurant to finish his snack. Then he and Vonnie went up to their room.

About fifteen minutes later, the band began playing louder than ever. The cheerleaders were leading cheers, and IU officials were talking on a public address system.

Brown came out of his room overlooking the pool and stood by the railing. Vonnie was right beside him to make sure he didn't get too upset. They watched and listened to several songs and cheers. Thinking it was almost over, they went back into their room.

There was one more round of "We are the Hoosiers." Then several IU fans shouted in unison, "That was for you, Dale." That merely reinforced his decision to leave the hotel the next morning. Of course, that would be a moot point if they lost.

Losing was the furthest thing from Brown's mind that night as the team bus left for the arena at 8:15. He was so keyed up by the Hoosier distraction and his attack approach to the game that he never really considered the possibility of being eliminated by UTEP.

His pregame comments were simple and to the point. "Coach Abernathy and I are in our ninth NCAA Tournament together. We've been down the road. We know what you have to do. You are one of nine schools that have been to the last six NCAA Tournaments. Johnny has played and started twice against Texas-El Paso, and we won them both. We know how to play them.

"*You* have got to be more aggressive than them. *You* have got to take the game to them. That's our approach tonight, and *you* will win." He never mentioned that this game was for the right to play Indiana, which was in the process of destroying George Mason.

The game plan was equally simple. They had to move aggressively in the matchup zone to prevent Hardaway and the other guards from penetrating. Most of UTEP's losses had come against teams that played zone defenses. That was LSU's defensive edge. Offensively, everything seemed to be clicking. Brown went over some adjustments in case UTEP tried a box-and-one or triangle-and-two. He expected his players to be effective against any defense.

Father Bayhi, who had flown in that day to be with the team, closed out the pregame session. First, he gave them a message from Jamie Roth. "He wanted me to tell you all that he loves you and he is going to meet you in Seattle.'' Then he gave a brief scripture lesson and led the team prayer.

In the early minutes of the game, everything went according to plan. Blanton, Jackson and Sims each had a basket and Singleton hit two free throws to account for LSU's first eight points. They weren't pulling away, but the ball movement and timing that had been missing for the last two weeks had returned. The Tigers led through most of the first seven minutes, but never by more than two points. There was no reason to believe they couldn't maintain that level of consistency.

But their last lead was 12-11 on a rainbow jumper by Sims with 14:38 left. The last tie was 13-13 with 12:55 remaining. Then LSU's offense dissolved. Jackson stopped looking for Blanton and Mouton on the wings. Sims and Singleton were stationary inside. They fought bitterly hard on defense, but the offense wasn't there to back them up. There was no rhythm, no teamwork, no points. They went 14 possessions without scoring.

Meanwhile, Hardaway spearheaded a fast break that helped send UTEP on a spurt of 15 unanswered points to build a 28-13 lead. The McKale Center was rocking with orange-clad UTEP fans that made it seem like a home game in El Paso.

During timeouts, Brown was fierce, screaming at his players to run their offense. He pulled Jackson temporarily, replacing him with Tracey. Then he tried Richard Krajewski for Sims. Nothing worked. His temper escalated.

The C.J. File—I was too emotional. I really thought we were going to play well, because Coach Brown had pushed us so hard in practice. I wanted to win bad and I was forcing too much. Coach Brown took me out and gave me a chance to think about it. I'm glad he did that. I needed that time. I realized I was trying to make too much happen. After that, I let the game come to me.

Singleton broke a dry spell of more than seven minutes without a basket. Still, UTEP's lead swelled to 19 points. LSU, aided by a four-point play by Blanton, made a late run but was still down 42-29 at halftime.

It had been bad enough for the LSU players out on the floor. But there was a Brownout waiting for them in the locker room. It didn't last long, but was as powerful as any of the season.

"This damn team can be beaten!" he roared, marching around the room. "But you guys don't seem to have enough guts to do it. We are going man-to-man, and we are going to spill our guts out there. I am fighting this damn game down to the last second, and you sure as hell better, too. We can win this game! We can win this game!"

Everyone who had played took some heat. Jackson got the most criticism he had received all year. He was responsible for getting back on defense, and UTEP had seven fast-break baskets. He had also forced too many shots and taken the team out of its offense. Blanton, Sims and Singleton were blasted for not hitting the boards hard enough, even though LSU had a 23-22 edge in rebounding. Mouton, for once, escaped with only a minor scolding.

Abernathy, who was mad at Craig Carse for continually telling C.J. to shoot, took the floor and pointed out some problems with the offense. That gave Brown time to simmer down. The Brownout was over. He gave some brief instructions on offense and rebounding. Then he reminded them they had come from farther behind at Georgia and could pull it off again. "Don't quit. Don't feel sorry for yourself. Get out there for warmups and get the right attitude and we will win this damn game!"

The switch to man-to-man was just what LSU needed to become more aggressive on both ends. UTEP missed its first five shots of the half. Meanwhile, the Tigers got two free throws from Singleton, followed by two Jackson jumpers. The lead was down to seven. Antonio Davis missed a short jumper for UTEP, and LSU had a chance to pull even closer.

On the next possession, Mouton had the ball up top. Blanton, trying to work free inside, was knocked to the floor by Davis. Brown screamed for a foul. There was no call. Instead, Johnny Melvin made a steal and fed Hardaway for a layup. Brown was still arguing with referee Leonard Wirtz when trail official Sid Rodenheffer blew his whistle and charged Brown with a technical foul.

Brown was furious. He couldn't believe that Rodenheffer had called a technical when he wasn't even in the vicinity of the bench and there had been no profanity used. Brown turned toward Wirtz and shouted, "Haven't you got enough guts to call a technical?" Wirtz did, and Brown got his second technical.

After the game, Brown wouldn't comment on the calls. Blanton did, saying they were cheap calls and that Brown had said nothing to warrant a technical.

LSU lost possession and UTEP got four free throws. Hardaway made them all, pushing the lead to 48-35. Even though Hardaway missed a three-pointer that could have stretched the margin to 16, LSU's momentum was broken.

Jackson had a 25-point half and finished with 33. The Tigers attacked to the end, but they never made a serious challenge. UTEP took an 85-74 victory and moved on to face Indiana. LSU, its season over, was heading back to Baton Rouge.

The C.J. File—We just couldn't quite pull it out. We got on that losing streak, and everyone was so tired. We needed to win one to get back on track. But we couldn't get it.

After the game, Brown went around the locker room shaking each player's hand again and thanking him for a season Brown would never forget, even if it were a finish he would rather not remember.

"We wanted to do the impossible," he said softly, in dramatic contrast to his halftime address. "Twenty wins was the impossible. We have to face reality, too. You should be proud as hell of yourselves. You didn't quit the second half. You had a wonderful season. I am sorry I cost you four damn points. I didn't help you one bit. But it's over. Wipe this game off your mind. If this is the worst thing that ever happens in our lives, then we should be overjoyed. We can thank God that we made it to the NCAA Tournament and had a miraculous season."

He nodded toward Father Bayhi, who led the final prayer. "You are a special group of young men. A very special group. Disappointments are going to happen in life. But we do have so much to be thankful for. Let's praise our God with the Lord's Prayer." They held hands and prayed for the last time.

In the next hour, Brown was sidetracked by reporters. When he finally did leave the arena, he went the wrong way around the building. By the time he reached the back parking lot, the team bus was just pulling away. The managers had looked for him, but had finally given up.

His anger rekindled, he took a taxi back to the hotel and bawled out Jim Childers and the managers for leaving him. Then the players complained because the hotel had packed only one tiny sandwich in their box lunches. Brown became even more upset. He ordered fifteen pizzas, but when they finally arrived, most of the players had fallen asleep.

That wasn't all. Childers found out they couldn't get the team on a flight home until almost 5 o'clock Saturday afternoon. Brown went to bed angry and slept late.

But in the morning, he was refreshed mentally and physically. He got a rental car and took Vonnie for a long drive around Tucson and into the surrounding mountains, all the while contemplating the events of the season.

"Last night I almost forgot how much God gave us this year," he told Vonnie. "I guess I expected so much out of them, I almost lost sight of reality. But if I hadn't expected so much..." He stopped talking and kept driving.

Nothing Will Change

Ricky's Diary, March 18—I'm hurting right now, but I've got to look ahead to the future. I want to keep playing basketball. My dream is to play in the NBA. But whatever happens to me, Coach Brown has really helped. He is someone who taught me a lot as a person and drove me as a player to be my best. We've been through so much, both good and bad. I think that's what friendships are made of, good times and bad times. If you had only good times, you don't know if you really have a true friend. We've been through some bad times, so I know I have a true friend. A lot of times people get caught up in winning and losing and forget about what's right and what's wrong. I think your first priority should be to learn and to mature as a person. And if you can do that, everything else is going to be successful.

Mingled with the inevitable disappointment of losing an NCAA Tournament game, hope sprang eternal for Dale Brown, his players, his coaches and his program.

Chris Jackson would be coming back with a full complement of what might become the greatest talent ever on a college basketball team. Ricky Blanton, though hating to end his college career, was eager to give the NBA his best shot. Ron Abernathy couldn't contain his excitement over being a candidate for several head coaching positions.

All the other players and coaches had aspirations of being a major part of making LSU the preeminent power in the game.

"Next year" had arrived for Brown. He sensed it was well worth the wait. He was already looking forward to October 15 when he could start blending them all together. For once, he had no urge to get out of the country or even out of town. He liked where he was at. He loved the kind of athletes and individuals who were with him.

Vernel Singleton had already made plans to work out with Jackson all summer; they would concentrate mainly on ballhandling. He was anxious to move back to off guard, his natural position. Who better to learn from than Jackson. They agreed to train on the beaches of Gulfport for part of the summer and practice on campus with their new and old teammates the rest of the time.

Wayne Sims was also ready to make a position change. He knew his best chance to start on this new team and later in a pro career was to play small forward. That meant he had to work on his outside game, shooting and ballhandling. He also had to slim down and become quicker. His offensive ability and experience would give him the early edge.

Another duty Sims had been preparing for was team captain. Through the season Blanton had taken him under his wing, showing him what is required in keeping all the players together and serving as the liaison between them and Brown. Sims was entering his fourth year in the program and probably his third season as a starter. He was the logical choice for captain. Jackson was the other choice because of his floor leadership.

Russell Grant and Dennis Tracey figured to be backup guards again. They could help themselves and increase their playing time with a good summer. Tracey had to develop a jumper to go with his defensive skills. Grant worried that he might need knee surgery, which would probably sideline him for a year. He knew he couldn't go through another season with so much pain. But he didn't expect what team doctors told him shortly after the season ended. There was really nothing they could do to improve his knee.

All his dramatic, fearless dives for the ball had caught up with him. He had sacrificed himself for the good of the team. He had set an example for everyone else. And just like Brown had predicted, Grant had won a game for them—probably several games. Following the doctors' recommendation, he chose to give up basketball and concentrate on getting his degree in finance from LSU.

Lyle Mouton was a special case. He had not met his own expectations or Brown's, but he had stuck it out and made the effort. And he had improved markedly in his overall performance, so much so that he even surprised Brown. By season's end, he was a respectable defensive player, perhaps the best on the team.

Despite his progress, he was unsure if he wanted to return or if he would be invited back. The constant grind of Brown's demands and embarrassment of Brown's verbal abuse made Mouton wonder if he could take another year of it. At times, he thought it might have been better for him to have left the program in December. Then he thought about what he and his teammates had achieved in the last three months and knew he had made the right choice.

After meeting with Brown, Mouton decided that he, too, was going to give up basketball. But his athletic career would continue. He followed the lead of Ben McDonald and switched to the baseball team. He was a power hitter and had enough speed to play almost any position. Many thought baseball was his best sport, anyway.

There were similar doubts for Kyle McKenzie, Lester Scott, Geert Hammink, Richard Krajewski, Stephen Ussery and Jason Cormier. Unless some players were injured or ineligible, they realized they would probably not get any meaningful playing time. McKenzie and Scott wanted to play somewhere, so they chose to transfer to smaller programs. Cormier and Ussery made the same decision as Grant, electing to devote their full attention to academics. Hammink and Krajewski remained on the team. They showed hints of progress and could still blossom late in their careers.

Brown hoped Jamie Roth would still be on the team. Maybe they had helped give him the will to live. Certainly, he had enriched their lives. Somehow he grew stronger during the late spring and early summer. Brown wanted his players to keep encouraging this courageous boy in his battle with cancer. He knew they would learn from their little captain, who had become a part of them all. It was an emotional moment for everyone when Brown presented Jamie with his very own NCAA Tournament watch at the team's awards luncheon. No, he didn't get a ring. But oh, that watch. It was something very special "forever to see."

All the decisions had been made. Six of the underclassmen were returning, and six were following other pursuits. Then there were the seven new players—Stanley Roberts, Harold Boudreaux, Maurice Williamson, Shaquille O'Neal, Lenear Burns, Shawn Griggs and late addition Randy Duvall—all looking ahead to their chance to play with Jackson. Mike Hansen also would be available for practice, but had to sit out a year before he could play.

Never satisfied with his performance, Jackson couldn't wait to start working out for next season. This was a happy time for him. He had thoroughly enjoyed his first season. He had set an NCAA freshman scoring record with 965 points and his 30.2 scoring average was second in the nation to Hank Gathers of Loyola-Marymount.

Even in his childhood fantasies, C.J. had not fathomed becoming the most celebrated freshman of all time. He had been raved about in every major sports publication and on every network in the country. He was responsible for generating hundreds of thousands of dollars in revenue for LSU and an immeasurable amount in publicity and good will. As for recruiting, Craig Carse had the easiest job in the world. It seemed everyone wanted to play on the same team with Jackson. Melvin Simon, a burly forward from New Orleans, committed to sign with LSU before his season ended in the state playoffs. And Stanley Roberts' former high school teammate Tim Burroughs, another powerful forward, told Brown he would join the Tigers after another year of junior college.

More importantly, Jackson felt at home in his new environment. He had a second family with the basketball team. He was best friends with Singleton. He had arranged a summer job with a Baton Rouge public relations firm, which enabled him to get a loan to buy a used car. There was also a girlfriend, Kim House, a sophomore from New Orleans. He shared his personal problems with her and went to her home to meet her parents. "She's very special," he said.

If anything would keep him coming back for three more seasons, it would be these people. That the team would not be undersized and undertalented any more wouldn't hurt, either.

Jackson expected to be a different player as a sophomore. Not so much because of his experience as a physical change. Taking Haldol for Tourette Syndrome, he had gained so much weight that his speed had decreased sharply and his jumping ability had declined to the point that he rarely dunked any more. Near the end of the season, he weighed more than 180 pounds and felt bloated.

Lil Jenkins and Joe Walters took Jackson to a specialist in Houston. After a series of tests, it was determined Haldol was not the proper medication for him. He was switched to Proza, a more sophisticated drug that does not cause an increase in appetite and retention of fluid. C.J. immediately started losing weight and started to get the spring back in his legs. Over the summer, he was expected to lose 15 pounds. There was no telling just how much that would improve his play. He couldn't wait to find out.

The C.J. File—I feel good about what we did. Most people didn't expect us to go very far and we did. Even though we didn't accomplish all of our goals, we got to the NCAA Tournament and we won a lot of big games. I feel good about that. And working with the guys all year long, that was fun. With the guys coming in, it should be a great year for us, but we have a lot to do before next season. I've got to work on my defense. Everyone has got to get better. I might take a day off during spring break and go home, but I'm going to mainly play ball every day. I still want to improve on a lot of things. I want to play better next year. I'm really looking forward to next year. There's no limit to what we can do.

Academics will play a big role in who will be playing in 1989-90, including Jackson. He was having difficulty keeping up with his studies and the demands of the season. But he worked tirelessly and gave it his full effort.

He was also encouraging Roberts and Williamson to stay on top of their academic game. They had struggled through the first two semesters. Even Jim Childers was getting frustrated at having to prod Roberts to hit the books. Boudreaux, though, had exceeded everyone's expectations and was close to becoming an honor student.

Of the new recruits, Burns took care of the Prop 48 requirements early and O'Neal made it in the spring. Griggs, though, was having difficulty meeting the test requirement. That wasn't necessary for Duvall, a transfer from Garden City Community College in Garden City, Kansas. The Baton Rouge native was eligible right away as a junior college graduate. A 6-5 guard, he was rated among the best outside shooters in junior college. It was readily apparent that Jackson would have help at his side when the season opened.

No matter who is eligible, they will be playing without Abernathy, who for 13 years was a crucial bridge linking Brown and the players. And they would have to do it without Blanton, the other link.

Abernathy had checked into dozens of job openings. Recently married and approaching his late 30s, he was serious about becoming a head coach. He anticipated getting interviews at Eastern Kentucky,

Tennessee State, Marquette, Illinois State and Loyola-Chicago. In late April, he was hired by Tennessee State.

"Ron has been fiercely loyal, like a brother," Brown said at Abernathy's going-away party. "He was always so upbeat, always smiling. He just made you feel good. He really lifted the players and lifted me. We will miss him here. But we're happy for him. He will be successful wherever he coaches."

Blanton, meanwhile, received invitations to all of the postseason all-star camps for pro prospects. He wanted to attend as many as would be beneficial. His senior season had greatly enhanced his chances of being drafted. Most scouts considered him a late first-round or early second-round pick. The Boston Celtics had shown the most interest, scouting him on eight occasions. But it turned out to be the Phoenix Suns who got him in the second round. His draft value had dropped because of a knee injury sustained in a pro tryout camp.

Meanwhile, Brown felt refreshed by the success of this season and prospects for the next one. He never dreamed he would be able to bring together so much talent on one team. There would be more All-Americans on this next team than in his previous 17 seasons combined. A new era was dawning for him.

The recruiting efforts of Brown and Craig Carse were displayed in the Dapper Dan Roundball Classic. All three of LSU's high school recruits—O'Neal, Griggs and Burns—played in the all-star game at Pittsburgh. Burns and Griggs turned in respectable performances, but O'Neal, the sculptured 7-footer who had just turned 17 and was still growing, simply overwhelmed the competition. He had 14 points, 12 rebounds and seven blocked shots in earning MVP honors for the West. Dick Vitale called him "the best big man in the country. He's got power and quickness. Put him on a front line next year with 7-footer Stanley Roberts and Dale Brown's team will be awesome."

For an encore, O'Neal went to Kansas City for the McDonald's All-American Classic and was even more devastating. Millions saw him on the ABC national telecast. He again earned MVP honors with 18 points, 16 rebounds and six blocked shots, despite being in foul trouble most of the game.

This time, Vitale called him the best prep player in the nation at any position. John Wooden was even more complimentary of the young man to whom he presented the MVP award for the victorious West team.

"I'm really impressed with him as a player and a person,"

Wooden said. "I'll have to tell you, it looked like a man among boys. I can envision him playing with Chris Jackson, and I know Dale has other good players, although I haven't seen them. With O'Neal and Jackson, Dale will have a chance to win the national championship next year. The only problem is they'll be so young. When Jackson is a senior and O'Neal is a junior, they should really have what it takes. I really think O'Neal is like a young Lew Alcindor [Kareem Abdul-Jabbar] or like a Patrick Ewing. He could play on several championship teams. I was extremely impressed."

Shortly after the all-star games, Vitale and Billy Packer released their early preseason rankings. Packer picked LSU third in the nation and Vitale placed the Tigers seventh. Several magazines were considering ranking the Tigers number one in the country.

Now Brown is king of the mountain. Everyone has to come after him. But how will he handle it? Everything will remain the same, he insists.

Is it possible to keep eight to 10 super talented players content and functioning together for the good of a team? Brown has no doubt it is, especially after consulting with Wooden about how he handled players like Alcindor and Bill Walton.

Another thing that won't change is the captain of the ship. Brown will be at the controls, and everyone will do things his way. He got that message across in a staff meeting immediately after Abernathy left for Tennessee State.

Johnny Jones was promoted to full-time assistant and would be the support man at practices. Carse remained recruiting coordinator and would also make recommendations during games. Jim Childers would continue as administrative assistant and would make most of the travel plans and some business decisions. No one would be added to the staff. In the final analysis, Brown would make all the important decisions in practices, games, recruiting and the business of running the program.

He also cleared the air concerning the friction that had been building between Carse and the other coaches. "We are going to do it my way, or else Craig, you can find another job; or Johnny, you can find another job; or Jim, you can find another job. That's the way it is. We are all going to work together."

As for the players, they would be given a similar message on October 15. The objective was to win the national championship, and nobody was going to get in the way of that. Brown's motivation would be simple: Do it my way or sit on the bench. He had not had that luxury in recent years.

Brown was the featured speaker at a banquet honoring O'Neal and his Cole High School teammates in San Antonio, Texas. A large gathering was on hand to honor the Texas AAA state champions. The Cougars had completed a 36-0 season, thanks largely to O'Neal. He had playoff games of 47 and 44 points and in one regular-season contest had 27 points, 36 rebounds and 26 blocked shots.

Speaking at a press conference before the banquet, Brown said his new players have the same character and attitude that his other players have had. For that reason, he plans to coach the same way and demand the same things of all his players, including O'Neal, who was seated next to him in front of the reporters and TV cameras. The handsome teen-ager towered above his coach, looking most suave in his tux. He bears a striking resemblance to David Robinson. Only he is already taller and much broader than the Olympic center.

Even though Brown has never had a center the caliber of Roberts and O'Neal, he looks at them simply as large Blantons or king-size Jacksons.

"Nothing will change," he said at the San Antonio event. "I am going to handle them just like I have every other team. I am excited about it. The family atmosphere will be there. The love will be there. That is a part of the program that will never change. I will still want them to help people and be kind to children and all that. And they're good kids. They will want to do that."

There will be one change for sure. Brown won't set a half-dozen or more goals for this next team. There will be only one goal: win the national championship.

Despite the likelihood of winning the SEC title, Brown said he won't put any emphasis on the conference. Kentucky will be on probation and under a new coach, Rick Pitino. Florida may be the only team capable of challenging LSU in the SEC.

"Everything we do will be geared toward winning a national title," he said. "Our goal will not be to win the league, or to win the conference tournament, or to win a particular game. We want to win the national championship. That is why these kids are here. Everything we do will be geared toward the championship. Every day we will have to make sure we're doing everything we can to win the championship."

Most of his San Antonio speech focused on family and team unity.

He said these are vital to any group, particularly his next team. "The first thing I'm going to tell them when we start practice on October 15th is the most important thing is not your size, your test score, your color or your religion. The most important thing is your mentality, that which is locked up here in this eight ounces of gray matter called your brain." He tapped his finger on his head and glanced at O'Neal.

"When we start learning that independence is impossible, we will start understanding ourselves better. We have to do things together. There is no way you can reach a goal without each other."

Then he recited a short essay he had written several years earlier and would share with the team on opening day.

"All things must be paid for. Mutual exchange is the law. You get, because you give. There is no such thing as independence. It is a hallucination of the most foolish sort.

"We are all dependent upon one another, for we are all component parts of a great whole. We depend on each other for our very existence.

"Mankind has never advanced a centimeter in the history of this world by fighting and hating and killing and jealously and bigotry. The only advances that we have ever made in the history of this world are when we've been brothers and sisters and labored toward a common goal.

"Yes, the best potential of me is we."

Brown will have to adjust. He must get enough out of his talent to avert upsets. In the past, his teams were molded on the philosophy that if they worked hard enough, they could be giant killers and upset the Kentuckys and Georgetowns of the world.

One of his favorite motivational theories is that attitude always beats talent. He survived on that for many years. Then he thrived on it. His new motto is talent, combined with a good attitude, is unbeatable.

The combination of Roberts, the prolific scorer, and O'Neal, the defensive intimidator, as a double post brings a gleam to Brown's eyes. But no more so than the backcourt duo of Jackson and Williamson.

Williamson, a wonderful player with a Jackson-like personality, could well be the biggest surprise next season. The son of former NBA player John Williamson, he has all the tools to become a big-time player. He wasn't a high school All-American only because he didn't attend the summer camps. Instead, he went on an exchange program to Africa. His jump shot isn't as effective as Jackson's, but he is quicker and has just as many moves. Together, they are the ideal guard combination. In pickup games, they perform like twin fighter jets flying down the court and attacking from every possible angle.

Which is more dangerous, Roberts and O'Neal inside or Jackson and Williamson outside? Brown says that is like asking a boxer to choose an opponent between Muhammad Ali and Rocky Marciano.

If that isn't enough, there are the wing players. Boudreaux has a sweet jumper. Duvall is similar to Indiana's Keith Smart, another Baton Rougean who attended Garden City Community College. Sims and Singleton have shown what they can do, and Burns and Griggs are offensive threats.

But like Wooden pointed out, LSU will be a young team. It won't have a senior. There will be a transition involved, and it might not come together in one year.

Brown has set up a relatively easy non-conference schedule with virtually all of the games at home. The only road trip is to nearby Houston to play the University of Texas.

One exception will be playing in the preseason NIT against some of the top teams in the country. The Tigers will open the NIT at home against Southern Miss in mid-November. If they win, they will likely get another home game, and then it could be on to New York City and Madison Square Garden for the NIT Final Four. Later in the season, they will also try to break the Superdome attendance record with a game against Notre Dame. Proceeds will benefit the homeless. Brown is trying deligently to get Mother Theresa to attend.

Also, Brown has arranged for LSU to play the Soviets in an exhibition game. It is certain to be a memorable experience for both the Tigers and their guests. Arvidas Sabonis and his teammates should beware of dark rooms.

If his dreams materialize and LSU becomes a powerhouse of the '90s, it will be hard for Brown to think about retirement. But that time will come. Vonnie has made it clear she wants him to retire before he gets too old to enjoy retirement. But that may not happen until he is 70. By then, he might have that elusive national title. More important, he will have had time to completely resolve his old self with his new faith.

In no previous year has he learned so much about himself and understood his strengths and weaknesses so well. He continues to pray for more humility and patience. He keeps getting more belief and faith.

"I really believe I am more alert and tuned in to my frailties now," he told Father Bayhi. "I know I still make mistakes. I've got ego, temper, selfishness and vanity. Before, I would harbor them. Now through my belief in God, I am quickly revitalized. That is such a wonderful feeling. I went through a slump for a while during the season. But I feel so much stronger in my faith now. I was in a valley, but I'm back on top of the mountain now."

As a coach, he also feels much better equipped. Not only can he lift his players with inspiring messages and drive them with his forcefulness, but he can give them a spiritual strength and unity that he never understood before. It comes through prayer and a common faith. Father Bayhi's presence and guidance complement Brown's own spiritual development of his team and himself.

Even when it concerned Bobby Knight, Brown was able to keep his peace. On the morning of the NCAA Tournament game between Indiana and Texas-El Paso, Brown told a friend that losing to UTEP was really a blessing in disguise.

"We weren't ready for Indiana," he said with a smile of relief. "We just didn't have enough firepower this time. God spared us the embarrassment. I understand that now. I don't need to beat Bobby Knight. I know it is all meant to be. And what a wonderful year it was. This has been the best year of my life."

That afternoon, Brown watched Indiana destroy UTEP. He could only imagine what the Hoosiers might have done to LSU, considering the way it was playing.

But Indiana didn't make it to the Final Four, either. Seton Hall beat the Hoosiers in the regional semifinals and went on to earn a trip to Seattle.

There was an LSU delegation in Seattle. Blanton went first to play in the National Association of Basketball Coaches All-Star Game. He was overmatched talent-wise, but he outhustled the opposition like he always does. Jackson and Brown, invited as finalists for national player and coach of the year, joined Blanton in Seattle. Carse came to be with Jackson, and Childers made the trip so he could attend some business meetings held in conjunction with the Final Four.

The media swamped Jackson with interview requests. He was the only one of 10 finalists for player of the year who was not a junior or senior. He was also the top scorer of the group, and everyone wanted a story on him.

Jackson's favorite part of the trip was meeting Julius Erving. He spent more than an hour visiting with Erving and his wife in their hotel room. They talked about basketball, career goals, education and their Christian beliefs. Jackson was elated, especially after Erving gave him his private phone number and invited him to visit his home in Philadelphia. They could have some interesting one-on-one games.

When the national award winners were announced, Jackson finished third, the highest ever for a freshman. Brown came in fourth. The only players ahead of Jackson were seniors Sean Elliot and Danny Ferry. The only coaches in front of Brown were Knight, P.J. Carlisimo of Seton Hall and Lute Olson of Arizona. Brown didn't seem to mind this time that Knight beat him for yet another national honor.

Although the Tigers didn't earn a trip to the Final Four, some of them got to Seattle. From October 15 to March 17, they had all believed it was possible. This time, the dream came true for Michigan, which upset Illinois in the semifinals and then held off Seton Hall for the national championship.

The 1990 Final Four is in Denver. Brown already has his players talking and dreaming about playing there for a national championship. Don't count them out.